JOINING AFRICA

JOINING AFRICA

From Anthills to Asmara

Charles Cantalupo

Michigan State University Press

East Lansing

⊗ The paper used in this publication meets the minimum requirements of
ANSI/NISO Z39.48-1992 (R 1997) (Permanence of Paper).

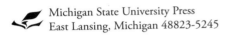 Michigan State University Press
East Lansing, Michigan 48823-5245

Printed and bound in the United States of America.

18 17 16 15 14 13 12   1 2 3 4 5 6 7 8 9 10

LIBRARY OF CONGRESS CATALOGING-IN-PUBLICATION DATA

Cantalupo, Charles, 1951–
Joining Africa : from anthills to Asmara / Charles Cantalupo.
    p. cm.
    Includes bibliographical references.
    ISBN 978-1-61186-036-8 (pbk. : alk. paper)
    1. Cantalupo, Charles, 1951—Travel—Eritrea. 2. Eritrea—Description and travel. I. Title.

DT393.34.C36 2012
960.3'311092—dc23   2011029503

Cover design by Charlie Sharp, Sharp Des!gns, Lansing MI

Cover photo by Ribka Sibhatu and author photo by Abraham Tesfalul are used with
permission.

Book design by Scribe Inc. (www.scribenet.com)

green press INITIATIVE Michigan State University Press is a member of the Green Press Initiative and
is committed to developing and encouraging ecologically responsible publishing
practices. For more information about the Green Press Initiative and the use of recycled
paper in book publishing, please visit www.greenpressinitiative.org.

Visit Michigan State University Press on the World Wide Web at:
www.msupress.msu.edu

Contents

Light the Lights

"LIGHT THE LIGHTS," I SPOKE INTO THE MICROPHONE. "LIGHT THE lights," the audience politely responded. "Light the lights," I said louder. "Light the lights," the audience responded, louder too. "Light the lights for the *getamay*. Light the lights for the *getamit*. Light the lights for the *getemti*. Light the lights. Light the lights!" The crowd began cheering and laughing, "Light the lights. Light the lights! Light the lights!" "Light the lights. Light the lights!" I joined them.[1]

A row of forty seated *getemti*, male and female oral poets of Eritrea, most of them old, half circled the stage. They wore white: long gauzy dresses and scarves, their hems brightly embroidered, on the women; white pants and shirts with white gauzy blankets, called *gabis*, on the men. Most gripped the curved handles of thin, smooth walking sticks. Many of the *getamo* also held half-liter, white enameled metal cups of *sewa*, Eritrea's cider-colored, traditional barley beer, which a few of the women, the *getemti*, held too. Its color and shimmer resembled their skin.

Behind the *getemti*, the hall the size of an airplane hanger buzzed with a standing-room-only crowd attending Eritrea's annual, eight-day summer arts festival that was happening all over the huge fairgrounds in Asmara, the nation's capital. The festival featured separate areas devoted to a wide range of Eritrean culture and arts, which included nine ethnic groups with different languages. Among these areas were agriculture, industry, technology, computers, painting, books from ancient manuscripts to new publications by the Ministry of Education, tool making, dance, examples of traditional housing from the below-sea-level deserts to the two-mile-high highlands, popular music, animal husbandry, camel herding, coffee ceremonies, textiles, varieties of firewood and more, including poetry.

During Ethiopia's thirty-year occupation of Eritrea before it won its independence in 1991, the "Expo" fairgrounds, as they were called, were transformed into a prison. Tonight I could have read a Tigrinya poem that I translated by a young woman poet locked up there during the war. She wrote about her beloved cellmate's execution by firing squad: "Abeba . . . flower from Asmara . . . / Who never blossomed."[2] Ironically, most newspapers, magazines, and websites around the world depicted Eritrea now as if it had become one huge prison suffering under a dictatorship. However, with the possible exception—although no one seemed to care—of a few elders dressed like the *getemti* and some of the Muslims in the crowd wearing their robes, turbans, and veils, the crowd in the hall resembled what I might find at an American state fair, although nearly everyone was black: parents in casual clothes and holding babies and children, teenage girls in tight pants and boys in baggy ones either chasing or pretending to elude each other, grandparents either tagging along or having fun with their own older friends: nearly everyone in jeans, khakis, T-shirts, polos, a few dresses and skirts, sweaters, sweatshirts, sneakers, comfortable walking shoes or sandals. ERI-TV cameramen covered the event and broadcast it live.

"Light the lights. Light the lights," I continued. Whatever few lines I excerpted from my original poem and wove in and out of the refrain didn't seem to matter: "Leave out most of the connections . . . / If I nail you down, what is left to question? . . . / Why are we here except to light the lights?" Most of the people in the audience knew enough English to understand me: "Light the lights for our dark inventions. / We can provide the story later."

I was not important. The audience packed the house for Eritrean poetry: *gtmi* or poetry in Tigrinya, Tigre, Arabic, Afar, Saho, Bilen, Bega, Nara, and Kunama. Putting aside their cups of *sewa* and picking up their walking sticks, one by one each oral poet took the stage. As they performed, many in the audience would spontaneously cry out, whether echoing or challenging the verse I couldn't tell, but unfailingly answered by the *getamay* or *getamit* with anything from a wide-eyed nod or a smile to a flick of the hand and a vicious curse—all of which would call forth more laughing and cheering.

Instead of having a separate word for poetry, Tigrinya uses *gtmi*, which means "joining."

With my background in American, British, and European literature, I found it roughly equivalent to the Scots *makir* or maker and the Latin *faber,* identifying the work of a poet as much with manual labor as intellectual. Yet *gtmi* also invoked the same power as the alternative Latin word for poet, *vates,* meaning prophet, since the *getamay* or *getamit* also had a spiritual power and traditionally offered verses on the rituals of life and death, although not officially religious. The poet as joiner or *getamay* and *getamit* also connected with the Greek mythological figure of Hephaestus, a blacksmith and great craftsman, who made or joined the shield of Achilles in Homer's *Iliad*. Described as containing gold, silver, and less precious metals, the shield portrayed and prophesied a city at peace and a city at war, pastoral and agricultural life, the earth, the sky, and the heavens, with all encircled by the ocean. A penultimate scene on the shield had richly costumed girls and boys dancing and whirling quickly yet gracefully—the boys waving daggers as the girls in fresh garlands weave confidently among them[3]—just like I had seen a few minutes before I entered the hall, when I had stopped to watch a traditional performance by Afars, pastoral nomads known for being fierce in battle and who lived along Eritrea's southeastern coast on the Red Sea, one of the harshest places on earth.

Contemporary poets who wrote their work, none of whom wore the traditional dress of *getemti,* followed the oral poets and received the same enthusiastic response. After the readings, I interviewed each one of the poets for a documentary I was filming with the Audio Visual Institute of Eritrea on contemporary Eritrean poetry.

My main reason for being in Asmara was to finish editing and translating an anthology of the contemporary poets' work called *Who Needs a Story?*—the first book of its kind ever published. I wanted readers finally to be able to take a book of contemporary Eritrean poetry off a library or a bookstore shelf the way they had for years been taking for granted that it would contain anthologies of contemporary American, Irish, French, British, German, Italian, Eastern European, Russian, Australian, Asian, and most any poetry—with the even greater exception of nearly all African-language poetry except in Arabic—written around the world.

Some of the poets kindly invited me to read my translations after they read their originals, but after two or three I demurred, since the evening had already lasted three hours. I had gotten up too early that morning to travel to Asmara back from Massawa—a trip of approximately seventy-five miles but a nearly two-mile climb—on Eritrea's Red Sea coast, where I had spoken the night before at the public library about the new anthology. The embassy of the United States in Eritrea had arranged the trip, and I traveled with the widely known Eritrean poet Solomon Tsehaye, who had authored Eritrea's national anthem. At one point the American ambassador invited us to join him—although he didn't mean "join" as in to provide poetry—in welcoming and touring a naval frigate, the USS *Hawes*. It had recently docked in Massawa and was supposed to signify a big breakthrough in Eritrean / American relations.

But what a difference between these poets asking me to "join" them and the ambassador's invitation. In Massawa, when our U.S. Embassy Land

Cruiser stopped at the gate to where the frigate docked, a skeletal guard in the tatters of a Fanta T-shirt and a sarong asked our Eritrean driver for a list of our names. The embassy public affairs officer, who rode shotgun, handed it over the driver directly to the guard, who then compared it with the list he had. Shaking his head to imply "no" each time he made the comparison in silence for the next three minutes, his first and only words were, "No Conloopoo," meaning me, at which three more, similarly clad guards, one with a Kalishnakov and another with an old, long pistol and a porkpie hat came up behind him.

"Your name is not on the list," said Solomon, as if expecting this. The BBC and Deutsche Welle journalists also with us could only sigh, fanning the 100-degree air that replaced our air conditioning through the open window.

"Let's drive or we'll be late for the ambassador's ceremony, and we will come back for you," said the PAO, not too sympathetically, to which Solomon added, "I will wait with you," sliding over on the now sweaty backseat and right behind me out the door.

Taking two seats on a bench constructed of Red Sea coral, Solomon and I watched the Land Cruiser pull away, and the guards began to lower the gate, a bleached tree trunk tied to thick and fraying, discarded mooring ropes, until suddenly it jerked up. Two black, tinted-glass Suburbans sped by, and the ambassador faintly waved his hand, not forward but backward like an Italian. He looked at us but didn't recognize me.

Solomon and I sweated, shifted on the uncomfortable bench and hoped the Toyota SUV would be back soon, at least at first, until an Eritrean in khaki pants and a polo shirt walked by and opened a door I hadn't noticed at first behind the bench. We were sitting in front of a rusty shipping container, which served as an office, and he invited us in to sit on plastic café chairs. Our host took a stool, sat at a desk with a few onionskin and carbon papers, and everything stopped except an old air conditioner that roared, stuck through a cutout hole in a corner of the container. No one talked, rapt with our frigid surroundings for the next ten minutes. Not caring if I was ever retrieved to visit the frigate, I stared at an icon of the Eritrean armed struggle: a kind of replay of the famous American scene of Iwo Jima—of GIs struggling to plant the Stars and Stripes on top of a hill—only here the soldiers wore short shorts, they all had Afros, half of them were women, and the flag was the gold, red, green, and blue of Eritrea.

Seeing the same icon twelve hours later over an exit sign as I tried to leave the hall inconspicuously while the poetry reading still continued strong, I also noticed two college students at a table near the door: a boy and a girl, whom I had seen back at the hotel around the pool. They had first said "Hi" when I passed, and I had said "Hi" too, recognizing that they were Americans as they recognized that I was. We talked a little. I told them that I lived in Bethlehem, Pennsylvania, and taught at Penn State. Their names were Scott and Abrehet. She was Eritrean, her father owning a fleet of taxis in San Diego and Los Angeles, and he was her African American fiancé, invited to come on vacation with her family, one of many wealthy Eritrean families who came back to Eritrea in the summer and stayed at its only five-star hotel, the Intercontinental Asmara, especially around the time of the Expo festival.

Abrehet waved and Scott came over to me. "Hey, professor, we couldn't believe it was you up there. Really great," he said.

Abrehet followed, saying "Hello, Professor *Charlus*," emphasizing my name, smiling and rolling her large, icon-like eyes to acknowledge how it was pronounced when I was introduced to the audience during the reading. "Why didn't you tell me you speak Tigrinya?" she scolded facetiously.

"I really don't," I replied.

She didn't want to hear it. "Wait until I tell my Eritrean friends back in L.A. I met an American *getamay* in Asmara."

"I'm really not," I answered. "I mean, do I look like one?"

"Maybe you do, maybe you do," joked Scott.

"But not until you start to wear a *gabi* over your jacket," Abrehet quickly added. "I'll call my cousin Saba tomorrow. She'll know where to get one, and we can all go together."

"Sorry, Abrehet," I said, "Tomorrow is my last day in Asmara, and I have too many loose ends to tie up. I would love to buy a *gabi,* but maybe next time. I'll stick with the T-shirt and jacket for now. I better go because I have to get up early." Before she could respond, I yawned, knowing that the students were only beginning their night.

"Professor, wait a minute," Scott said, in a half-joking, half-serious tone. "I want to ask you one question. How does an American white guy get so wrapped up in Africa?"

"Yeah," Abrehet spoke slowly, "and why Eritrea? But before you go, what's the name of your book? *Who Needs a Story*? Where can I buy a copy?"

"That's it. The book will be out in October," I replied, thinking fast and unsure about how to answer her first question. "I have good friends here. But to answer your question, too, Scott. Why did I—or did you say how did I—get involved with Africa? Do you remember the first line of the poem "Who Needs a Story?" that Ghirmai Yohannes read tonight? It goes, 'I needed a story.'[4] Around twenty years ago, when I was in Jericho, in Israel, I began to realize that I needed a story, too. It led me here."

CHAPTER ONE

From the Other Direction

I LOOKED DOWN AT MY FEET IN THE SANDY DIRT ON A SITE OF ANCIENT Jericho. Ants tunneled where twenty cities had risen and fallen. I couldn't look up, blinded by the pallor of the Dead Sea to the east and the cliffs and caverns of Qumrum to the south where, according to one account, a Bedouin shepherd searching for his stray goat forty years before had found the Dead Sea Scrolls. To the east, a rickety administration building flying an Israeli flag in tatters between the water and where I stood and, to the north, a seemingly endless, abandoned Palestinian refugee camp also forced my eyes to look down at the ants digging around my feet. I could not connect with anything I was seeing or feeling. I felt as if I didn't exist except as an illusion.

Before this, I had been in Jerusalem as a kind of religious pilgrim in search of consolation. To a great extent, although I would not have said so at the time, I thought I could get over my wife's death from breast cancer two years before in the United States if I saw how—not if—the Holy Land could be real: not a Holy Land of violent newspaper headlines or fundamentalist faiths, but of a Bible rich with rhetoric and ambiguity and looking like a Renaissance Italian painting—a Holy Land of beauty.

I was drunk on death and had had enough. It made me religious, going back to being a Roman Catholic, attending predawn daily Latin mass and singing from the oversized illuminated Psalters in a Cistercian monastery a block from where I lived, studying Bernard of Clairvaux on the Song of Songs and St. Augustine on the Psalms instead of reading Jacques Derrida and Michel Foucault, as a professor of literature at that time was supposed to.

I had traveled to Israel to follow a dream I had one night of my dead wife's being back with me in bed and alive. The dream ended when I reached for her and awoke. It made me think that I could understand her death and how to go on with my life if I became or at least wrote from the perspective of a kind of Orpheus, seeing her as a Eurydice. Trying to hold my dead wife in a dream resembled his leading her out of hell and, turning around to see her, making her disappear.

As I walked through Jerusalem, my willing suspension of disbelief, my poetic faith, became indistinguishable from my religious faith—"the substance of things hoped for, the evidence of things not seen,"[1] as Hebrews 11.1 defined it—that seemed to be growing everywhere like wild rosemary lining the paths. Why not conflate the voices of Samuel Taylor Coleridge and St. Paul? The ancient olive trees of Gethsemane bloomed as golden as the Dome of the Rock. What Middle East war? Bright limestone walls enclosed cisterns of dark waters and whispered healing. I watched a prophet finding her way amid the sheep shearing and goats grazing along the sides of the Valley of Judgment. The bread on the slab of the claustrophobic tomb of Jesus in the Church of the Holy Sepulcher, where I huddled at midnight with six others, readily became His body. Outside, a flood of voices, dead and alive, requiring no distinctions between "I am" and "Let there be," flowed down Mount Zion and out of the city of David. Feeling that I witnessed the "repetition in the finite mind of the eternal act of creation,"[2] Coleridge's definition of the primary imagination repeating like a mantra in my head, whenever I looked up, a swallow showed how to live. She could find a nest for herself and her young nearly anywhere and make it an altar. Whatever the direction, she flew exactly among a multitude of swallows—all looking the same but none seeming to follow another or in each other's way. They flew like the prayers of the faithful at war with each other below—Muslims, Jews, Christians, and all their variations—only made perfect and at peace with one another in the sky.

Before Jericho, I had also been to other places in Israel. I reached into a hole in the floor in the Church of the Nativity in Bethlehem to touch the ground supposed to have been soaked by the blood of Mary giving birth to Jesus. I listened to how the cave in Hebron that contained the tombs of Abraham and Sarah, Isaac and Rebecca, Jacob and Leah echoed the footsteps of Jews and Muslims, which sounded the same. They shared the surrounding building but worshipped at different times, when it became either a mosque or a temple. I relaxed buying donuts in a Palestinian bakery in Ramallah and sharing French fries with the armed and bandoleered Israeli guards at the tomb of Joseph. I read the Beatitudes of Matthew 5:3–5 engraved on the wall of a chapel built on the spot of the Sermon on the Mount, surrounded by the green hills of Galilee bathing in the sunlight of the sea that I heard rattling the pebbles on the shore below:

Blessed are the poor in spirit: for theirs is the kingdom of heaven.
Blessed are they who mourn: for they shall be comforted.
Blessed are the meek: for they shall inherit the earth.

I could hear the angel Gabriel's *Ave, gratia plena, Dominus tecum* yet see the words as they appeared on Simone Martini's *The Annunciation*: the long, thin bar of raised gold letters extending from his pursed lips to her pinched and hooded face shrinking in fear while she gathered her dark robe to her throat. I heard the words again but thundering ominously in the Golan Heights looming over my shoulder as I crouched beside a charcoal fire and ate fish netted the night before in a part of the Sea of Galilee where fishermen often saw their departed loved ones walking. I dreamed of collecting the bones of my own lost love and, as they stung my hands and made them bleed, taking an entire day to place them in an ossuary twelve months after she died. I greeted the eastern star as if it had not been born countless times before. I witnessed the making of the first frescoes and icons of the Christian pantheon on the lower slopes of Mount Sinai. Echoes of any injunction against graven images only sweetened the dawn and strengthened the herbs on the summit as it seemed to burst into honey, and I gulped the cold air.

Yet other images in the Sinai became more troubling. The huge jagged rocks made me nauseous. Could one rubber hose running impossibly for miles and miles along a road a few degrees away from catching fire be the only source of water? Did I really have to wait to hear a voice on the bus radio from Mecca announcing the sunset before I could eat? A moment later, could I refuse to tear a chunk off the greasy chicken passed around the bus for everyone to share? I chewed more sand than flour in the pita. The land looked like a huge accident: a head-on collision of all the gods—of the Torah, the Koran, the Old and the New Testament, the Zarathustrans, the pre-Christian Axumites, Byzantium and more—who had emerged from the Red Sea.[3] I felt them following me back to Israel into a room piled high with only the eyeglasses of executed Jews and another room piled high only with their shoes in the Holocaust museum in Tel Aviv, Yad Vashem.

I went to Israel for consolation. My grief felt cured. Why become a troubled pilgrim? I decided to leave Israel and take a flight to Egypt. Orpheus or not, I wanted to see the pyramids, the Sphinx, and other exotic sights and stay in a luxury hotel built on an island in the Nile to celebrate the opening of the Suez Canal. Let the serious part of the trip be over.

Fifteen years before, during my first year of college, nearly all of my preconceptions and values had been undermined by the Vietnam War and the protest movement against it: soldiers roaming the quads and firing on students, campus buildings on fire, universities shut down, hallucinogens and the answers to all problems in Eastern religions and mysticism.

Then I read Dante's *Divine Comedy*. Enthralled by the terza rima, his vision, and all that it resisted and affirmed, I decided that I had to devote myself to knowing and accounting for my own, Western culture before seeking out or learning any other. Like most first-year students at my university, I really only knew a slice of the contemporary American culture of my origins: white, middle class, and suburban. But reading Dante made me want to know more. In the early modern literature in England and painting from the same period in Italy, the Ring of Kerry, the monasteries of Mt. Athos, the ruins of classical Greece, Ukraine if I could get there, modern American poetry, London, Paris, and most of all in Rome I would find who I was. I decided that the Africa of black nationalists—like the poet, Amiri Baraka, in my hometown of Newark, New Jersey—the Asia of the Beat poets, Native American ideals of environmentalism or even American literature before 1900—around when my grandparents on both sides immigrated to the United States—had nothing to do with me.

But what I read and wrote in the next fifteen years didn't prepare me for Cairo, Al-Qahirah, "The Victor." Fifteen million people and no traffic lights? The morning after my arrival, trying to ignore contemporary Cairo as I had also tried to disregard contemporary Jerusalem, I walked from my hotel to the national museum. As I entered I felt that I could have been on Mars: floor after floor packed with what I didn't know, never learned, and didn't understand; glittering gold, black, and uncanny angles, minutely detailed drawings and symbols painted into an infinite perspective. Less than a week after I had seen the ants digging in the dust of Jericho, again I felt totally disconnected and ephemeral compared with what I saw. I entered a maze of images and messages, almost as if I had followed the ants into their tunnels and chambers below Jericho. At the entrance, I felt disoriented, but I left feeling overwhelmed with desire and starved. In between, I lost who I was.

Something beyond measure confronted me in the dust of Jericho and now in Cairo. I could only express it by trying to describe the art I saw as another kind of holy land: of the Nile not the Jordan; lotus and papyrus, elaborate illustrations for the dead, fertility in red mud, black soil, yellow mountains, little rain, deserts and green irrigated fields. Had I been starving in Israel like a son of the biblical Jacob? I fled to Egypt. Its ancient gods welcomed me to eat. They cried out to me in the museum and crowded the streets. Seshat gave me her ink, a mixture of night and stars. Thoth provided his durable, precise, and ageless style. I rose above the city on the long wings of Nephthys. The falcon, Horus, picked the old world out of my eyes. Requiring no authority or sacred power, Isis bathed me in her milk. She led me to Osiris, who said he thought I had died. When Ptah said he put me back together after I had fallen apart, Anubis laughed.

I can't remember walking from the museum to Qarafa, Cairo's "City of the Dead." As a child on his bicycle touched my arm, I looked through the gate of a garbage dump. I wanted to hide but couldn't decide between Misr Al-Qadima and its Coptic compounds dark with the earliest ideas of Christ or the thousands of mosques, enfolded in marble and palms and pointed with minarets to tell Allah exactly where they were. Whose voice was that? "I am the sand. I am the sand." Was it mine? "I am the sand of Egypt. Everything comes to me and falls." The same words lined the walls, pulsing in the veins of basalt and red granite where I slid my hands descending a passage into a pyramid's inner chamber at midnight a few days later. Was this the wisdom of the desert? The secret of the Sphinx? Raw fear in the shadow of a crow's wing on the limestone cliffs at noon? Did Amen Ra rise out of the Sinai, fade into the soft gray Nile, and weave between the tombs of Memphis and Thebes and their massive columns a rainbow from underground? Did it reach a disembodied finger two hundred miles east to write on two porphyry tablets handed to Moses, which he destroyed, only to write once more what would eventually become lost in the wisdom of Sheba?

I felt a flush and vertigo in the dust of Jericho, the piles of shoes and eyeglasses at Yad Vashem, the Sinai landscape, Cairo's national museum, the streets of Cairo's City of the Dead, the bright hieroglyphics—in thousands of sarcophagi and on wall after wall of the underground tombs, deeper and deeper in Luxor—and in the everyday Egyptian eyes I was afraid to meet. Whatever Western knowledge and religion I had, they couldn't explain what I experienced now. My pilgrimage to witness the beauties of the Holy Land took an unexpected, disturbing turn. It gave me a sick feeling of having made a big mistake somewhere—of having missed something. I didn't realize it then, but my decision fifteen years before to focus primarily on my European cultural origins was coming apart. The bottom—quite literally, considering their geographical relation to Israel and Egypt—was falling out. Most of all, I didn't understand I was in Africa.

Two years later I wanted to go back. In the interim, the Latin rites of the Cistercians and the beauties of nature in the deep forests surrounding my house in Pennsylvania helped me to put in perspective the gaping shadows of the Sinai and my feeling like the easy prey of an ancient Egyptian pantheon—at least enough to write a long poem called "Orpheus the Pilgrim." Published the year before in a literary journal that focused on mystical experience, the poem didn't include seeing the ants in the dust of Jericho—that I decided to omit—or the relics of the Holocaust, which seemed too political. Now I wanted to travel to Senegal, Gambia, and Togo to see and write about how Roman Catholic theology, rituals, and iconography adapted to African cultures. Thinking that Catholic saints and sacraments could resemble African worship of ancestors and animism, I eagerly anticipated discovering a kind of African and Catholic syncretism. Since I had a friend working in the American embassy in Kenya, I could visit there too and explore the game parks and the coast of the Indian Ocean. Combining what I thought would be the theology and spiritualism of West Africa with the natural beauty of East Africa, I wanted to write another long poem. Thinking about it brought back an experience of ten years before.

Staggering in Athens's summer sunshine after a fourteen-hour flight from New York and wanting nothing more than sleep, I found a high-ceilinged, hot, and shuttered hotel room. Street clatter and neon lights awakened me at dark from a dream in which I felt sure and full of a sense that I had reconciled something, but I could remember nothing more specific. I started to say a word I remembered from the dream—*meh*—but couldn't finish it. Two years later as I retold the story, the word came to me: *metamorphosis.*

After a few days in Greece, I couldn't understand how classical Greek art and Byzantine or Christian art originated in the same rocky soil. Each seemed epitomized by its sky: dazzling blue or gleaming gold. Did the ruined temples, columns, and caryatids—or the bright mountainous expanse of Delphi—and the Orthodox icons of Jesus, Mary, and the saints enclosed airlessly and deep in the churches drink the same wine? The two visions seemed so opposite.

Reading Yeats, I wanted to explore the art of Byzantium and experience what he imagined when he wrote,

> O sages standing in God's holy fire
> As in the gold mosaic of a wall,
> Come from the holy fire, perne in a gyre,
> And be the singing-masters of my soul.[4]

I planned a trip to Mt. Athos in the north of Greece to visit its Orthodox monasteries. Staying for a day and a night in Thessalonica, a kind of staging point for the trip where I also had to obtain a license to visit Athos, I visited the municipal museum and saw a golden vase of scenes from the life of Dionysius. Like the ants in the dust of ancient Jericho ten years later, it challenged as illusory everything I thought had led me to this point.

On Athos a few days after I saw the vase, as I tried to focus on the icons, books, and relics in the monasteries set high in the mountains, I kept seeing the vines and blossoms, the proffered cups brimming with wine and the curves of the bodies in love on the vase. As I climbed the forest trails alone, I began to scream and sing that the hills, the sea below, the streams, hundreds of birds and the drone of bees in the lush plants all around could not be merely shadows of some greater spiritual reality. Repeating the traditional pilgrim's greeting of *Evlogite*, "Bless me," like a mantra, why did I want to be lost amid the wild orchids blooming along the ancient stones? Frustrated that I couldn't concentrate, one minute I was cursing and kicking my bags, and the next I was feeling overwhelmed by the natural beauty of the place as if it existed, like "the tree . . . in the midst of the garden," as Genesis 3:3 recounted, offering a godlike knowledge of good and evil.

My bags became too heavy with my beliefs. I wanted the icons' abstract bodies, the impossibly curved fingers held out against the gold skies of Byzantium, and what I imagined I would find in the monasteries of Mount Athos to signify the Catholic doctrine of transubstantiation: that the bread and wine of communion became in substance if not appearance the body and blood of Jesus, "the real presence," unchanging and eternal. The vase and what I saw along the trails leading from monastery to monastery challenged such spirituality with natural beauty, yet a beauty subject to change and death.

Two years later, when I remembered that the word I had first dreamed of in Athens was *metamorphosis*, it seemed like a synonym or translation of *transubstantiation*. I also realized that like Ovid's poem, *Metamorphoses*, the vase in Thessalonica portrayed human passion in the extreme: the kind that led to an experience of the supernatural.[5] Transubstantiation named the miraculous transformation of everyday bread and wine into the sacred, unchanging, and eternal. Metamorphosis also began in the everyday— flowers, animals, and people struggling with one another, the earth and the sky—but gloried in profane and innumerable instances of change and mutability. Gold sky, Byzantium, transubstantiation; blue sky, classical Greece, metamorphosis—I wanted them to add up to one answer.

Regardless, any ideals of natural beauty or intimations of transubstantiation seemed absent in the monasteries themselves. Their supposed abiding by the edict of Constantine that allowed no female presence on Mt. Athos— the chickens in the barnyards notwithstanding—had become a drawn-out death warrant. Worms hollowed out the few remaining ancient manuscripts on the shelves. As I carefully slid an eighth-century *Aeneid* off one of them, the pages fell apart in my hands. The script with gold, red, and blue illumination looked like a piece of construction paper after a child attacked it with a hole puncher. Most of the monks interpreted a request to see a manuscript or a work of art as a sexual solicitation to walk behind a shelf with a stranger whom they thought wanted nothing else but their toothless, oniony gums and their bodies that resembled abandoned corpses under their robes. I found no "singing masters of my soul": only recluses, unabashed in expressing their hatred for Jews and making slaves of the retarded boys of women from far-off villages who sent them in the hope that they might be saved and provided for on earth.

One night I watched them serve the monks a lavish feast of fish and octopus, platters of mountain greens and vegetables, massive loaves of bread and huge jugs of wine poured carelessly into tall clay goblets. Earlier one of the smaller boys had served me a meal of mushy pasta like maggots floating in rusty water. He had brought it to the attic of the monastery's auxiliary chapel, where the abbot had ordered me confined since I had sprained my ankle a few days before. I had slipped, and a donkey had to carry me up the precipitous, foot-wide path. Now I was summoned to a feast. Why? No one offered me food.

Several minutes after I arrived, I saw the abbot, his long beard like dead straw glistening with so much grease and wine that it appeared to be on fire, signal to the largest and most muscular boy to take a huge pot of boiling water off the stove and place the vessel at my feet. As the monk waved his hand, the hairiest I ever saw, repeatedly up and down, his glassy eyes grew brighter and brighter. When the boy realized that the monk directed his gestures at him, he immediately, before I could say a word, lifted my leg and plunged my bare and swollen foot into the water. As I screamed, the room rumbled with laughter. After a few minutes, the monk gestured the same way again. Slowly but surely responding, the same boy approached me again and lifted my foot out of the pot. Then he took a pitcher of olive oil, poured it from my knee to my toes and rubbed my ankle until the abbot, after draining three glasses of wine, one after another, which the small boy from the auxiliary chapel smilingly filled, signaled me to pull away my foot.

With the gift of a freshly carved walking stick from the abbot and barely feeling the sprain, I climbed down the mountain early the next morning for a boat to join others who traveled from monastery to monastery. They included a few monks who never said a word and acted as if no one else could be seen or heard, retarded serving boys who traveled with them, and a handful of visitors like me.

As they talked about the relics they had seen—a finger bone of John the Baptist here, a girdle of the Virgin Mary there—I was thinking of Ovid's story of the metamorphosis of Adonis into anemones that grew out of the ground drenched with his blood transubstantiating into the story of anemones that sprung from the ground soaked with Jesus' blood at the foot of the cross. Becoming devoted to a kind of correspondence between Christian and Greek classical art, I saw it arc like a dolphin in the Aegean, swarm like bees in the olives at dusk, and tower like a sphinx over a grave. The power of metamorphosis made the air rattle at Delphi, the light as intolerable as the flies at Mycenae, and the moon turn copper at midnight over the forests of the island of Andros. Metamorphosis broke down Corinth into cheap chandeliers. Transubstantiation in fiery boats like fiery birds entered all the harbors, indifferent whether they were discovered or destroyed. It broke every stone column with the same chorus, over and over: "The stones wash up on shore, / And we throw them back in the water." Metamorphosis turned the amphitheaters to face the sea, danced in a stiff, hot breeze, drank hard preferring sweat to shade, wielded an axe no one could lift, taught the spoon players in Heraklion's alleyways the holiest of numbers, weighed every law against a flower, encouraged octopus cults, revealed the gods in the shadows disguised as grapes and grain, found putti intact in the rubble, rippled church walls with the dead praises of Minerva, stretched up the slopes of the dead volcano, and buried believers like me in torrents of stone only to emerge again, muttering flesh and word.

Muttering ten years later and wandering like Orpheus amid the ants in the dust of Jericho, the roomfuls of shoes and eyeglasses at Yad Vashem, the Sinai's violent terrain, and the Martian strangeness of the objects in Cairo's national museum, I glimpsed but tried to turn away from another kind of metamorphosis. But two years later it returned with a vengeance, despite my Orphic plan to wander from Dakar to Nairobi and Mombassa in the hope of finding and writing poetry about common ground between Catholicism and African animism.

As I was checking in for my flight to Dakar at the Air Afrique desk in Kennedy Airport in New York, a tall and very dark African male asked if I would include two of his suitcases in my luggage, since I was traveling light with a small bag. I had never seen such huge suitcases and politely declined, not knowing that such a request—at least in the days before post-9/11 security requirements about packing one's bag and watching it all times—was the norm when flying between Africa and America. Yet stuffed in those bags were Jericho, Yad Vashem, horrors of the Sinai, a predatory Egyptian pantheon, and more.

Half awake and anxious as the flight to Dakar prepared to land, I felt driven. "East into an unclear dawn of new republics," I heard, as if in a speech out of nowhere, while I envisioned a mountainous jungle, an abandoned brick hut, and a small plot for me to try to plow a straight furrow. But why were we crashing into a peaceful blue and yellow pool? The wheels touching down opened my eyes.

I was too self-conscious to notice the airport. Taking a taxi to my hotel, I felt warm and dizzy, as I had in Jericho and Cairo, only now at the strong smell of dust in the air, sweet and bodily. Was it the red peppers set out on bright, printed cloths by women—wrapped in even brighter cloths but with similar patterns—who lined the road all the way into the city? I couldn't tell if the lot after lot of seemingly empty buildings I was passing were new and under construction or old and falling down. Vultures circled everywhere I looked, as if they thrived on whatever the city exhaled. I followed their shadows. They wound over desert dwellers picking vast garbage dumps for food and any other scraps of value all the way to the entrance to the first-class European hotel where I had a reservation.

After checking in, I went down to the hotel pool. Surrounded by French tourists getting a suntan, the pool area bordered a steep beach and a seemingly angry, green, and towering Atlantic. Trying not to glance at the deeply tanned and worn breasts of the topless French women, I was surprised by a loud drum and a procession of black dancers. Performing around the pool, they wore costumes of animal skins, feathers, large jangling beads, and necklaces over bright printed cloths like what I saw on the way from the airport. Leaping, whooping, and always smiling, most of the women dancers were topless too. To stop from staring at their breasts, I tried to stare at them, but neither offered much pleasure, and both made me nervous. Although I could only imagine and fantasize an original setting for the performance, the incongruity of wrenching it into such surroundings and the touristy staging numbed me. I decided to leave.

The only way out passed through the troupe. I wanted to close my eyes but looked straight ahead as I brushed through a thicket of sweaty arms, feathers, jangling and rattling. I took a breath and the smell again of dust and red peppers clouded my eyes like too much burning incense. Almost colliding with an incredibly thin and tall male dancer dressed in greasy rags, I lunged for the closest pool chair and dizzily plopped down. He burst through the front of the troupe and began bending and twisting his limbs into the most grotesque shapes I had ever seen. As the applause of rich, white pool goers grew louder and louder with each new contortion, I thought he turned and looked either to see how I was or to tell me with his eyes that he

perfectly understood and expressed the traditional meaning of the performance. Recovering, I stumbled back to my room and slept for sixteen hours.

Late the next morning, I walked out of my hotel through a suspiciously
neat, tropical garden and past the fence that surrounded it. As soon as I
reached the street, I was surrounded by wispy clouds of beggars thickly
laced with very dark young men offering themselves as guides, touts, pimps,
and prostitutes, pressing themselves physically into me and pushing cowry-
decorated leather charms into my hands. With the smell of sweat, including
my own, but also the incense-like mixture of dust and hot peppery air, I
became terrified and almost turned around to go back into the hotel. But
seeing the eyes of the contortionist flit through the crowd, I went forward,
neither speaking nor acknowledging anyone until eventually I was alone,
outdistancing the throng.

As I went further into Dakar, the stereotypical romantic images I had
in my mind of an Africa of magnificent fauna, flora, landscapes, color,
and gleaming brown bodies draped in exotic tribal accessories—the stuff
of high-powered photography, popular anthropology, and the performance
around the pool the day before—fell away almost as quickly as the crowd
of indigents outside my hotel. Gray streets strewn with paper, iron-screened
windows, not a single surface of fresh paint in sight, dilapidated buildings,
and urban anonymity embraced me instead. I relaxed for the first time since
my arrival and saw at the end of the street—which ran back to Mt. Athos,
through Jericho and Cairo—the ostensible reason for my leaving the hotel:
to visit Dakar's outdoor, central market.

Yet the street ran back farther too, to places I understood or felt connected to not much more than here. What did my vow about exploring to
the roots my own Western culture before seeking any other really mean?
Where did deciding to focus on European culture because my Italian and
Ukrainian families had been in the United States only since the beginning of
the twentieth century really lead? Would traveling over and over to England,
France, Italy, Sicily, Eastern Europe, and Greece tell me much more about
my origins and myself than it would tell anyone of any background who was
equally attentive and enthralled with the experience? Why wouldn't Shakespeare's English and Kent's pastures, Paris's gutters flooding in the morning
and all the art history in the Louvre, Duccio's *Maesta* in Sienna, every layer
of religion like sediment in Rome and the rest of the European cultural tradition like any continent's cultural tradition reveal the riches of humanity
and the universals of identity to any pilgrim devoted to them?

Didn't any more individual kind of European cultural identity for myself
as a second-generation American also lead back to a place less grand but

more like the dust of Jericho and the rooms of shoes and eyeglasses in Yad Vashem yet at least as strange as anything I could experience in the national museum in Cairo? Didn't I come out of the steerage compartment on boats coming to the United States from Europe early in the twentieth century?

If I went back to *Know thyself,* as the legendary Delphic oracle counseled, at my first stop I joined millions and millions of others. It was not even a place but a piece of paper filed on Ellis Island in New York City's harbor: a ship's manifest. For others it could be a plane's, a train's, or a bus's and for more and more no paper at all but merely a memory. I read "Ignatz Skula: ethnicity, Austria; last place of residence, Bukacziza, Galicia; date of arrival, January 27, 1911; age at arrival, 25; ship of travel, Rhein; port of departure, Bremen"—my Ukrainian grandfather. I read "Carlo Cantalupo; ethnicity, Itali; last place of residence, Altomonte; date of arrival, June 15, 1894; age at arrival, 20; ship of travel, Scotia; port of Departure, Napoli"—my Italian grandfather. I read "Katarzyna Skula; ethnicity, Austria, Polish; last place of residence, Bukaszowce, Austria; date of arrival, July 22, 1913; age at arrival 22; ship of travel, Rijndam; port of departure, Rotterdam"—my Ukrainian grandmother. I knew my Italian grandmother's name, Pasqualina Bertoli, and when she married my grandfather in New York City in 1898, but I couldn't find her on any ship's manifest.

I looked at the ship's pictures—the *Rhein,* the *Scotia,* the *Rijndam*: antiquated smokestacks and masts perched on seagoing wombs giving birth to my grandparents' new lives. I read that a few hundred at best traveled in first and second class, while thousands including my grandparents packed into third. They existed like ants in the dust of Jericho. Their bags looked like the African's I declined in Kennedy Airport. I pictured my grandmother's eyeglasses and my grandfather's shoes. Stories as complex and strange as any Egyptian god's trailed behind them.

Where could I find these people? How could I join them? By going back to Galicia, Austria, Poland, Italy, and Ukraine, which they fled? By finding some birth records in addition to what I already had on the manifests; some family gravestones; a relative who wouldn't have known them since they died too long ago; their names and mine on an office or a store or in a telephone book? Or perhaps I could see this bulbous nose in Galicia or that double chin in Altomonte like my own? Perhaps I could trade a knowing look, recognize or even spontaneously duplicate a gesture over some kind of cabbage dish or pasta?

Didn't traces at least as real or strange of my past families' lives lie ahead beyond the archway at the entrance to Dakar's Marche Sandaga, as they would in any such open market in the world?

Squeezing between the only eight inches I could see in a tight line of dilapidated, idling taxis, I hopped three piles—basketball sneakers, Korans, spare parts for wheelchairs—like a moat around a striped brick doorway. In its cool shade after Dakar's bright streets like steam rooms, my mind went blank as if it had been erased. I saw a table of vultures, split open, gutted and spread for sale in the hot, peppery air. I saw another table covered with roots. Taking the lowest denomination of paper currency that I had in my pocket, I bought a stick and chewed it. The seller, veiled and dressed in straw, chewed the same kind. A leper held out her white-crusted stump of a hand for some coins, and I knew I should give, if only to feel safe.

As I went to the next table covered with incense for sale, the smell of whatever was burning overwhelmed me with its entropy. I would have fainted but held on to the table's splintery edge, clenching my teeth on the root until it burst with a bitterness and heat that flashed from my tongue to my eyes that immediately began to tear so that I couldn't see—but then just as suddenly cleared. I saw myriad colors with woven or waxed patterns on stacks of cotton fabric for sale—the women on the road from the airport pressed deeply within them. Did they know my recurring dream of hand-drawn pictures of the uses of petroleum from my sixteen-hour first night's sleep after arriving in Dakar? Ghosts with no hands and wings like goat horns picked over piles of jelly shoes decaying in the sun. I saw debtors and creditors locked together in a single chain that dangled coins. A fashion model removed one to wear as an earring. Worms and bugs caressed endless tables of obscene vegetables, not one of which I recognized. Could I taste one, please? No one answered. The birds depicted on miles of rugs flew off like prayers into a labyrinth of green walls. A disembodied high-pitched voice offered ivory for my bones and dung to burn. "Are you cold?" I heard the words as if they were spelled by a pitch-black face with heavy crude stitches where I would expect to see eyes, a nose, and mouth. The next stall offered a corpse fresh from the gallows. I ran my hands lovingly over a table of huge bras mixed with equally large flowers that, when I asked their name, the saleswoman called "God." Chubby children sold Kleenex, short children sold gum, and the skinniest children sold cigarettes—but only one by one and not in packs. I sorted through baskets of hands and feet belonging to thieves who begged beside them. After tasting various sweat-flavored oils in between licks from a bar of salt offered to me by a mother as toothless as the baby sucking her breast deep in the green and yellow leaves and letters of the alphabet on her dress, I took notes on all the different horns that can grow from a human mind. Between a table of roasted rats and three boiling vats of fufu, I felt cleansed of my sins amid so many lost husbands and dead wives sharing the good news in the gonging bells. Selling cassettes with a claim that they guaranteed peace, a writer closed his journal to tell me that he cloned children out of the museum fantasies of secret police. An old man with a face shaped like a heart and neither selling nor buying anything offered me half of the water he carried in a plastic baggy. Drinking in this kingdom of fetish ruled by the drunk and lonely, I prayed that I would either become so white I would be invisible or that, from when I first entered the market, the leper's blessing—which stayed with me throughout but modulated from a purr to a shriek—would make me black. Playing it back on the small tape recorder I carried and trying to sing along, I envisioned storks consuming swarms of locusts blocking out the sun until it shined again between thunderstorms. The first hand of a line of hands to shoulders, the blind leading the blind, pushed me out of the way. I landed at a table with a chair. A waiter brought a beer I didn't order. When the rat running back and forth underneath the table and the man hanging over it with a gun became too much for me to bear, I clutched the black cat skin I bought—although to this day still afraid to say from whom—and said my name out loud so that I could disappear.

I awakened, back in my room again. Around five minutes after I had entered the market the day before, nausea and stomach cramps forced me to turn around and go back to the hotel. I fell asleep but woke up feverish and had been back and forth to the bathroom many times during the night. Luckily I had bought three liters of water, a baguette, and bananas at the market, which made me feel better now. I was also better prepared—I said the word "initiated" out loud—for the next time I walked out of my hotel.

I tried to pick my way through the hotel gate's impoverished throng who offered every possible way to help me, but this time one of them persisted even more. A young man named Mino stood at my shoulder as I waited at the corner for a break in the traffic two streets away. "No thanks, no thanks, no thanks," I told him, but he continued to remain by my side, striding in the previous year's model of Air Jordan sneakers, his half buttoned and ripped flannel shirt hanging out of baggy pants flapping in the hot and soggy air that I had followed the day before through the streets of Dakar. I tried and tried to lose him, but he hung on.

When we reached the market, it seemed to say, "Here you need him too." The dust of Jericho, Sinai's unforgiving stone, Cairo's labyrinth, and all I had seen thus far in Dakar reinforced an inescapable stereotype I had hoped to avoid: white tourist, indigo black guide. Over a beer, we set a price.

A week later when I was about to leave Dakar, I invited him into the hotel lobby. A few tourists raised their eyebrows, and a few staff lowered theirs. As we sat down and I was about to pay him, he doubled the price. I refused and, although he quietly persisted, the lobby's darkness lined with mirrors amplified our haggling to a point where I felt I had at least to offer him a tip. He had said his family needed more money than we had initially agreed upon, especially since the day after the next was the prophet Mohammed's birthday, which would require a sheep for the feast. I offered to buy the sheep, and he agreed. The next morning on a beach near the hotel, we both stood knee deep in the waves, foamy and pink with the blood of his sheep and many more being slaughtered in the surf.

The day after Mino and I struck our initial deal, a Sunday, he said we should take a ferry to the island of Goree, one of the first places in Africa to be visited by fifteenth-century Europeans and a marginal debarkation point for slaves a mile and a half out in the bay of Dakar. Halfway there I saw red stucco buildings lining its shore, and a famous line from *Macbeth* squirted into my mind to describe how Goree's history and the entire West African slave trade would eventually "the multitudinous seas incarnadine, / Making the green one red." Shakespeare and Senegal? The line's iambic rhythm blended with the small, quick waves lapping Goree's welcoming quays that opened onto a vision of palm trees, baobabs, and bougainvilleas in a cool and flowery breeze. I never expected to realize and experience the line's literal meaning, especially amid such a tropical, peaceful scene. It also seemed to reach out into every winding Goree alley and street, up and over any mortar or human wall of fear or doubt and drift in the clouds of ganja smoke rounding every corner—as if Goree required so much peace to shush and still every other possible disturbance that might detract from someone's hearing what Goree also launched.

A few days later, Mino led me to a shore outside of Dakar heaped with sharks, blue marlins, and tuna like giant coins. Wooden boats painted with divine eyes crashed through the warm, rough surf and up the steep beach. Along the way I saw a lake—shallow, pink, and surrounded by foam—where women panned salt the way I wanted to understand what I was beginning to see and had, in my earlier planning for the trip, mistakenly thought was my religion.

We ended every day in poor clubs in the outlying districts of Dakar. Reeking of pombe, palm wine, and lager, my teeth red with cola nuts and bangi smoke, I danced until I fell down, danced and fell down again, happy to lie in the mud and hear a drum like an oracle. It told me that I should start my life again, only this time with no pretending that I wasn't at least equal parts animal and soul, West and East, my family's past, my children's future, and most of all what I found in between.

The day I was to depart Dakar, Mino went with me to the airport. Still very drunk from the birthday celebrations for the prophet Mohammed that had continued the night before—religious fundamentalism having no place in his pantheon and less and less in my mind—he told me along the way that he would be starting a new job on a shrimp boat owned and run by Greeks.

"Do you like them?" I asked.

"They are seagulls. They steal everything," he spat. He thought that Greeks and their culture—modern or ancient—stole everything they had from Africa. I had heard such Afrocentrism before, although not as spontaneously expressed, arguing for a surge of civilization from Egypt to Crete to Athens. A dozen years earlier I had wondered, "Classical or Byzantine? Blue sky or gold? Metamorphosis or transubstantiation?" Now I was beginning to see things from another direction: from Jericho, Cairo, Marche Sandaga, and Goree.

At the airport, after an hour of my struggling through the crowd at the check-in desk, an agent told me that I had no seat because the flight was overbooked, and that I should return the next day for another flight. "*Non confirme, non confirme, non confirme*," she said over and over, shaking her head.

Drenched in sweat and panicking that I would never get out of Dakar, I could only answer her with "*Impossible, impossible, impossible.*" I went back to tell Mino. The same fear that almost made me turn back the first day I left the hotel and the same feeling of dissociation and being lost that I felt in Jericho, in Cairo, and again Dakar's central market came all at once rushing back into my mind. Seeing Mino passed out drunk and sprawled over two chairs, I ran away and took a taxi back to my hotel.

Neither the doorman nor the two clerks at the check-in desk showed any surprise that I was returning—bags in hand—three hours after I had said good-bye with a tip and an unfulfilled wish for some reassurance that I would not be returning. I went straight to the hotel manager's office, Mr. Diop, to whom I had given an even larger tip. A good businessman but not an actor, he obviously feigned surprise at my return but compensated with directions to the Air Afrique office two blocks away and the name of the person whom I must demand to see. For the price of another sheep, I felt secure once more.

Leaving my bags in his office, I ran to Air Afrique as if I knew the way; as if I knew the lepers whose hands I filled with coins in exchange for blessings at the door; as if I knew everyone like family in the crowd even worse than at the airport pushing and squeezing and stuck between *non confirmé* and *impossible*; as if I knew that for the price of one more sheep, I would leave the crowd behind and enter the inner sanctum of a dwarfish manager at a huge desk, and that his high-pitched *Merci* would confirm my ticket to depart the next day while I still felt as if I barely escaped with my life.

My next stop, Togo, wiped out once and for all any interest I had in seeing how Catholicism adapted to an African cultural context. I took a day trip from Togo's capital, Lomé, where I was staying, to an island that the pope had visited a year or two before. To get there I had to hire a boat and someone to pole our way across a blindingly silver lake reflecting a chrome sky. For most of the trip I could only see the boat boy's dark skin and a few distant mangroves. Stumbling up the dock when we arrived, I took his hand, and he led me to a building.

Inside I met a blind old man in a stained pink djellaba with a matching skullcap. Acting official, he proudly pointed to a huge wicker chair and said, "Pope sat there." A few pictures of his visit hung on the walls, but nothing and no one else seemed to register that anything out of the ordinary had happened.

Mistakenly taking a left turn rather than a right out of the building, I walked further into town instead of back to my boat. Less than a block away from where the pope sat, I stopped. In the middle of the road and about knee high, I saw a crude gray statue of a man with an oversize penis sticking straight out; the statue was lodged in a kind of red shrine littered with a few spent candles, a broken Coke bottle, and some plastic flowers. Becoming self-conscious and afraid that I was alone, I ran back to the boat.

A week later in Lomé, I wanted to visit Togo's famous "fetish market" before I departed for Kenya. I hired a cab, and about halfway there, I saw people running and screaming in a huge cloud of dust. The driver stopped, and I asked him what was happening. He said that the people had caught a thief.

They surrounded him in a ravine, his shirt already in tatters. At quick, random intervals someone would jump out of the crowd and hit him. At first he met them with his own anger, standing straight and yelling in their faces. But as the crowd, refusing his intimidation, continued to draw a tighter and tighter ring around him, he began to cower. A woman calmly approached with a corrugated aluminum Coca-Cola sign. I turned away and, closing my eyes, heard a loud slam. Opening them, I saw him on his knees with blood running down his face. As he lifted his arm, a barrage of stones and garbage fell upon him, and he crumbled in the dust. A clean, well-built man in a workout suit ran up with a huge stone and dropped it point blank on the thief's chest. His legs and arms flapped a few times, and then they stopped. Everything stopped. A few guilty minutes passed, and the crowd began to disperse. We drove on.

I recognized the man who delivered the final blow. He was one of a group of bicyclists and boxers with whom I had been hanging out in Togo's bars at night, doing whatever they did except ending the night with prostitutes, since I was afraid of catching AIDS.

I met him one day when I was wandering past a huge soccer stadium in a dusty, windy and iridescent expanse at the edge of the city in search of a bicycle rental shop I never found. Seeing him standing authoritatively near a doorway into the stadium, I asked him if he knew about the shop, but he asked in reply why I wanted it. "To get some exercise," I said. He pointed toward the door and said a gym was inside, and I was welcome to workout there. Out came two bicyclists only slightly lighter than their black bicycle tights emblazoned with *Liberté, Egalité, Fraternité* in neon red, yellow, and green. Telling them I wanted a bike, he translated their speaking in Ewe into French. They said the shop had closed for lunch. He insisted that we should all have lunch too and called a taxi driver idly standing near his cab with an open trunk full of cloth in fifty yard bolts of bright magenta, chartreuse, and orange printed with soccer balls and what I supposed were pictures of Togolese soccer stars. The driver slammed down the trunk immediately and pulled over to us. Remembering Mino and how I had been unnecessarily cautious and afraid when I first met him, I got into the taxi without a second thought. Two more men in their late twenties whom I hadn't seen before now jumped in the car. They carried fraying plastic shopping bags with boxing gloves inside and wore tight T-shirts: the red one had *boxeur* written in white across the chest; the other reproduced the Togolese flag, with five equal horizontal bands of yellow and green, yet emblazoned with red squares containing dollar signs instead of the usual white star.

Barely able to see out of the crowded cab and wondering why the road kept getting worse and worse to the point that we all had our hands above our heads to protect them from hitting the fabric and padding-stripped roof with its sharp, rusty bolts, I realized the driver was asking me a question. I had to ask him to repeat it three times before I understood: "You like *choukoutou*?" I knew the word meant a local beer made from millet, and I wanted to taste it. Before I could say yes, the cab hit another deep rut and lurched so hard that I pulled back my answer and wondered if *choukoutou* was worth this strange ride with six Togolese whom I had only known for a half hour and that maybe I was in danger. Why should I die for *choukoutou*? Five seconds later we stopped, and everyone got out without a word.

I followed them through a gate of bound-up gray sticks. We entered a mostly empty dirt yard with low benches barely carved from trees and set in a rectangle around a huge, black, boiling cauldron on a smoky fire under a canopy of very dry palm fronds. A topless, toothless, and smiling woman, as fit as any of us although looking much older and in a head scarf and skirt dyed by the dirt and the ash, handed me a weathered and hollowed calabash brimming with the beer, a cooled-down version of what was still brewing in the pot. We sat on the benches, but still no one spoke except for the first man I had met back at the stadium, who said over our third refill that the brew became stronger and stronger the longer it aged but that each batch had to be finished by the end of the day.

As I saw him from my taxi window the next morning slightly lift and then let go of the huge rock that crushed whatever life remained in the thief whom the crowd caught and tortured to death, our eyes met. As he turned his back and walked away toward the crowd, he began shaking his finger at the sky and slowly repeating, "*Chou-kou-tou, chou-kou-tou, chou-kou-tou . . .*"

The fetish market was a huge, open field with many lean-tos and tables covered with dead and dried vegetable and animal parts. The arrangements, however, were orderly as a supermarket's, including items like antelope horns, large skulls of birds, lineups of progressively larger claws, similarly laid-out skins—and then, in the vegetable section, pods of every hue and size, tiny straight sticks, crooked big ones, gourds and seeds, mounds of leaves, and fetid liquids looking like a mixture of them all in corked bottles long missing their original labels. I bought a monkey skull. It still had some hair and meat that were indistinguishable from one another, but I thrust it in my vest pocket.

Toward the end of the market, I entered a cinder block building with holes for windows. Inside I saw a pile of burnt wood, wax, bones, seared paper, and thick gooey blood. A little boy poked in his head.

"Stay, stay. Priest is coming."

At first I wanted to meet him, but not after I saw him. Barefoot, filthy, wearing a ripped tweed jacket, shorts almost falling off, one bloodshot eye open and the other swollen closed, he was drunk. I said hello and asked about the pile at our feet. He started to explain, but I couldn't understand if he was even using words or was only managing slurred syllables amid long gravelly "urrrrrrrrsssssss." Feeling intimidated and replying *Merci* in an unintended high voice as my fingers gripped the monkey skull in my pocket, I backed out the cinder block door and hurried with the little boy running beside me toward the taxi. Along the way his filthy blue shorts and red T-shirt reflected every stand in the market like a mirror. He ran as if it were simply part of his job. His eyes glanced back and forth between what we were passing and me as if he saw no difference.

Returning to my room in the hotel and dazed by all I had seen, I felt my pocket and remembered the skull. I took it out, gagged and didn't know what to do with it. What if it did have some kind of power or disease? Guiltily, I wrapped it in toilet paper, gently placed it in the bottom of a garbage basket and put it out on the balcony.

The next morning I was at the airport to begin my flight to Kenya. Over coffee, I decided I should take a few more notes while I had some extra time and a lot of details fresh in my mind. I reached in my pants pocket for my notebook, but it wasn't there. I panicked. All of my fresh, on-the-spot observations and insights were gone: the precise words of the exact moment as it happened—my supreme superstitions of *le mot juste* and *le ligne donnée*—upon which I based my most precious possession, my poetry. Who needed people, traveling companions, or even love when I had such dispatches from what I imagined to be an African muse and in my own words? Thinking I lost the notebook at the hotel, I called the desk attendant, whom I had tipped before I left, although with less than I tipped in Dakar, and asked him to search my room. He said he would call housekeeping and that I should call him back in ten minutes. Ten minutes would only leave a half hour before my plane departed.

When I called him back, he told me that nothing had been found. I insisted that the room be searched again more thoroughly, and he said I should call back in ten minutes. When I did, in five minutes, he told me that the notebook had not been found, but the maid did say she found a monkey skull.

Embarrassed and desperate, I remembered that I had had breakfast in the hotel that morning and that I had been writing in the restaurant. I asked that it be searched, too. Again he said I should call back in ten minutes. When I did, again five minutes later, the news was what I wanted to hear. The desk attendant drove to the airport with my notebook. Clutching my own fetish, I ran and caught my plane to Kenya a minute before its cabin doors were sealed.

Flying over central Africa, I looked down. Darkest Africa? No darker than the Atlantic I flew over from New York to Dakar; certainly less dark than the Atlantic to my immigrant grandparents deep in the womb of steerage on the *Scotia*, the *Rhein*, and the *Rijndam*. They traveled a lot further physically and mentally from Galicia or Altomonte to New York than I from New York to Dakar, around thirty-eight hundred miles. But Dakar to Nairobi, West Africa to East, now doubled my distance from New York.

How much would Nairobi differ from Dakar? What made me think that flying nearly four thousand miles more I would find roughly the same Africa, except for the landscape and the game parks? Was my assumption based simply on race, since nearly everyone was black? Nearly everyone in Europe was white, but a distance of four hundred or sometimes even forty miles revealed huge differences. Flying thirty-five hundred or four thousand miles from New York to Europe—London, Paris, Rome—revealed them too. Why did I consider Africa as a single entity, not merely as a continent but culturally too, when I knew and thrived on the differences I saw among these other places? If I thought of race as color, white had no great advantage over black in registering difference other than in shades. If I saw so much of it in white culture, why didn't I expect to find at least as many differences in black? I might not have seen central Africa through the airplane window as any darker than the Atlantic, but something out there, as in Jericho, Yad Vashem, the Sinai, Cairo, Marche Sandaga, and Togo, kept challenging the darkest parts of my mind.

If I had more readily embraced rather than run away from what these places were telling me, I might have known a way to see a kind of unity about Africa not merely based on race or ignorance yet beyond its simply being a continent. Ironically, since I was flying to Kenya, I didn't know that around the same time as I had vowed my fealty to Western culture fifteen years before, a Kenyan novelist and professor, James Ngugi, had proposed that his Department of English at the University of Nairobi be abolished and replaced with a Department of African Literature and Languages. It would establish the "centrality of Africa" and "African literature . . . [as] the major branch of African culture." Professor Ngugi insisted, "Things must be seen from the African perspective."[6] I also didn't know that since then his novels and essays had established him throughout Africa and worldwide as one of Africa's leading writers and that, now known as Ngugi wa Thiong'o, he was proclaiming literature—both oral and written—in African languages as the key to Africa's unity and development.

Still tightly holding my notebook as I took a taxi from Nairobi airport to a beautiful green suburb, I had never heard of Ngugi. Arriving at my old friend's lavish house behind a huge fence with an armed guard at the gate and his shack with eight members of his family in the back, I also had no idea that Ngugi or anyone else had been imprisoned in Kenya for their writing. I could never have imagined that a mere character in one of his books had frightened the government into issuing a warrant for the character's arrest. Sipping deliciously cool and plentiful Portuguese green wine, I felt consoled by my friend's British-style colonial housing—even down to the shape and particular mechanism of the doorknobs. Driving her new Isuzu through herds of giraffes in the game park on Nairobi's outskirts, freely coming and going in the American Embassy, and lingering in its substantial library, I didn't see any of Ngugi's Kenya. I wanted to see my own.

It didn't include the British gin and biltong set in a sleek and rich, mahogany-paneled flight club at Nairobi's municipal airport, where my friend introduced me. Unlike most of the members, I neither aspired to nor could act like a character in updated versions of Beryl Markham, Ernest Hemingway, Elspeth Huxley, or Karen Blixen. At dinner parties and embassy gatherings when their books were continually pressed into my hands with warm recommendations about seeing the real Kenya, I demurred. They seemed so strong, assured, self-asserting, and individualistic. The recurring moments of profound vulnerability I had been experiencing from Jericho to Togo made me feel the opposite, even though I fit these authors' stereotype—although I was also not conscious of it at the time—of the wandering white writer from Europe or America treating "Africa as setting and backdrop . . . as a metaphysical battlefield,"[7] which Chinua Achebe wrote about Joseph Conrad's *Heart of Darkness* a few years after Ngugi had proclaimed Africa's "centrality." Seeing the ants tunneling through the sand at Jericho, walking through Dakar's Marche Sandaga, and wandering in Togo overwhelmed me and became the foreground, pushing who I thought I was either into the background or almost totally out of the picture. Initially I had come to these places, as Edward Said wrote ten years before, feeling like I had "the relative upper hand"[8] and "as a European or American first, as an individual second,"[9] self-proclaimed at that. Until then I embraced and wanted no more than to know myself as "a part of the earth with a definite history . . . since the time of Homer,"[10] again in Said's words. But experiencing the rooms in Cairo's national museum stacked with a different "definite history" and seeing a makeshift animistic shrine in Togo supplant one man's "definite history" with its own, my American and European, individual concerns disappeared. Overpowered, I felt like an erased slate, and these places and their people began writing on me. Between the sun and the ants in the sand at Jericho or what lay on the tables in the fetish market in Lomé, I felt like little more than a shadow.

Like most foreign visitors to Nairobi, I wanted to leave the city to see more of the country: the Rift Valley, the savannas, the lakes, the wildlife, Mt. Kilimanjaro and all the way down to the Indian Ocean. Countless travel agencies, most of which were painted bright yellow and run by Indians, offered safaris, and their low or high price reflected the quality of the vehicle and accommodations.

Grouped with half a dozen travelers who like me could not afford to travel in a new air-conditioned Range Rover, on one trip I rode in an ancient Nissan four-wheel with holes in the floor and the ceiling. They allowed the red dust and rain to enter freely, depending on the weather of the moment. I traveled with an austere but nature-loving Swedish mother and her adolescent daughter who were continually annoyed by the driver's playing Janet Jackson tapes and smoking Marlboros. A Saudi Arabian couple rarely spoke and slept most of the time, although she, veiled and swirled in turquoise chiffon, would awake to spray perfume when the dust inside the car became thick, and he had an endless supply of Johnnie Walker Black. He was happy to share it with me in the evenings as long as I smoked his Marlboro Golds when we drank. An Italian couple occupied the third bench seat in the very back. They were impeccably clean, urban, and tailored in safari khaki. Whenever I would turn around, I would see them frowning and gesturing as they muttered "*Sporchi, sporchi, sporchissimi*" (dirty, dirty . . .). A glaze of red mud finished the scene.

As we approached Mt. Kilimanjaro from the Kenya side, and at a left turn on a road that bordered Tanzania, I looked up. Nothing but the mountain filled the windshield and sky.

Did the car and its inhabitants disappear? Did I? It felt that way.

Two hours later I crouched in the dust next to the skull of a wildebeest. We had passed it earlier in the car on our way to a camp. I left it just before dusk, walking by myself around half a mile back to where I had seen the skull because I wanted to take a tooth from it home with me. The camp rules were that no one was supposed to go out alone. They reminded me of what most of my family and friends said when I told them I wanted to go to Egypt and then to West Africa and Kenya—don't go. I looked at the skull. It wasn't threatening me, no more than the few scraggly bushes nearby and the light brown dust all around. I picked up the skull by the horns and took it back to the camp.

Seeing the mountain blot the entire windshield brought back the vertigo of my own unreality, but the skull literally gave me something to hold on. Its intricately engraved wood texture against my palm made feeling overwhelmed familiar and even welcome. Kilimanjaro's massive scale and the wildebeest skull's deep, hollow eyes originated in a specific place, but that didn't prevent them from becoming a part of anyone's self-understanding, no matter where he or she was from or going. I happened to be moving from west to east, from America to Europe, to Israel, and then south to

Africa—my own kind of ant tunneling through the sand. But finding such places and trying to fathom their meanings could no more be limited to one direction than the winds.

We camped on a river and slept in box tents set up on platforms with front porches. Hippos floated like detached, dark clouds down the stream. A leopard perched in a nearby cedar crowned by a martial eagle belying its name by looking peaceful. I wanted a style like the sharpened bones of sunbirds and weavers. Could I get them to build their nests somewhere between my ears and my eyes? I wanted words like a wand of carved teak from a nearby tree that I could wave in the form of a question at the throne of creation surrounding me wherever I looked.

Later that night, necklaces of impala eyes like yellow stars draped the trails around the camp. We drove out to spot game and parked beside a Tanzania-bound tsunami of wildebeests. A lion leaped in the headlights and landed on one's back, scattering the herd. The second I saw blood, I heard the cry of hyenas and saw her cubs approach. An ivory ring I had bought in Nairobi cracked and fell off my finger. I knew I could not tolerate being alone much longer.

Three days later, the same feeling drove me to the end of a beach jutting far out into the Indian Ocean near Mombasa. Seeing no one else around, I couldn't tell what pounded louder in my ears, the surf or my bloodstream. I imagined finding a pearl and throwing it as far into the waves as I could. Their fading dark gray except where they broke brighter and brighter white made me look up. I was caught in a hard rain and a harder wind. Where could I go? I saw a big bush. Its branches easily parted, and inside I sat on the sand. I saw another person's eyes but felt no fear.

CHAPTER TWO

Connection

Blinded by the sunshine in the park outside of Casablanca's peroxide white cathedral, I could only think, "Mint, mint, mint." I was chewing a sprig and shuffling two more between my fingers. For a moment, the city's colonial name, "Casablanca," better represented its overwhelming brightness than the original Arabic name, "Al Maghrib," referring to sunset. As my sight returned, I saw Barbara walking toward me. I gave her a sprig and remembered what she said when she first saw and then took off the chain of religious medals I always wore around my neck: a cross of poppy petals, a dove, a corn god, a shell from Senegal, an image of St. Benedict. Did I "wear them for or against?" Both, I replied, *for* protection and *against* harm. But protection and harm from *what* was the harder question, which the mint itself answered for now.

The cathedral reminded me of the wildebeest skull—only immense and bleached white. I had gone inside. Stepping around the piles of ripped newsprint swirling around its door and passing the dry holy water font, I entered a kind of cavern lit only by daylight through half boarded-up, color-less windows. I expected the cool, damp air but not a vacant building. The emptiness made me hunch over and anticipate a bullet, since I was unsure if I should even be there. What used to be a cathedral now felt like a trans-gression. As I walked—or was pulled—toward the main altar flanked by two smaller ones, a flock of pigeons whirled overhead, their wings and coos sounding like quick, high-pitched cries of "no, no, no, no, no, no, no." At the altar I found blood and feathers where the tabernacle would have been. The glass had been removed from the two-inch hole gouged in the center of the altar stone for relics, but I rubbed my finger inside it. Looking up at the blankness of the altar's backdrop, I wanted to project a word, which I whispered: "Desecrated." As soon I heard it, I knew it was wrong and thought of "desacralized." Or did I mean "deconsecrated?" With the noise of traffic coming from outside droning louder and louder like some new kind of plainsong, as I was leaving I found an old man sitting in the doorway. He quietly sang "Allah, Allah" amid empty medicine vials, amber beads, shreds of a flowery shower curtain, bits of colored paper, and a large, fresh bouquet of mint. He pointed to it and held out his hand. Leaving alms at his feet, I took three sprigs.

Barbara and I came to Morocco to produce a play that I wrote, focusing on the closeness between the words "animal" and "anima"—spirit or soul—and centering on my experiences the previous year in West Africa and Kenya. I wanted my lyric poetry to be performed, including a cast of college students and reinforced with original music, dance, and slide and video projection.

Due to our sponsor's being related to a Moroccan general currently waging a successful war against antigovernment insurgents in the western Sahara, the play avoided being censored, which would have occurred if we were forced, as one municipal official demanded, to translate it into French from English. The official's cramped office with three desks, a raging out-of-control storm of documents in French and Arabic, typewriters everywhere and no air conditioner, all of which added to his hysteria, couldn't compete with our calmly invoking the general's name and his autocratic approval of our work that, of course, he hadn't read and wouldn't see. From before we entered the office until after we left, the official never stopped talking—again in a chaotic mixture of French and Arabic. The sense of what he had to say only registered as an increase and decrease of the speed and volume of words: an unpredictable sequence—fast, slow, soft, and loud—in which I never actually heard him say *oui, aewa, iyeh,* or *yes.* Nor did he stop or seem to notice when my sponsor, the general's brother-in-law, signaled we should leave.

When we descended the slippery-with-sand two flights of gray marble steps from the office and passed through a hallway to the other side of the building that housed the city hall, I began to understand what had happened. A door opened and one of my students appeared. "Great theater," he said. The city hall and the municipal theater shared the same building. I felt like a fool thinking that my staging lyric poetry as a form of multimedia performance could be avant-garde in a place where politics and theater officially and literally shared the same roof, although one had to turn right or left at the entrance for one or the other, even though they could seem indistinguishable. The battle-scarred general knew that neither he nor his government should fear a play from the United States featuring rock music, bizarre costumes, modern dance, and good-looking American students, most of them African American, performing obscure poetry in English that few in the audience of the sold-out theater could understand but that they still enjoyed.

I fell right into the mix—although also for me the confusion—of politics and performance one afternoon as I walked to rehearsal. A passing, beat-up Renault with bullhorns on its roof blared what I thought was a political message to support one candidate over another in the upcoming election. Mixing English and French, I asked a shopkeeper selling cheap pastel chiffon women's clothing—whom I chose so that he could not delay me for long with too many invitations to buy something—exactly what the loudspeakers were booming.

"Ah, you don't understand," he said. "It is in Berber and from the mayor inviting everyone to a play tonight."

"That's *my* play," I replied, but he only acknowledged it with a smile and a nod before he lifted a huge pile of chiffon veils and pushed them into my arms.

When Barbara and I began to bond—beginning after an earlier performance of the same play in Pennsylvania—I wanted a different kind of connection instead of the spiritual sense of the word "anima" and the more ordinary meaning of the word "animal," which the play was about. I remembered the myth in Plato's *Symposium* about a time when "The race was divided into three. . . . Beside the two sexes, male and female, which we have at present, there was a third which partook of the nature of both, and for which we still have a name, although the creature itself is forgotten."[1] Was this as imaginary as Eurydice? I tried to imagine it. Four arms, four legs, two faces on two heads, four eyes and two necks? Two sexes knitting one body and one bloodstream with never less than two dreams yet both understood a desire easily rolled apart and back into one ball of difference and *yes?* Eight spokes of happiness strong and sensitive to their tips cartwheeling across any boundary to touch? Did this creature have to be split on every hair of judgment sharp as a razor? Broken into sexes, races, species, politics, families and inevitably alone? Unable to understand a dream of walking away with an armful of dead leaves that look like children's faces on old gravestones? I gave Barbara the mint from the beggar in the doorway of the cathedral in Casablanca as I gave her a sprig of lavender on the day a couple months before when we decided that we would travel here together because I felt the answers to these questions connected us.

Before we met, we had wandered like two separate halves, two myths: two fables with nothing to feed or to eat, having said and committed too much to too many other myths; both unable to prevent betrayal, abandonment, failure, and death. We saw each other in torn mattresses, ripped and burned photographs of abandoned steelyards and curling paper covered with rules that no longer applied. We wanted a beaker not a vase. We wanted to connect a chorus of dogs at first light and a cat claw in the dirt; an interstate trucker's evil eye and a stop sign; a riverbank planed lower than the rapids it contained and a black butterfly too close to the water to survive. Now when she put the religious medals back around my neck, I realized that they were for and against when she was gone, and they meant I missed her. The lavender and the mint meant we were together.

Traveling to Casablanca for a few days to relax after the play, we found a sleek hotel room and made love near constantly for three days and nights. I had proposed marriage to her on the way as were driving in the desert from Fes. She said "Yes" framed by our tiny, rented, white Renault's passenger side window as the blurry charcoal mountains and colorless, scorched plains whizzed by. Casablanca was our last stop together, after traveling north from Agadir, where the play took place, through Marrakech and over the Atlas Mountains to Fes.

After she left Casablanca, I drove south down the coast to stay a week more on the ocean. Watching twenty-foot green surf crash and carve an inlet through a volcanic jetty, from my dilapidated balcony room with white shutters, I realized I knew no one on an entire continent behind and below me as I looked east. I felt even more isolated as I thought of Barbara being on the opposite coast, far beyond the furiously impenetrable barrier of wild surf. It seemed to leave me helpless: once more the unwitting prey of ants in the dust of Jericho, mountains of eyeglasses and shoes at Yad Vashem, strange gods of Egypt, soul-crushing rocks in the Sinai, confusion and chaos in Marche Sandaga and fetish fears in Togo; flattened by Kilimanjaro and twisted as the wildebeest skull's rictus; even more exposed and vulnerable than I was when the storm hit the beach on the Indian Ocean. Instead of turning away from such enigmas and looking back like Orpheus, hoping for some consolation from what I knew had to be false, I now understood that connecting myself with these places and things led to connecting with Barbara and a new life. But where was it as I woke alone and opened the shutters to look out? This separation from her at once embodied all of the disconnects I had felt being in Africa up to that moment. Yet again it pushed and cast off like a dead skin the person who I thought I was into the background, only now the foreground was not the Egyptian pantheon, as it was when I first experienced such a feeling at the entrance to the national museum in Cairo, but the pain of separation from Barbara. For the next week I would again have felt insubstantial as a shadow and merely ephemeral or more like an illusion than a person except for the surroundings and remembering our experiences together south of this exploding emerald ocean and sultry shore pouring into my sense of absence and bursting it open.

The always damp, salty, and sandy coating on everything in my room, including the bed, and the wind from the ocean rattling the windowless shutters kept waking me up the first night I was alone and drove me out before dawn. On the beach, as the sun rose, I watched a candle burn all the way down on a rock beside a deepening tidal pool. A woman in a tight and shining black suit that barely covered her stepped into the pool, immersed herself totally and began a kind of dance of prone moves like a giant eel in a secret cleft. She arched her back, twisted, stretched, splashed, spread her long hair, and whipped the water with it. She went under again, reemerged floating on her back and repeated the moves more slowly than the first time until, after pausing a minute—that seemed unending—and as her long hair floated out into the water, she stood up. As the dark pool looped and dripped off her full body with no apparent need or desire other than an innate, lifelong impulse to split into two and curve back into one, I felt the third sprig of mint from the beggar in the cathedral doorway in my pocket.

Barely up an hour, the sun already burned across the rocks and the entire beach like an unaimed spotlight. I went back to my room, closed the shutters, and, as I watched the slats become more and more starkly black and white, fell asleep.

Did I want my room cleaned? I woke up saying, "Yes, you can come in." Drawn again to the big green surf that I heard constantly crashing through the circular jetty, I opened the shutters and pulled them closed behind me as I stepped out onto the balcony.

Fog had rolled in off the Atlantic, all the way up to the balcony and outlining it in chilly pearls. Yet the zero visibility echoed with voices, and the longer I sat there, the more they echoed. They echoed like what I had heard high up in the Atlas Mountains. We had pulled over to the side of the road just before dark. There were no other cars. The steep drop, the snow-draped peaks still higher, the dark pines stretching up and down—"The wilderness!" I had thought. I didn't know until a few minutes later that no such thing existed in Africa. The feeling of being in the wilderness in the United States meant being alone—or only with one or several others—and beautifully isolated by such a scene. Entering the wooded mountains of my home state of Pennsylvania, many a colonial American poet described such a scene, remaining unaware that the romantic vistas uplifting the European-articulated spirit to transcend the grim reality of its origins and cruel propagation concealed a Native American audience suspiciously tracking such an oddly costumed, solipsistic display of affection for the inhuman. We had barely stopped for a minute when I heard voices and a bell tinkling on a goat, as if in Africa one could or should never feel alone.

Seeing nothing but hearing an endless stream of voices from my balcony confirmed this. But so did an experience of two weeks before: one early evening as Barbara and I streamed naturally as sand and water through the souks and archways of a small town not on our map. When the light became too dim, we guided ourselves with our hands along walls furry with pink and yellow moths. When they flew away and the walls changed back to stone, we wanted to write in each other's flesh a history of ourselves before we were born because our words ever since until now felt like lies. Unable to go on, we found a table at midnight to eat gazelle with or without the prophet's words seared into its skin. But before it arrived, we mistook for unexpected rain a young man's splashing a silver flask of turquoise, perfumed water secretly behind us.

From my balcony I couldn't see the source of any of the voices echoing through the fog, even when they seemed to be passing by closely, but could I understand them? I listened, not knowing the language but only what I had seen in the weeks before.

One voice carried mint, water, and dented tin to a charcoal fire between the least of a tree with its inch of shade and a door of flattened sardine cans. Behind it lay salt, nothing but salt. It attracted more voices down the hill tracks timeless as the generations, worn flat, unnumbered and not caring who came down their vague parallels and kicked their years of pebbles, bones, and claws. Passing the donkeys dreaming in sewage and irrigation ditches—where one day I retrieved a goat horn without thinking—and easily climbing over the flagstone walls half built and half decayed, broken and fused but equally needed and used by flesh and clay, cactus and snail, red lichen and marble, mud and light, still more voices lugged brushwood for a fire beside the door to grill corn to have with tea.

One official voice asked, "How did you like your drive out to the ruins and your lunch in the village?"

A naive voice replied, "Lovely. But I didn't know there was so much poverty in Morocco."

"Poverty?" The questioner answered in surprise. "There is no poverty in Morocco."

Hearing this, feeling threatened and hoping to survive, a local poet responded, speaking directly to no one, "We will hear more from the disloyal opposition in the services of the Imperial Market. They mean to waste our time and resources. But I will not let them waste my poetry."

Where was the voice I heard when Barbara and I rested along the way in a rose garden between Marrakech and Fes? Oven-sized tombs of local saints appeared every mile or so under a helplessly glistening sky. I pulled off the road to look at one more closely: the white dome and cube painted green inside; its ledge holding a few pieces of plaited straw left as offerings.

Pounding the jetties through the fog blanketing my balcony, the twenty-foot emerald surf also drowned voices of tar and whitewash, broken car parts made stronger than new, spent cartridge coppers, old tires made into plates and no utensil that ever began life as itself. How would I find my way through the fog back to the local souk's dim space beneath canvas, planks, reeds, and rusty metal forming a town under one roof with seeming random openings to let in the sun, rain, moon, stars, and anyone else who would wait for tea with heaps of yellow, black, red, and brown dates? Now the surf started to make me long again for Barbara and home. Turning around to open the shutters and go back inside, I saw that the room had been cleaned. The light wood table had its wicker chair pushed in—draped with my green T-shirt—and my notebook and pen set at right angles. Beside a fresh bottle of water lay a small braid of straw.

As soon as I returned to the United States, Barbara and I made plans to be married. Our church would be an old barn on the property I owned. Our rose window would be the barn's wide-open doors, and our altarpiece would be a deer walking across the green meadow and woods of the state game land the property bordered. The pews would be twenty bales of fresh and local, bright straw.

Making room and rearranging a few old bales of straw already in the barn, I found in one of them a mummified wolf—curled and at rest, tanned and stiff. Another bale contained the intact skeleton of a snake. Not removing the totemic remains but only making sure they would be out of sight, I thought again of Barbara's question: were they for or against? For protection? Against harm? And what lurked in the new bales of straw? Feeling the Moroccan braid of straw in my pocket, I pictured the fields further up the mountain and still to be mown.

We used the barn because the prior at a Cistercian monastery down the road refused to marry us. Barbara and I had made an appointment with him to ask if he would perform the ceremony in the monastery's plain, small, light chapel, with its abstract stained glass windows and prayer desks holding the old, Latin Psalters. We walked there along the same path I had traveled many a morning over the previous years for mass. The prior had written on phenomenology in the writings of William James. Also a medievalist and very learned in the writings Bernard of Clairvaux, he fed my hunger for the beauties of early church rhetoric, and I fed his, albeit cloistered, to hear of their coinciding and colliding with contemporary thought. Never once did we let moralistic, divisive issues of an ever more reactionary church curdle our conversations—I want to say *sacra conversazione* because it felt, as in Italian Renaissance painting, like two mystics communing intensely as if in the presence of the Madonna, the infant Jesus, and the saints.

I was totally unprepared for our meeting with the prior about the marriage. Brought up Ukrainian Catholic and divorced with two children, Barbara was willing to let me try to convince her that he might think differently than the autocratic and pampered clergymen in charge of Catholic Charities, where she worked in Buffalo for ten years as a social worker. He greeted us with hugs and smiles and "I've heard so much about you" to Barbara, which she happily returned. We entered the living room and sat on three different sides of a small table with Barbara in the middle. When I explained to him that we wanted to be married and for him to perform the ceremony in the chapel, he flatly looked at Barbara and said without emotion, "This sexual attraction won't last and is no reason for him to leave the church."

Directly across the table and surprised that he referred to me as if I weren't there, I didn't know what to think at first. Did I hear him correctly? I looked at Barbara and her expression hadn't changed. I looked at him and he looked back at me as if he hadn't said anything, but it hung in the air and I understood. We didn't argue and quickly left. The door closed weakly behind us. Did he really believe what he said? Decades and four children later, I would ask myself this question when our family would drive past the monastery—and "the mean old monk," as he was now known—after a hike in the woods from where we had moved. I had left the church and had been leaving since I found another kind of *sacra conversazione* where, if all my holy communions at dawn meant anything, they had to lead: to Jericho, Yad Vashem, the national museum in Cairo, the Sinai landscape, Marche Sandaga, the waves around Goree, Togo, beneath Mt. Kilimanjaro, across some lonely sand dunes on the Indian Ocean, Casablanca's cathedral and Morocco's green Atlantic shore. As we walked back up the hill, we thought of other places to be married. As soon as we got home and saw the barn, we knew where.

CHAPTER THREE

Both Sides

IN THE FIVE YEARS BETWEEN FINDING THE ANTS TUNNELING AT MY feet in the sands of Jericho and a braid of straw in Morocco that became the bales of straw filling an old barn on a steep mountainside in rural Pennsylvania, I undid my vow of roughly twenty years before that I would devote myself to learning my own, Western culture before I would seek out any other.

The earlier vow resulted in my intensely studying the writing of English and other European writers since the ancient Greeks and similarly absorbing European art and architecture as well as music: Gregorian or plain chant, Machault to Monteverdi, Renaissance and Baroque, classical, Romantic, and modern to minimalist. I wanted to memorize all of Edmund Spenser's *Faerie Queene* and trace every detail in the cathedral windows from Canterbury to Chartres. I compared looking over "Shakespeare's Cliff" in Dover—having climbed through many a backyard and stepped in a lot of sheep shit to get there—with the passage describing it in *King Lear,* as Edgar outlines it for his blind father, Gloucester, planning to jump to his death. A kind of young and naive Edward Casaubon, the character in George Eliot's *Middlemarch* who thinks he can write a "Key to All Mythologies," but also as many a young American ever since the nation had emerged in the eighteenth century, I felt that I had to learn the achievements of European culture and go to Europe as well to be truly educated. I thought I saw the ghost of Coleridge standing in my room in an otherwise deserted bed-and-breakfast on a farm near Lake Keswick. I unashamedly committed idolatry seeing the panels of Duccio's *Maesta* in Siena and Michelangelo's *Statue of Night* on the tomb of Lorenzo d'Medici in Florence. I prowled every room and corridor of the Louvre like a starved animal in a drought lasting all summer. I wrote poetry about the Elgin Marbles and followed the principles of Keats's letters as if I knew no one and nothing other than them. I let them tell me who I was. Amsterdam to Athens, Milan to Palermo, I saw and listened. However well worn, they were new to me, and news that stayed news, as Ezra Pound—a prime example of an American who ransacked European culture to find himself—said literature should be.[1]

But whatever road I took in this intellectual and physical journey, it led to Rome nearly every year. One summer night in Trastevere at an outdoor restaurant a block from the Tiber, I had to share a table with a young priest studying at the Vatican, since we were both alone and neither of us wanted to argue with the burly, sweating maître d' who, putting us together, simultaneously laughed and swore with everyone else in the restaurant as if he thought they wanted him more than the food.

Half British, the same size as me, wearing heavy black glasses, bearded like an apostle and with seemingly colorless eyes, yet also, like me, half Ukrainian—and midway through our second of three icy liters of Frascati—the young priest said, "I would love to learn more about Africa, to read a book by a great African author, but how can I when already I have no time to learn everything I must before I leave Rome next spring?" He was studying the differences between Ukrainian Orthodoxy and the Ukrainian Catholicism that still remained in the Church of Rome. He felt that Roman Catholicism needed to reconcile with Orthodoxy. Seeing the schism in Ukraine as a microcosm of the split between Orthodoxy and Roman Catholicism, he practiced the latter but said he wanted to be in love and get married, which was only permitted in the dispensation of the former.

"How can we know another culture if we don't know our own," I replied, recounting my own vow about limiting myself to Western culture before I would look to any other. We both felt that we needed a complete knowledge, at least as complete as possible, of our own traditions before engaging any more, and we ended up in Rome trying to find it.

Such a sense of completeness, a kind of key to all cultures, or at least to what we both thought were our own—yet at the time we never talked about how different our orientations were from each other—was, of course, an illusion, as if a culture could be a continent, a boundary, an island and a separated ocean instead of a bridge, winds, currents, and the light of the sun, moon, and stars. Jericho, Yad Vashem, the national museum in Cairo, the Sinai landscape, Marche Sandaga, Togo, Mt. Kilimanjaro, a dune on the Indian Ocean, Casablanca's cathedral, a sprig of mint, a braid of straw in Morocco and a barn full of bales of straw in Hecla, Pennsylvania, "broke down with rigour pitiless,"[2] as Spenser himself phrased it in my beloved *Faerie Queene* in 1596, my illusion of thinking any one culture could or should be my own. My immigrant grandparents on the Italian and

Ukrainian sides never maintained such an illusion. They left their old cultural identities behind them and gladly became Americans, letting old lives, smelling worse than the steamships' steerage to America, burn behind them.

Especially in Rome, the Ukrainian Catholic priest and I should have known better. We came to Rome to find ourselves, but where did Rome come from? From Romulus and Remus, born of Rhea and Mars—the twins floated in a basket down the Tiber and nursed by a she wolf—as depicted on the manhole covers in the city around us? What culture was that and who was a part of it, then or now? Or did Rome come from burning Troy, in the person of Aeneas, the son of Venus and Anchises, whom Aeneas carried on his back to the shores of the Tiber, as recounted in Virgil's *Aeneid?* Instead of myth and legend, could archaeology tell us more? Instead of reading the stones, and instead of in the Latin of poets like Virgil, Ovid, and Horace, could we find Rome's Rome—I mean its cultural origins and our own, in the Latin of St. Jerome's translation from the Hebrew of the Old and New Testament at the end of the fourth century—the basis of Roman Catholicism and its dominance in politics, commerce, art, and literature in Europe for the next one thousand years? Following Jerome, I would end up not too far from Jericho, since he was said to make his translation in a monastery in Bethlehem. Or, if Rome were inseparable from the Church of Rome and thus so was I, should I follow Jerome's junior by a little more than ten years, St. Augustine? No writer could be more important in the immediate development of Christianity from its Roman origins. But Augustine came from Africa. Following his origins, I could reverse the famous opening words of the third chapter of his *Confessions*: "Veni Karthaginem," "I came to Carthage." Augustine encountered the African city as a kind of midpoint in the course of his life before he traveled to Rome. Moving from Carthage to Rome, he changed direction—most of all, the direction of his life. After roughly two thousand years, he wanted to be amid a new cultural cycle, in his case, Christian Rome. Obviously these were literal places, but their significance was figurative, symbolic, and historic, too, and they still are. My journey had been the other way from St. Augustine's: to Rome first and then to Africa.

Too much cold Frascati numbed the brains of my newfound friend and me. We couldn't see that the boundaries that we had both set up as a result of our supposed devotion to our cultural origins immediately excluded the place where we sat and the city humming and bursting at every angle of seeing and hearing around us, which we even tasted. And what about all the different faces in the restaurant: the different kinds of Romans, Italians, Europeans, Americans, Asians, and Africans? Getting over our initial shyness, wasn't the feeling that the big maître d' laughing and swearing in his sweaty T-shirt at everyone in the restaurant made us one big family what we most enjoyed?

Draining the last of the Frascati, I wondered why we thought that what happens in the world could be measured, judged, and even dismissed by ideas, beliefs, and abstractions that only existed in our minds without any physical reality other than, perhaps, chemical. Yet Rome was also the perfect place to contemplate such an absurdity. Didn't the Vatican represent the most elaborate, pristine, and impossible levels of unreal and unattainable abstract concepts thoroughly belied by its own equally extreme, all too human, bloody history still thoroughly in tune with the city surrounding it?

Sitting on a bale of fresh straw in my barn in Hecla, I knew now what I didn't fifteen years earlier in Trastevere. I came to "Rome" the way that Augustine came to "Carthage," but why stop there? The same year I first read Dante's *Commedia,* I also first read Augustine's *Confessions.* It too prompted me to decide to devote myself to my own culture before learning any others. I was excited to talk about the book with my friends in college. However, when they told me in Comparative Religion 102 on a cold spring morning in St. Louis that they hadn't read the book and didn't plan to, I had forebodings, which turned out true, that we would drift apart and follow different roads. But then I didn't follow Augustine back far enough, and now I could—through Rome to Africa. Neither culture was exclusive of the other, intellectually or even biologically. Informed by one, I was becoming informed of the other. Following Augustine to his first home in Africa, I also retraced from the other direction what linked all human beings to a single migration of a few hundred people out of Africa roughly sixty-five thousand years ago. Furthermore, the full capacity to use language, developed approximately one hundred thousand years ago, came with it.

Yet whether I or anyone traveled from Africa to Rome or Rome to Africa, or along any of the countless paths of migration around the world, mattered little compared with what and how they connected. Twenty years before or now, in Africa or Rome, I still sought the image and the word to tell me who I was and about humanity and nature. Neither their cultural origin nor mine made much difference. In Trastevere, Giuseppe Belli's sonnets in the dialect of nineteenth-century Rome praising the eternal city's rats and mocking the pope spoke to me and for me. In San Luigi dei Francesi, Caravaggio's disembodied torches glaring in the dark oils he mixed with the legends of St. Matthew opened my eyes. Borromini multiplying stone *trompe l'oeil* by straight lines of oval space that didn't really exist showed me how to measure. But now I found objects and images of African art—not because they were African or not, but simply because they were there—telling me about my newborn, the nature of power in Washington, DC, how democracy works, what my immigrant grandparents dreamed crossing the Atlantic, and about my father's dying.

The day after Barbara told me she was pregnant, as I read a book on central African sculpture, the illustrations seemed to reflect my excitement. A darkening female power figure stuck with tacks, part rough crust and part rubbed smooth, expressed my awe. Her hands grew with her stomach to protect and open it. Dreaming of amnion, I traced ten feet of snaky soul around her neck, leopard teeth, ivory ears, nostrils like berries, a coat of quills, and a navel filled with sticks. We aspired again to the birthing country, the innocent and first fruit. Where was the sling to hold the powerless and meek? Head-to-toe blossoms gestured "freedom." A world made by one creator instead of polygenesis and catastrophe seemed useless. Unpainted bricks, a money of needles, a cane and papier-mâché quadruped without a name, a three-headed heart, a chameleon mind, a crocodile pillar, a sharp and deep vagina of one being, and two doves in the sky expressed the newborn. The combinations of seemingly random materials expressed it, too: beans that would never be planted, two small horns, uncapped pens and arrows in thin wet leather, a petrified bird, a stone shaped like hips, dust that seemed to bleed, a dateless ball of wax holding pins, hair twine, and porcelain chips. I wanted to add my grandfather's hammer, drop cloth, and extension cord—the only physical mementos I had of his life. I wanted to empty a divination basket onto my table: cowries, chimp and lizard skulls, somehow intact dragonflies, buttons, nuts, turtle shells, bits of chrome, mushrooms, broken watches, newspaper shreds, anteater scales, red parrot feathers, a tight package of suet, and a crystal pulled by a midwife out of the sillion of a newly plowed field along with the name only our baby would truly know.

The carved wood power figures I saw in the African art museum at the Smithsonian in Washington, DC, spoke at least as much about my nation's capital as its colonial French street layout. They formed a dialogue, too, colonial and neocolonial, exemplifying what Said had written: "The great imperial experience of the past two hundred years is global and universal; it has implicated every corner of the world, the colonizer and the colonized."[3]

I also saw each power figure offer its own eloquent denial of Hegel's infamous charge that they came from "no historical part of the World . . . [with] no movement or development to exhibit. . . . still involved in the conditions of mere nature" and not having "attained to the realization of any substantial objective existence . . . entirely wanting . . . completely wild and untamed" with "nothing harmonious with humanity to be found in this type of character."[4] Furthermore, when I tried to separate any African forms of knowledge as it appeared in the power figures from Western forms of knowledge, they came together, like a magnet and metal, yet which was which? I didn't see them separating into politically charged abstractions, so popular in academic writing, of "self" and "other"—the former meaning powerful Western and the latter meaning African or, by extension, the entire non-Western world—either in themselves or in what I might see or say about them. The power figures expressed a kind of unabashed universality.

Geographically I wasn't from where they came from. But wasn't the wonder and even the miracle of, for example, a great play by Shakespeare that it was not limited merely to communicating something in Elizabethan London from the mind of a man named Shakespeare but that it prompted someone hundreds of years later and thousands of miles away and even in a different language to say, "Yes, this is what I think? This is like who I am." All of my experiences since I first saw the ants in the sand of Jericho up to knowing no one on the entire continent as I longed from a white balcony facing the towering break of green surf on a beach in Morocco for my loved ones on the opposite coast—to walking out of the Cistercian monastery and shaking its dust off my sandals—said "So what?!" to much if any self-consciousness about one's place or origin.

As Said wrote, "Cultures [we]re too intermingled, their contents and histories too interdependent and hybrid" to continue with such "fictions" as "East" or "West," "self" or "other,"[5] American or not. Yet the remains around Jericho and the creation as I witnessed it according to the market of Sandaga and the empty space of Casablanca's cathedral also confirmed the historical and political horrors that such abstractions tried to convey: the danger of deep disaffection in using nouns like "other" and "self" before simply saying "human." Their message paled in comparison with the power figures and what they said about power; paled too if compared with the power one might hear in Bach played by a great cellist, whatever his or her geographical, ethnic, or national origin. I could no more control such notes, play or silence them than I could make a decision to give my voice or any voice to the Holocaust remains at Yad Vashem, apostasy and fundamentalism every which way in Cairo, the collision of altars in the Sinai landscape, the creation according to Marche Sandaga, the fetishes including my own of Togo, Mt. Kilimanjaro casting its shadow over the entire world, sheltering in a bush on the stormy Indian Ocean, or to the skull of a wildebeest in the Serengeti. *They gave me their voice.* Otherwise I could say nothing since they were so powerful in their own right and in comparison with anything else of art or life I had seen before. I could only listen and try to repeat what I heard.

With their horns, mirrors, shells, and iron nails—with or without the secret and supposedly magical ingredients sealed in their hollow cores—the power figures looked like concentrated personifications of all that churned the twentieth century into the twenty-first. However local to communities or individuals of central Africa, in their expression these figures could no more be contained in their climate-controlled clear museum cases than the ideas of any great writer in the pages of his or her book. They had African knowledge but also world knowledge. They embodied Francis Bacon's sixteenth-century maxim, *Ipsa scientia potestas est,*[6] knowledge is power, to the hilt. Images of power performed as if it could never have been born or came from a slit gong that once entertained a perpetual stranger; power never once scratching backward like a chicken with hyenas clawed into its back; power forwarding itself against all denominations, leaving behind no crumb, bone, or even a trace of what it ate, and needing no memory, song, or feast to ordain every day with vacancy. Nameless and big, concentrating its attention for only seconds at a time, power dismembered itself at high speeds and, depending on who was watching, looked like poured concrete, foreign cash, easy credit, or simply homelessness with a new price tag and lit up sodium orange. Power played a bell of double deals and rivet lines: one eye an unfired bullet, the other an old teat; six ridges in one brain with green bolts; claws like bars across lips stuck to a smooth cheek scarred like a fossil rock but glued with feathers and fur and twitching while it waited for another mask to enter the room, and wearing my face, too.

The power figures also drove me back to Dakar, where I hoped to find Mino again, who had taught me so much the last time I was there. To celebrate our newborn, he had sent us a huge package of Senegalese cloth: yellow leaves adrift in a blue sky; burgundy and silver clamshells rising out of the greenest sea; fine black zigzags combing green nuts out of brown soil; formations of blue ants marching through fire-orange concentric circles emerging from sand; a dark green and white waxed batik of two vast, abstract, and winged eyes flanking the cross section of a gargantuan spine. Mauritanian silver bracelets—one very small and with our baby's initials—and doughy feeling necklaces with small clay beads on thick, waxy string lay within the folds. The cloths reminded me of my first drive into Dakar from the airport: the roadside with Senegalese women wrapped in their bright prints and colors and selling hot peppers, which the new cloths smelled of too.

As the taxi pulled into the driveway entrance that I had once hoped I would never see again, instead of feeling disorientated as when I first visited

Dakar, I felt reassured to be back. We stopped behind a huge black limousine, I paid the taxi driver as uneventfully as if he had been dropping me off after a brief ride in Manhattan, and I grabbed my own bags. Pouring out of the limousine, an entourage in a riot of more bright Senegalese cloth, coiffures of braids, cowries and beads, reflecting sunglasses, gold and silver chains, muscular men and women like fashion models hesitatingly moved toward the entrance. They revolved around a hulking, slightly tired looking, elaborately braided man in a one-piece suit of alternating ankhs in red and gold entwined by grapes and monkeys. A similarly heavyset woman in an orange and brown Muslim headscarf and robe modestly led him by the hand. Stevie Wonder was checking in ahead of me.

I called back to the taxi driver who couldn't leave since the driveway was blocked and asked if he would watch my bags for a moment. With a flick of his gold-ringed pinky toward the limousine and the crowd, he obliged, as did I him with a five-dollar bill. I weaved myself through the entourage, and no one seemed to mind or even notice amid their high-tempo arrival. Everyone sounded American. I had to talk to Stevie.

Walking slowly, he looked straight ahead with his trademark sunglasses shielding his blindness. His double chin moved up or down according to the level of the ground under his almost shuffling feet. Three feet away, I thought of my opening line: "Stevie. I'm just arriving at the hotel and from America too. A lot of us coming to Africa are following you. Thanks." Two steps later I began: "Stevie, I'm . . ."

Before I could continue he turned to me and held out his hand, replying, "Yeah man, yeah man, yeah man." We shook and he said, "What's your name?"

"Charles," I said in a normal tone of voice that I feared he might not hear amid the commotion.

"We're only staying one night, Charles, and leaving tomorrow for the states." He looked directly at me but the tilt of his head suggested an awareness that he needed to keep moving with the crowd.

"I'm leaving too," I replied. "But first I'm going out into the countryside and down to Casamance with a friend from here."

Even moving slowly, the entourage started pressing and rattling louder as it pushed him along, and I started falling behind. "Hey, Charles. I wish I could go with you. Let me pay your hotel bill tonight and promise me you'll come back and tell me someday what you saw."

I looked sideways, abashed by his offer yet grateful, and saw the concierge, whom I recognized from my last visit by his bright blue eyes and the circular scarification down his cheeks, give me an emphatic okay sign, pinching his forefinger and thumb and holding out his other three fingers, his pinky wearing a ring like the taxi driver's. I looked back toward Stevie. He disappeared amid his Afrocentric Detroit entourage like a fabulous sunset draining through the hotel's dark glass doors, across the lobby and seemingly into the Atlantic.

As I entered behind them, I passed the same sign I had followed the last time I was here, which advertised the hotel happy hour by the pool to feature "native dancers." I saw a bunch of tanned, middle-aged French women in halter-tops with their older husbands in billowy thigh-length shirts over their tiny Speedos. They headed for the pool, the husbands and even a few of their wives ogling the statuesque prostitutes like ebony wrapped in orchids peaking out of the lobby's corners. No thanks. I had joined that party before.

I went up to my room, upgraded on Stevie's orders to a suite of chrome, red and black leather, champagne and feather pillows, a steam room, fresh fruits and vegetables, baguettes, French cheeses, and six kinds of olives. I ordered local fish, a 1985 Châteauneuf-du-Pape, and drank to Stevie and Africa, remembering his songs from the seventies and the eighties, even back to 1966, when I saw him come onstage in Yankee Stadium in a chartreuse zoot suit and sing "Fingertips." Wanting to sing "Isn't She Lovely," I remembered my newborn and started to cry from the proverbial pangs of separation that I felt from Barbara and the children. Too much love . . . too much wine.

The next morning, when I gave Mino the money I had saved on my hotel bill, he replied with a deep nod and a smile, "Last time you were here you gave me enough to buy a sheep to celebrate Mohammed's birthday. Now I will buy five."

Around ten in the morning, Mino called me to come down to the lobby where he was waiting. His letters since I last saw him passed out and draped over two chairs in an Air Afrique lounge at Dakar airport told me that he would be changed. He now said that he had quit working on the Greek shrimp boat after two voyages over a year. I didn't recognize him standing near the lobby's beige in-house wall phones because he appeared, at least at first, almost as pale as they did, instead of gleaming indigo black as I knew him before. Wearing a gold cotton, Western-cut suit printed with different color turtles, he looked half the size I remembered him. When he saw me and waved, he looked dark again. We hugged, and he had almost no muscle. He had a bag of clothes—two pair of Senegalese-style shirts and pants all made of a patchwork including every print and color I had ever seen or dreamed. I asked him almost immediately, "Are you all right?"

He pointed to the men's room and, as we walked in, I noticed that he limped. I carried the clothes. Once inside, in front of the glistening mirrors and sinks, he pulled down his pants and pointed to a gash like folded and unfolded bat wings running the length of his inner thigh and circling his knee. When one of the French husbands from the lobby the day before—now dressed in yet another billowy shirt with tight white jeans—entered the bathroom, he saw us, thought "sex" and smiled as if he expected us to invite him to join in. Mino had tears in his eyes and seeing the scar made me nauseous. Realizing at the same moment what the French tourist intended, Mino and I burst out laughing.

As we walked back into the hotel lobby, he told me that on his second voyage with the Greek shrimper, he had been guiding a heavy net when a rope broke. It spun wildly overboard and became tangled with a chain that caught around his knee. As the net sunk and the boat speeded forward the chain squeezed Mino's knee. As he fell head first toward the water, the chain pulled him upside down, wrapped up his thigh and hoisted him in the air. Tighter and tighter embedded in his flesh—until the captain broke it with a .357 Magnum he fired near the winch—the chain eventually had to be cut out of Mino's flesh. The ship was off northern Morocco when the accident happened, and the same captain required a shipload of shrimp before returning to port in Dakar.

As he counted the cash for a second time, Mino said we should leave the next morning for the lush palm groves and forests of Casamance in southern Senegal. For now he invited me to join him as he went to vote in Senegal's parliamentary elections. Looking even happier than when he anticipated the birthday celebration of the prophet Mohammed during our last time together, he equated the achievements of democracy in Senegal with the stark and ancient baobab trees that studded its savannas. He began walking, even on a shattered leg, with a swagger. He beamed as if he was about to enter a feast, yet he maintained a kind of reverent air as if the feast included the most important ceremony too. Expecting that the experience would differ from what I saw on election days in the United States and in Europe and stoking Mino's now confirmed prejudice against all things Greek, I remembered and told him what the first President Bush had once said: "At a time when peoples around the world are beginning to establish systems of representative government. . . . [w]hat better way to celebrate the origins of democracy than with . . . [an] exhibition of ancient Greek sculptures."[7]

"Greek? Greek sculptures?" Mino shrieked and spat like he did the first time I had asked him about his new job on the Greek shrimp boat. "Those seagulls stole democracy from us! Now you'll see!"

The usual throng of beggars, touts, souvenir salesmen, pimps, and prostitutes at the hotel gate parted for Mino to pass and didn't bother me following him. He hailed a gray, beat-up Citroen cab and jumped into the ripped front seat, and I slid into the back, my body wiping a layer of red dust off the gray cracked morocco. A strong smell of gasoline, more red dust, and the stuffy air—since the windows weren't open—created a kind of lens or filthy veil between my eyes and Mino talking with the cabbie in Wolof to the visual rhythm of Muslim, animist, and soccer amulets dangling over the dashboard.

The red dust and urban grime on the windows also fogged my view of the passing streets of Dakar. I recognized a corner near Marche Sandaga: the child vendors selling cigarettes, gum, Kleenex, chloroquine, cowries, aspirin, packets of salt, sugar—each one by one; the uneven walls of the used and used-up all atilt: boom boxes, refrigerators, telephones, faxes and copiers, furniture, shoes, auto parts, plastic pipes, pans and tubs. We were driving to Pikine, where Mino lived and where he had to vote: a poor city that, only established in 1952, had since swelled to over one million people, most of them under twenty years of age, not counting the spontaneous and teeming neighborhoods that formed and unformed during the frequent floods, around ten miles outside of Dakar.

My eyelids closed like a flue, and I smelled fire. The window felt like cold lips. I was gouging clay and riding the ruts like a razor between layers of music I couldn't identify and my own familiar prayers: "Our father . . ." We passed a tall albino wearing copper plate pants, a wooden shirt, a belt of nails, a cartridge shell wig, a hot pepper beard, and a straw cloak. He waved and pointed at twelve naked hags beating a pregnant girl. I caught myself waving back. In the rearview mirror, a jackal emptied a wheelbarrow of distended squashes at the feet of a wolf. My palms felt like burlap as I watched a boy with a stick spinning two oil-drenched rats in a flaming tire rim. The "u" sounds of Mino and the cabbie now seemingly arguing piled up like hooves running faster and faster, but we were stuck in a line of trucks slowly hauling lumber with even slower bulldozers scraping the road down to its bedrock, flooding with water. Mino's hand caught my forehead before it smashed the back of the front seat. His "We're here. I will now vote" opened my eyes, and he also told the cabbie in English to wait so that he could drive me back to the hotel.

At first the men and women at the polling place, most of them holding children, appeared like they were posing for pictures, but then I saw people forming six or seven lines through a kind of small athletic field that had long been mud instead of grass. The lines snaked toward four enlarged, sample ballots tacked on a makeshift, cloth bulletin board half visible through thick black smoke coming from behind. "The candidates," Mino told me, as I strained for a closer look: a pudgy male executive; a scowling marabout in traditional robes; a smiling woman with a green and white headdress; a young man with a thin face, a cold stare, and a baseball cap. Half a dozen haughty policemen with batons watched the crowd as if the process were of no concern. Following Mino and watching where I walked to avoid what looked like either some kind of land crabs or scorpions, I tried to ignore the big flies landing on my exposed arms, neck, and face and felt my feet slipping and sinking into previous footprints. Curls of burning incense distracted me from the reek of sewage in the air. Every few feet a different pop song played from a radio. Mino whispered as if to no one a kind of mantra, *Rien de plus merveilleux que les gens, rien de plus merveilleux que les gens,* nothing more wonderful than the people. *Les gens, les gens* I joined in, but also so no one could hear me.

After an hour we wound up in front of a cinder block, thatch, and corrugated aluminum, one-room house held up by posts thicker than anyone in line. A cool, chapel-like atmosphere inside greeted each voter, who, leaving the lines behind, was individually given his or her ballot and a seemingly ancient, thick pencil behind a black curtain. Mino went in, and I sat on a low stool, a tree stump, next to the election official. No one said a word. Even Mino and the official only used gestures, nodding yes or no and then with one big, shared nod extending into a bow, which meant "Now, vote."

Sculpt this, I thought. Make me a monument that also moves. Brightly paint it. Give it large nipples, juicy lips, and a belly never denied. Make the eyelids copper, the eyelashes wire, and the eyes out of seashells set with black and green enamel. Hide effective drugs and medicine in all the body's cavities and drape it—as it seems to breathe gold, silver, and ivory—in goatskin, fresh bronze, a little lead for protection, and soft, caressive hair. Sculpt a marble, unpretending gaze of eternal regret. Then pour blood, porridge, fruit juices, pulp, flour, seeds, tar, burned herbs, dyes, butter, soil and three kinds of oil down this body's upraised arms and over its head and shoulders so that a crust forms to obscure the original sculpture. Also, make a new one every sixty years out of the truth that can be known and the not true that can never be known.

Wiping a few drops of rain come through the thick stalk roof off my face, as I continued to wait for Mino to finish voting, I saw a single being of mammal, reptile, bird, and human: abstract and figurative, carved and knotted, fruit and blossom, rectangular and curved. I wanted to fix the sandal of this naked victory, adorned and pulsing centers upon center of belief in one body. My eyes couldn't move from the natural flesh and liberties unforced by any god, symbol, harmony, ability, sex, politics, or beauty other than this act vibrating with freedom of choice. Letting there be no more distance between education and experience, a vote here challenged all the violation, guilt, and shame of slavery played out on Goree and the other slave embarkation points up and down the coast. A vote here could call up anyone's ancestor. A vote here could bless anyone's child. I cast mine, finding two short sticks on the ground and winding them tight together with thread from my pocket, a little paper from my notebook and some spit.

The next morning Mino picked me up at the hotel door with the same cab and driver from the day before, and we left for Casamance. As we drove through billows of diesel exhaust piled up like storm clouds along the sides of what seemed like Dakar's only major artery clogged without any hope of a bypass, a repeat performance of the drive to the polling station began to unfold, only not merely along the roadside but on the median too. But this time I was not lulled asleep. Instead, I wanted to join in the conversation—zigzagging from Wolof to French to English at a proportionally high speed to the slowness of the traffic—between Mino and the driver. "Amadou," I said, having heard Mino use his name, "where are you from?"

He looked like Mino: round headed, physically fit, light framed and loose limbed, only with more brown than blue in his very dark skin. He wore jeans and a blue and orange tie-dye shirt with a three-eyed half human / half devil face. Mino had given me a shirt with a similar face when I had first visited Dakar. Mino wore baggy jeans, too, and the same green flannel shirt from the day I had first met him two years before, when he refused to leave my side. Pausing with every syllable, Amadou replied, "Gam. Bi. A."

"He is an immigrant to Senegal, like your grandparents to America," Mino added with a laugh after exchanging a quick, almost respectful glance with Amadou.

"Your grandparents had to be good swimmers," Amadou joked. "Are you?"

"Yes," I said, "at home I work out, swimming three times a week to stay strong. Are you a swimmer too?"

"This man is the best swimmer," Mino jumped back in, slowly pronouncing every syllable the way Amadou said "Gambia." "He swam to Senegal."

I had been leaning over the front seat, but now I leaned back in a small cloud of red dust. "How did you do that, Amadou?" I asked, hoping that maybe by the end of the trip Amadou would also at least partly answer the more difficult question of *why* he swam to Senegal. But Amadou made no such distinction between how and why, his story eclipsing whatever we passed outside as he continued driving and began to speak as if he had entered a trance.

"Ponds, reeds, rivers, mud, ocean . . . I swam through it all, and I was watched the whole time too, if not by soldiers and the police then by my ancestors. My wife had died giving birth to my first-born. He died a little later the same night. When the midwife came to me as I waited with my uncles in a yam field far enough away from my house so that I could not know what was going on there, they barely let me cry—although I might have lost consciousness too—before blindfolding me and taking me a kilometer or so out into the bush, where they sat me on a large smooth stone. They took off my blindfold, held my head down, and I saw a messy circle of feathers centered by the remains of a sheep's throat. In violent thin lines I saw my name written in blood and strange shapes that I thought were symbols. I asked what they meant. My uncle, whom I had always called Papa since my father had died only a year after I was born, replied, 'They are the names you don't know but will someday spell with love as the names of your new wife and children. Now take this finger bone of your father and go. Go far. Swim if you must. Find them and come back.' His eyes shone bright as the full moon. We both shed tears and it started to rain.

"I left not caring what would happen to me. I ran all night until the rain stopped and ran all the next day through swirling dust. I ran not caring if the policeman who caught me would skin me alive. I ran not caring if my eyes had to be cut out with a knife to be truly opened. I ran not caring that the spun barrel and pulled trigger of a gun held to my head fired what I ran from.

"I ran not caring about anything but those symbols in the dust and their prophecy coming true. Then I would be free, a strong link in a chain with all the others who ran with me looking for a new altar of earth and to bud and grow like the saplings I planted around it.

"When I had nowhere else to run, I dove into the river. I only saw black except when I looked up at the sky, where I couldn't tell if I was seeing letters or animals. I felt as if the river had unclasped a stone belt that I didn't know I was wearing. Without it, I swam effortlessly and fast as the black river changed to a mirror. But I lost all sense of direction. Forward? Why was I in reeds? Backward? I choked on a mouthful of salt. A wave slapped me as I tried to breathe. I pushed through dust, dew, petrol, rain, and mud and found myself no longer alone but surrounded by other immigrants, all of us heavily inhaling and exhaling the horizon that settled in our knees. Yes, I swam to Senegal."

Amadou stopped in the middle of the road, which was by now hard, blonde dirt and barely two lanes both ways, leaving the city far behind. As he told his story, Mino had fallen asleep, but the stop jerked his head up. A procession filled the road in front of us. Breaking out of his trance, Amadou spoke quickly: "Roll up the windows. But it's better than being stopped by Casamance rebels."

Mino facetiously disagreed, as if to wake up both of them. "That's not so bad. At least they would make us Christians and get us stoned before they killed us."

The procession approached and split in the middle as it flowed around the car. Costumes and drumming poured through all the windows as if they were video screens, but the fast-moving, sudden crowd and my anxiety blurred them. Through the driver's side, did I see a collection of United Nations flags, all faded and weather shredded? Following them, were the men dressed like monkeys? A few of them held elaborate and empty gold picture frames above their heads. Why did the young men who followed them seem to be half costumed as women, and the young women who followed them seem to be half costumed like men? Why were some holding sheaves of unhusked corn? Looking out the windows on the passenger's side, I saw hands waving boughs of what looked like tiny cherries. The remaining marchers—who crinkled their eyes, pursed their lips, and varied in age from young children to women and men so old that I was surprised they kept up with the group—held up old photographs, many of them charred, of young adults and children.

As I watched the last of the procession pass by the Citroen's back bumper and disappear from the rearview mirror, I asked Mino and Amadou, "What was that about?"

Neither answered. Staring into the rearview mirror and as the clamor of the procession faded, Amadou floored the accelerator, the wheels spun up a cloud of white dust, and we sped off like an escape car from a robbery. Both men rolled down their windows.

Looking straight ahead, Amadou muttered a few sentences in an African language that didn't sound like Wolof, as if he were annoyed. Mino didn't answer, and I imagined a translation: "They are commemorating children who have disappeared from their village and pretending to look for them." I leaned back and opened the window. Air like a hot, dank summer attic hit my face. In a minute we came to a village's outskirts: an open field beside a baobab, maybe forty feet in diameter and forty feet high—half dead, its other half sticking up three green legs. I saw a thin, old man in tattered shorts and T-shirt beside an empty cart. He seemed as if he had stood there forever, doing nothing but watch us and others like us speed by.

To my question, "How much longer?" Mino replied, "Another hour," in a deadpan tone that told me he no more wanted to talk than Amadou after passing through the middle of the village procession. The savanna around us opened flat and wide with baobabs at distant intervals that seemed to echo each other's massive, earthbound, and squat loneliness. One by one they pinned an inscrutable message of themselves across a vast expanse pockmarked in places like a bulletin board where any other idea fell away like an out-of-date announcement. Symbolizing the power of Senegalese democracy for Mino, these trees also reputedly entombed the land's griots and griottes, in Mande language the *djalis*—the flesh and blood, singing books of praise, history and poetry. Buried in the tree, a good griot made it thrive, a bad griot killed it. As we sped by the trees, I thought that most of them looked half dead and half alive, like the first one I saw. Whether they entombed good griots, bad griots, or no griots seemed to make no difference. Heat and humidity blasting in my face, I could barely form a thought beyond "tree . . . tree . . . tree . . . tr . . . ee."

I woke to a very different scene. Red mud splashed the window. I didn't remember rolling it up. The car lurched like a children's amusement park ride. Enveloped again in a continuous cloud of diesel exhaust, we followed a line of slowly grinding trucks, taxis, and cars that should have fallen apart years ago. Amadou sharply pulled off the road, squeezed the car between two piles of rotting lumber that looked like they might have once been outdoor market stalls, and said, "Better we should walk from here." Mino pulled a flat, grease-stained brown paper bag out from under his seat, and we walked down the road together, Mino struggling with his leg more than I had ever seen him, in the direction of the traffic, only faster.

Was this our destination? Why a one-street border town on a river? Chameleons crawled everywhere. Dragonflies chasing gnats and mosquitoes transformed the air into a crazy grid. We walked past at least fifty small shops, many of them no more than the width of a doorway, identically stocked with short-lived batteries from China, brochures about vaccinations, sand bags, bungee cords, sisal rope of varying thickness, Bic pens and shavers, Lux soap, Asian action and Indian romantic videocassettes. A couple steps ahead, Mino beamed and gestured toward a few plastic chairs and tables beside a red bar and under a gray thatch roof. "We are here! Time for palm wine."

As we sat, I saw him gesture with three fingers to a girl behind the bar. She smiled with gold teeth and bright eyes. As she approached with a green plastic pitcher and three large, murky plastic tumblers, I marveled at her huge and bare strong arms and legs like mahogany wrapped in a strapless, stained yellow sarong. She had snaky red hair pushing out from under a half black half pink net grasshopper print headscarf. Maybe I was too far or too long away from home, but her slow walk and open-mouthed smile seemed to exude a promise of consummate sex. As she placed the palm wine on the table with its myriad of stains from other drinkers, we sat dazed and gawking like three just-chopped tree stumps. I watched her pour my glass first, but three black chunks rising with the milky wine to the brim stirred me out of my trance. "Flies are in my wine," I said to Mino.

He looked indifferently at the waitress and pointed to them. She turned to me, came close to my face and smiled, saying nothing for a few seconds. I wanted to lick her patina of sweat, but only smiled back. As she pulled away, she swept up the glass and drained it in one gulp, flies and all. We all laughed as she licked her lips, her gold teeth gleaming through them, and poured three more glasses.

Over two more pitchers, I told Amadou about my various adventures with Mino and also about meeting Stevie Wonder back in Dakar a few days before. I noticed that Mino drank two glasses for every one Amadou and I poured. Also, Mino's eyes kept circling the bar as if he expected someone.

Stiff from too much palm wine and sitting, I got up to take a walk. Wanting to find a gift for Barbara, I found a shop selling hand brooms made out of thin, hard fronds. I bought four. The heat and humidity, the industrial air gathered over this small, single town near the mouth of the Gambia River, the palm wine soaked up by my brain with nothing but the peanuts served on a pink plastic plate to continue to make us thirsty, and my longing for home made me envision each broom with a kind of symbolic use: one for fire, one for dance, one for the unknown, and one, more practically, to sweep the house.

I said "for the unknown" aloud, picking up one of them. I thought of the line from St. Paul's writing in Acts 17:23—"I passed by . . . and beheld . . . an altar with this description, TO THE UNKNOWN GOD." It typified for now at least how I thought about much of life. Paul went on to claim and even boast that he knew the name of this God and wanted to convert people in His name. However, I now came to this phrase from St. Paul, as I did to St. Augustine's origins in Africa, from the other direction. The ants in Jericho, the domestic relics of Yad Vashem, Cairo the victor, the rocks of Sinai, Marche Sandaga, Togo's tables of fetishes, Mt. Kilimanjaro's shadows, that bush beside the Indian Ocean, Casablanca's white cathedral, a sprig of mint, a braid of straw, more bales of straw in my barn in Hecla, Barbara, and now this border town in Casamance led me back to the unknown god whom I had missed before: agnostic, not one creator but many, no regulator threatening deserts or ice ages, no self-proof, interpretation, or any other kind of rationalization.

I envisioned the hand brooms for fire and dance burned down to butts. They formed the eyes of a mask: a face barely visible through painted leaves, rope pouring through its nose, with the rest of the mask left unfinished and unnamable in the hope that it meant Barbara and I would have another child, whose room would be the first we would sweep with the fourth broom.

By now I had wandered all the way to the riverbank where the road and the town stopped. The near end of the day had replaced the swallows with bats jerkily swooping the river for bugs and what looked like small chunks of fat in the oil slicks on the surface. I saw a huge, rusty barge about to depart and filled with black, oily silt and tree trunks. Amadou caught up with me and said, "Look at that man, his left foot on the shore, his right foot on the dock and watching like a vulture, only with white feathers and so perfectly clean. He is the town judge."

Just then I saw Mino near the dock. He seemed to be the only one moving. He looked at a pirogue that, floating in the shadow of the barge, held a beautiful pregnant woman in a matching bright green and blue sarong and headscarf. She had two children with her and held a baby. Mino opened the flat bag he had brought with him from the car and took out some kind of animal skin. Putting it over his shoulders, he slipped off the dock and disappeared into the water, and the pirogue started moving up stream. I turned to Amadou, who smiled and said, "*Ba beneen yon. Fo tuma du. Au revoir.* Now he is the swimmer. Don't worry. For the price of a sheep and a goat, I will drive you back to Dakar tomorrow morning."

CHAPTER FOUR

The Journey Provided

I stood at my father's deathbed. After a long day's vigil, Barbara had taken my mother home. We had decided to detach his water and feeding tubes, since they had been all that were keeping him alive—along with morphine—after seven years of cancer that spread from his prostate to his bones, lungs and brain. He lay unconscious and beyond pain, but every few hours he would wake for a few seconds and speak.

My son and I had returned from Cameroon two weeks before, cutting our trip short and rushing home when Barbara called with the news that my father's condition had suddenly worsened. Now our journey had to be joined closely as possible to his, about to end.

I planned to stay with him through the night. I brought the journals of Christopher Columbus to read and the beginnings of a long poem that I had been writing based on them. The next year would mark the quincentenary of Columbus's arrival in the Caribbean in October of 1492. Were his voyage and its legacy evil or good? Words traditionally associated with him like "discover," "New World," and "first" underwent deconstruction. How many voyages from Europe and elsewhere preceded his? Since the Americas contained many ancient, indigenous cultures who met Columbus and his followers, who discovered whom? Words like "discovery" and "New World" sounded like euphemisms to justify or cover up the destruction of most of these cultures by westward European expansion and colonialism: the way that George Orwell writing in the wake of World War II identified the word "pacification" as meaning "defenseless villages . . . bombarded from the air, the inhabitants driven out into the countryside, the cattle machine-gunned . . . [and] huts set on fire with incendiary bullets."[1]

A sixteenth-century historian full of praise for Hernando Cortés's ruthless siege and extinction of the Aztec empire, Francisco López de Gómara, considered Columbus's voyage to be the greatest event in world history, next to the incarnation and death of Jesus Christ.[2] In *The Wealth of Nations,* Adam Smith in 1776 echoed Gómara, yet, more secular and concerned with economics—a little like Columbus's modern adversaries, although with opposite sympathies—Smith considered the European eastward expansion of trade with Asia to be equally monumental: "The discovery of America, and that of a passage to the East Indies by the Cape of Good Hope, are the two greatest and most important events recorded in the history of mankind."[3]

Smith only mentioned "the Cape," but Europe's "discovery . . . of a passage to the East Indies" precipitated its large-scale colonization of Africa that, furthermore, historically overlapped with the European colonization of America. With slavery, the former fed the latter: fifteen million African slaves shipped across the Atlantic; perhaps five or ten times more if the likely casualties that led to one's slave's arrival were counted. Was this wild speculation? Cut it in half or quarter, the fact by definition was wild! Yet how many tens or hundreds of millions more if Africans and Arabs enslaving Africans in Africa were counted too? The clattering and bloody tons of all their chains joined Europe and Africa and dragged in the Americas too, reducing a desire to consider these places separate from each other or one after the other in some orderly or pure sequence a delusion. The European destruction of indigenous American civilizations and grasping of economic plunder along with the toll of African slavery made Gómara's "greatest" and Smith's "most important" sound like euphemisms for the *worst* and *most violent* "event[s] in world history," at least until then and on record—which the name Columbus and its quincentennial celebration epitomized.

Still I heard another word in the name "Columbus": *columba,* the Latin word for dove, a symbol of peace. It echoed in the drip of morphine down the intravenous tube and in my father's breathing becoming shallower and shallower. His father, Carlo Cantalupo, left Altomonte behind, boarded the steamship *Scotia* in Naples, sailed to "the new world" of New York City in 1894, and lived a life of peace as a quiet, gentle barber and father of seven who liked to cook and play mandolin. His son now rested peacefully, and I sat at his bedside on a deathwatch.

Opening his eyes, he blinked several times. I heard him whisper as I leaned closer to his drained but still soft face: "I'm satisfied. Happy. God made me." I listened for more and his dry lips started to part, but then he stopped blinking and his eyes closed again.

The night nurse poked her head in the door and asked "All right?" as she set down a fresh pitcher of ice water and gave me a pillow. She sounded Hispanic and also looked part Indian and part black. "I will be here all night, if you need anything," she said.

She looked like women whom I saw in Mayagüez, Puerto Rico, where the year before I had staged a play, or rather "an ode in performance," called *Colonial / Neocolonial* at the university. It presented one set of voices named the Verge and another set named the Curse that turned and counterturned like a strophe and antistrophe between Senegal and Gambia and London and Paris, respectively. At the conclusion they resolved themselves in a kind of epode spoken by a third set of voices called the Oracle. As in Morocco, the cast consisted of college students (members of the campus Ethnic Coalition) wearing bizarre costumes—the Curse in masks looking like devils, the Verge like insects, and the Oracle like cats—and performing modern dance to rock music. Barbara designed the production's poster, featuring a picture of a carved, wooden predatory cat with jaws opened wide to chew the upside-down names on a collaged language map of the world.

The project required elaborate lighting and a huge sound system including amplifiers and instruments that we brought with us, except for one major component with which we performed the play in Pennsylvania but that I thought would be readily available in Puerto Rico: eight conga drums to be played by either the Curse or the Verge when one of them wasn't speaking. Although I asked the University of Puerto Rico at Mayagüez, our hosts, to supply the drums previous to our arrival, and I continued to ask every day of the week that we rehearsed, the drums never appeared until the local students supplied them on the day of the premier. Roughly consisting of two choruses challenging each other across the colonial divide between the colonizer and the colonized—the Curse and the Verge—the production blurred and subverted the distinction between them in an attempt to embody the neocolonial dilemma as articulated by Wole Soyinka: "The contemporary artist . . . has to do a double retrieval; first from the colonial deniers of . . . [the] past but also, second, from the . . . neocolonial deniers of . . . [the] immediate past and present, even when that immediate past is the history of . . . [a] struggle for self-retrieval at the hands of the colonial deniers."[4] The convoluted process of the university denying by failing to provide the play's conga drums—that only the local student stage technicians could eventually supply—exemplified the dynamics of Soyinka's almost as convoluted explanation of colonialism and neocolonialism. But the stark contrast we saw outside of town between the rundown housing and barely subsistence farming and the gleaming new and vast factories of U.S. pharmaceutical companies also reinforced the intractability of what Soyinka described. We saw them off the highway as we drove with a UPRM professor to an archaeological site reputed to have been a settlement of the Taino, an indigenous people thought to have been the first to greet Columbus and also the first to have been driven to extinction—with the help of their traditional local enemies, the Caribs—by the Spanish conquest.

To pass the time during my deathwatch at my father's bedside, I read the journals of Columbus and catalogued their intricate imagery. I also took my research on the Taino and the European conquest of the Caribbean and South America and the notebooks I had filled in Cameroon as well. In my mind they all floated together on a black Atlantic, connecting Africa and the Americas, yet connecting Europe too, and its raging millenarian storms of conquest and black slavery. I felt I was seeing the same grass floating at sea, strangely familiar birds in need of nests, and the same inexplicable sources of light—clung to by a lost and desperate Columbus in his journal as evidence that land had to be near—in the Caribbean as in Cameroon.

I read one of my notes on a passage in Genesis about when the dove that Noah had released, since he needed a sign that the flood was receding and not all of the earth had been restored, returned to him: "and, lo, in her mouth . . . an olive leaf pluckt off" (8:11). I was looking for a spirit like this dove's, this *columba,* with its branch of peace on my own journeys, returning to and immersing in some of the same currents that once flowed into the horrors of conquest and colonization in the name of Columbus and the fifteenth- and sixteenth-century expansion of western European civilization into Africa, the Caribbean, and South America.

Ironically, perhaps, historical currents touching these same places pushed my father and me in almost opposite directions in and out of Africa. Four years after immigrating to New York City in 1894, his father married, moved to a tenement on Orleans Street in Newark, New Jersey, and moved again several years later into an elegant house on Highland Avenue in the Forest Hills section bordering Branch Brook Park in Newark's mostly Italian Fourth Ward. Born and raised in Newark, my father returned there after having been stationed in the Aleutian Islands in World War II. He received a degree in law from Newark University, which later became a part of Rutgers, and soon thereafter he joined one of the first waves of "white flight" out of Newark to the suburbs in 1952. Newark had a thriving Italian immigrant community, but African Americans migrating from the South began to outnumber and outvote them: much as the Italians had done to the Irish immigrants who preceded them. By 1967, roughly 150,000 blacks had replaced half of Newark's white population now ensconced in suburbs north and west of the city.

Although my father served as the chief probate clerk in the surrogate court of Essex County in the Hall of Records building located in Newark, as a family in the fifties and sixties, we never went back to the city together except to shop at the huge department stores, since this was before shopping malls in the suburbs, to visit my uncle's restaurant, the oldest Italian restaurant in Newark, or to go to the doctors, who were nearly always Jewish. Such trips included trying to navigate around or simply to have as little contact as possible with the increasingly black population. Going to Newark for additional reasons that most suburbanites now visit a big city—to visit museums, attend concerts, movies, and lectures, eat at ethnic restaurants—was never an option. We were afraid of black people and acted as if, as my sister said decades later, since she still believed it, "they have no culture." These were the years leading up to the Newark riots—although "rebellion" may be a more accurate word—in the "long hot summer" of 1967. They lasted five days, left twenty-six dead, and caused ten million dollars in property damage.

If anyone had "no culture," at least comparatively speaking, it was the white suburbs where we lived: where most Italians along with other recent immigrant families—for example, Jews from Newark, memorialized by Philip Roth—wanted little of the sound or color of their urban counterparts, except maybe on holidays. Moving out of ethnic Newark, my parents opted for assimilation, blending into a mix of indistinguishable identities—at least on the outside—ethnic in last name only. Italian, Jewish, Scottish, Irish, German—all white and of European ancestry—they had houses, food, clothes, cars, politics, entertainment, schools, furniture, and windows—covered with three layers of drapes, curtains, and shades—that looked almost identical because they were suburban and middle class. The same on the surface, the surface was our lives.

Yet the surface was thin, and telltale signs of confusion often popped through. In my parents' house, peanut oil replaced olive oil and scotch came before dinner instead of wine with it. Going to Roman Catholic grade school, I thought the world was Roman Catholic, until my father told me that he was voting for Eisenhower in the presidential election of 1956. If he wasn't Catholic, I somehow thought at age four, the only alternative must be that he was "public." When I left Catholic school to go to public junior high, I came back to my old playground one day to play basketball and wore a brightly colored shirt. The priest, who was Irish, told me scornfully and spit, "You look like a Jew." My high school reading list at its best dwelled on Ernest Hemingway and Edward Scott Fitzgerald—with a dash of Samuel Beckett—as if they were the only salvation amid West Orange's mores of assimilation and cover-up as the way to achieve and maintain middle-class status.

My uncle's restaurant in Newark, called Fucci's Italian Kitchen, and our traveling through the black towns of Orange and East Orange to get there, were my only reminder of a culture other than suburban. Popular with Italians in the city, the restaurant also attracted Newark's business and political leaders. The former were mostly white insurance executives, but the latter mixed Italians, Irish, Germans, Jews, and blacks into one big, jostling order of outrageous claims and laughter fueled by Chianti and pasta. Somewhat quieter and a little more demanding, Italian Mafia figures had their regular tables too amid the red walls covered with thin wood-framed black-and-white photographs from the forties and fifties of local and even some national celebrities—all of whom dined at 13 Central Avenue. Most frequently pictured were Jerry Lewis and Dean Martin—since one of my uncle's sons was his look-alike in Hollywood—and Fred Allan Hartley—the Republican congressman who at different times represented New Jersey's Eighth and Tenth districts. He co-sponsored the anti-labor Taft-Hartley Act that, overcoming President Truman's veto, passed in 1947. Pictures of parties at "Fred Hartley's farm" hung next to long-legged bleach blondes in heels and a little flabby in polka dot bikinis as they leaned over big, gleaming black cars. Pictures of first Holy Communions and massive and elegant gatherings of formally attired family surrounding stiff and shrunken Italian immigrants celebrating their wedding anniversaries hung next to heavy and dark-suited men with shiny hair and shinier faces looking up, mouths full, their arms resting on white, starched tablecloths spread with platters of mussels, veal cutlets, and chicken cacciatore. The restaurant's ebony bar, usually tended by my cousin, Charlie, another son of my uncle, reflected nearly a hundred Mexican masks hung above it. My father and his brother—a powerful Newark lawyer and leader of the county's Republican party—brought them home since they trained for World War II at the army base in Eagle Pass, Texas, along the Rio Grande. The masks' grimacing faces reflected the near constant self-glorifying and derisive laughter that Charlie provoked from whoever sat there. Whenever my family visited, and even later when I was in graduate school and stopped by to pick up a case of wine, I wandered around the restaurant like it was a second home where I could help myself to all the provolone, salami, and bread I wanted. The Genoese chef, Samarone, his Italian English always slurred, especially at the end of a night when he had had plenty of wine, which was every night, never failed—over thirty years—to take my hand and tell me that I should marry his daughter since we were born in the same year and the same month.

Fucci's revealed more history, tradition, culture, change, and different kinds of people than I saw anywhere else. Yet so did even fleeting glimpses of the old streets of the black cities of Orange and East Orange that I saw through the windows of the locked car doors. Still I witnessed two histories, two cultures, which when they joined, since they had to, as in most major cities in the United States at this time, joined violently. One of Charlie's jokes hinted at the troubles to come. Several white Newark politicos had invited their black counterparts to join them for lunch. Charlie came to the table and offered them wine, "white or black." No one thought he was funny, and the blacks angrily walked out. The restaurant withstood fifteen years of aftershocks—in the form of break-ins, vandalism, and unresponsive police—from the Newark riots before it perished: bulldozed for a parking lot.

On the first night of the Newark riots I walked with my father in Orange, a mostly black town "down the hill"—a phrase that signified a shift in class and race as much as geographical elevation—from West Orange. We had gone to dinner at a Jewish deli, Eppes Essen (Yiddish for "I will give you something to eat"), located between the YMCA and the Rheingold brewery. When we came out of the restaurant, I saw national guardsmen wearing white helmets and speeding around the streets in army jeeps. Getting into our aquamarine 1964 Ford Galaxy, my father turned on the radio. A news story about someone named LeRoi Jones—years later known as Amiri Baraka—reported that he had been imprisoned for inciting the riot. When the announcer said that Jones was a poet, I couldn't understand how or why he would incite a riot with his poetry. I was writing protest songs, a genre that was popular at the time. Since my friends at school liked them, I thought I was a poet, too. The soldier's white helmets, black people filling the streets, the air crackling with their uneasiness and walkie-talkies from the jeeps combined with news bulletins about the riots and a poet prompted me to ask my father, "Who is LeRoi Jones?" Our Galaxy powerfully climbed the hill back to the humdrum of West Orange, where black culture amounted to little more than Motown songs on Top 40 AM radio, cleaning ladies, and a few professional athletes on television and radio. The civil rights movement, Martin Luther King, Malcolm X, and the Civil Rights Act of 1964 barely rippled the white suburban surface. My father muttered, "He's a god-damned nigger."

Amiri Baraka went to the same Newark high school, Barringer, as my father, only twenty years later. When I asked Amiri about it in 1995, he chuckled, "I went to high school in Italy."

I stared blankly through the windshield then as I did now into the dimly lit hospital room's gray. The turned-off television mounted on the wall became a memory screen. Newark went off the air with an image of overflowing banks of blue hydrangeas around the steps leading up to the dark green porch on Highland Avenue. I flipped through a few other channels on the memory remote: sports—Yankee Stadium in the early sixties,

Mantle and Maris hitting home runs; news—my father, a diehard Italian Republican, calling me in Greece to say the resignation of Nixon in August 1973 had signaled the end of an era; music—as a young man Dad managed Ted Fiorito, his cousin's big band; cooking—Dad loved to eat and cook and taught me how; home movies of the family parties.

Providers, husbands, faithful, hard workers: six Italian uncles ate in their sleeveless T-shirts at an enameled metal kitchen table in the garage basement of a small home at the Jersey shore where their wives cooked for them. Ralph, who owned Fucci's, and my father's youngest sister's husband, Teddy, argued in half English and half Italian as if only to see—who can remember the issue?—whose voice could be louder.

I went to Teddy's funeral. The last of them who died. A cold-type printer built like a freezer, he finished two six packs of Pabst by noon on every Sunday. An old florid Irish priest eulogized him with analogies about golf—which Teddy never played, although the priest did regularly. He reminded us of Teddy's gentle nature, love for God, and faithfulness to the authority of his holy mother Church—more fictions. We would see him transformed at the Last Judgment. At his grave near the edge of a forest, the priest forbad anyone from tossing a flower on the coffin before it was lowered into the ground since, he said, this was "pagan." The next morning I took a thick, dark branch I had found in a rainy forest near Mayagüez. I crudely whittled its sides until it looked half corn, half beast. After sharpening one end to a point, I pounded it into a corner of my garden: my hammer, heart, and sweaty hands praying for fertility, abundance, and protection. Doctrine and ideology wiped out the inconvenient details of a man's life and death and sucked on his sons' and daughters' bones. His dead body wanted new words and new wine. The stake meant sex, the individual: two snuffed candles' smoke drifting into each other and one last flame of an unlit match to guide us into the future. I pounded the stake and a breeze swirled at the base into a tongue. It sang like vines entangling a naked, nursing mother, her power in her daughters and sons. All of them adopted a new land to live again, again and again, growing in and out, athletic, with words growing in and out of them too. They formed an icon engendering a race of grassy flesh, fertile beds, the protection of fire and water and no fearful face lighting the lights, lights, more light . . .

"Do you want more light? I can light the light." I heard the nurse, Elena's voice. She saw me staring straight ahead with my book, *The Four Voyages of Columbus,* and my notebook open in my lap.

"No, thanks. I can see." I watched her go to my father's bedside and ask as naturally as if she had met in the hall, "How you doing, honey?"

"Satisfied, satisfied," he whispered without opening his eyes. As she put her hand on his forehead, they opened, and as he rolled his head to look at me they opened wide. "Generous," he uttered slowly.

"You're generous, you've always been generous," I said back to him, hearing myself sound oversolicitous. I wanted to change the tone by saying the Italian word that he often pronounced like a dance step when he saw something plentiful and delicious—*abbondanza*. But before I could he responded in a normal voice and sounded perfectly lucid.

"Why be any other way? We need help."

He looked up at Elena, who nodded and closed her eyes as she took away her hand from the pulse in his wrist to leave the room. He looked back at me, closed his eyes, and said as if everything was normal, "When did you get back?"

I didn't know whether he meant "back" to the hospital room, which I had left a few hours earlier, or "back" from Cameroon. I looked down at the page in my notebook and read silently,

In the aperture,
On the page, on the horizon—
No being apart.

"Two weeks ago," I said. "Remember I told you that Chris and I came home early because the day before we got there twenty students were killed in a riot at the university in Yaounde, and their bodies thrown into a lake near the campus?" At the time I was afraid of what happened and of many incidents over the next two weeks. Ironically they made me grateful for the call to cut our trip short and to come home early because my father was close to dying. I knew my hosts at the university, among them the writers Bole Botake and Kashim Tala, would understand my needing to leave prematurely to be at the deathbed of my father. But what if I said to them what I was also feeling: that the killings and threats of growing disorder and violence made me want to take my son practically from the day we arrived and get on the first plane out of Douala back to Europe?

Although my Cameroonian friends carried on as usual and expressed no fear for their own lives but only rage at the students' deaths, I went to the United States embassy in Yaounde repeatedly to ask if my son and I were in danger and should leave the country. Both the embassy's deputy chief and cultural affairs officer assured me that we were safe. As Christopher and I were driven back and forth between the Francophone south and the Anglophone north, seeing angry soldiers at government roadblocks every few miles pushing muzzles of machine guns into our faces through our car's open windows told me otherwise. When I saw the embassy's deputy chief and cultural affairs officer sitting in the Lufthansa lounge and waiting for the same flight to Brussels that I had been desperate to book the day before—that the embassy couldn't help me with but that a girlfriend of one of Bole's students who worked at Cameroon Airlines confirmed at the last minute—I realized that the embassy people were as afraid of the political situation as I was—and also afraid to admit it. When I passed them they didn't say hello, but I did, with a mock surprise, "How are you?"

"We're great," replied the deputy chief with similarly mock cheerfulness, adding, "We're going on vacation."

I spoke to my father again. "We got back two weeks ago. Remember I told you about the one small wax candle we had burned for three consecutive nights with no power, the pillows filled with pebbles, and the vinyl sheets we slept on sweltering under mosquito nets heavy as blankets?"

As his eyes stayed closed, I heard his breathing becoming louder, shallower, and harder. I tried to talk with him again, knowing that it didn't matter what I said, suddenly feeling desperately sad and not really knowing what I could or should say.

"Remember the branch of fire, your first grandchild's birth salty eyes that you drunk dry, the dolphins leading with their powerful shoulders to food when we were hungry, the left-to-right waves, the chunks of mast floating away from your hands, the patch of red canvas, and the delicate green grass floating on the ocean?

"Remember I told you about the trees? The pines growing amid palms? The bananas hanging like diamonds as we drove up the mountain out of the rain forest and then down the conch shell highway to the turquoise bay and the black sand with roots rippling in every direction of the great tree full of other trees? Remember I told you about the trees? Baobab, banyan, ginkgo, peach, olive, oak, and more I can't name—all full of bees, snakes, flowers and birds and ripe with cloves, turpentine, oil, and mastic? Remember some parts of the tree continuously burned and smoldered, while other parts looked like stumps, some of them sprouting new shoots? Remember the countless pods opening and closing, each like its own sun on its own day shining between antipodes of earth and rain, sound and echo, loss and invention, ascension and burial?"

I started flipping the pages of my notebook faster and faster. What could I find to tell him when I knew he wouldn't hear me? "You shall live, shall live, live," I read audibly but softly, again expecting no response.

As a form of thanking him for all the good he gave me and as if to close a circle with a triangle and three points of father to son to father to son inscribed inside, I wanted to tell him about my son traveling to Cameroon: what he saw through the eye slits of a thirty-foot-long python skin offered to us by a rain forest Pygmy with two more skins under his arms as we walked through an outdoor Yaounde market; how Chris watched a six-inch blue beetle move an inch a day on a path outside our university rooms surrounded by cacti, half their surface crawling with chameleons; how a cricket chirped in our room all night, "Never tired, never tired"; how Chris stepped ever so lightly through a field, the red earth and bent poles that looked like a kind of shrine but was really only a field of cocoa yams; how he realized he was the first white boy that the other boys in a remote patch of northern Cameroon had ever seen; how he and I ran away terrified by the hissing and taunts of angry prostitutes on a street with no lights in Yaounde; how the rain every other minute turned on and off like a big faucet near the top of Mount Cameroon.

"Why was I going back to Africa again?" I had thought on the bus to Kennedy Airport a few weeks before. The miles of graveyards and graffiti we saw in Queens and Brooklyn through the windows blurred into a strong, two-way current. Two floods alternated, pulling in seemingly opposite directions, as I first felt when I went to Dakar, only now they pulled much harder. Should I go or stay home? No beginning and no end but a second start and a kind of providing abyss bit deeply as a spear tipped with teeth into leaving my dying father. It ripped a wider and wider hole, letting in more and more anxiety and forming a sense of absolute loneliness that no discovery could appease or even distract me from for a second. The thought of being away from Barbara nursing our two-year old daughter, Alicia, smashed me apart like a ton of melting steel. Our lives and our love depended on holding each other, desperate for our family, flooding with each other down a bad road's history, crossing a bridge of corpses, running faster and faster, more and more muck sucking at our sneakers, the shots behind us getting closer if we didn't try to run faster and faster to return to the denial of our never being apart even on two opposite horizons. "Let there be" or don't exist? Orpheus or father? I forgive or I forget? Rain on. Rain off. I reached for Chris next to me. So much rain flooding the windshield I couldn't see.

Opening my eyes, I saw Elena in the room's brightly lit bathroom as she emptied and refilled the yellow plastic pitcher of ice water and put it back on the table near where I sat. "Thanks. How is he doing?" I asked her.

"His heartbeat keeps getting slower and slower," she said softly and matter-of-factly, meaning he would probably die tonight, and I should be there.

I thought of the Cameroonian writer Mbella Sone Dipoko living in an empty, corrugated aluminum storefront in Tiko, near a deserted palm oil plantation. Since he had decided decades before to remain in Paris and not return to his mother dying in the village where he was born, he now barely wrote or spoke, he was so haunted by her.

Part of my dream had evoked the surprisingly sharp and sudden sense of separation I felt from Barbara in the few first hours of our trip. I had realized facing the roaring twenty-foot green surf on the coast of Morocco when she left to return to the United States and I stayed—and I had been reminded in Dakar as I feasted on the unexpected gift from Stevie Wonder of a night in a first-class hotel only alone—that the continent and culture and where I felt the greatest sense of belonging was not in any one place but in love. Late in the sixteenth century John Donne named it "my America! my new found lande," but the name didn't matter as much as his desire to "License my roving hands, and let them goe / Behind, before, above, between, below."[5] We traveled, father and son, and our continent of love stayed with us the way slaves carried the seeds in their hair of the lands they left.

Three years later, I guiltily thought I should have been tougher and should have traveled alone. Every other night for six days at exactly 11:00 p.m. Christopher broke out in a fever approaching 106 degrees. We called every physician we knew. The third night the fever struck him, we brought him to the local hospital's emergency room, but no one could explain what caused the fevers as we panicked between wrapping him in blankets when he seemed to shiver beyond control and lowering him almost unconscious into a bath of lukewarm water as he sweated the fever out. Coincidentally, I had a Cameroonian student at the time, Ajua Alemanji. As I desperately described the symptoms to him one day on campus, he didn't seem upset but almost lit up in joy and said, "This is what my mother used to call night fever."

I asked him "What?" and he said "Malaria." The image of my naked twelve-year-old son standing in a white tub placed in the middle of a bright bathroom in a cheap Yaounde hotel and bathing out of a bucket as he slapped mosquitoes off his body haunts me still. Chloroquine failed us the way it was failing most Africans, and people worldwide—over a million of whom die from malaria every year, most of them children–who lack the knowledge, the money, or both to get a more effective prophylactic. Our hospital in Bethlehem had one infectious disease specialist, but he served as an administrator, presumably because it saw no need for his expertise. I called him. Also suspecting that the symptoms might mean a strain of malaria, he immediately admitted Christopher for three days of intravenous antibiotics, after which the malaria left him as suddenly as it had come and never to return. I knew only a few people where I lived and taught who recognized the overwhelming power of African cultures. Still fewer around me could recognize a common African disease that almost killed my son and had infected close to three hundred million people annually.

While we were in Cameroon, Kashim Tala insisted that we should take an afternoon to drive to pay homage Mbella Dipoko, since he was one of Cameroon greatest living poets. On the way I learned that young men in tattered shorts and T-shirts who would jump out of the weeds along the side of the road and wave were not simply being friendly or asking for rides but selling black-market gasoline in whatever container they could find to hold it. Gas was scarce and rationed, although we had seen many oil refineries in our travels around the country.

We stopped for a beer and for Chris to have a *pamplemousse* soda. As Kashim told me about Dipoko's reputation as the ultimate Bohemian in Paris when he was young—sleeping in doorways after all-night parties, spontaneously proclaiming his verses in long intervals wherever he was and always accompanied by at least three women—my son emptied his Cameroon Brasseries and filled the bottle with dark brown earth from a tomato garden along the road. Similar gardens grew close to the medians all along the roads because larger plots had been choked off by mile after mile of useless rows of palm oil trees. Kashim's stories about Dipoko made two beers feel like four.

Aglow but stiff, we rose to walk back to the car. Kashim saw one of the boys from whom we had bought gasoline now lingering near his early 1980s Toyota Celica and looking inside. Kashim screamed, "You will not look like that," took him by the shoulders, and repeated over and over at a higher and louder pitch each time, "You will not look like that." Our friend who had seemed so gentle and urbane, a loving husband and father and expert in oral poetry in six Cameroonian languages, had almost lost his mind. Yet he smiled as he brushed off and straightened his tweed jacket and khakis and repeated once more in the quiet tone of voice that we had become used to hearing before the last few moments, "You will not look like that." As we drove away, I turned around and saw a woman who could have been the boy's mother in a kind of orange burlap sack dress and only half his size beating him before he fell into a ditch and fetally tucked himself into a ball.

The ruts on the road into Tiko cut so deep that Kashim had to park his car beside the first building he saw. Windowless with paint-chipped benches inside and out revealing at least a dozen colors, it had a big homemade sign above the open doorway—GIN—and no one inside or out. The porch and large room also looked freshly swept. Remembering our last stop, I asked, "Do you think the car will be all right here?"

"Don't worry. Nobody will look at it. We visit Dipoko." Kashim lengthened his stride between the crevices in the road.

Just then a young girl with long braids and wearing jeans with a sweatshirt emblazoned by a yellow lion bursting through a red and green soccer ball peaked from behind the car and called me: "*Etes vous entendez avec mon père pour voir Dipoko?*"

Kashim laughed—"She thinks you look French"—and said without turning to look at her, "My daughter. Speak English like your Uncle Mbella, or I will not see you at my university in Buea." His voice trailed off bitterly so that only I could hear, "Your French will only get you killed in Yaounde." The student murders in Yaounde ten days earlier made him more adamant than ever to establish the University of Yaounde's branch campus in Buea as an independent university to serve the northern part of the country's mostly Anglophone population.

The town looked deserted with empty porches lining both sides of the street and the only movement an occasional cloth flapping over a window or door. The hot bright sunlight intimated that the buildings—all one story— had been painted before: shades of peach, turquoise, chartreuse, and red glimmering out of the stucco now gray as the road. When I tried to hold Christopher's hand, he pulled it away and turned around to look for the girl who spoke French. As we walked down the middle of the road, Kashim would peer into each building, and my head would swivel the same way three seconds later. Nobody came out, and I wasn't sure if anyone lived inside to come out since the interiors looked as dark as the soil Christopher had poured into his empty soda bottle. "Here," Kashim beamed, pointing to a building that appeared no different from and as empty as the others.

We stepped onto the porch, which felt solid despite its appearing ready to collapse. Kashim called through the empty door into the darkness, "Mbella Dipoko. I am Kashim Tala from Buea, and I come with an American professor and his son."

"His son," I heard a low voice echo. "Then come in."

Christopher found my hand. We followed Kashim into a long narrow room, again only with benches, which I couldn't see—my eyes accustomed to the bright sun in the street and not to this cool dark interior—but only felt as their splintery edges grazed my shins and guided me deeper in. I saw the outline of a man with long dreadlocks and beard. He seemed to be wearing a sarong and a button-down shirt. He sat on a bench, his hands and head on his knees, his beard and hair extending between them too.

"Let me light a lantern," he said slowly and evenly, "and order us some lunch of spicy goat sticks," but he didn't get up.

The girl whom we first saw when we entered town ran from the back of the room and out into the sunshine. I didn't see the two lanterns next to him on the bench until he lit them. Kashim went out after her.

In the lamplight and throughout the visit, Dipoko seemed unable to blink. As he got up slowly he seemed to recite, as if in a poem and heavily stressing the accented syllables, "America. America. Let's talk about America." He smiled and stared at me, "How can we perform modern poetry in Cameroon, professor, when we don't have your powerful microphones, amplifiers, light shows, and theaters?" His question addressed what I had said in an interview broadcast the night before on Buea's radio station about using popular media and technology to reach a broader audience with contemporary poetry. Either he had listened or someone had told him about it.

Further introductions were not going to be necessary, so I replied, "Mbella Dipoko. I'm glad we can talk. Maybe we can ask Kashim if the university can support your work and perform it."

"If we don't perform our poems, they only fly like dreams back to the bookshelves where they belong," he said, his voice trailing off as he stared through me at the wall.

The girl ran back in, repeating, "Five minutes, five minutes." When she reached the back of the room, she pulled back a large, dark, tattered curtain that covered an empty doorway and two window frames. Dipoko blew out the lanterns, their flames overcome by the wide burst of constant light.

Kashim reentered from the front with two jerry cans. "Buea *wata,* my friend. I went to the spring myself this morning before dawn."

Delicious water from Mt. Cameroon soon sparkled on all our chins and created a red paste on all our lips from the spice on the goat meat that we ate off the sticks, which were actually twigs.

"Better than gold," Dipoko muttered, his face, beard, and even his dreadlocks gleaming with water. "Now get us six Guinness," he added, looking at no one but knowing the girl would hear him.

As she disappeared into the light out the back door, Dipoko ambled back to where I first saw him sitting, slumped, and spoke to no one in particular: "Gold. Gold and a good harbor. The people are open mines of gold. Deep rivers of gold. Shores of gold. Gold eyes and gold fingernails. Gold earring and bracelets. Mountains, gardens, and burial mounds of gold. Solid gold trees and bunches of gold flowers. Lapis men and raw sapphire women. Gold ducks and dogs. Pearl birds. Horses invisibly pounding gold shields with helmets of dust so golden that rocks burst gold at our touch to free prisoners from their gold chains. I drink this water from a gourd of gold. I drink to America. Black and white gold. Gold babies in gold cradles. Plenty of nights and days of gold. I drink to America. Because of women, I drink to America, to gold. Because of slaves, America, the gold of slaves."

Glancing quickly at Kashim for a nonverbal hint on how to respond, I saw him leaned back from his bench all the way to the wall, with his chin on his chest and dozing. By this time, Christopher had decided, after tasting only a shred of the goat meat, to leave the room and go out and explore Tiko.

Dipoko now looked at me instead of through me. I opened my eyes as wide as I could, although not as wide as his, and spoke in a businesslike tone: "Okay, Dipoko. I will trade you for your gold. I'll give you paper, brass, and salt. Guns and bullets. A box of knives. Glass necklaces for your lover, chains for your enemies. Whistles, whiskey, all the guitars and amplifiers you need, and a foolproof generator that runs on sugar!"

Dipoko exploded, "Master, master. Take my canoe! Kashim! You said 'Cantalupo,' but this man is Columbus!"

Kashim woke up with a grimace and looked startled, but then immediately started laughing, "Columbus, Cantalupo, what's the difference? Time to go home."

Now three weeks later, I sat by my father on his deathbed. I had written at odd angles on the page before me what he had said that night so far: "I'm satisfied. Happy. God made me. Generous. Why be any other way? We need help? When did you get back?"

I touched his hand. "Home," he whispered, "home." Another word or syllable came before "home," but I couldn't identify it. I wanted to think he said, "I'm home," or maybe he simply said to me, "Go home."

I pulled my chair closer, and the book of Columbus's journals slipped onto the floor. Seeing the book and then glancing up at my father's face, which now resembled my earliest memory of his father, when I sat on his lap and he tickled me with his clipped moustache, made me think again of the ship's manifest with the words "Carlo Cantalupo . . . Altomonte . . . *Scotia* . . . Napoli." On June 15, 1894, ninety-seven years before, a careful, slow cursive recorded him as number "127" in a list of fifty Italian names. Registered as having sailed in the ship's "forward" compartment, he arrived with one bag. A "yes" straddled the line between the two columns under the heading "Able to / Read Write." Was he or the immigration officer responsible for the fictitious "Calling or Occupation" of "Shoemaker"? Yet "Shoemaker" and "Labourer" alternated three times in a row as if either weariness or the sudden need for a credible lie required a momentary antiphon to keep the line of immigrants moving, hopefully on their way to discover a new world and gather a little more gold than they had when they came, although far less than they were promised.

Sliding my hand over my father's chest, I felt his heartbeat getting slower and fainter. He too set sail, only now for the proverbial "undiscover'd country,"[6] sparing no one from being a kind of immigrant with no chance of ever returning. Any voyage to America, Europe, Africa, or anywhere else led there, and no one came back. Any other boundary in comparison could come down. I let my fingers and my kiss trace the power of his life up and down the full length of his limbs—his pale face, his limbs, his loins, and his chest—and prayed *Our father* forehead to forehead with him. Placing my fingers again on his heart, I felt it fade to its last beat and then nothing. As his lips parted ever so slightly for one last, almost imperceptible breath, which I took with him, I saw the first seep of wine grapes—his favorite color—that his father pressed. I walked home, lay down next to Barbara, and the first light of dawn through the window revealed the same color in the dusty pigment on a life-size, smiling mask that I had found the day before leaving Yaounde and that now hung near our bed.

Interpretation

FIVE AND A HALF YEARS AFTER MY FIRST VISIT TO KENYA, I INTER-viewed its greatest living writer, Ngugi wa Thiong'o. By then I had published a lot of poetry in American and British literary magazines based on what I had seen in Africa—Egypt, Morocco, West Africa, and Kenya—but I had not read a single book, except Ngugi's latest, by any African writer. Ngugi proposed "a pan-African property. . . Ama Ata Aidoo . . . Wole Soyinka. If you travel anywhere in Africa, people . . . recognize them as their own writers. . . . Not . . . a Ghanaian writer or . . . a Nigerian writer."[1]. But the concept remained foreign to me, in letter if maybe not in spirit.

I had the idea to edit a special issue of one of the journals in which I had published and to devote it solely to Ngugi's work because three months before, in October 1992, I had heard him speak at Penn State. He gave a great reading from his latest novel, *Matigari* (1987), and talked about African literature and politics, particularly about African literature in African languages. He also discussed his imprisonment in Kenya in 1978, detailed in his memoir, *Detained* (1981).

By the time of the interview, I didn't remember much of what he had said, beyond his great anecdote about writing a novel in prison on its rough toilet paper. However, I had immensely enjoyed his reading a comic passage from *Matigari* as well as talking with him before and after: so much so that as we said good-bye at the entrance to the Hotel Bethlehem, where he was staying, I pressed into his hands a manuscript of my poems about Africa, inscribed to him with one of their lines: "In black and silver light of independence." I thought of him as a great writer first, a great African writer second. I knew that I should be reading African writers, and now I would also be getting to know one.

As he glanced at the manuscript and its inscription, total puzzlement clouded and darkened his face. His lips slightly parted and his teeth looked sharp, like they did earlier in the shadows backstage just before I introduced him. At such a moment, what I said or thought about didn't matter. He sent me back to the sands on the site of ancient Jericho, the victorious maze of Cairo, the predatory rocks of Sinai, the teeming Marche Sandaga, Togo's spirits, Mt. Kilimanjaro's shadows, a bush in a storm on the Indian Ocean, Casablanca's skull of a white cathedral, the coast of Morocco's towering wall of green surf, a one-street border town in Casamance, Cameroon's choked-off freedom, and my father's deathbed. I was there not to know but to listen: in the background not the foreground; not the light but a shadow; with no upper hand, closed fist or open; not the writing but the erased; the controlled not the controller; the silenced not the speaker; at best some questions, not the answers, not one or a thousand lines of poetry, not in Africa or on the streets where I lived and taught for a dozen years; and not even five minutes from where I was born and raised, since I would be interviewing Ngugi at his home in Orange, New Jersey.

On a bright and freezing January Saturday morning I drove there from Pennsylvania with the photographer Lawrence Sykes, whom I had invited to provide images for the journal, based on a recommendation from the Malawian poet Frank Chipasula.

I had read a poem called "Singing Like Parrots" from a book of Chipasula's poems, *Whispers in the Wings* (1991), while I was looking for books by Ngugi in New York City's St. Mark's Bookshop to prepare for the interview. The poem's title derived from Daniel Arap Moi's saying, when he took over Kenya's presidency from Jomo Kenyatta in 1978, "I would like ministers, assistant ministers and others to sing like a parrot after me. . . . That is how we can progress."[2] Formerly Kenya's vice president and minister for home affairs, Moi also signed the 1977 detention order sending Ngugi to Kamiti Maximum Security Prison without charges or a trial for the next year. Frank wrote, "And so the mind, emptied, rots / into a parrotry of sing-song praises / . . . for the right / to sing in the beak of a hawk."[3]

I found out that he lived and taught in Nebraska, in exile from Malawi, a country of perhaps even worse "parrotry," ruled by the longtime dictator Hastings Banda, who would feed Frank and anyone else who opposed him to the crocodiles of the Shire River. When I called Frank, he sounded depressed, his own mind "emptied" and harassed by the narrow Afrocentrism of his university's Black Studies department, which couldn't abide a great African poet with a scholarly and passionate expertise in Sterling Brown *and* Yeats and who as a teenager in the early sixties and glory days of Malawian independence studied with a young Peace Corps volunteer named Paul Theroux. When I told Frank that I was calling him about his poem, which I loved and wanted to include in the journal on Ngugi, Frank responded like an incredulous prisoner who thought he had been forgotten in solitary confinement when suddenly a friendly hand instead of his jailer's opens the cell door. "You are calling me about my poem? You are calling me about that poem?" He even admitted that he could barely remember it. But within a week and without my asking, he sent an annotated list of names of addresses of scholars and writers whom I should also invite to contribute to the journal—including Larry—with a note to look up his visual work for the poet Michael Harper and a conference on Sterling Brown. Based on one phone call, I received more contacts from Frank than I had in fifteen years from colleagues working in the European Renaissance *and* modern poetry. Similarly, when I called Larry and introduced the project and myself, he immediately offered to drive down from Boston to shoot the interview.

The way he shot it would reveal to me as much as, if not more than, the interview itself.

Larry showed up at my house in Pennsylvania around ten at night with two bottles of Shiraz and two pounds of Ethiopian coffee beans. All the Shiraz and a lot of the coffee disappeared before we left the next morning. As we were driving the interstate across the Delaware River, a cloud of nonstop talking about art and politics seemed to lift, and Larry told me a little about himself. By the fourth sentence, his focus was "Scottsboro."

The son of a dentist, Larry was born in Decatur, Alabama, sixty miles east of Scottsboro, the same year as its infamous trial of the Scottsboro Boys over the alleged gang rape of two white girls by nine black teenagers, aged thirteen to nineteen, around noon on a Southern Railroad freight train from Chattanooga to Memphis on March 25, 1931. The belief that a black man would always rape a white woman if he got the chance ran wild through the green and rolling hills of pastoral northern Alabama. The boys had to be killed—"The nigger must be kept in his place"—whatever the evidence or what anyone said.

Decatur being the site of the trial, since it was the Morgan County capital, Larry's father worked with the sheriff to bundle the boys to a safe location whenever lynch mobs gathered outside the jail, which was often, until the original judge for the case—also fearing the mob—swiftly handed down eight death sentences and one sentence of lifetime in prison for the thirteen-year-old, with an order that they be just as quickly carried out. Appeals ensued at every judicial level, eventually reaching the U.S. Supreme Court. It overturned each of the sentences, although all of the young defendants but one—who escaped—suffered years of appalling, Depression-era Alabama prison conditions.

With three sons, the oldest only six, and seeing that the crosses burning on Decatur lawns would all too soon burn his family, too, Larry's father decided to move his dental practice to Baltimore, repeating a move north that he had made once before when he went from Atlanta Baptist College, which became Morehouse, to Howard to get his dental degree. He opened a second-floor office above a bar near the John Hopkins University hospital in the surrounding, busy, black neighborhood mostly filled with orderlies and other hospital workers—with a school a block away and not much further the row houses of Slavic women mopping not only their doorsteps outside brightly painted screen doors but the street, too, providing enough sanctuary in apartheid America for the Sykes children to leave the fate of the Scottsboro boys behind. Eventually, Larry's preference for playing basketball at Morgan State instead of fighting in Korea metamorphosed into a tall quiet black man with short hair and wearing an overcoat taking a black-and-white photo of himself reflected in a store window in New York City, where he taught for ten years before moving to Rhode Island and setting up his studio on Hope Street in Providence, where he became a revered visual arts professor and artist.

Hesitating at first to ask Larry about Scottsboro, I still wanted to know if the experience affected him. "So what does Scottsboro make you most think of now?" I said looking straight ahead.

His answer surprised me. "Now that's one question you can't ask Ngugi," he laughed. "But let me tell you. Alabama during the early thirties and all the oppression going on: the trial, the state convictions, the Supreme Court reversals and acquittals and all the fury swirling around it—I really didn't see any of that as a child. I just learned it later on. Back then I only saw my loving parents. There is no substitute for the way they give you your start, the images and feeling that you carry until the last day."

I had no trouble finding Ngugi's house. He lived on the edge of Orange's "Seven Oaks" neighborhood—an affluent African American enclave and semigated community within Orange. The early afternoon January sun and its reflection in the remains of the previous week's snowstorm blinded and chilled Larry and me as we climbed the front porch and knocked on the door of "Limahouse," as Ngugi called it.

Ngugi's wife, Njeeri, answered, and she was all warmth and welcoming. She told us that Ngugi had not yet returned from New York University, where he had enrolled in an intensive language course in French to prepare for a documentary he planned on Africa's greatest filmmaker, Ousmane Sembene. As we sat and waited at the dining room table, Njeeri offered us a bowl of the new crop of clementines from Morocco and glasses. She would refill them often after only a few sips of a kind of tropical fruit juice that I had never tasted for all the years I lived practically next door. Three of Ngugi's daughters and one of his sons also greeted us warmly and, at Njeeri's insistence, told us where they went to school—including a private all-black academy in Newark—and about their latest school projects.

The large house looked lived-in and not lavish. Njeeri ran it without fuss. Stacks of papers, magazines, and books lapped at the feet of tasteful yet unexceptional African sculptures—a tall, thin ebony girl; a large, soapstone bird; a dusty, black male spirit or warrior mask one might as readily find for sale on a sidewalk in Manhattan as East Africa. In one corner a pile of papers and knocked-over sculptures blended as if they washed up together on a beach.

Hearing Ngugi let the back screen door slam behind him as he entered the kitchen, Njeeri smiled and declared, "Here he is. You are late again, Baba. Please don't forget to close that inside door. It's cold out there."

"You guys better get started because I know you love to talk, and you don't want to be too late," she softly said in time with her steps as Larry and I followed her into the living room where he had already set up two banks of lights. As I settled onto a large, curved, beige velour couch, the only furniture, Ngugi came rushing in. He wore a scruffy winter parka that he kept on throughout the next three hours of our conversation, until he could no longer resist the smell of roasting goat and samosas from the kitchen, when we returned to the dining room for a huge meal.

Ngugi easily answered all of my questions, based on my having just read his latest book of essays, *Moving the Centre* (1993), published coincidentally on Martin Luther King Day, a week before, and took them as opportunities to express additional concerns of his own. Hearing echoes of his lecture that I had heard a few months earlier, I prompted and recorded a kind of primer: Ngugi's thinking about his now writing primarily in Gikuyu instead of English; African languages, their power and their marginalization; the development and empowerment of cultures and writers other than European; the continuing legacy of racism and "the West . . . bleed[ing] the Third World";[4] the Marxist solution despite the recent collapse of the Soviet Union and other countries that were Marxist; and the political failures of Africa—with the exception of the release of Nelson Mandela in 1990—since the late 1950s and early 1960s' dawn of independence. For Ngugi, as he wrote in *Moving the Centre,* "Those days at Makerere, in east Africa! It was a replica of the Wordsworthian bliss at being alive at the birth of a revolution and the possibilities of a new future. Africa, our Africa, was coming back."[5]

Ngugi testified, and Larry and I witnessed, but Africa wasn't "coming back," at least not yet. How could it, when thousands died of AIDS every day, tens of thousands of mothers died every year just giving birth, and more than a million babies died every year in their first month of life? Coming back? A continent with only 10 percent of the world's population, 1 percent or less of international trade, and widely afflicted with the harshest kinds of natural environment? Coming back? A continent poorer than it had been in thirty years, with population growth out of control, agriculture in steep decline, and most of the best-trained youth and skilled graduates unable to find employment and justifiably fleeing to the West? Where was "The birth . . . of a new future" in neocolonialism's virulent reproduction of the barely faded horrors of colonialism? How could Africa come back, if it continued to suffer mass starvation, pandemics, racial and ethnic war, genocide, murderous national debt and suicidal borrowing, colossal corruption, and billions and billions of mostly futile, stolen or wasted foreign aid?

As I read *Moving the Centre,* the most recurring word I heard was "struggle," and I asked Ngugi about it. He replied by first citing Hegel's principle, "Without struggle there is no progression."[6] He added, "Culture develops within the process of a people wrestling with their natural and social environment. They struggle with nature. They struggle with one another. . . . What is often officially paraded as authentic African culture today is virtually a repeat of the colonial tradition: tourist art, dances, acrobatic contortions emptied of the content of struggle."[7]

I had myself experienced and joined precisely such a parade for tourists—exotically costumed, gleaming black dancers whirling and whooping, the stock contortionist from central casting too—around the swimming pool of my hotel on my first day in Dakar five and half years before. Since then I had struggled to understand an alternative and ended up here. What did Ngugi propose? It sounded like a categorical opposite, for example, of what Baudelaire wrote, "*De la vaporisation et de la centralasion du Moi. Tout est là*" ("The dispersion and the reconstitution of the self. That's the whole story").[8] However, Baudelaire's depiction of a writer also highlighted struggle, albeit only of the individual.

I wanted to interview Ngugi because I knew of no writer in Africa or the world with as many major, lasting achievements in such a wide range of genres, including novels, plays, short stories, essays and scholarship, criticism and children's literature, in English and Gikuyu. I also liked his writing about politics in Africa and the world, which did not make him unique except for the large, worldwide audience and similarly extensive critical attention he attracted, again like no contemporary writer I knew.

In my own writing and thinking about Africa until then, I was little more prepared for what Ngugi wrote and said than I was five and a half years ago in Kenya, unaware of Ngugi's work and for the most part comfortably in bed with the U.S. Embassy and buried under blankets of neocolonial Kenya's tourist mentality. Ironically, perhaps, my previous work on early modern or Renaissance writers in England, particularly on the philosopher Thomas Hobbes, now provided me with more insight into Ngugi's achievement. For example, in 1651 Hobbes wrote that he felt "beset with those that contend, on one side, for too great Liberty, and on the other side for too much Authority."[9] Although Hobbes was referring to the specific political conditions surrounding the restoration of the Stuart monarchy in England and how many more freedoms—particularly of expression—it might allow than the previous, more Puritan regime, the situation he described, more generally, seemed no more settled in the world now than then. Ngugi himself seemed to straddle such a divide and, furthermore, he struggled with it: as authoritative a voice in African writing as there could be but thought to have exercised "too much Liberty" in his work, as evidenced by his imprisonment and exile.

Another of Hobbes's observations provided me with an ultimate measure for Ngugi's work: "If there be not powerful eloquence which procureth attention and consent, the effect of reason will be little."[10] Hobbes's "powerful eloquence" and his language interested me more than his philosophy, politics, or theology. I considered as inseparable his ideas and the highly rhetorical language with which he expressed them. Similarly, Ngugi's eloquence, his language, and his writing about language in Africa and the world interested me most, exemplifying not merely his formulations based on black and white or rich and poor but his struggle and unresolved conflict precisely between "too great Liberty . . . and too much Authority" when he wanted to claim, as he did in the beginning of *Moving the Centre,* "I am an unrepentant universalist."[11] Was he? Was I? Could anyone be?

Despite one writer being Kenyan in the twentieth century and the other being English in the seventeenth, they both exemplified nearly throughout their work the-hand-in-fist art of language and politics. But not only did Hobbes's writing provide me with an insight into Ngugi's, so did Hobbes's historical period: the European Renaissance. At least my African travels had prepared me to recognize many of its most distinctive characteristics from Dante in Italy to John Dryden in England and as chaotically swirling through Africa and around Ngugi: widespread political and social upheavals (particularly identified with nationalism, ethnic rivalry, and class-restructuring); the transition from an oral to a written culture; the rise of vernaculars and literary colossi; literary and fine art with little self-consciousness and more public than private purposes; the specters of colonialism and neocolonialism (the Renaissance Roman church and twentieth-century European and American colonialism playing similar roles in the government of new nations); leaders unwilling or unable to lead responsibly; popular and frequent practice of religious rituals that made spiritual systems (fundamentalism and/or animism) and their performance central to everyday life; little access to the amenities of running water (drinking, bathing, sanitation); crude and limited medical practices and facilities with fatal results, including high rates of infant mortality and short average life expectancies; religious fanaticism and resulting intolerance, persecution, and war; profound factionalism ("tribalism"); an even more profound lack of public recognition of the abilities and rights of women; rapidly developing materialism; an influx of new science and new wealth; recurrent plague and pandemic; conspicuous consumer consumption by select individuals; unprecedented and unpredictable cycles of economic boom and bust; largely intact systems of caste according to social standing yet also to profession; near universal censorship; out-of-control militarism; genocidal living conditions regarding health and welfare.

The list could go on until the analogy broke down with the further realization that, unlike Renaissance Europe, contemporary Africa had nothing as extensive as a "New World" like the Americas for plunder and expansion, including its equally myriad opportunities to prosper on slave labor.

Nevertheless, I saw the deluge of cultural and historical currents that flooded Europe in the Renaissance recurring now in Africa. Despite his exile from Kenya, Ngugi writing in Orange resembled Dante in Florence and Ravenna, Marlowe and Shakespeare in London, Montaigne in Bordeaux, and the nomadic Cervantes in Spain.

Ngugi's traveling through "Renaissance" Newark—as its politicians called it—to commute to his job as a distinguished professor at NYU provided the requisite twentieth-century irony to qualify such an observation.

The lights that Larry had set up in the shadowy living room to photograph our exchange seemed to brighten not only the room but also Ngugi's responses, especially when he talked about language. He envisioned

> beautiful ones who will grow their roots in African languages and cultures. They will also learn the best they can from all world languages and cultures. They will view themselves as scouts in foreign linguistic territories and guides in their own linguistic space. . . . They will take whatever is most advanced in those languages and cultures and translate those ideas into their own languages. They will have no complexes about borrowing from others to enrich their own.[12]

Focusing on language, Ngugi's answers seemed to yearn for even more light than Larry provided. When I asked Ngugi if English was a kind of first love—despite Gikuyu being the mother tongue he spoke at home as a child—that had betrayed him, his eyes flashed around the room as if he wanted to purge any remaining shadows when he answered:

> There's nothing wrong with the English language. There's nothing wrong with French. There's nothing wrong with any language in the world. It's very important that what has been produced in these languages—in Chinese, in Japanese, in Finnish, in Swedish, in whatever—is a part of human heritage. They're all very important. Equally well, what's produced in African languages—in Swahili, in Gikuyu, in Yoruba—is also a part of human heritage. Suppressing . . . languages, we are suppressing . . . human heritage. For persons growing up in Africa, fully in the world of their languages, in the literature of their languages, there's nothing wrong with them acquiring other languages as well, and enjoying fully whatever has been produced in those other languages.[13]

Knowing nothing about African languages, beyond what I heard and understood barely a word of when I was in Africa, I thought again of Renaissance Europe as Ngugi spoke. My mind flooded with questions I hadn't prepared for the interview. Didn't the rise of European vernacular languages like English, French, German, Italian, Dutch, and more parallel the European Renaissance as well as the growth of separate, European nations?

And didn't European vernaculars—including their translation into each other and of classical languages—feed a vast array of creative fires besides literature burning into each other that became the European Renaissance itself? Wasn't the European Renaissance inconceivable without the growth and development of vernacular languages, not only in literature and the arts, but also in science, government, politics, philosophy, religion, education, medicine, economics, and more, even including the individual self?

Ironically, as Ngugi spoke I drifted from thinking about Africa to the Renaissance writers I loved throughout undergraduate and graduate school and who had been my specialty when I first became a professor. I remembered Petrarch's *Canzoniere,* written in the third quarter of the fourteenth century, and the book's subtitle: *Rerum vulgarium fragmenta,* "Fragments in the Vernacular." It sounded a little rough and humble, but it announced the most significant event in the history of European literature: the shift from writing in classical languages, especially Latin, to local languages. Over the next three centuries it shrunk over the horizon and disappeared nearly everywhere except in religious or academic cloisters—never to rise again.

Even my favorite writer, Thomas Hobbes, compared the contemporary use of Latin in 1651 (even though he sometimes wrote in it, too) to "the Ghost of the Old Romane Language."[14]

Would African writers now who only wrote in colonial languages someday be similarly relegated, only to be read by the cloistered few, while African writers in local languages—the greatest languages of everyday African life—created bodies of literature above and beyond whatever we could imagine now?

Would there come a day in Africa when its writers would consider writing in colonial languages as little more than their ghost in comparison with writing in African languages?

Could reading African authors who only wrote in English, French or other colonial languages look as obtuse as someone only reading authors who wrote in Latin during the European Renaissance? If not now then in the future, could there be as many books and handsome volumes on my shelves of African-language literature as there were of my beloved English and European Renaissance literature? What would I know about it without writers like Petrarch, Dante, Chaucer, Shakespeare, Donne, Rabelais, Montaigne, Cervantes, and more? As I sat on this couch in a house on Berkeley Avenue in Orange, New Jersey, did I listen to one of their African counterparts in Ngugi, now predicting how African language literatures would grow like theirs?

Meanwhile, Ngugi continued speaking:

> There's even nothing wrong in African languages appropriating whatever is best that has been produced in and through other people's languages. There would be nothing wrong with any languages appropriating the best that has been developed in African languages in a healthy give and take. When economic structural imbalance is corrected, the borrowings from each other would be a natural, organic, healthy development without competition, if you like. Acceptance or rejection would be a part of a healthy dialogue.[15]

Having drifted off into my own questions, I barely followed him until Larry, switching off his lights, seemed to wake me up. Seeing Ngugi taking off his coat and getting up, I became anxious that maybe he had sensed my divided attention. Larry unbent his six-foot, eight-inch frame from around his 35 millimeter Nikon and said as Ngugi stretched and smiled, "Something's cooking besides you under these damn lights."

If I had remembered the word Ngugi stressed most in talking about African and European languages, "dialogue,"[16] I might not have been so shocked by Larry's pictures when he sent them to me two weeks later. I expected pictures only of Ngugi, but the contact sheets revealed a roughly equal number of shots of both our faces in clear and sharply contrasting black and white responding to what each other said: in other words, a dialogue. In the tilt of a head, a determined parting or a tightening of the lips, a reflection off a forehead, a furrowing brow, shadows around the eyes and their closing for a moment to reflect, Larry also caught a "struggle" to communicate and understand between us both. Larry heard and just as importantly captured in his images the point Ngugi made in our conversation about ensuring "a content of struggle" and not merely "colonial tradition . . . tourist art, dances . . . [and] contortions." Larry heard and snapped "languages and cultures . . . translat[ing] . . . ideas into their own languages . . . no complexes about borrowing. . . . what . . . has been produced in and through other people's languages" and "nothing wrong with any languages appropriating the best that has been developed in African languages." The pictures found an "imbalance . . . corrected," a "give and take" without background or foreground but a middle ground of light and shadows and two distinct faces not abstractions: neither silenced nor silencing, controlled nor controller, dominating nor dominated, framed nor framer; neither with an upper hand but wanting to find the best hand for opening, not closing, any circle of interpretation. Interviewing Ngugi I expected his intense scrutiny to bring me back to feeling overwhelmed, erased and negated by all I didn't know, like I was in Jericho, Cairo, Sinai, Dakar, Togo, beneath Mt. Kilimanjaro, on a Kenyan beach on the Indian Ocean, in Morocco, Casamance, and Cameroon. I certainly didn't expect to be in Larry's pictures.

On the way to the interview, I asked Larry what he expected. Cramped in the front seat, his knees against the dashboard and his head pressed against the inside of the roof, he sparkled as he said, "I take the picture that I don't see until it happens."

Before we arrived at Ngugi's house I wanted to show Larry a little of Orange. As we drove through an old Italian neighborhood that had become dilapidated and boarded-up buildings where we only saw blacks living, I was saying, "There used to be a great fish store there. It had the best *bacala* for Christmas" and "Here there used to be a great bakery. My father argued with the owners to put their scale on the front counter since they were cheating him when they weighed things in the back."

The first question I asked Ngugi, but informally while we were sitting down in his living room, with Larry still arranging his lights and tripod, was, "Why do you write?" No longer hurrying but pronouncing his words calmly, slowly, and emphatically, Ngugi replied in exactly the same words that he had written in *Moving the Centre:* "Writing has always been my way of reconnecting myself to the landscape of my birth and upbringing."[17]

Larry saw one of Africa's greatest writers living in exile in Orange, New Jersey, now "reconnecting" with the place where he was born and raised, outside of the village of Limuru, Kenya through writing in his mother tongue, Gikuyu.

Larry also saw me talking with Ngugi by returning to where I was born and raised, struggling to reconnect by coming back to Orange for the first time since my father had died eighteen months before. When I asked Ngugi why the word "struggle" recurred so often in his writing, I saw Larry smile as I stumbled on the word and had to repeat it for Ngugi to hear me. Larry found and photographed a new connection, yet my struggling with its incongruity, in coming back to the town where my father carried me as a newborn out of the hospital a few blocks away and finding forty years later one of Africa's greatest writers living in the same place.

Hearing Ngugi asked why the word "struggle" recurred so often in his writing, Larry also saw Ngugi lose his equanimity and speak urgently: "People wrestle with their natural and social environment. They struggle with nature. They struggle with one another. Struggle is central to my art and to my history."[18] But when I asked Ngugi what he meant by the title of his book, *Moving the Centre*, its subtitle, *The Struggle for Cultural Freedoms*, and the subtitle of his book's title essay, "Towards a Pluralism of Cultures," Larry saw him relax, sigh, and almost sing in a gentle tone, reaching for my copy of *Moving the Centre* and flipping through its first few pages to read what he called "the possibility of opening out the mainstream to take in other streams"[19] of "moving towards a pluralism of cultures, literatures and languages"[20] and "a plurality of centres all over the world"[21] with "its roots in regional and national individuality":[22] a "true humanism with its universal reaching" yet "rooted in the histories and cultures of the different peoples of the earth." Ngugi was leaving no one out of the picture, and Larry shot what he saw when it happened.

What Larry also saw eventually took up more pages of the journal to come out of the interview a half a year later. Collaging his images of Ngugi with illustrations readily associated with critical issues from his books, Larry pictured the silhouette of a young man in Kenya, hands on hips and standing *contrapposto* on a lush green bank overlooking a river cascading through the Mau escarpment of the Kenyan highlands. Curtains of British, French, and other European flags closed off the sky. Ngugi had run there after school and his bright mind struggled with the missionary who scolded him in geography class. "When will you learn to speak civilized languages like

English, French, or German? You are not interested in knowing the rivers, mountains, lakes and trees of Europe. You say that you want to first know those rivers, mountains, and animals in your own country. When will you ever learn?"[23] Trying to cope with the missionary, at the same time Ngugi was saying in his mind, "*I thiomi cia kiiriu, thimo cia uthitarabu n uthil na mbera ta King'enu, Giitariani, Kiibaranja, na Kiinjeremaani.*"[24] Ngugi pictured the missionary dead, his skeleton like the one hanging in the science classroom, and fantasized scribbling the Gikuyu words for "Frontal Bone," "Jaw," "Sternum," and "Humerus" on the skeleton's labels.[25]

Larry also saw the signature of Kenya's "minister for home affairs," Arap Moi, as big as the seal of Kenya, and growing bigger, at the bottom of a paper dated "December 31, 1977,"[26] in Moi's thick handwriting, ordering Ngugi detained "for reasons of public security" but no other charge. A window with three bars and the left profile of Ngugi behind them opened amid the insistent Pica typed with dirty keys and a sketchy ribbon. Larry saw no jail cell but only Ngugi, his eyes on the horizon and a part of the landscape, as he spoke, near the end of our interview, "of changing seasons, the season of harvest, the season of planting, the season of things growing."[27] A crow flew through the bars.[28]

Larry also superimposed Ngugi's profile on a black-and-white diagram of the center of the solar system. His head grazed earth's orbit and he wore a halo of the orbits of Venus and Mercury. His high, broad, dark forehead scribbled with thin bright pencil lines reflected the snow of Mt. Kenya behind him and gleaming limbs in ancient African cave drawings of dancers, some standing straight and others bending back and forth, all of them retracting their necks into their shoulders and pulling up at the same time to extend their arms. The profile emerged out of an ocean of tenement blocks and slums with their shantytowns of Nairobi. More thin pencil lines scribbled across his dark, strong jaw and outlined the threads of his warm wool turtleneck and tweed jacket. Only where he parted his lips to speak remained unclear. It formed either a blurry abstraction, sunlight finally breaking through damp grass, or a collage of maps cut up and rearranged in the patterns of historians, philosophers, and poets instead of cartographers.[29]

A few months later, with a torrent of thinking and writing in essays and poems about Ngugi pouring in, I realized that interest in Ngugi ran faster and deeper than what the journal I was planning could ever contain. In the beginning of the project, I never expected the "The World of Ngugi wa Thiong'o," as I titled the issue, to attract so many different kinds of writers and writing: distinguished professors, fledgling professors and graduate students, undergraduates, everyday African Americans, African poets, Gikuyu and Kiswahili scholars, and Ngugi's contemporaries. I saw the collection moving toward a "pluralism of cultures, literatures and languages,"[30] in Ngugi's words, unlike most of the contemporary poetry and scholarly journals that I knew. I watched a flow of Marxist analyses, poems, literary history, classical modernism, postmodernism, close reading, biography, popular culture, orature, and interviews welling up around Ngugi but also revealing, again as he observed about culture in general, "people wrestling with their natural and social environment. . . . struggl[ing] with nature . . . struggl[ing] with one another."[31] The writing focused on trial and error, vision and revision, liberty and authority, not merely analyzing Ngugi and his work but joining him. Like a power figure, Dogon sculpture, or shrine, if unlike a Grecian urn, Ngugi's work became a site of accumulation: added to, embellished, encrusted, and in some places even obscured by writers sounding a little desperate: as if they wanted to communicate not only through it but to it and in the process ravage any kind of beauty wanting to remain untouched, pristine, or static. As Ngugi began his novel, *Matigari*, "To the Reader / Listener,"[32] writers about him seemed similarly intent to respond, "To Ngugi / Reader / Listener." The inseparability of political action and the action of writing overshadowed any comings and goings of the self. Yet in John Keats's words about William Wordsworth—the Romantic dimensions of whose work Ngugi's most resembled in English literary history, which he well knew through his secondary and university education (including Makerere University in Uganda and Leeds University in England)—the credibility and beauty of Ngugi's struggle also contained a broader, deeper dimension not necessarily as explicitly political: an "anxiety for Humanity," compelling a question about whether he had "in truth epic passion, and martyrs himself to the human heart, the main region of his song."[33]

Great writers often become the subject of a literary conference. The invocation of "Ngugi / Reader / Listener" reaching so many centers cried out for it, too. As a result, I planned a three-day conference for the following spring called "Ngugi wa Thiong'o: Texts and Contexts." It became the largest conference on an African writer ever held in the United States or anywhere else, including Africa. Over two hundred writers and scholars from Africa, Asia, Europe, Canada, the Caribbean, and the United States, all reading their work on or related to Ngugi, formed, again in Ngugi's words from *Moving the Centre*, "A pluralism of cultures, literatures and languages"[34] and "voices coming from . . . a plurality of centres all over the world."[35]

We also moved the center, holding the event at a branch campus of the Pennsylvania State University in Reading, a small originally Pennsylvania German city and now largely Hispanic: a relatively obscure place with little of the traditional power and prestige associated with more famous American universities; a land grant university campus that enrolled only first- and second-year students, most of whose parents did not have the opportunity to go to college. Acclaimed and unacclaimed professors, writers, artists, cultural activists, publishers, graduate students, undergraduates, secondary school students, university staff and administration, Africanists, a wide range of academic disciplines and members of the surrounding city and towns became their own cultural center, although with one gaping whole.

No one could come from Kenya. Of nineteen scholars and writers—many of them from a new, second generation of Ngugi's readers—who currently lived in Kenya and whose proposals had been accepted, none received the kind of university or government support required for such a long, expensive journey. At one point and after much effort, I received a verbal commitment from the U.S. State Department to fund ten scholars, but it never materialized. Subsequently, their letter after letter expressed a tragic question hotly echoed from every conference podium and in every conversation for three days in the cold spring of southeastern Pennsylvania: why wasn't such a historic event being held in Kenya, as it should be? Uprooted from Kenya, the words in Gikuyu that translated the title of the conference would be heard more than ever: *Ngugi wa Thiong'o: Mandiko Maake Na Kiria Meege Maine Nakio.*

With no other prescribed agenda or preconceptions, more questions and commentary—some of the best examples sounding like testimony—about Ngugi's work spontaneously accumulated like a canon of large, uncertain, and yet to be discovered proportions. Ngugi's publisher in Kenya, Henry Chakava, revealed for the first time after fifteen years how in 1980, two days before receiving the printed copies of Ngugi's Gikuyu original *Ngaahika Ndeenda* and *Caitani Matharaba-ini—I Will Marry When I Want* and *Devil on the Cross*—he pulled up to the gate of his house around 7:30 P.M. In Chakava's words, publishing history became a crime report:

> When I was waiting for the gate to be opened, I noticed a car behind mine that was now so close to me that I was virtually sandwiched between that car and my own gate. With lightning speed, four people armed with *simis, pangas,* and clubs set upon me, broke the windows of my car and cut me badly in my face and hands. . . . I lost use of my index fingers because the tendons had been severed in two places by a *simi*. My attackers were never apprehended.[36]

From Barbados, the poet and scholar Kamau Brathwaite revealed how at age forty-one he unexpectedly received the Gikuyu name Kamau, and dropped his Christian and very British name, Edward, three years after receiving his Ph.D. from the University of Sussex. Recommending Kamau for a City of Nairobi fellowship, Ngugi invited him to the University of Nairobi. Ngugi also invited him to Limuru, the village near Kamiriithu, where Ngugi was born and, before he changed his name, where Ngugi was baptized "James." One afternoon, Kamau met Ngugi's grandmother, surrounded by, in the poet's words, "the whole large family and many others from the neighbourhood + those who had motored up from Nairobi with me or to meet me." They came to "witness the ceremony, although . . . [Kamau] didn't know anything about it."[37]

Kamau continued as if he had become a player in a kind of African rewrite of the stark beginning of the Gospel of Mark, when the prophet John baptized Jesus "in the wilderness" and "the heavens opened" (1:4, 10).

> I was there, kneeling on the ground with the wind on my face & the great sky of Eden all around me in front of these old women who like ripped open my shirt & like spat upon my chest (the water of baptism / though I was very much alarmed to say the least at first) & began chanting deep deep down inside their chests & deeper down into their very bellies searching for . . . my name.

From the United States, from Newark, the poet from my home soil who lived in the next town east of Orange, Amiri Baraka, read a brief elegy focusing on the life of Okot p'Bitek, the Ugandan poet and novelist. It evoked with an uncharacteristic gentleness for Amiri the painful exile of Ngugi "in the West" where

> plainly, each evening
> . . . the sun goes to die. . . .
> here w / us
> In hell. . . .
> I have heard
> his songs
> felt the earth
> drum his dance
> his wide ness
> & Sky self[38]

Picking up on Amiri's mood, the poet and professor from Philadelphia,

Sonia Sanchez testified sadly and quietly at first, "Ngugi has eaten a little of this earth. . . . We all have to eat a little earth before we die. And we who come from the earth will finally taste of ourselves. This earth. Which will seep from the corners of our mouths and make us whole."³⁹ Yet slowly and surely rising to a piercing crescendo that might be heard back across the Atlantic from West Africa to East, she broke into the Ghanaian language of Twi:

EBE YIYE, EBE YIYE
EBEYIYEEEEEEEE
Ebeyiyeebeyiyeebeyiyeeeeee
it'll get better . . .⁴⁰

Joining their distinct voices to Ngugi's, Chakava, Brathwaite, Baraka, and Sanchez came from different places but sounded like the progenitors of a new yet growing tradition of not one logos or word but of many tongues at a center, albeit it relatively momentary and shifting, of many centers, epitomizing Ngugi's words about "retaining . . . roots in regional and national individuality"⁴¹ and being "an unrepentant universalist."

Such testimony flowered into a barrage of questions from the "The Reader[s] / Listener[s]" who heard it. Larry built two room-size art installations for the conference, the first titled *The Colonial Classroom*. A wide wooden panel, it featured a window in the center looking out on a bluish Mt. Kenya in the background and silhouettes of elephants grazing green plains in the foreground with bushes constructed of delicate, lacy coral. The flags of Africa's European colonizers and the United States hung over the window and two blackboards flanked either side of it. One began "Good morning, teacher" written in perfect cursive, followed by the conjugation of "to be." The other blackboard vertically listed the countries, "England, France, Germany, Italy, Switzerland, Spain, Portugal, Russia, United States" with their respective capitals. A microscope and field hockey stick propped on top of the blackboard's ledge, which held different colored chalk. Illustrations of Chartres cathedral, the Roman Forum, and the British Parliament building hung from the walls. While the window invited a look out onto a lush and hazy, blue and green Kenyan landscape, the mundane walls of the classroom with their oppressive rote and visual clichés faced down the viewer as if to remind him or her of who was in charge and of the message, albeit less viciously expressed, directed at Larry as he grew up in Scottsboro in the thirties that was also a pedagogical premise of most colonial classrooms in Africa and around the world: "The nigger must be kept in his place."

Extending from the gallery to the conference rooms and auditorium and confining Ngugi's "The Reader[s] / Listener[s]" for three days, Larry's colonial classroom transformed them into uncontrollable but very smart students firing questions from all directions at any assertion of its authority and inspired by what they saw looking out onto Ngugi's Kenya surrounded by all Africa and the world. Did Ngugi's education—Gikuyu to Christian to British—make him who he was? What made him different from countless other Renaissance, Enlightenment, Romantic, modern, or postmodern writers jailed for their art and forced to defend it? What informed his testimony and made it unique? Did it defy and transcend Western critical categories and evaluation, or could they with enough self-consciousness adapt to what he had to say? Did Winston Churchill in 1957, filmed sitting at his desk and warning "the problems of East Africa are the problems of the world,"[42] set off, in Ngugi's phrase, a "cultural bomb"[43] in Nairobi that sent shrapnel flying all the way to infamous sites of the American civil rights movement like Birmingham, Montgomery, and Little Rock? Did the same bombing also burn American moviemaking so badly that that it was afraid to go outside the colonial classroom? While the Danish Karen Blixen, who wrote under the name Isak Dinesen, and the Gikuyu Ngugi both chose English to write about Kenya's threatened survival, did colonialism's lurid dissection in Ngugi's novels, compared with the romance and romantic writing in Blixen's—although Ngugi used plenty of it, too—disqualify Blixen's *Out of Africa* from being "a good book," as its "faithful servant Kamante" says?[44] Why were the title of Blixen's novel and Conrad's *Heart of Darkness,* the two most commonly used phrases in Western writing about Africa?

No one, not even Ngugi, could have answered all of the questions shaking Larry's colonial classroom. Did Ngugi's choosing to write in Gikuyu, or any African writer choosing to write in his or her mother tongue when it was not the official language of the state, present an unresolved conflict, and did it threaten the state? Could an answer to the question of the relationship between the arts and political commitment be expected to come from a political party instead of an individual and still produce good art? Was a writer's choice of language—if there were a choice—more important than the audience he or she appealed to—if there were an audience? Since African writers advocated political revolution for African countries, did their widespread degeneration into neocolonial failures as independent states make African writers, at least in their political roles, failures, too? If so, if they wanted to continue writing, wouldn't satire be their best choice? Even then, didn't what a writer expressed about female circumcision reveal most of all, regardless of any politics, where he or she was from? Furthermore, how could such concepts as language, place, or time—tradition or change—truly signify anything exclusively or truly African or European, especially when considered at the present moment? Was the connection between them a kind of muse or language hidden in the colonizing and enslaving language of English that burst out like an updated Sycorax—the witch and mother of Caliban from Shakespeare's *Tempest*—speaking her own revitalized diction, syntax, and rhythms out of the tree in which Prospero was said to imprison her? Was her liberation mystical, pragmatic, or both? Why did she speak more in circles than straight lines? Were all of the voices she used locked in the tree with her? Why did voices that sounded like hers want her sealed back up in the tree? Did her testimony make them too nervous? Was the tree a kind of solution to identify insiders and outsiders who otherwise might not be told apart? Was the tree even her story and, besides its being smashed open, not what she remembered: not the history that needed to be heard and that was stranger than fiction?

Such questions echoed in Larry's second installation, too. On one side of the room he placed a large box as tall as a soda machine, roughly half the width and painted silver. It had a gun scope perched on one corner to aim six sharpened yard-long penlike rockets at Ngugi's and "The Reader['s] / Listener['s]" classic yet real-life adversary—the second part of the installation—across the room: "The Dictator." A life-size frontal male figure in military dress formed the center of a massive, heavy, rough wooden panel painted bright green and orange. With the face of an upside-down horseshoe crab—its pointy tail piercing a cockeyed, too small officer's hat on his head—he stared emptily through eyes of cowry shells. Brass merry-go-round rings hung from both of his pierced ears. He wore a nine-inch, empty cartridge shell for a medallion and shoulder boards of scrubbing brushes. Two oversized silver buttons etched with lions, one at his neck and the other at his navel, tightly clasped his Serengeti-red clay officer's jacket, splattered with a brighter red that could have been blood. Black machines guns—plastic water pistols—set at angles, with one pointing up and one pointing down, formed his arms. A holster hanging from his patent leather belt pulled too tight held the legendary Colt .45—a child's shiny silver plastic version—of cowboy movies and a short billy club of greasy, ominous woven leather. The frame cut off where his stiff thick thighs pushed up into his belly.

As Ngugi entered the auditorium stage to deliver his final words on the conference's last night, I thought of the gallery next door with the dictator and the rocket launcher. As Ngugi's lips parted to speak his first word into the microphone, he gripped the barrel of his ballpoint pen and, with his thumb on the button to launch, he clicked it.

At a reception in the gallery later that evening, Ngugi said he wanted to introduce me to a publisher but then disappeared. My head spun with fatigue and too many chocolate-covered strawberries. I wanted to be home with Barbara, our new baby, Alexandra Leila, and hear my four-year-old daughter Alicia Kiah's first notes on her violin.

A medium-size man who wore a graying goatee and tinted glasses introduced himself: "Kassahun Checole. I am a publisher." Neither his looks nor his name told me he was African. What did I know?

"Ngugi told me you would be here," I answered.

Kassahun replied, "I would have liked to have been here earlier to hear more, but Ngugi didn't tell me about it until the last minute, no?"

Kassahun seemed to end every third or fourth sentence with "no?" I didn't know how to respond, especially as he told me that he was the president of Africa World Press and Red Sea Press in Lawrenceville, New Jersey, and I felt embarrassed by my ignorance, neither knowing about him nor his publishing house that was barely an hour away. Or maybe there was no such thing?

I listened as he spoke about his press and about where he was from: the way I listened to Ngugi when I first met him and, as Kassahun continued to speak, the way I listened going all the way back to the sands covering ancient Jericho, and later as I wandered through Cairo, Sinai's landscape of Red Sea gods, Dakar's outdoor markets, and Togo with its angels and devils; as I listened from the abrupt slopes of Kilimanjaro down to a bush where I could hide on the Indian Ocean, to Morocco's emerald ocean pounding up its white phosphorus beaches, to its even whiter Casablanca cathedral and to the braid of Moroccan straw binding Barbara and me wherever there was straw; and as I listened through the endgame, one-street border towns of Casamance to the time bomb I heard ticking in Cameroon, which would continue to tick with or without me when I had to leave as my father's final breaths back in Bethlehem, Pennsylvania, ticked down to nothing, and he gave me his spirit to be happy and for my children to know.

Kassahun continued: "No? No? 'The World of Ngugi wa Thiong'o.' And then 'Ngugi wa Thiong'o: Texts and Contexts.' We could consider publishing two collections of essays? No?"

Distracted by the din of half drunk laughter and loud, dragged-out good-byes echoing through the gallery, I could barely hear or believe that a publisher would approach me, and in a five-minute conversation say he wanted to publish my work when I had spent decades of paper, postage, and phone calls seeking publishers, only to receive the usual, near eternal response: silence or no (and emphatically without any question mark).

Immediately drawn out of my distraction like a cat to a bird, I answered quickly, "Yes, that would be great."

"You would edit them and write the introductions, no?" Kassahun nodded.

In addition to not telling Kassahun about the conference until it was almost too late, I thought that Ngugi probably hadn't shown him the journal, "The World of Ngugi wa Thiong'o," since it had been published three weeks earlier, and I had already written the introduction. I had already been planning to combine it with what I had learned during the last three days and to write a paper for a conference I had been invited to in Israel at the University of Tel Aviv the following summer called "Breaking Boundaries: Beyond the Land of Cush. New Critical Encounters with Languages and Literatures of Sub-Saharan Africa."

When I told Ngugi about the conference, his eyebrows leaped up his high, round forehead, and he gently groaned, "This separating Africa from itself with a term like 'sub-Saharan' is a form of racism and more 'divide and conquer.' Africa is Africa. Sahara is Sahara. Sub-Sahara is no different than above Sahara."

To reaffirm my interest in working with Kassahun, I told him about the essay I was already planning for the Tel Aviv conference and about Ngugi's feelings about it so that Kassahun wouldn't think I was blind or deaf or ignorant—as I was about his own efforts—to the kind of objections Ngugi had raised. But then Kassahun's response surprised me. "While you are in Israel, you should take some time to go a little farther and visit my country, Eritrea."

CHAPTER SIX

Rome's Rome

I HAD FIRST VISITED ISRAEL AS A RELIGIOUS PILGRIM. SEEKING consolation and the kingdom of heaven, I floated over the wildflowers and thorns in the valley of Kidron, knelt at the burial slab of Jesus, ate His body at dawn in the Church of the Holy Sepulcher, and watched the gold of the Dome of the Rock reply to the sunset and settle in the olives of the garden of Gethsemane. The fingers of my right hand grazed the Wailing Wall and my left reached down through a hole in the floor of the Church of the Nativity in Bethlehem to touch the dirt and the birth spot of Jesus. I listened to the bones of Abraham and Sarah, Isaac and Rebecca, Jacob and Leah still stirring deep in their cave in Hebron and walked in the footsteps of a mythical "St. Orpheus."

Was I kidding? No, I was a believer, and still was, but just before I left Israel ten years before, I looked down and saw ants tunneling through the sand where twenty cities had come and gone, my faith changed, and I opened my eyes in places like Cairo, the Sinai, Dakar, Togo, Kenya, and Morocco. Or if my faith hadn't changed, I had just enough of it—maybe spurred on by the holy places of Israel and reinforced by a thousand Holy Communions—to know that if they meant anything, and I wasn't kidding, I had to change and be open to a different kind of communion, which led me to Africa. It led me to Barbara, our having to get married in a straw-filled barn instead of a church, and our having four beautiful children and a family. It led me through "the valley of the shadow of death" and now led me "beyond the land of Cush." Where? Again, was I kidding?

Cush, or "Kush," meant "dark" in Hebrew. In the Bible, Cush, the son of Ham and the grandson of Noah, settled with his descendents in northeast Africa, extending from southern Egypt to Sudan and the Horn of Africa, yet also including both sides of the Red Sea. The term "Cushite" provoked contempt, as in Numbers 12:1, "Moses married a Cushite,"[1] that is, he married a black woman, and Jeremiah 13:23, "Can the Cushite change his skin,"[2] immediately followed with "or the leopard his spots," and the implication that the Cushite like the leopard would always be up to no good.

The conference on African languages and literatures that I traveled to in Tel Aviv obviously didn't ascribe to the negative connotation applied to Cush in the Bible, and by extension to all Africa, but now, confirmed in another faith than what I had ten years earlier, I looked forward more to actually leaving behind any sense of Cush, biblical or otherwise, and leaving Tel Aviv to go to Eritrea.

I still traveled as a kind of pilgrim. I wanted to witness the site of one of Africa's greatest, harshest, and most recent revolutions for independence: Eritrea's thirty-year armed struggle—the longest war in modern African history—to liberate itself from Ethiopian colonial rule, added on to Eritrea's seventy-year struggle to liberate itself first from Italian and then British colonial rule before Ethiopia took over. Yet I also traveled, as I had to Israel ten years earlier and to Africa after that, as a literary pilgrim: to write about what I experienced but now toting some of my own books, the two volumes of essays on Ngugi published by Africa World Press, to deliver to its offices in Asmara, to Kassahun's uncle, Arefine Tewolde, who would look after me.

"*Ah, Cantalupo. Benvenuto a Asmara. Avete un buon viaggio? Venga all' interno e rendasi comodo.*" Arefine stood in a huge glass and iron open doorway under a red, yellow, black, and green sign with "Africa World Press / Red Sea Press" superimposed on an image of the earth with Africa in the center.

Kassahun had told me that after I arrived I should ask at my hotel, Albergo Italia, for directions to the post office, and I would find the press nearby. I stumbled down an iron and marble staircase that morning, after arriving in Asmara after midnight from Cairo. Built in 1899, the hotel only had two floors. The slightly dingy mirrors, the pink and white plaster walls with laughing putti and overripe grapes over the doorways, the marble, the restrained dining room with white tablecloths and wine glasses seemed strangely familiar and comforting, even though the trip made me feel dazed and uneasy. The bulkily sweatered but neatly dressed, middle-aged desk clerk didn't understand what I was trying to say until I mentioned "Africa World Press."

With an open hand held vertically and slowly chopping the air in the direction of the hotel's front door, he said slowly and gently, "*Diritto. Su. Su Diritto.*"

Walking on a wide cement sidewalk up a finely paved street, I quickly felt short of breath and stopped to look at a building at the first intersection: again two story, with two symmetrical and sloping staircases, their balustrades opening onto a street corner as if inviting a passerby to ascend into a pilastered, baroque temple conferring its dignity and importance on whoever would be lucky enough to pass through its portico and columns to have a meeting scheduled inside. I started uphill again and in a few minutes came to a line of small taxis: six orange Fiats from the 1960s, *cinquecentos* and *seicentos,* some of them battered, but their interiors—like the nearly empty metal dashboards with a few tiny dials and two black knobs—still gleaming, however worn.

"*Buongiorno, signore. Taxi?*" Men older than the hotel clerk, gray haired but dressed similarly, exuded calm and confidence as they spoke an almost stately Italian.

"*Per favore, signore. Dove desiderate andare? Benvenuto a Asmara. Prova la mia machina. Siete stanco 'sta mattina. Siedasi giu.*"

I faced a man who looked like an African, older version of my cousin Charlie, who tended the bar at Fucci's Italian Kitchen in Newark. The taxi driver held his car door open and slapped the torn green leather seat for me to get in.

"Africa World Press? *Per favore, dove Africa World Press?*" I asked wearily.

Quickly closing the old Fiat's door, which creaked and required an added push to fit back into the frame, the driver rubbed the three-day's whiskers on his reddish brown face until it sparkled. He gently turned me around by the shoulders. "*Diritta. Giu. Giu. Diritta. Siete vicini,*" he answered in a kind of melodious staccato, again with an open hand vertically chopping Asmara's low-oxygen air laced with morning traffic fumes at seventy-six hundred feet.

"*A la Posta Centrale,*" he said, and I kept repeating it to myself as I walked down the hill I had just come up. Where was I? Church bells began ringing down the street to the right, and I saw a Franciscan cathedral. Next minute I reached an open square and heard my mind saying, "*Che cosa e questa piazza?*"

I stopped at a barbershop. Old bright silver and deep brown leather revolving chairs hung with straps for straight razors in front of mirrors with short marble counters bearing Rococo-labeled ointments and hair tonics that mustached barbers in white jackets handled like artworks. The scene burst with the light of one of my earliest childhood memories: Grandpa Cantalupo's barbershop.

On the opposite side of the square, a large archway in the middle of a one-story building painted avocado and lemon and lined with almost as tall, classically corniced windows crowned by a white frieze of veils and flowers looked like a fancy version of the back entrance to the courthouse where my father worked in Newark. I finally got my bearings when I saw "Central Post Office" in thick black letters in English painted across the pediment under equally thick characters that looked like the bones of the Hebrew alphabet—the Ge'ez script used for Tigrinya, Tigre, and Amharic.

Directly across from the barbers, I saw a row of high-ceiling shops and watched an old man in a bulky wool, double-breasted three-piece suit tap his cane on the window where inside two men dressed more casually sat at a long, low, polished, light wood counter, both their fingers touching a picture in an opened newspaper. I took my books out of my bag and walked in, happy to have found the heavy iron gate over the top of the storefront pushed all the way up and the place wide open for business.

"*Buon giorno. Mi chiamo Carlo Cantalupo. Un amico di Kassahun. Ho portato questi libri. Ecco. Sono per lei. Vi ha detto che stavo venendo?*" I had not planned to introduce myself in Italian. It just came out, as if the streets, the buildings, and everyone else whom I talked to, who also spoke Italian, made me forget my English.

Small framed, trim, with a head that seemed too large for his body and wearing oversized, plastic aviator glasses that, when they would slide down his nose, he would push back up disconcertingly with his middle finger, Arefine naturally responded in Italian. But by then I had used up most of the Italian vocabulary I could remember because I never spoke it anywhere else, except at my favorite pizzeria back home in Bethlehem, with the Neapolitan, wise, and friendly owner, and always with a glass or two of wine he offered me. For a split second as I listened to Arefine and only understood half of what he said, I wondered how I could suddenly feel as comfortable here, after ten minutes in the streets of Asmara, as I did back there? Arefine looked up, his glasses sliding down his nose, to see how I would reply.

"*Per favore, Arefine. Ho dimenticato il mio Italiano perche io solo parlo Inglese nella America. Possiamo parlare Inglese?*"

He smiled, "*Certo. Non e una problema, Charlus.*" He pronounced my name CHAR-lus.

"When did you get into Asmara? How was your flight? Kassahun has told me you are staying at the Albergo Italia. *E bellisima.*" He brought the fingers of his right hand together and kissed them. "Kassahun also gave me a list of some people you should meet."

I joined the old man with the heavy double-breasted suit, who went into the bookshop before me, to sit at the counter. His two hands resting on the top of his cane, he didn't say a word, as if he had sat down to watch a play, in which I was now a background extra flipping through a stack of newspapers. At first finding two versions of the same paper, one in Tigrinya and one in Arabic, going three weeks back, at the bottom of the pile I eventually found the English editions, titled *Haddas Eritrea*, meaning "New Eritrea." I also looked through the most recent Ethiopian Airlines in-air magazine, featuring a glossy picture of the Rock Church in Lalibella, and a year-old issue of the Italian magazine *Oggi,* with a similarly glossy picture of Pope John Paul II, crowned and mitred, and seemingly cringing as he was giving a blessing. Meanwhile, Arefine stood in the doorway and held court with a near constant stream of well-wishers greeting him warmly in Tigrinya frequently laced with Italian as if *he* were the pope or at least the mayor of Asmara. The severity of the titles of the books about Eritrea in the shop window—some of which I also had back in my hotel room—*Against All Odds, A Painful Season, Even the Stones Are Burning, Never Kneel Down, Riding the Whirlwind*—seemed to belie the easygoing atmosphere.

It rolled on for the rest of the morning, interrupted for only a few moments when a young German backpacker came into the shop, oblivious to Arefine at the door and almost knocking him over before he scurried after him.

"I want a phrase book in Tigrinya? Do you have?" the backpacker seemed to demand.

"*Scusilo, Charlus, per favore,*" Arefine said as he quickly rounded past me and behind the counter. The backpacker gave me a skeptical look and repeated his request to Arefine, who replied, "It is coming, but we don't have it yet. I am sorry."

As the backpacker turned around without a word to leave the shop, Arefine quickly ducked and, as he stood up, put both open hands together, raising and shaking them up and down in a kind of mock prayer and rolling his eyes as if to heaven. At the same time a little boy in a school uniform came running into the shop and scooted around to the back of the counter to hug Arefine, only reaching his waist. Arefine hugged him back, bent over, whispered in his ear and straightened up to make a kind of announcement.

"Ah, look who is here. We have an American from Kassahun. Meet Charlus."

The boy ran over to me, kissed the top of my hand, placed it on his forehead for a second and ran back to Arefine. I turned to look at the old man, but he had left without my realizing it.

Arefine continued, "Charlus. We close for lunch. Come to my house for some pasta. Then later we will make plans for you for tomorrow."

"*Grazie molto,* Arefine, but I'm still tired from my trip and need to go back to my room to take a nap. Is there somewhere near where I can get a sandwich to bring back with me?"

We repeated this exchange around four more times, in varying mixtures of Italian and English, until he told me about a small market called Senay, a block past the piazza and toward the cathedral. Passing through the market's doorway piled with plum tomatoes, beans, peppers, apples, mangoes, and bananas, I waited at the counter as two Italian nuns in full habits that I hadn't seen since the 1960s in grammar school filled their bags with meats, cheese, vegetables, olive oil, bread, pasta, and two bottles of wine, Lachrymae Christi, red. I took one off the shelf myself. When my turn came, I ordered what I never expected to find in Africa, the same kind of sandwich I could have had at Fucci's in Newark: prosciutto and provolone. The owner behind the counter nodded, quickly sliced the prosciutto, cut the provolone, and, taking the roll, pulled out the doughy inside: "gutted it," as I would say at home, the same way as I learned from my father. Both men even looked the same and could have been brothers.

Nearly half a million refugees. Famine. ELF / EPLF civil war. Eritrea versus the superpowers. Civilian massacres. Emperor Haile Selassie. Lion of Judah. Hundreds of thousands of troops in months-long battles. Round-the-clock bombing. Mengistu. Human wave attacks. Napalm. Chemical weapons. The third, the sixth, the seventh Ethiopian offensives. Red Star. President Isaias Afwerki. "A handful of bandits in the hills." Back in my room at the Albergo Italia, I read about an Eritrean reality as invisible but at least as important as God—only it had be to be believed in because it happened—in the almost painfully bright Eritrean air. It gilded the deep red wine. But as I drank and read more, my experience of walking in Asmara in the morning felt like a kind of false cheer: shredding, going crooked, haplessly hanging like the flimsy banner I saw when I arrived the night before in Asmara airport, proclaiming "Welcome to Free Eritrea"; the only expression of warmth, caring, or concern I could feel as immigration and customs officials performed their duties like automatons, never lifting their eyes, all wearing old, used clothes and enforcing a spirit of general depression that all visitors also had to adopt if they wanted to enter.

I looked out my hotel window. The old man who had disappeared in the bookstore sat alone in a shaded doorway across the street and chewed his handkerchief. He looked up at me and had no eyes, but tears poured out of his empty eye sockets.

I turned away, but when I looked again, he was gone, and I was standing in the stationary store that also sold books where I had stopped on the way back to the hotel. Flipping through an Italian-language catalogue of reproductions from Asmara's National Museum, I saw a picture of a headless body yanking out its left limbs with its right. Another by the same artist pictured bodiless huge bones breaking each other into tiny pieces. A photograph captioned with "EPLF" showed the face of soldier with a slash running from his eyebrows to a rifle butt, or was it a donkey's hoof where his chin should have been? Another photo had two lonely tanks exploding at each other across a grove of papaya and oranges. A headless soldier's body flew at a sixty-degree angle above it. I could smell sulfur and burning meat, and the heat felt like an overwhelming kiss of half laundry bleach and half flies. What I thought at first was an abstract painting became mashed up tendons, blood, bone and marrow, titled *Martyr*. A painting labeled "materials: berries, clay, canvas, battery acid" showed a parade of skeletons marching across a broken bridge. Some chewed straggly hair and others dropped along the way into an open graveyard already too full of corpses, many of them half stuffed in ragged sacks and ammunition crates perched on by crows. Two men with gasoline cans dowsed the scene and another two men ran away, their uniforms catching and ripping on thorn bushes, the only vegetation. A dark acrylic diptych of an Eritrean woman, her head tightly braided on top but loosely unfurling down her neck—traditionally dressed in a kind of white gauze shawl and dress trimmed with green and golden ribbons—showed her on one side running into the shadow of a palm tree. On the other side the same woman emerged from the palm's shade in fatigues—with a big Afro and short shorts. She carried the bloody head of an Ethiopian soldier as if she was a kind of biblical Judith having just slain Holofernes. I turned to a landscape of salmon, tangerine, fuchsia, and white bougainvillea, bamboo, mimosa trees, and cypress. In a kind of time-lapse effect repeated across a green and blue sky, something like a sun but really a bloody flag rose and set.

Why was I hearing constant machine gun fire? Muffled drums, hoof clatter, rumbling iron wheels? The cathedral bells wouldn't stop. Where were the men in this city? Why were piano wire and tin cans strung across the sidewalk? How did it get to be dawn? Was that the beautiful teenage girl whom Arefine had spoken to this morning in Africa World Press doorway now lying half in the street and half on the curb? Her dress was bloody and pulled up. Was she dead? Why were all these broken dishes, jugs, and smashed ovens all over the street? She was alive. She had a grenade and was pulling the pin. My face was wet. She exploded like a sack of grain. Why was the page wet?

Rain? I opened my eyes and rain was coming in my hotel room's window. A pink puddle filled the bottom of my wine glass and rain splotched my books. I heard thunder. I looked outside and huge cumulus clouds rolled up as far as I could see from the square, deco rooftops with laundry left out and satellite dishes everywhere. A jackhammer or maybe just two men with sledgehammers were knocking out a wall down the hall. Obviously the break for lunch was over by now, 3:05 P.M. I looked for information about the museum in the guidebook Kassahun had given me and that he had just published. It was right about this being the rainy season with afternoon showers, but then I remembered my appointment with Arefine.

As I walked there, I wondered why I had not noticed this street full of tailors before. I saw one in a creamy silk jacket that contrasted his dark olive and bronze skin as he fit four boys with suits. Their mother, her gauzy shawl thrown back over her shoulders, her sleeves and dress trimmed in purple and brown satin, sat on the tailor's stoop, hand in chin, wide eyed, her teeth like so many of the other Eritrean women's, pinched and prominent beneath her narrow lips. Shops with a hundred slight variations on what she wore lined the next street.

On the next, I found two huge pavilions covering an outdoor market. As I watched finches and sparrows flying through it and gleaning what fell out of the open sacks of grain onto the ground, I saw a child, around six, my daughter's age, walk by. She laughed at herself as she passed a mirror and two steps later reached for some grapes hanging off a forbidding garden wall. I was lost, having gone left instead of straight when leaving the hotel, but I felt no fear and kept aimlessly walking.

If I had only read about Eritrea and the wars and destruction it suffered, I wouldn't believe it could exist anymore. But then what was I now seeing, getting brighter and brighter after the afternoon's shower? And what was I hearing? A kind of drumming kept getting stronger and closer as I walked. Did I breathe at a center of the opposition to death, where every word now had to be guaranteed by life? The city felt like an expansive, bright, empty pedestal. I saw epic survival in an old wife wiping her face on her husband's shoulder and in a blind young man's counting and measuring out dried chickpeas in a bowl.

In a shop window I saw pictures of the liberation of Asmara. Finally without a war, people waved palms and flags. They blurred into each other, creating flags of leaves and leaves of flags, yellow stars and olive branches: flags on fire with leaves as the people holding them, waving leaping and dancing also blurred into hands and mouths turning round and round—east, west, north, south—with leaves and flags ripping in their mouths and spilling from their hands. Still, despite their overwhelming joy, it stopped short of consolation, or so said their eyes.

I saw a nation stripped of every myth except of itself: unsure but not in fear, beaten down to nothing and almost as if in the middle of nowhere since nearly everything around it had been destroyed, too: a nation taking a few steps back to leap an absolutely unbridgeable valley and landing in a place of nearly total disrepair, where every sign fell down or hung only by one hook, or a string, or the symbol of a hook or a string, and where the fast and epoch deal that led to such a situation seemed equally lost and alien in that gesture I remembered: the schoolboy kissing a friendly hand and touching it to his forehead. No longer walking aimlessly, now I was following the drumming.

I came to a towering brick gate, crowned by three arches and a balustrade through which the blue sky poured while a tight flow of trucks clogged and squeezed into the gate below. From behind the gate, the drumming expanded louder and louder into one all-out, deafening pounding that would imperceptibly fall apart into a thousand different rhythms washed over by the huge diesel engines of the trucks and their grinding gears. Two palm trees on either side of the gate exuded an unthreatened sense of harmony and order, whatever might be heard.

As I squeezed between the gate's left side wall and a truck piled high with metal mattress springs, a hanging wire hooked my shirt and began to pull me. I had to run for a few seconds until the truck stopped, although I couldn't hear it since the drumming drowned it out. Pinned to the truck and looking up into the wiry, rusty chaos of the mattress springs, I panicked, ripping the wire out of my shirt and afraid that the truck would start up again without my knowing. When it did, and as my palm felt the wire scrape it and let go, I looked into a labyrinth of nothing new or wasted under the sun, and all metal: pounded, sawed, folded, heated, blowtorched, snipped, welded, soldered, sanded, steel-wooled and polished into something entirely different from what it was, to be made new. Tire rims, air ducts, surviving window frames and doors, wheel-less barrows, car hoods, legible and illegible business signs, chests of drawers, beams, bailing, presses, gutted couches, balconies and stairs without buildings, ingots, shields, rails, and an endless supply of shell casings and cartridges drummed and drummed by old men and young intent on hammering "swords into ploughshares" (Isaiah 2:4): a cannon into a bucket, a lamp, a pair of crutches, and a washboard; an ammunition box into a school desk and chair; fuel drums into shiny coffee pots, pans, platters, and bowls; sledges, axes, hoes, shovels, and a stove out of machine guns.

I listened, my ears ringing, and put my fingers into a three-inch divot of rainwater on top of a thick shaven stump used as an anvil as if it held holy water. More than faith or miracle, transubstantiation and metamorphosis became physical. But I smelled more than fire, propylene torches, sweat, and the steam off burning metal, as if they still longed for something else. I looked around and saw a circle of stalls with faience beadwork doors, women and children. As I walked closer to one, the drumming quickly subsided, and I smelled spices. Inside I sat down in the dark amid bowls of mint, oregano, garlic, nutmeg, almonds, cumin, ten shades of pepper, sunflower seeds, and so much more I couldn't name. A laughing woman appeared. She had broken teeth, skin seared like meat, and golden wheels in her ears. She wore a dress the color of spring grass with deep blood red and purple folds enclosing patches of sea and sky. I kissed her hand and touched it to my forehead, which made her children laugh too. She brought tea with a drop of fermented honey. I bought Arefine some oregano.

After less than a day in Asmara, I felt as if I belonged to the streets I was rushing back through, late for my meeting with Arefine. Unsure where I was, I stopped at a corner to catch my breath. Leaning against a wall, I felt it crumble a little. Running my hand over the lime and burgundy stucco, I put my fingers into still unrepaired bullet holes from the Ethiopian occupation during the war. At the same time, I felt hungry. Standing in front of a doorway with no sign or windows, I smelled bread and saw a bakery inside. I stood in line in a dark room with a table at one end, roughly divided in half between long rolls and short. No one spoke, as if everyone was in a hurry just to get home after a hard day's work. I watched the people in front of me and did what they did: handing over the right amount of money—a few Ethiopian birr—and taking two loaves in a small piece of waxed paper. Continuing in what I thought was the general direction of Africa World Press, I tasted the same bread, the best bread, I had as a boy, going with my father to "the stoop" in the old Italian section in Newark thirty-five years ago: before it was demolished for a high-rise housing project, itself now in ruins, with broken windows and occupied by squatters, far worse than any building I saw in Asmara after thirty years of war.

Finding Arefine sitting behind the counter and reading the story in *Oggi* about the pope, I gave him a bag of oregano and a loaf of bread with a "*Sono spiacente che sono in ritardo.*"

"*Ah, Cantalupo,*" he smiled looking up, "*Non si preoccupi.* It's fine. What's late? *Non fretta. Parla un po di Tigrinya? Dehan, dehan. Grazie per l'oregano e il pane. Dove siete stati?*"

I told him I found the recycling metal market, where I also bought his oregano.

"*Medeber. E chiamao Medeber.* Did you like it?"

"That's the name? Everyone there is a poet! *Tutto la e un poeta,*" I said happily.

"*Tutto la e un poeta,*" he laughed, "*tutto getamay, tutto getamay.*"

"*Che cosa e un getamay?*" I asked.

"*Getamay? Getamay.* Dante. A poet," he said, seeming surprised that I didn't know the word.

"Arefine, when a *getamay*," I replied, but I was interrupting, and Arefine continued.

"We have an appointment in *quindici minuti* at the Constitutional Commission. *Andiamo*, Charlus."

As Arefine was shutting off the uncovered, long fluorescent lights that lined the fifteen-foot ceiling and splashed brightness over the office's gray leather furniture and chrome, I headed out the door, wanting to hear more about a *getamay*, with Arefine crashing down the heavy iron, chipped pale green security grate and locking it.

"*Si, Si,*" I replied to everything he said, while we walked up the street together and I thought, "What does a Constitutional Commission have to do with me? What is it, anyway? Sounds official and boring."

Arefine floated ahead on a constant stream of "*Ciao . . . Dehan Amsi . . . Dehan Hider . . . Com' esta . . . Arefine . . . Arefine*" over the two blocks between the office and the taxi stand where I had asked for directions earlier, and I followed.

At the corner I said, "Arefine, across the street, what's that?"

"Cinema Asmara," he answered in a stately tone. "*Desiderate prendere uno sguaurdo rapido?*"

"I'd love to see it, *grazie*," I replied, since it sounded a lot more interesting than our appointment, which I hoped, if we were late enough, would be cancelled. I wondered: a cinema? Raised above the street and behind a large shell-shaped fountain, two symmetrical staircases entwined into a loggia with seven huge arches and a long row of Corinthian columns. It looked like a Romanesque and Renaissance brick *mista*—part castle, fort, and palace—or a stage set for a production of *Romeo and Juliet* actually taking place on a street in Verona. As Arefine rushed me up the stairs and through the entrance, I saw a blur of massive wooden doors, the sunset gleaming through a ring of different-sized semicircular windows and lintels curling with plaster vines, grapes, and lilies.

Moving straight into the auditorium, Arefine declared, "*Mille novecento veinte. Construito da un Italiano. Cavagnari.*" He did such a good imitation of local guides who stationed themselves in the historic buildings of Italy that I half expected he would conclude with "*Cento lire, grazie.*"

Lifting my eyes past two balconies and a gallery, I circled the vaulted cupola, delicately painted with eight beautiful women—but not quite muses—all white and obviously Italian, joining hands and dancing yet tied together with ropes like ribbons. In stark contrast, the theater walls were smeared with a gruesome, chalky red. Why paint it like that, I thought. "*Per che questo colore per la mura?*" I asked.

Arefine shook his head. "*Mbwa.* The Derg. The Ethiopians. *Brutta,* eh Charlus?" As we reached the stage, I smelled sewage and saw pipes on both sides leaking water.

Outside again, we kept walking uphill. A man walked out of a block-long, pistachio-colored school where the sidewalk narrowed and clogged with students standing around and trying to stay out of the street. A small, hand-lettered sign above the door read, "Asmara School of Art" in English and Tigrinya. Arefine stopped, raising his hand as if to call us both to a halt and intoned, "*Dehan amsi, Feshaye.*"

"*Arefine, inehelka bel nebeserat! Selam,*" the small, thin man with a scraggly beard and dressed in khakis, open-collar white shirt, and a tweed jacket replied.

"Don't be surprised. *Sono dappertutto sempre,*" Arefine beamed.

"Everywhere at all times"—I was translating in my head and drifting back into the horrible images I dreamed of in the afternoon until Arefine snapped me back to attention.

"Professor Charlus, meet Feshaye Zemichael, the director of the Asmara Art School."

Deliberately responding in English, "My pleasure," I was beginning to feel self-conscious speaking mostly Italian when it was the language, after all, of an oppressive and murderous colonial regime, despite its making Asmara look like its own little "*nuova Roma.*" Italian colonial rule took over the Eritrean economy, denied Eritrean children an education beyond fourth grade, and kicked Eritreans off the sidewalks so that Italians could walk there by themselves. Yet for me, at least, Africa and especially this northeast chip out of the Horn, wasn't Rome simply because of the way it looked. Instead, Africa became my Rome because what I thought were my European cultural origins led me to further cultural origins. St. Augustine came from Africa to Carthage to Rome, but I wanted to reverse the direction: from America to Rome—for much the same reason as Augustine—but then back to Africa: his Africa, my Rome—Rome's Rome. Asmara filled me with nostalgia for my Italian grandparents and new Italian American immigrant ways of my father's family in Newark, New Jersey—which was truly remarkable and unexpected—but if I hadn't traveled beyond such sentimentality, literally, I would probably still be there as a lawyer living in the suburbs and commuting to Newark's courthouses—shaking my head and locking my doors as I drove through Newark's black ghettoes.

"Why does an American English professor come to Asmara?" Feshaye asked, shaking my hand and weirdly intimating my train of thought. He held a sculpture.

Arefine pointed to it. "*Aye kezebeg. Belllisima,* eh Charlus? *Ahagwiskanna Feshaye!*"

Feshaye nodded. I looked at a four-string harp—"*krar,*" Arefine added— attached to a bronze, smiling mask of comedy, flanked by a palate and brushes on one side and a quill, inkwell, and book on the other. A woman— "Hedareb," Arefine pronounced slowly, "one of our ethnic groups"—danced behind the *krar*'s strings. She offered a laurel wreath and did not look very different from the women I saw dancing on the Cinema Asmara's ceiling, only she clearly was a muse.

Feshaye answered Arefine, "*Tesfa negeber,*" and Arefine raised his eyes.

"*Speriamo,*" Arefine said, looking a little skeptical. "Let's hope so, right Charlus? The government will like it, but what about the artists? They're tougher to please. This is the model for our Oscar. This year we will make the award for the first time: one each for poetry, painting, and drama. *Ciao,* Feshaye. We are late for an appointment with the Constitutional Commission." As we walked away, I wondered if Feshaye thought our going there was as strange as I did.

A half block up the street, we stopped at a two-story house built like a miniature Cinema Asmara. "*Ecco qui,* Charlus. Just go in. I must go see my sister. Ask for Dr. Bereket. Bereket Habte Selassie. *Va bene?* Come to the office in the morning, and we will go for macchiato. *Harrai!*"

Before I could get him to stay and at least come inside to smooth the introductions, he turned around and started to walk away, immediately greeted by another "*Arefine, zegerem'yu.*" I heard him reply again, "*Sono dappertutto sempre,*" as he disappeared down the hill with another fan.

Feeling unprepared and lost in the doorway, I tried to remember the name of the person whom I was supposed to see. "Selassie?" As in "Haile Selassie," the Ethiopian emperor who, preying on the sympathies of the United Nations and the ignorance plus arrogance of the United States, forced Eritrea to become federated with Ethiopia in the 1950s, with England, which had won Eritrea from the Italians in World War II, happy to hand it over? Even my minimal knowledge of Eritrean history made me not want to make a mistake and ask for a "Selassie" in the office of Eritrea's Constitutional Commission. I might as well go in and ask for "Mussolini." Becoming a little paranoid, I wondered if Arefine might even be joking.

A vigorous, slightly heavyset, balding man with a short gray beard came to the doorway from inside, although I didn't knock. He immediately said, "Are you Cantalupo from Africa World Press? Running late, I just got here, and I'm glad not to have missed you."

We went into a one-room library with dark wooden bookshelves built into all four walls floor to ceiling. Where was the commission, I wondered: the offices, the secretaries, the metal files, and conference rooms? His desk blended almost indistinguishably with massive wooden library tables in front of shelves that overflowed with open books and stacks of papers scattered everywhere. Sitting at one end of a table and signaling to me to sit at the other, he said in a deep, precise voice, "You teach literature at Penn? I teach at North Carolina, Chapel Hill. Kassahun has told me about you." I wished Kassahun had told me about him, whoever he was. Selassie? He seemed to be in charge.

I heard a knock at the door, and he got up to leave the room. I saw a pile of English versions of *Haddas Eritrea,* the same small, tabloid newspaper I had seen in the Africa World Press office, with an issue from a year ago on top. It showed his picture on the front page. I glanced quickly at the article from my seat, first seeing his name and finding phrases like "Attorney General of Ethiopia," "EPLF Representative to the UN," "Chairman of Constitutional Commission," "process with tens of thousands of Eritreans participating," and "women . . . 47% of Commission." He came back into the room followed by a young man in jeans and a sweater and holding a tray with two espressos and sugar. It would be my sixth coffee of the day.

"So how is the constitution going?" I asked. What else could I say, also asking myself how in less than twenty-four hours in Eritrea I could be sitting in the office of its Thomas Jefferson.

"It's a big, long process, but we have to get it right," Bereket replied in a professorial manner. "Too many have struggled and died for us not to. I assume Kassahun has told you about it." I nodded yes, even though he hadn't. Bereket continued, "Some issues are easy. Everybody agrees about what the flag should look like. Some are hard. Today we argued about whether an official oath of office should be sworn in the name or Eritrea's martyrs who died in the independence struggle or in the name of God or Allah."

"Which are you for?" I asked.

"Right now I'd say the martyrs, but Eritrea is a deeply religious society." His answer was undecided, but his tone was confident.

As I thought to myself, "How could Eritrea be religious since Marxism played such a large part in the books I was reading from Kassahun," Bereket continued.

"Our religion and culture are so inseparably woven together that it is sometimes difficult to separate the priest from the layman. Take those very colorful cotton dresses our Eritrean women wear. They are adorned with designs of the cross and probably woven by a Moslem."

Sensing that Bereket loved to talk, especially about a topic of so much passion, and that I would not need to contribute much to the conversation, I relaxed and asked, "Any other tough issues?"

"Language," he said, his eyes brightening and bulging. "Should there be a national language? National languages? Tigrinya and Arabic? Tigrinya and Tigre, the languages of 80 percent of the population? All three? Then again, Eritrea has nine languages and why not all of them?"

"All of them?" I asked, "Would that work?"

"I don't know," Bereket replied, rubbing his beard, "but the secretary of the commission, Zemhret Yohannes, is really adamant about this. He wants a simple declaration of the equality of Eritrea's nine languages based on the principle of the equality of all nine ethnic groups."

I thought of the sculptor, Feshaye's dancing Hedareb woman, and wanted to talk to her.

Bereket continued, seeming to lapse into repeating an argument that a weariness in his voice suggested he had heard too often: "Every Eritrean citizen has the need and, therefore, should have the right to use the language of his or her choice in education, legal matters, court cases, and whatever else comes up that's important."

"Sounds revolutionary, almost too much so," I answered, sensing some friction between the commission secretary and Bereket and wanting to support his view if only because he was being so gracious in our meeting.

Suddenly he got up, took two old books off the shelf behind him, handed them to me, and said, "We should be talking about Eritrean poetry. What are you researching here?"

Wishing I could remember the Tigrinya word for "poet" that Arefine had told me less than an hour before, I looked at the books and tried to think of an answer. They weren't Eritrean but in Italian; the authors' names were Rossini and Gasparini, and I turned a few brittle pages with sepia plates of picturesque Eritrean landscapes and what I thought might be Italian translations of Eritrean poetry. What could I be researching in Eritrean poetry? The land of Cush? Rome's Rome? How the metal workers at Medeber seemed to me to embody the craft of poetry itself? Wanting to sound more academic, I responded, "I'm hoping to make some translations of Eritrean poetry."

I felt like a first-year graduate student struggling to come up with a paper topic to please my professor as Bereket said, "Rossini has some Italian translations of oral poetry and you should try them. Do you speak Italian? But let me tell you. Tigrinya can't be translated."

"Maybe not," I weakly replied, wondering what could be so uniquely difficult about it.

"Is this your first day? You must be beat," Bereket then said, getting up. I handed him the books, we agreed to meet again, if not in Eritrea then at a conference in the United States, and I found my own way out as he settled back into his papers. "I must get back to rewriting the draft of article 7 on human rights, especially for women," I heard behind me as I left the room.

Barely remembering where I was or how to get back to the Albergo Italia, I thought if I simply kept walking downhill from one stray streetlight to the next, I would make it. However, I couldn't remember whether I got lost or not when I woke up in my bed at 12:30 P.M. the next day. I had missed another appointment with Arefine.

Waiting for him in front of the closed grate to open up the press around 2:00 P.M., I looked across the street at the barbershop from where I had first spotted the office. A tall thin man with a clipped moustache, a plain cotton African leisure suit, and sandals ducked into the shop. He looked familiar. The three barbers' faces lit more brightly than their mirrors and the chrome and porcelain of their chairs. The visitor waved them off, as if to say "No fuss."

Just then Arefine showed up and said, "Charlus, are you watching the president get a haircut?" Now I recognized him. But if it were the president, how could he travel alone without even one security guard? As if in a trance, I barely heard Arefine unlock the heavy steel grate and glass door until he said, "Charlus, maybe your Bill Clinton should come here too."

"*Buongiorno,* Arefine," I replied, coming back to reality. "Clinton should. He would learn something, too. I certainly am. *Me piace Asmara, molto.* But I'm sorry about this morning."

Arefine lifted his hand, opened his palm, and looped it in the air. "It's okay. *Non si preoccupi.*"

I continued still feeling guilty. "*Chiedo scusa.* I overslept. *Ho dormito in ritardo questa mattina.* Maybe I did too much yesterday. *Ho fatto ieri troppo.* Looking around, Medeber, Cinema Asmara, and then meeting Bereket. I liked him. *Nella America, Thomas Jefferson. Nella Eritrea, Bereket Haile Selassie* and a few more, *ed alcune piu, forse?*"

"*Si, alcune piu,*" Arefine laughed, "but don't remind Bereket of that."

Arefine's good nature put me at ease, and I changed the subject. "*Ma, basta cosi.* I'm taking it easy today, Arefine."

With this he shook my hand to agree. "*Buono, buono. Bisogna oggi di un certo resto.* Tomorrow you go to Massawa. I have a driver for you. You will leave early. Be ready at your hotel at six o'clock."

With a few hours left in the afternoon, I wanted to visit a site I had read about: Asmara's Tsetserat, or the tank graveyard. The walk up to the taxi stand was starting to feel familiar—the busy post office, the shoe store, the stationary store, the appliance store, the little grocery, the line of 1960s Fiats, the "*Buongiorno, signore. Taxi,*" the dignified and unhurried invitation, "*Per favore, signore. Prova la mia machina. Siedasi giu.*" The place seemed timeless, anything but a graveyard. The Fiats had outlived the tanks.

"*Tsetserat, per favore,*" I said with some embarrassment as I got into the front seat of the first taxi. With so much life around me, life that had survived so much death, why go there? As we drove, I continued to be amazed by the city. I saw a new nation at peace and in action—with women fighters serving in the government, children learning in their mother tongues, a grassroots constitution process coming to fruition, and so much more— developing itself with confidence, joy, and incredibly hard work. The place seemed to embody the enlightened political and social vision so fervently expressed by Ngugi and many other great African writers I was beginning to read—like Chinua Achebe, Okot p'Bitek, and Nawal El Saadawi—but in reality and not only on paper. Thinking of the book Kassahun Checole had given me and that I had left back in my hotel room about the Eritrean revolution, *Against All Odds* by Dan Connell, I realized that the same phrase—*against all odds*—also characterized the struggle of these writers. If only they could all gather together in Asmara and see their aspirations for Africa embodied in the everyday of Eritrea.

Traveling up Liberation Avenue, we passed two more exquisite "cinemas"—named Roma and Odeon—their facades a mix of rationalism, cubism, expressionism, classical Rome, and outright fantasy. A little up the road, why were those huge airplane wings stuck on a building labeled "Fiat" with cars lined up at its gasoline pumps? Nearby I saw a creamy deco hotel with long windows, cantilevering balconies, gray slated turrets, sweeping towers, rich gardens, bronze statues, and reflecting black and white marble tiles—yet none of it looking luxurious—inviting me to stay there on my next visit. Forget the graveyard. I wanted to ask the driver to let me stop and drink at that bar of turquoise and pink Formica. Or maybe I would take a seat on one of the chrome stools around the warm marble tables where gold and silver mirrors trimmed with frost held each face perfectly in its own, individual angle. Why not linger in the shadows where long diaphanous curtains grazed whimsically geometric tiles? Could I also stop and take a picture of the bicycles resting unlocked against lavender and avocado walls shadowed by a stop sign? Resting my eyes on the open windows and doorways framing massive rows of palm trees that lined the wide boulevards where men and women walked to and from work and children to and from school, I saw everyone perfectly safe.

"Martyrs Cemetery," the driver said five minutes later, pointing to a weak fountain and depressingly symmetric, hundreds of rows of white marble tombstones, half of them decorated with plastic flowers. "*Desiderate arrestarsi?*"

"*No, grazie,*" I answered. Stop for what? To marvel at all the recent dates and brief life spans? To feel their presence and pay my respects as I walked the narrow paths among too many graves and the obligatory cypress? I had enough cemeteries in my own life and didn't want to wander in any others. The driver looked straight ahead, more seriously than before.

"*Continuamo a andare, per favore,*" I reiterated. The spirits of these graves seemed impossibly confined here and challenged my upbeat feeling over the last two days that Asmara was anything but the gruesome and dire specter of its history.

The taxi skidded on some gravel and stopped at the edge of a field, and the driver smiled, "*Qui e. Attendere?*"

"*No, grazie. Ciao,*" I replied with a wave of goodbye. I didn't want him to wait and run up the fare, although for a second I wanted to get back into the cab and go back to town.

Instead of following narrow paths through the gravestones, I now walked on a hard dirt road through wide pastures of tanks, troop carriers, armored trucks, and rocket launchers resting beside each other and overgrown with thistles and bougainvillea. The superpower emblems on the rust brown Soviet T54 and British Mark tanks didn't seem to want to fade. Their turrets aimed nowhere and at nothing or at each other, which amounted to the same thing. I thought of the photograph I had dreamed about the day before: the tank battle with flying body parts. Was the soldier who destroyed one of these tanks or who was destroyed by one of them buried next door in the martyrs graveyard? "Rest in peace?" Like the old Italian railroad car—its quaint insignia with "*Ferrovia Eritrea*" also visible—that I found strangely alone in a patch of cactus? "Peace" like I found climbing through the blasted open hatch and down for a few seconds into the rank darkness of an American M48? I wanted out, again preferring the living Eritrea to the skeletons and ghosts who wanted it, too. I wanted the Eritrea of the resurrection and the life, in Christ's words from the Gospel of John (11:25), only in absolutely human terms—punctuated by the drumming and hammering of Medeber—and not the death and useless oblivion of Tsetserat, the anti-Medeber.

I began running deeper and deeper into it, following the ever narrowing road in the hope of finding a back exit until a soldier in fatigues with a machine gun gestured to me to stop.

"*Tetenqeg*," he said slowly coming right up to my face. "*Tetenqeg.*"

Did he mean stop? Go? Get out? Who are you? I didn't understand and said, "*Non ho capito*," once again thrown back on using the colonial Italian.

"Be careful," he said slowly, impossibly rolling the "r" and recognizing my American accent.

"*Ah, grazie*," I still replied in Italian, asking, "*Dove l'uscita?*"

I never saw a straighter arm than when he pointed back the way I came and smiled. After a few minutes, I once again saw the battered orange-yellow Fiat *seicento* that had dropped me off. Glad that the driver hadn't listened to me and stayed, I greeted him like an old friend. "Africa World Press, please," I said getting in. "*Iwe*," he replied, and neither of us said another word all the way back to town.

I was hoping to find Arefine for a few moments of more human warmth and liveliness than the wasting carcasses of superpower weaponry from an unnecessary proxy war could provide, but the iron grate on the Africa World Press office was pulled down and locked. Across the post office piazza, however, the white fluorescent lights under the hand-lettered "Senay Super Market" sign still offered the food I grew up with and would be eating right now if I were home with Barbara and our children. I bought my dinner and another bottle of Lachrymae Christi red and joined the rest of the Asmarinos shopping and walking home for the night.

My room's marble floors, high ceiling, long mirror, plaster molding, cavernous neogothic wardrobe, and otherwise sleek, deco furniture—all well worn—and the vase of deep purple statice on the table where I ate, along with the wine, helped me forget Eritrea's unfailing, maybe insuperable, evidence of war. I wanted something to read besides the books I had brought from Kassahun that, for the most part, only reinforced that evidence.

What about the first one, called *Kebra Nagast*, that I had tried on the flight to Israel from New York and that had seemed impenetrable? The title peered out from under *Never Kneel Down*. I reached down, opened to the title page, and read the long subtitle: "The history of the departure of God and His Ark of the Covenant from Jerusalem to Ethiopia, and the establishment of the religion of the Hebrews and the Solomonic line of kings in that previously pagan country."[3] Opposite the title page was a photograph of an iconically posed Haile Selassie in an expensive, European double-breasted suit (similar to what the old man wore in the Africa World Press office the day before), with a high starched collar, skinny regimental tie, and breast handkerchief emblazoned with a crown. Similarly imposing, or trying very hard to be, the caption beneath him read, "H.I.M. *Negusa Negast*, His Imperial Majesty . . . (Power of the Holy Trinity), Emperor of

Ethiopia, King of Kings, Lord of Lords, Conquering Lion of the Tribe of Judah, Elect of God, Light of the Universe," and more.[4] If I had read this ten or fifteen years before, that is, before coming to the ants in the sands of ancient Jericho and then coming to Africa, I might have been immediately interested and wanted to read on, intrigued at least by such language that sounded more in the tradition of the biblical Israel and Europe, what I had vowed to learn before I would learn another tradition, instead of referring to a king of Africa. However, my vow long past and gratefully broken, as I read the description now, it seemed opaque and like propaganda. Ironically, it seemed more related to where I left to come to Eritrea and where I would be flying back to—Israel—than to where I was at present. "The Glory of Kings"[5] sounded like just another version, albeit elaborate, of a king's self-glory. Still I wondered, why did it mention "Judah" and resonate with references to the Old and the New Testaments?

Turning the book over, I read on the back cover, "These pages were excised by royal decree from the authorized 1611 King James version of the Bible." African Apocrypha? An illustration reproduced the "Original Ge'ez (Ethiopic) text," while writing like what I saw on all the papers, books, and signs all over Asmara decorated the back cover. Promising to reveal "ancient secrets. . . . long suppressed. . . . hidden truths. . . . and the present location of the Ark of the Covenant," the book also sounded occult.

Scanning the table of contents and chapters with grim titles like "Concerning the Glory of Kings," "The Greatness of Kings," "Concerning Envy," "Declaration of the Patriarchs," and "The Glory of Zion," I stopped at "Part II. Solomon and Sheba." "Excised . . . from the . . . King James version?" Something salacious, perhaps? What did the King James say? I had the same, small red leather copy with me that I had bought for my trip to Jerusalem in 1985. Starting with the second book of Samuel, I found nothing and tried the first book of Kings, offering a second version of many of the same events. Finally I read at the beginning of chapter 10, "And when the queen of Sheba heard of the fame of Solomon concerning the name of the Lord, she came to prove him. . . . And when the queen of Sheba had seen all of Solomon's wisdom . . . there was no more spirit in her." The description built up Solomon to be all-powerful and out of reach, the way the introductory pages of *Kebra Nagast* built up Haile Selassie.

I went back to the *Kebra*. The editor sounded like a crank, claiming that his "modern translation" would prove that "the lawful kings of Ethiopia were descended from Solomon, King of Israel" and that "the God of Israel transferred His place of abode on earth from Jerusalem to Axum, the ecclesiastical capital of Ethiopia."[6] And the translation didn't sound modern but more like the language of the Revised Version of the Bible in the 1880s. Rhetorical claims about the absolute authority of one culture over another didn't interest me, since my own similar presumptions had crumbled to dust to join a lot of others on the site of ancient Jericho. Rome's Rome?—yes—a cultural continuum between Europe and Africa: but not the setting up of yet one more kind of cultural superiority to replace another.

Or could there be a Jerusalem's Jerusalem? Thinking of how in 1985 before I fell apart in Jericho I visited sites like the Church of the Nativity in Bethlehem and the slab of Jesus' tomb in the Church of the Holy Sepulcher, I said aloud, "Why not?" Hadn't I once invested them with the same kind of absolute belief with which the *Kebra Nagast* endowed the chauvinist and nationalistic claims about the "kings of Ethiopia" and ultimately Haile Selassie? Hadn't I once been a victim of my own absolute distinctions about what was American or European about my cultural origins and what wasn't? Didn't I know that every tenet of the Old and New Testament emerged from a welter of authors, editors, languages, translations, transcriptions, centuries, and political and historical concerns that did not prevent Christian and Jews—and followers of Islam and the Koran—each from claiming that Jerusalem was particularly their own God's "place of abode?" Finding myself traveling between two places that literally made such a claim, what could I do but read on? Unlike Israel's Zion, which characterized Sheba as overwhelmed by Solomon, Africa's Zion made them more like equals, or at least that was the way I wanted to read it.

I thought of Barbara and when we were married. Knocking the dust of the Cistercian monastery off our feet, the barn and freshly mown straw to be married in. But who would marry us? Would our friend, Jack Barton, an easygoing Presbyterian minister? What was he doing in Asmara? In a room down the hall where I had heard hammering before, I saw him beside a simple shrine of an obsidian anvil and a half Athena, half mother figure who seemed taken from a ship's prow. Jack read aloud from a scrap of goat skin. "Walk to the river's edge. Stretch out your right hand. Fill it with water and sprinkle it on your shadow. Look. Fruit."

"Where did you get that?" I asked as I tried to read the words. "Were you fossil hunting again?"

"I found it in the garbage," he said with a smile and continued. "Look. No grim messages. No 'Forgive them. I'm thirsty. It's finished.' No 'You left me.' Forget those purple vestments. Listen to your daughters playing violin. Look at Sheba. She is dancing to their music, like she did even before the creation. Remember what I read at your wedding?"

The book falling from my hands onto the floor woke me up. I remembered

Jack had read a passage from Ecclesiasticus that seemed to be about a female god. Later I asked him about it. Who was she?

He replied smiling, "Maybe she was Sheba. Maybe she wrote the Song of Songs."

Awake now, I tried again to read on. "No more spirit in her?" Sheba came from Ethiopia, traveled to Jerusalem, and had an affair with Solomon. She left him when she grew homesick. "Nine months and five days" into her trip, she gave birth to a son by a stream in "the country of Bala Zadisareya." She named her son Bayna-Lehkem. The birth was joyous "with pride and delight. . . . great pomp and ceremony" and without a hint of shame or regret since Sheba "loved wisdom and God strengthened her kingdom"[7] as a result. "No more spirit in her?"

I was distracted. Why did the dogs in Asmara bark so loudly all night, or was I imagining this? What were they barking at? Wasn't the city at peace? "No more spirit in her?" God's daughter? She danced and spun before creation. Or was she a cheap perfume? From too far away? Write a book about her if you want, but it was only about sex. It disconnected. Ask the priest. Ask the editor. "No more spirit in her." Bruises, broken bones, cut up, a heap of bloody rags thrown in the sand. She got up muttering, "What do I know? What do I know?" My poems dangled from her waist.

La Illah ila Allah, wa Mohammed rasul Allah. The call to prayer from the Great Mosque woke me up. *La Illah ila Allah . . . As salatu khayrun an naum.* Unsure if I could get back to sleep, I looked at the page in my lap and could barely focus: "And Benaiah, the son of Jehoiada, Commander of the army of King Solomon answered and said to Bayna-Lehkem, 'Solomon the King is better than thy mother, and this our country is better than thy country. . . . Thy country is a land of cold and cloud, of glare and burning heat . . . when the sons of Noah, Shem, Ham and Japhet divided the world among them.'"[8] Where was I? In Cush? Who was Ham's son? Closing the book and my eyes, I pictured Asmara's mosque. I saw the minaret—visible from everywhere in the city—like a fluted Roman column, its two platforms with rococo Italian balconies and the mosque proper below with its tripartite neoclassical loggia, its shimmering double travertine columns with Carrara capitals and the outstretched gold and green mosaic facade inviting the faithful into a honeycomb with fresh blue water.

CHAPTER SEVEN

Where a Camel Roams

I woke up thirsty with only fifteen minutes before I would be picked up to go to Massawa. Five hours later, seven thousand feet lower, and fifty-five degrees hotter, I remembered the mosque's blue water as I thankfully put my mouth to a rusty pipe in a cement cistern two feet below ground the color of light ash to drink hot mineral water from a spring called Mai Wei. My driver had three red plastic jerry cans that he filled after taking a much longer drink than I did. "*Questi sono per il Asmara,*" he said, straining to keep the huge container's opening directly under the warm trickle and with the sun glistening on his wet, bristly round face.

I had been surprised at 6:00 A.M. when I saw him, the same driver who had taken me back and forth to Tsetserat the day before, waiting for me in a relatively new, white Nissan.

I asked him, "*Siete amico dei Arefine? Stiamo andando a Massawa insieme?*"

Wearing a royal blue Nike tracksuit and rubbing the sleep out of his bloodshot eyes, he replied, "*Si. Iwe.* Yes. *Buongiorno.* We'll stop *per il café lungo il modo.*"

"Si, *bun. Ma,* where is your old Fiat?" I wondered aloud, and as I opened the Nissan's tinny door and sat on the gray, stained cloth seat I felt the springs.

"*Questa e la machina del mio nipote.*"

"*Nipote?*" I asked, forgetting what the word meant.

"*Si,* my nephew," he answered. "*Mi chiamo, Berhane.*"

I shook his hand with "Thanks, Berhane. I'm Charlus." I thought that I might as well go by the pronunciation of my name that I first heard from Arefine.

His gravelly response, "*Allora, andiamo,*" gave me a second of vertigo, triggering a thought of all the vastly different kinds of circumstances and people the same phrase had served in Asmara over the years.

We left Eritrea's capital and largest city, but no larger than a typical rural county seat in the United States, at what seemed like the same speed as the last bits of twilight in the rising sun. As every man, woman, and child I saw seemed absolutely intent on walking straight to their appointed tasks and nothing else, I wondered if in all of Asmara there could be two lovers who ignored the sun and turned to each other in bed. As the road wound through the silver light under the eucalyptus trees and reached the edge of town, Berhane gestured to the side at roughly one-minute intervals and said, "Italian cemetery," "English cemetery," "Zoo." I didn't answer, asking myself without an answer if too much wine, too many tomatoes with green chilies, the altitude, or the rough night's sleep kept me feeling woozy.

Suddenly straight out the windshield, I looked at a huge cumulus cloud in the middle of the road. I tried to remember the word in Italian for fog. "*Nebbia, Berhane?*"

"No," he replied, pronouncing the word like a raindrop. The cloud moved across the road like a wave breaking in slow motion. As we passed quickly through it, I stared out into an abyss. Varying shades of green, deeply slashing mountains, and remnants of the cloud I saw trailing down one of them opened into a fuzzy blue horizon far off and below us.

For the next forty-five minutes, we clung to a precipitous mountain-side of jagged rock and prickly pears—"*beles,*" said Berhane—which scruffy children in long pants and heavy acrylic sweaters were already picking, knocking the cactuses with long poles tipped with small sacks to catch the ripe fruit. It piled up in lines of indistinguishable baskets overlooked by more children standing on the road's shoulder and usually accompanied by their seated mother looking straight ahead and unmoving as if she had to conserve her energy for some huge task ahead. Meanwhile, more cumulus clouds tumbled down the mountain at unpredictable intervals around us. From the passenger's seat, I looked down the impossibly steep ascent to the road, but my eyes always stopped before reaching the bottom—or as far as I could see—at a person or two, usually with a goat or donkey, slowly walking up. Often a flash of the white or yellow paint of a car or truck that had gone off the road and tumbled far down but still within view made me close my eyes and open them looking hopefully at Berhane calmly varying his speed, although never really going slowly, depending on whether the road curved, hair-pinned, or unfolded relatively straight. "*Buona strada, si?*" I said.

"*Constuito dagli Italiani, trascurato dai Britannici, ravinato dai Ethiopians.*"

"And now fixed by Eritreans," I added as we passed one of many local road crews: skinny men dressed in colorless rags, shorts, turbans, and wearing no shoes.

"*Si,*" Berhane nodded, "*riparato dai Eritreans.*"

"*Tutto,* everything *e riparato dai Eritreans,*" I repeated, adding "and no one else." I was about to say, "*Riparato dai* Eritreans, like *getamay,*" to see how Berhane would respond, but before I could, he interrupted.

"*E nessun altro, no one else,*" he said, once loud and once soft. For a couple seconds he took both hands off the wheel, moved them in unison up and down twice, and looked up to heaven uttering in exasperation, "*Mbwa.*"

Feeling warm and still a little sick, I rolled down the window and stared into the air blowing in my face and at the mountains looming ahead and not any smaller than what we were on.

At one curve we passed a group of boys on the shoulder. One of them had cut open a *beles,* a prickly pear, and he held out his index and middle fingers together, which he thrust in and out of the fleshy red fruit. The older boys around him laughed, but the younger ones looked a little hesitant and wide-eyed.

"Berhane," I asked, "what are they up to?"

Berhane chuckled. "They like to practice on the *beles* before they get a real girl. Do you need some practice, Charlus?"

"I'll pass for now and wait until I get home," I answered with a laugh but wishing I didn't have to wait so long.

"I know what you mean, Charlus. But here—we are almost at Nefasit, where we will visit Kassahun's sister." Arefine had said nothing about such a stop, but I started noticing one-room, one-story stone and cement houses at closer intervals and bushes and short trees instead of mostly cactus. When we passed an ominous gate with a guardhouse and I asked what it was, Berhane said, "*Riserva del petrolio,* in case we have to fight again." No one seemed to be there. Ten feet behind the gate to the fuel dump, I only saw dirt and rocks that led up another mountain.

At a sharp left turn that became the main street of Nefasit, Berhane gestured out my passenger's side window, "*Su, su, in alto!*" I looked up. As we entered the valley, I looked up a steep mountainside. Was it crenelated? Berhane continued: "*Debre Bizen, monastero.* You can walk up, *ma no donna.*"

"Just what I want," I thought to myself. "A monastery I can hike up to but with no women. At home, on Athos or in Africa, what's the difference?"

Trying not to sound rude or ungrateful, I answered "No, *grazie.* Maybe next time."

Sensing that my tone meant "never," Berhane replied with a smile, "It's good exercise *e una vista bella* but forget *tutto altrimenti.*"

"*Veramente,*" I agreed, as we pulled off to the driver's side of the road at a cafe with an open door near a bus stop. "*Ma, qui siamo?* Let's drive a little further."

"*La sorella*, Kassahun's sister," Berhane said, adding, "You know we have come down almost two thousand feet?"

He got out of the car, and I followed him in. Everyone spoke only in Tigrinya: Berhane, the young woman, and a slightly younger boy behind the bar, both of whom looked related and wore fashionable jeans and sweaters, and two older men who sat a table: one of whom wore a white blanket over his sport jacket and held a smooth, peeled walking stick. Berhane joined the two men, signaled to me to sit down, told them who I was—or so I assumed since several times I heard the words "Professor, Charlus . . . Kassahun"—and proceeded with a ten-minute, often animated conversation I couldn't understand another word of. Unbidden, the girl behind the counter brought us Cokes, with "Coca-Cola" written in Ge'ez letters, and sparkling water—*mai gaz*—that she mixed half and half in all our glasses. Draining his in one gulp, Berhane said, "Kassahun's sister is in Asmara. But we can meet her husband."

After several rounds of "thank you" and "good luck" in Tigrinya, Italian, and English, we got up, and I followed Berhane through a bead curtain into the house behind the shop and eventually into the backyard: a red clay terrace overlooking a ravine and facing a similar terrace on the other side with a pen full of goats.

Berhane introduced me to an old man, again with a white blanket over his sport jacket and holding a peeled walking stick with a crook at the top. He sat in a deep wooden chair. Almost bald, white whiskered, and with face burnt a dark brown red, he held his leg to signal that he had trouble getting up. We casually shook hands as he spoke Tigrinya and I responded, "Thanks, *piacere*, great to me you; it's an honor."

He spoke a little more with Berhane, and I listened, understanding nothing, but here I didn't need language, or not much of it. Instead I saw a life in balance: ancient shining eyes, a body at dusk, a pulse of long life and peace at home in old clothes—free of war in a backyard corner looking out on goats and terraces of tumbled red earth. "*Merhaba*, welcome," the old man said to me in a low, scratchy voice when he finished speaking with Berhane.

"Welcome one useful leg. Welcome tons of scrap metal. Welcome bombed-out, crazy angled masonry, and nothing wasted. *Merhaba*," I thought to myself. His *merhaba* echoed in the most everyday miracle of birth, as I heard a baby crying from one of the rooms inside. "*Merhaba*," I thought again.

Berhane tapped me on the shoulder. "I have asked him to show us what he has built."

The old man shuffled with his stick, and we followed him out of the house, across the road, and halfway up the facing hill where he had built a new school, its front frescoed with four maps: of Nefasit, Eritrea, Africa, and the world. Coming back to the car, we got in, and he took us halfway out of town the way we came in and off a side road until the town was no longer in sight, where he had built its first hospital. The size of a small motel, it had one room apiece for a pharmacy, storage, labor, delivery, pre-op, operating, inoculations, recovery, and rest. Without this building, I imagined almost everyone now using it would be dead.

As we drove away from the hospital, I heard the old man repeating a sentence, and I asked Berhane to translate: "He says, 'These are only a few of the poor, and this solves only one of their problems.'" On the way out, we passed a woman pulling a homemade stretcher with a sick child. She wore bright coral and yellow robes and a headscarf. Two huge bronze rings hung from her ears and one from her nostril. Without acknowledging the car, her eyes burned through us. The child appeared almost camouflaged: wrapped in burlap, palm fronds, and shreds of blue plastic tied to wooden poles with leather cords—some of them dangling beads.

Again I had to ask Berhane what our host was telling him: "She is a nomad and has been traveling for days."

Coming back to the café and telling Berhane I wanted to explore a little more before we left, I walked again up toward the school and past it. I found a small outdoor market selling flour and rice in burlap bags much like what I saw on the nomad woman's stretcher, some of them marked "USA" and others with Arabic writing and "Saudi Arabia" in English. I also walked past baskets of tomatoes, green chilies, eggplants, and *beles* whose owners acted as if they didn't see me. I stopped at one man who sat in the dirt in tattered shorts and T-shirt but also with the same white blanket that Kassahun's brother-in-law had. Old and gnarled, he had three heavy, peeled, and carved sticks in front of him, each around two feet long and in the rough shape of an "L."

"*Cos'e questa,* what is this for, *per favore?*" I asked.

He took one, grabbed the straight end, and motioned with it as if he were hoeing the ground.

"How much, *quanti costa?*" I asked.

"Eight birr," he said in slow, clear English.

"Over a dollar," I thought. "I'll give you five," I said taking a crumbled five-birr note out of my pocket.

"No, eight. Eight," he said nodding, slightly smiling and looking straight into my eyes.

Reaching into my pocket again I found a ten-birr bill. "Eight, here. Thanks."

As he gave me the mattock, I tried to wave away the two birr in change that he gave me with it, but he put both his hands together and nodded "no" harder and harder until I put the coins in my pocket. As I walked I realized that I had bought only the handle for a metal blade to be slipped onto it.

Turning around and following the rocky path back down the mountain, I felt ashamed of bargaining for such a small item from an obviously poor man, but when I started swinging it in the air to try to get rid of this feeling his image and the tool made me start singing each time I swung it in a circle, "No more spirit in her. No more spirit in her. No more spirit in her."

I saw some children in similarly tattered shorts and T-shirts only more brightly colored playing down an alley, and they must have seen and heard me. "Hey mister. How are you?" they shouted and repeated, laughing. I got closer and saw their bare feet and legs were covered in red dust, and no one watched them.

No more war, I thought as I answered, "I'm all right. *Va bene.*"

"*Va bene. Va bene. Va bene.* All right. All right," they shouted. The mountains wrapped themselves around their echoes.

Two hours later I thought I heard them again as I walked away feeling refreshed from drinking the warm mineral water from the pipe at Mai Wei. We had descended another five thousand feet. Forbidding gorges opened wide under half-destroyed bridges where once there had been a railroad—"*Constuito dagli Italiani,*" Berhane said again. The road zigzagged down mountain after mountain like a wildly erratic yet ever precise fever chart, which also required my needing again to roll down the window and concentrate my attention on the air—which became warmer and warmer—blowing in my face to distract me from feeling nauseous.

Often we had to slow down, and I would quickly roll up the window. We would be caught behind a heavy truck piled high with bottles, sacks of grain, or motor parts and grinding its gears as a black spume of diesel exhaust filled the road like an infernal parody of the gorgeously pure and puffy cumulus clouds that surged over the road when we began our journey down the escarpment that would eventually come to an end at the beginning of Africa's famous Rift Valley and the shores of the Red Sea.

Berhane would roll up the window even faster and make sure I did the same—"*Charlus, rotoli in su la finestra. Subito, eh?*"—if we happened to slow down as we passed a family of orangutans, flashing their claws, sharp teeth, and raw red behinds. "Get your weapon ready," he joked, referring to the mattock.

Further down as the road became less steep, lone rocks the size of big houses and acacia trees whose only shade was their thorns seemed even more threatening, until I looked up and saw terrace after terrace above them and all the way up to the sky. They continued tighter and tighter as the mountains finally lowered themselves into hills, and we wound past patches of corn with long and bright silk glistening amid the stalks pressed tight in the backyards of windowless, one-room houses, half going up and half falling down. Pointing at one particularly lush row where a thin dark woman in a fuchsia head scarf and a long blue dress stood straight and unmoving amid the thick stalks, Berhane joked again about my purchase, "*Possiamo fare un giardino con quella arma,* just like a true Eritrean." Using my weapon to make a garden: I heard the drumming and pounding of Medeber again, the swords of tanks and bombs in modern warfare beaten into plowshares. I thought of the famous lines from Isaiah. "The wolf shall dwell with the lamb . . . and the lion shall eat straw like the ox." Did that apply to the Lion of Judah too, whom I had been reading about the night before? Thirty years of war gardened Eritreans for just enough blood to grow a little corn and to keep a camel unperturbed on a hilltop close by.

Mai Wei had a row of five turquoise shower stalls, their doors half broken off their hinges, if they were there at all. The showers smelled like toilets. A vegetable garden thrived on the runoff behind them. A thatch-roofed café with pitchers and metal cups ready to be filled with the spring water at no charge invited everyone to stop and drink. Predatory yet seemingly protective of the spring at the same time, the overwhelming heat reflected like an alternating electric current off the chalky white dirt and the distant marble cliffs, the spring's source, reducing everything in between to no importance. After getting my shirt, pants, and feet soaked from climbing into the shallow pit of the spring, I joined others under the thatch, unable to tell who if anyone among them actually owned or at least ran it. For a long time no one spoke, as if in a place of perfect meditation with no religious trappings or appearances except the rickety Formica tables and tarnished metal chairs, the pitchers and glasses—full where there were people and empty where there were not—and the certainty of pure water when everything else, even the stones, might burst into fire. "No more spirit in her," I thought again and gulped three glasses.

The road from Mai Wei to Massawa stretched out flatter and flatter, hotter and hotter with sharp little hills like scar tissue remaining on a colorless expanse of third-degree burns. But "so what?" said the lean-tos of scrap metal, plastic, and broken wood gathering thicker and thicker until they formed a steady wall on both sides of the road with a row of tiny saplings planted between them and whatever passed. Every hundred feet someone crouched next to a pile of bags of salt for sale. As we drove further, I saw fields of it drying on the shore of shallow lakes, beyond which over a causeway through a bay I saw our destination, Massawa.

Over the causeway I saw three tanks perched on a kind of traffic island. As Berhane stopped, I remembered reading in *Against All Odds* about the terrible battle for the liberation of Massawa from the Ethiopians in 1990, Operation Fenkil. I thought I saw flaming lakes of oil billowing black smoky clouds in the pictures of it, but now seeing that they could only be the bay and the lakes of salt, I knew all too well what was burning. I read the English version of the monument's inscription, "In memory of the heroes who fell . . . who gave their lives to . . . the light of freedom . . . today and in the future." Another plaque explained that the three tanks were Ethiopian, one that Eritrean soldiers had captured, the first ever, at another battle, and the other two during the fighting in Massawa. The tanks looked like well-preserved versions of what I saw in Tsetserat and also along the way, upended and half buried in a gully or standing stark as any other object withstanding the ashen hills and fields just before Massawa.

"The light of freedom," I read again. I saw the water of Mai Wei, Nefasit's school and hospital, its laughing children, eagles soaring down the escarpment, the new life of Asmara, its old beauty, Eritrea's constitution, weapons beaten and transformed into homes and gardens instead of destroying them "today and in the future." But what if these same tanks, bigger and better versions for more and more Tsetserats, and an expanding Martyrs Cemetery, and one after another after another nomad woman, "No more spirit in her" and dragging her dead child to the throne of the Lion of Judah, also said "today and in the future?" Could the freedom last?

I looked around for Berhane, but he had taken the car for gasoline to a Mobil station across from the Fenkil monument. I walked over and found him inside. A row of bottles alternating between Johnnie Walker Red and Black behind the cash register looked inviting. I told Berhane that I wanted to explore the city on foot and that I would meet him again there in three hours. He protested at first, but I could tell he was more interested in taking a rest from all his driving than in playing tour guide.

Leaving the tanks behind and based on what I knew of the history of Massawa, I expected to see the usual: old buildings falling down and new construction in the same place so that I couldn't tell the difference between the two. And within minutes as the streets tightened around me, I couldn't tell what was collapsing on its own and what was being demolished; what was being built anew and what was enduring and prevailing from the past. Yet I couldn't even tell what I was actually seeing: the materials, their shapes and combinations, even more than in Asmara, seeming to have escaped from dreams and nightmares. I began to feel overwhelmed by a sense of what was invisible, what had come and gone and been lost, as being even greater than what I saw. Its overpowering ghostliness made me feel like a ghost too, but from when and where? People walked by me as if I weren't there or they didn't want to notice someone who looked different from them, which meant that he was there to control, collect, possess, or own something that they no longer had. An abyss greater and deeper than what we had driven through to get here seemed to open at every angle, beckon at every alley, and pour through every archway. Each window and doorway told a story. The outside recounted in its own language what it had witnessed. Inside remained what it had suffered and could not yet reveal except as echoes from mass graves of all the shootings, clubbings, stonings, sieges, kidnappings, detentions, genocides, pogroms, beheadings, bombings, fevers, torture, and starvation that had occurred here.

For now, the outside had to be enough: marble and coral, a palm tree becoming the minaret of a crumbling mosque. The rusty corrugated iron of a stable roof kissed the turquoise tracery of a chapel. Worn-out tires stuffed the two-story stage set of a gutted palace like a Palladian theater. Pockmarks of Israeli cluster bombs dropped by the Ethiopian air force punctuated every surface, echoing the British, Italian, Egyptian, Turkish invaders before them: in and out with the tides building up, tearing down, and burying the ancient city of Adulis, older than Axum and its Sheba lore gone almost without a trace. Coming to one arched doorway three times my size in a fading, whitewashed wall that had been blocked up hurriedly with stones, I didn't need a tour or guide but only to continue wandering, willing to be lost in what I saw as it happened, as Larry Sykes had shown me. As I paused to look through three concentric archways filled with honey-colored rubble opening smaller and smaller into each other with a hastily nailed together fence of scrap wood and a locked, weather-beaten door at their end, I was startled by a boy running into and then out of them to retrieve his soccer ball that I didn't see at first. A traffic sign in Tigrinya, Arabic, Italian, and English give me the only other instruction I would need: *adagio,* slowly.

I walked doorway to doorway. One looked ecclesiastical: a church of weathered and splintering planks, corroding sheet-metal, with scraps of plywood and sheetrock covering only half of the arch above it set in stucco, marble, bricks, and last week's cement. I stopped at another towering arched doorway stuffed with stones, perhaps not as hastily as the last but with forty sheets of corrugated iron and a few tree trunks piled against it. Down the street, a double door, maybe a gateway once, perfectly balanced its frame and lintel set in a coral block wall, but five huge planks of the same rusty blue nailed it shut at every possible angle: with more nails hammered all over the door at random as if to be certain it would never open again. The sunshine on the next street made me realize that I had been walking in the shade of the frame of a hull of an overturned boat reaching from house to house.

I walked from window to window. None had any glass, although a few had empty panes. Did I see trees inside, a veiled woman walking alone in a field, a tank about to fire, and a tiny wheelbarrow made out of branches and a broken flywheel? I was no longer sure. More weathered wood, chicken wire, logs, ropes, and steel bars closed off the frames, but always something delicate hung there too: a twisted cord, a bundle of sticks, dry flowers, feathers, a bunch of red and black berries, the last remaining shreds of a piece of brightly colored silk, a ripped bag of leaves, a half-stripped piece of yellow insulated thin wire strung through some otherwise seemingly useless stones.

Blinded by a sharp flash of light, I realized that it was reflecting off the Red Sea and that I had reached a long quay. At the end I saw a palace standing alone: the opposite of the way that the windows, door, walls, buildings, labyrinthine streets, and sandy alleyways where I had been before seemed totally, maybe even hopelessly, connected with one another. Counting the seven arches on each side of the huge marble and blue-enamel square topped by a high silver dome with a jagged, gaping hole in the center, I realized that I had come to Haile Selassie's winter palace in Massawa. I had read about it back in Asmara. No more King of Kings, Lord of Lords or Conquering Lion of the Tribe of Judah. The sparkling harbor light poured through the grand entrance stairs blasted in half and overflowed across the missing floors and crumbling walls. Nothing ceremonious or commemorative attached itself—not even an identification sign, a *Keep out* or *Vietato*—to the railings' shattered filigree, the massive foundation full of cracks and the viscera of masonry dangling in the attenuated, Moorish doors. The grandness of the palace reminded me of hearing about Eritrea's constitution a few nights before, only as the building decayed the document grew, yet both magnificently and with an approachable, provisional, take-it-or-leave-it kind of ready access.

Other than for a shirtless dockworker walking by barefoot in a sarong, no one was around the building or even seemed to care about it besides me. As when I told the taxi driver in Asmara that I wanted to go to the tank graveyard in Tsetserat, my interest felt morbid and trite, superficially gloating over a monumental toll of death rather than engaging the life that death could not overcome. Still I went ahead, climbed onto a balcony, and peered through brittle and breaking slats of shutters at a rich table and chairs lined up for a meeting that would never happen. I also looked down a three-story elevator shaft missing its cars and cables and looked up at a belfry stripped of its bell, now deaf and dumb. In the side yard of the palace, an empty delivery van and a boat in drydock had banished the Lion of Judah forever, and they didn't seem to care. Noticing some Ge'ez graffiti on a column near the top of a stairway leading into nothing but air, I thought it should have translated, "No more spirit in her," and laughed. The man in the sarong, the fishing dhows, and the container ships in the harbor had better things to do than be haunted or reverent. They saw and heard every day and moved on from what I stood amazed at: a raven perched on a construction cable fallen out of the corner of a destroyed loggia. Not exactly "Perched upon a bust of Pallas just above my chamber door," like Edgar Allan Poe's "ebony bird," it still said, "Nevermore" to any such delusions of grandeur.[1] Emperor and King of Kings, legendary Sheba, liberator, enemy soldier, invader after invader after invader, survivor, momentary visitor—who didn't cling like a particle to a grinding stone on the Red Sea shore?

Following the quay until it reached the water and walking south along the beach, I passed a girl of ten or eleven who had tethered her camel to part of an airplane or helicopter propeller sticking out of the sand. Barefoot and wearing cutoff shorts with a red Reebok T-shirt under a black sweater, she seemed unfazed or not to notice my being there, until I stopped, took off my sandals, waded into the water, and took a sip from my water bottle. The sea was tepid and barely refreshing. Even as the heat had begun slightly to subside from earlier in the afternoon, I didn't want to go any further and, when the little girl glanced at me, I offered her a drink of water with a tip of the bottle toward her. Her flashing eyes told me she saw it, and I smiled. I offered the water again, and we shared what remained without speaking but smiling every time either of us took a drink.

As I turned around to walk back into the city and find Berhane, she quickly ran a few yards to a pile of beach scraps: rusty palm fronds, plastic bags, collapsed water bottles, and dried tangles of seaweed clinging to broken branches. She grabbed what looked like a shell and gave it to me. I gave her five birr for not exactly a shell but the top part of a large fish's long snout. Its underside revealed a network of ridges and thin bones forming an attenuated and curving Crucifixion: cross, legs bent at the knees, extended arms, emaciated body, and Jesus with His head hanging down. Running my index finger over the figure for a moment, I looked at her and smiled: "*Yegeniyeley,* thanks, *grazie.*"

"*Genzebka,*" she said matter-of-factly and ran back to the spot near her camel, where I first saw her, crouching and staring out at the water.

A week later, taking a break from the Tel Aviv conference on African languages and literatures, I visited Jerusalem. What had happened over the last ten years to make me look for and find the consolation and mystery of "*Hoc est enim corpus meum. . . . Hic est enim calyx sanguinis mei*"—"This is my body. . . . This is my blood"—in the overflowing gunnels of the souk being hosed out at the end of the day? Any mention of biblical kings made me think of Arefine gently reigning in the Africa World Press office and on his rounds around Asmara. Isaiah's "A child is born" referred to my children with Barbara. I prayed at the Wailing Wall, and wrote our names and "more spirit in us" on a piece of paper that I, like everyone else, squeezed into a crack in the masonry. Back in the Church of the Holy Sepulcher, I prayed with burnt matches, candle stubs, tin foil, and unidentifiable broken bits stuck to what might have been a picture or an icon—since it had a frame— now blackened beyond recognition. I compared every Crucifixion and cross I saw with a fish bone that a child gave me from the Red Sea. It parted for Moses, looking for the Promised Land. It parted for me, on no such important mission but coming from the other direction and seeing endless promise somewhere between Rome and Jerusalem in Africa.

CHAPTER EIGHT

I Carved a Dream

"I want you to see my country. In ten years it could all be over." I remembered the conclusion of the conference on Ngugi in Reading, Pennsylvania, when Kassahun Checole told me this after I first met him and he urged me to extend a trip to Israel to include Eritrea.

"In ten years it could all be over?" What did he mean? Having returned from there feeling so inspired and overpowered by the experience, I didn't understand how "it could all be over" ever, much less in ten years. It had barely begun, and I had witnessed it going strong. As I sat in the waiting room of the Africa World / Red Sea Press offices just outside of Princeton, New Jersey, I saw plenty of examples, too, of Eritrea's strength: stacks of new books Kassahun was publishing about Eritrea, their bright colorful covers intimating a triumphant future; stacks of new cassettes of Eritrean music, journals and magazines; huge Eritrean paintings on the walls; a variety of NGO studies offering Eritrea as Africa's newest democracy and the avatar of a resurrected Africa.

In the two years since we had first met, Kassahun and I had become friends, based on the warm response and editorial care he gave to the two books of essays I edited on Ngugi, and in the process a lot of conversations about Africa and African literature, yet extending to more general matters about writing and more personal concerns like our families. Talking with Kassahun was like talking with Ngugi: a generous, instant, and comprehensive education in countless different aspects of African literature. Our talking about family matters, however, became less one-sided and more balanced, since we had children of roughly the same age. As middle-class parents we had to deal with difficult economic issues like private school tuition and college, and we weren't celebrities like Ngugi. Also we shared a lot of Italian habits, his from Asmara and mine from Newark.

When I had first visited him at his office soon after the Reading conference but before I visited Eritrea, I saw, in addition to all of the materials on Eritrea, Africa, and the Horn, at least as many things about African American culture. I felt incongruous and uncomfortable waiting on the couch to see the president of a black-owned and black-operated corporation with an explicitly Afrocentric vision. Every employee was black too. I asked myself, what was *I* doing there, and I feared that they were asking themselves even more, what was I doing there?

I remembered Ngugi first telling me I should meet Kassahun because of "reasons of politics," even though a more prestigious publisher, Heinemann, Ngugi's own publisher, had said it wanted to publish my two books. I wasn't sure what Ngugi meant, beyond suggesting that a smaller, more local publisher might be more responsive than a corporate-extension publisher and, more importantly, perhaps, that Kassahun exemplified a radical, ideal form of African and black political advocacy and solidarity. "Politics" was a pejorative word in my lexicon, meaning crass manipulation, self-aggrandizement, and making decisions based on expediency instead of true value.

Nevertheless, in meeting with Kassahun at the press, the first time and several times after that, even though I trusted Ngugi's judgment and followed it, the politics that I saw as I waited for Kassahun to come out of his office felt intimidating and foreign until I came back from Asmara. My race was not a question there. Across the piazza from the *Posta Centrale*, Arefine had made me feel at home in the Africa World / Red Sea Press office—where, of course, everyone was black too—and like a member of *la famiglia*, the family, *sedrabiet*. Kassahun was no different.

Over the last two years in getting to know Kassahun, I heard him repeat to others what he said about Eritrea the first night I met him—"I want you to see my country. In ten years it could all be over." He couldn't be serious, I thought. He had to be joking. Didn't he sound as if he were joking? He only pretended to be paranoid, justifiably perhaps since Eritreans had paid so dearly for their independence. It was too good to be true. Don't spit on your luck.

Now as I sat across from Kassahun at his desk and our conversation was interrupted by a phone call, I heard him say into the receiver once more, "You should go to Eritrea, no? You should see it. In ten years it could all be over," and I wasn't sure if he sounded as whimsical as I wanted him to be.

In one move hanging up the telephone and pushing a pile of manuscripts to the side of his desk so that he could see me better, Kassahun said, "That was your friend, Frank Chipasula. He wants me to come to a conference he is heading in Malawi called 'Singing for a New Dawn.'"

"He invited me too, Kassahun," I replied, "and Larry Sykes too. He's going to do a show for it. I'm not sure if Frank has the funding, but Larry says not to worry about it. Africa will deliver in its own way in its own time. I hope so."

I couldn't tell if the resigned smile and raised eyes of Kassahun, an African as well as an American businessman, wanted to confirm or deny Larry's proposition, as Kassahun asked, "So, Charles. What can I do for you?"

I was flipping through the new Africa World Press / Red Sea Press catalogue. "Great cover, Kassahun. I'm going to frame it."

"I am getting grief for it from some of my friends," Kassahun sighed. The cover had the 1623 Droeshout engraving of Shakespeare from the first collected edition of his plays—the long face, starched ruff, oversized bulbous forehead, hair falling over the ears, crescents under the eyes—framed by the African continent. I could understand how someone could see the image as smacking of the imposition of English and colonial culture—with Shakespeare as its icon—and burying African languages and cultures. But I saw the face of Shakespeare not pressing down but emerging from the continent: that is, an African Shakespeare who would do for an African language what Shakespeare did for English; whose "imagination" and "poet's pen,"—also pictured on the cover dipped into an inkwell of the world—would "bod[y] . . . forth / The forms of things unknown," "Turn . . . them to shapes, and give . . . to aery nothing / A local habitation and a name"[1]—an African habitation and an African name.

Kassahun continued, starting to laugh. "So I am getting myself in trouble by putting white authors on my book covers, no?"

"Not my picture," I joked back.

"But did I ever tell you that I used to think Shakespeare was African?" Kassahun quipped. I hoped he didn't mean the dubious way that Alexander Pushkin could be called African, based on his mother being the granddaughter of a self-proclaimed African prince in the early eighteenth century who became a leading general in the army of Peter the Great. By such a fungible measure I might find out that I was African myself, but no one knew my mother's or father's grandparents once their parents made the United States their home. Nor did I feel any need to know.

Kassahun continued, "As a child at school, I read Shakespeare and saw his plays in Amharic. I didn't realize they were translated. When I went to college at SUNY Binghamton and saw the name 'Shakespeare' on a booklist, I said, 'Great. We are reading an African author.'"

"Did anyone ever translate Dante's *Inferno* into Tigrinya, Kassahun?" I responded. "Eritrean history has plenty of imagery to match it. Marxist revolutions require greater than life-size saints and sinners as much as churches did. Also, forget any problems with Dante's *terza rima*. What I hear of Tigrinya, it rhymes even more easily than Italian."

"Charles," Kassahun answered, "You have eaten too much pasta in Asmara."

"You're right," I replied," "Now I want to make tomato sauce with that same Eritrean pepper, berbere. What would my Italian grandmother think?"

"That's easy," Kassahun said, "She would disown you, no?"

"Seriously, Kassahun," I continued, "I think I have an idea for another conference. Only this one would take place in Asmara. It's such a great city: safe, crime free, clean, open, easy to get around by walking, inexpensive. Asmara is beautiful and inspiring, and it has great politics. The people are so honest and friendly. At first I thought we should have a conference there for Amiri Baraka. You know the way the conference on Ngugi had to take place in Reading, Pennsylvania, since he could not get his proper recognition in Kenya? Maybe Baraka could only get his due in a place like Eritrea with its revolutionary Marxist politics, their long struggle and victory, all the explicitly political art, not just fiddling with language but always stressing content, struggle, and a 'useful shared vision'—isn't that the phrase he uses to describe the point of his writing so many eulogies?[2] Asmara even has the black / Italian connection, the love-hate relationship that Baraka has in Newark. I told you that he went to the same high school there as my father, right? After Baraka's reading at Ngugi's conference, I spoke with him, and he started joking about my name, being from Newark, and that he loved Italy because Italians eat as much corn and watermelons as black people. When I invited him to give a poetry reading last year at Penn State, he offered to bring good Newark Italian bread since he knew I'd be hungry for it since I lived in the anthracite outback. Listen to this from his new book, *Eulogies,* which includes a eulogy for his sister, who was murdered in 1984. I just read it while I was waiting in the hall. Baraka says he wants to write, 'In that African American tradition. In that democratic tradition reflected against a rainbow of nationalities and languages, telling of that growth through struggle of something beautiful, something wonderful . . . which we know to be the positive legacy of our lives on the planet earth.'[3] Doesn't this sound a lot like Ngugi's line in *Moving the Centre*—I've written it in the margin here—about his unrepentant universalism, 'retaining its roots in regional and national individuality yet upholding true humanism with its universal reaching out . . . [to] flower among the peoples of the earth, rooted as it is in the histories and cultures of the different peoples of the earth?'[4] Eritrea fits the same pattern: rooted in such an intense self-determination and awareness—plus speaking in a rainbow of languages 'that growth through struggle of something beautiful' for Africa and the entire planet to witness. At least that's what I saw."

Kassahun stretched to reach a pile of manuscripts on the far corner of his desk and started going through them. I continued, "But then I had what might be an even better idea for a conference in Asmara. Maybe the Baraka connection is too much, 'a bridge too far' as Larry likes to say. What about holding a conference in Eritrea on African writers? When I was walking around Asmara, I felt that it embodied so much of the kind of enlightened political and social vision that writers like Chinua Achebe, Wole Soyinka, and Ngugi express while the political reality of their once independent now neocolonial countries now represents the opposite. I might even have a name for the conference. Remember you gave me a copy of Dan Connell's book to take on my trip? He called Eritrea's armed struggle and victory "against all odds," but considering the political and social problems of twentieth-century Africa, the same phrase—*against all odds*—perfectly describes the struggle of these writers and many more of their African contemporaries in literature and its study. If only they could all gather in Asmara to see the dream becoming reality."

Kassahun found what he was looking for and gave me the typescript of a manuscript called "Black Lions." As I skimmed and tried to make sense of the subtitle, "The Creative Lives of Modern Ethiopia's Literary Giants and Pioneers," Kassahun put his left hand on his side desk to balance himself and leaned back in his huge swivel chair.

"That's a great idea, Charles. I have already had it and discussed it with Ngugi. He too has wanted a conference of African writers to take place in Africa. The first time I went back to Eritrea after the war was over, I said to myself I had to bring writers from all over Africa to see my country. I'm going to publish that manuscript you're holding. It's a series of portraits of twentieth-century Ethiopian writers. They have been writing in their own language, in their own script all these years. I want these writers—those who are still alive, before they die—to come to Asmara to meet with writers from all over Africa and be recognized for the first time by their peers. Let's set up a meeting with Ngugi about the conference after we come back from Malawi, no? Maybe we will get some more ideas there."

Malawi joined Eritrea on the bottom of any charts, tables, or statistics on the poorest countries in Africa and the world. A century of colonialism from outside and inside Africa and thirty years of war had emptied Eritrea's economy to the point that in trying at first to recover it could only manage to manufacture sanitary napkins and artificial limbs. Malawi's unspeakable degradation, however, could be attributed to one man: its first and only president since Malawian independence in 1964.

Frank Chipasula convened his conference to celebrate the demise of Hastings Kumuzu Banda, "president for life," or at least for thirty years. With a choice of exile or death, Frank was only one of his casualties. Banda's infamy included his penchant for throwing his opponents to the crocodiles in Lake Malawi and his Anglophilia, leading to the establishment of a school where African children wore elaborate, British school uniforms and straw boaters on their heads. His power beginning to unravel in the early 1990s, by 1994 he was a sick old man voted out of office in the country's first election. Frank returned to his country for the first time in twenty years to organize a gathering of Malawi's writers called "Singing for a New Dawn" in Blantyre, the capital of what was left of Malawi's economy.

Flying into Blantyre, I saw the Rift Valley, whose beginning I had scratched in Massawa and whose long dry grasses I had caressed in Kenya, open into a wide deep trench and the long Lake Malawi. Larry met me at the airport. As we sat for a moment in the snack bar overlooking the runway, I wanted to describe what I saw from the plane: "The color, Larry, the color of," I started, but he interrupted and, handing me a beer, said "Carlsberg green?"

Frank got us rooms in Blantyre's Mount Soche Hotel, thanks to a last-minute UNICEF contribution to the conference budget, but it was too late for Kassahun, who stayed home. A forest surrounded the hotel, built on a series of wooded terraces overlooking translucent green hills and valleys stripped of every tree, bush, and branch to make charcoal, the biggest local industry. What could have been a pastoral or tropical tapestry looked instead, due to unchecked erosion, like piles upon piles of slashed and shredded, bright cloth with burnt candles—the tree stumps—poking through.

Malawi's second biggest industry seemed to derive from such a landscape: bright African cloth from a company called Whitetex; a purple and black net of sky with exploding orange stars; Lake Malawi's best fish to eat, *chambo,* encircled in turquoise and maroon concentric circles of shrinking and expanding yellow dots; abstract magenta spears at rest on lime and lavender soil. Before the conference Larry and I bought several yards, decided we wanted new shirts, and had our pick of tailors, their feet pumping their sewing machines on sidewalks near the entrance to the outdoor market.

Between the extremes of a kind of spectrum from charcoal to vibrantly colored cloth and Malawi's godlike green, the market wound downhill into a dingy middle: broken tables half empty and littered with threadbare underwear, soiled bandages out of their packages, and pills long past their expiration date in cloudy plastic bags beside open cans of worm-eaten peanuts for sale. At least that was all I saw until the brightness of the lower oval of the eyes of a traditional healer caught me. Their color reproduced his colorless old clothes and gnarled beard. He stood inside a square of tables, no surface empty but covered with small bundles of sticks, dry flowers, rows of different kinds of bark and burls, piles of porcupine quills, water he said he had soaked a tortoise in, anteater scales, woodchips in alcohol, spirals of dried beans and grasses, wizened empty yellow pods, powders, roots, tiny bird's nests, soda caps filled with ashes of different colors and textures, unnamable composites packed into circles of pink wax, oily pieces of the local newspaper rolled like cigarettes, and one whole table of mosses squeezed into carved wooden scoops. They had to be bought together, and I bought six for a few kwachas.

As I gave him the money, I saw the market opening up into stalls of fresh vegetables, and his eyes caught me again. They seemed to overflow. Hundred of pounds of rich, creamy milk came crashing down through the red dust of the market like a tidal wave, tumbling the vegetables out of their baskets, washing the useless piles of rusty hardware shiny clean, and flooding the tables of his cures with bowl after bowl of light, pouring from rift to rift to rift, where three dark pillars haloed by stars shimmered in the moss I felt as I pushed my finger under the paper of one of the scoops. He blinked and smiled, and I was with Larry again, climbing back up the steps of the market and back to the hotel.

"You have met Malawi's answer to Dr. Livingstone," Larry said, offering me a taste from his bag of peanuts and adding, "Tomorrow let's hear the answers of Malawi's writers. But first let's watch the local edition of Blantyre's evening news." He signaled to walk with him across the street to a baobab on the corner surrounded by people buying and selling bananas, fish, nuts, and fried grasshoppers out of huge baskets. The tree's bark had been completely covered by pages of the day's newspaper with such an excess of staples that it seemed as if it couldn't be pulled down until it was believed. One page featured a picture of Frank sitting with Malawi's new president.

"Dr. Livingstone, I presume?"[5] Back in my room for the evening to prepare for the conference the next day, I read the famous words as I flipped through several old biographies of David Livingstone, replete with journal entries and letters, that I had brought with me, hoping to connect what they recorded in the middle of the nineteenth century with what I saw now nearing the end of the twentieth. "Dr. Livingstone, I presume?" I had grown up hearing and seeing cartoons in which a mustachioed, roly-poly, pith-helmeted explorer-journalist, Henry Stanley, directed the question to a ragged, emaciated, crazed-looking white man in an African jungle. But in Malawi, Livingstone was real, having explored it extensively. England's most famous, predatory missionary, with an alliterative love for using "commerce" and "Christianity" in the same phrase, named Blantyre after his birthplace in Scotland, claimed to have discovered the lake at least two and a half million years after a human ancestor first walked on its shore, and, in a quest as convoluted as intestines to find the source of the Nile, depended for his physical survival on the same Arab slave traders whom he had originally traveled to Africa to drive out.

Livingstone's response to Stanley, "You have brought me new life,"[6] could have been my own, I thought, as I paused in my reading and remembered the effect on me of the eyes of the healer in the market. The ants in the sand of Jericho, the doors and windows of Massawa, and the green walls of surf crashing onto the shores of Morocco had also left me with the same feeling. Still, I hoped the "new life" I meant was different from Livingstone's.

His words signaled the rejuvenation of his messianic impulse, echoing the words of Jesus at the conclusion of the Gospel of Matthew 28:18–19 that Livingstone applied both to himself and to his going to Africa: "All power is given unto me in heaven and in earth. Go ye therefore, and teach all nations, baptizing them in the name of the Father, and of the Son, and of the Holy Ghost: Teaching them to observe all things whatsoever I have commanded you: and, lo, I am with you always, even unto the end of the world." Looking up the quote in the pocket-size King James Version that I had carried from Jerusalem in 1985 to Eritrea in 1995 to here, I wrote "Livingstone" in the margin next to "All power . . . all nations . . . all things . . . always" and "given unto to me . . . even unto the end of the world."

A fundamentalist megalomaniac, Livingstone hated Africans, as one of his journal entries of 1853 revealed:

> The more intimately I become acquainted with barbarians, the more disgusting does heathenism become. It is inconceivably vile. It is lamentable to see those who might be children of God, dwelling in peace and love, so utterly the children of the devil. . . . They bestow honors and flattering titles on me in confusing profusion. All from the greatest to the least call me Father, Lord, etc. . . . They need a healer. May God enable me to be such to them.[7]

Nevertheless, he readily adapted his mission, cooling its rhetoric of religious fervor with the more measured, imperial language of "Her Majesty's Government," which "explicitly stated" that the main object of . . . [his] Expedition . . . was to extend the knowledge already attained of the geography and mineral and agricultural resources of Eastern and Central Africa—to improve our acquaintance with the inhabitants, and to endeavor to engage them to apply themselves to industrial pursuits and to the cultivation of their lands, with a view to the production of raw material to be exported to England.[8]

Code switching between Christian and colonial rhetoric, Livingstone constructed and set off a cultural bomb that rumbled for the next hundred years and more, and its fallout still rained not only in Malawi but in every part of Africa where I went. "You have brought me new life" read the caption under my imagined cartoon of a personified England greeting Livingstone with a personified Africa in tow.

"You have brought me new life." As I repeated the phrase and imagined Livingstone in the cartoon, I suddenly realized that he had my face. I continued to read the journals and began trying what Livingstone wrote on myself. A lot of his observations and attitudes seemed to fit, and I started copying them at random into my notebook.

"Africa was a wonderful country for the appetite. The mere animal pleasure of traveling was great. I was opening a path. I liked to investigate other human beings. I had my map, my mission, and I scrambled. I wanted the raw materials. Enjoyed traveling the unexplored. My time was now and the future. Who had a culture? I had my tools, my pencil. I would never build on another man's foundation. I promised them great buildings and great ruins in a thousand years. Poetry was the center of my life. Get that rat off my crotch. Yes, I wanted to speak English. Why not? I believed in independence. I liked the appetite and wanted the answer. They lived by force. Huddled in each other like sacks. Ate by force. Hung their dead up on hooks to be smoked. Believed in force. In blood up to their throats. Legitimate commerce opened them up. I broke down the middle wall for something higher too. Ordinary judgment fell short. I discovered what they hadn't for two and half million years. I discovered the great lake, its center of pure waves and fish swimming in my words. When I wrote about the place it became my name, my appetite, my mission, my map, my own. Dr. Livingstone, I presume? You have brought me new life."

"Dr. Livingstone? Dr. Cantalupo? Dr. Cantalupo? Cantalupo. I'll meet you at breakfast. The bus leaves in half an hour." Larry's knocking on the door and calling my name woke me up.

I met him on the bus. He had saved me a seat—the last one left on the bus, too—and was talking with two older men in the seat in front of him.

"He wants to put his picture on kwachas, just the way Banda did," said the shorter of the two, with the body of a twenty-five-year-old bantamweight.

"So what's the difference?" said the other one, laughing and elegant in a finely pressed sharkskin suit clinging tightly to his plump frame: "As long as he lets us have the same videos that the chairman of the censorship board banned but kept for himself."

"Yes!" retorted the first, standing up as if he was ready to fight. "I also want to see Central Bookshop stock every book with sex, social reform, or communism in the title that he wouldn't let me read until I found them in the library of the prison where he thought he'd shut me up."

"Charles," Larry said, also getting up but stooping to avoid hitting his head on the bus ceiling. "Please let me introduce you. Meet Kanyama Chiume, a great Malawian patriot since the forties in Nyasaland: the man who fought Banda and won! And here is Aubrey Kachinque, Malawi's first modern novelist who is now the retired managing director of the Blantyre Steam Laundry."

"It's a pleasure and an honor," I said as we shook hands, and I sat next to Larry, who was about to continue when Chiume spoke first.

"What we don't need is worshippers. Just be curious—that's enough. Don't stop. Ask questions no one else does. I have seen my small country—with so much energy, so much gentility, so much wealth and so much generosity—rise and fall too many times. What's next?"

Kachinque answered, "Our sausage of a country gets sliced and sliced until there's nothing left for the people to eat. I don't know how our way of life still survives. Call it our undying history or—"

Chiume cut him off. "It won't survive if we don't bring it out in the open. No more secrets someone wants to show me around the corner."

Larry looked out the window. "I'll bet they have some secrets," he said in a low voice. A white Land Rover without a speck of dirt sped by.

"Who's that?" I asked, before seeing "British Council" imprinted on the car doors. Just then our own bus door slammed shut. I had to slide closer to Larry as the aisle filled with twenty more people who had just boarded.

"And we're off to see the president," Larry laughed as the bus lurched forward and everyone on it, seated or standing, jerked back a foot.

With the engine noise and everyone talking, I could barely hear him but asked, "Is Frank already there?"

"No," Larry said. "He's in the back of the bus. You can bet that those British Council folks get there first, though. They're the big writers."

"The big men?" Kachinque laughed. "I thought we Africans were the big men."

Larry almost roared, but again could barely be heard. "They're big all right. Big women too. And we're all packed on this bus to climb the holy mountain to meet the president in his palace."

As the bus started to climb, filled with mostly Malawian writers and scholars from Malawi and abroad, I could see that we were behind the British Council Land Rover. A few blocks past the Mount Soche, I noticed that the buildings had abruptly stopped, replaced by stalls and lean-tos that made the outdoor market where we had walked yesterday look light, airy, and rich. Yet even these buildings became progressively smaller and flimsier until soon we were speeding past crowds of people standing in vacant lots with puddles and smoky fires.

Kachinque turned around to Larry and me and said, "Prepare to see a miracle in this part of Malawi." In a few seconds, the crowds of people disappeared and, as we passed through a gate with four soldiers, Kachinque pointed out the window, "Look. Trees!"

Chiume now turned around too. "We will see more when we go up to the Zomba plateau next week."

"And we will climb even higher," Kachinque added.

"Higher than this? Impossible," Larry quipped.

As the road spiraled higher and higher up the small, steep mountain, I saw only evergreens and clouds. We seemed to have left Malawi and all of Africa behind. The round and round, the continuing climb, and the bus's grinding gears made me spellbound, not realizing at first that John Donne's lines about truth from his third satire played like a tape loop in my head: "On a huge hill, / Cragged, and steep, Truth stands, and hee that will / Reach her, about must, and about must go, / And what th' hill's suddennes resists, winne so."[9]

I awoke when Larry said in mock seriousness but closer to the truth than I was, "Welcome to Mt. Olympus," as the bus passed through the ornate palace gate and stopped near an entrance on the side of a sprawling yellow Chatsworth-like palace without the gardens of Derbyshire surrounding it.

We entered a room that had a long table spread with a creamy lace tablecloth, teacups, plates, and a small parking lot of silver spoons. An aroma of freshly baked muffins filled the room, prompting the Macmillan Malawi publisher's representative to comment, "Just what hospitality experts recommend. Welcome your guests into your house with the smell of muffins. And the bone china," she continued, turning over a cup to see the Spode imprint.

Being curious writers and scholars, most of us wanted to turn it over to identify it, too, before getting our tea, which was a mistake, since before more than one or two cups could be poured and a single muffin touched, two frowning men in black suits, one with a red and one with a green tie—both representing the colors of Malawi's flag—clapped their hands in unison, one on each side of the room, and announced, also in unison, "The president will see you now." Just then I looked around to see if the British writers had joined us, but the only two other white people besides me were an Australian African theater specialist who taught in Botswana and an elderly, dapper Italian Marxist professor from Turin.

Still frowning and moving quickly, one man in the black suit pushed us and the other pulled us into a circular room divided between a semicircle of concentric pews and desks and a huge ebony table reflecting ornate chandeliers and tapestries on the wall featuring eighteenth-century European nobility enjoying the outdoors. I couldn't tell if the tapestries covered any windows, but the room seemed to be designed to let nothing in from outside that wasn't invited.

As we filed into our seats, a loud clap and then another let us know that we should stop talking. As soon as we did, a small entourage in shiny suits and ties entered from stage right behind the ebony table and, following a prompt by our two frowning escorts now seated in the front row, we all stood up, expecting to see the new president, Bakili Muluzi, but it was only a member of his cabinet, and we sat down. The same process recurred three minutes later, only with a slightly larger entourage, and the same again two minutes later, again with the entourage increased.

One minute later, the president walked in alone. Asking us to "Please, be seated," he welcomed us graciously, saying that he joined us in "singing for a new dawn" in Malawi. He praised Frank and offered to commemorate our gathering with a promise to reduce the exorbitant tax on paper for newsprint and books: a levy that was the most effective kind of censorship since any local publisher who wasn't government subsidized could not afford to buy paper.

Looking across the room, I saw Chiume roll his huge, bloodshot eyes. As Larry started to get up, saying, "Mr. President, Frank Chipasula has asked me to give you . . ." the lights went out. I heard shuffling from the sides of the room, expected machine gun fire to pierce the darkness, grabbed my book bag beside me, and felt to see if there was enough room under the desk to crawl under it. After maybe ten more seconds, I heard a loud motor somewhere outside and realized that a generator had started. The lights came back on. Still standing in his Yugoslavia yellow soccer windbreaker that he had bought the day before to ward off the cold—maybe the only "XXL" piece of clothing in Blantyre—Larry didn't miss a beat as he continued, ". . . this image to remember our gathering here today." The president wasn't listening, but instead he looked wide-eyed back and forth to his ministers flanking him on either side of the table, who looked back at him wide-eyed too. The brief spell of graciousness was broken. Larry held up the picture, which had five naked, bottom-heavy copper-colored women in a row viewed from the side and running with sticks in a kind of green dawn.

"Thank you," the president replied and without another word left the room followed by everyone at the table. Maybe Larry should have dressed the women in T-shirts with Muluzi's picture, I thought: the way all the women in Banda's time who attended his rallies had to wear T-shirts with his face on them. Sliding down my pew to tell Larry this, I saw one of our frowning escorts signaling me to turn around and slide the other way toward the door where our entire group was being directed now not only by our escorts but by three more heavily built men who looked mean and like burly soldiers unused to being stuffed into suits too small for them.

As all of our escorts were repeating the phrase "Please board the buses immediately," I realized at the palace door that I had forgotten my book bag under the desk.

As I turned around, I addressed the guard. "I'm very sorry. I forgot my book bag. I need to go back and get it since"—I added hoping for a little understanding with some humor—"I probably won't be coming back."

The beefiest escort, who now stood next to him, glowered and replied, "No, you won't be coming back."

As we rode down the hill in our beat-up and rickety bus again I saw the spotless, white British Council Land Rover in front of us. Suddenly our driver accelerated. As we passed and saw three stony faces staring out the windows, everyone on the bus as if on cue started cheering and laughing. The good mood carried us all the way to the conference site, the cultural center of the Alliance Française, swaddled in all sizes of palm trees and bushes, also on the outskirts of Blantyre but in the opposite direction from the president's palace.

As we deboarded the bus at the door and filed into the building, I caught up with Larry carrying his picture under his arm. I still wanted to goad him about his presentation *interruptus*. Also I could see that he was enjoying taking mental pictures of our new surroundings and yet another cultural shift beginning to unfold.

Amid the commotion of the entrance, he had to bend his huge frame close to my face to hear me. "Who needs Mt. Olympus when we can have a Malawian Montparnasse?"

Before he could answer, we were swept up into a crowd, none of whom I recognized from the bus. Instead they were Malawian writers of all ages and levels of experience and accomplishment—students to newly released detainees who had stood with Banda in the beginning of Malawian independence but who were soon thereafter betrayed—poured into the building. For the next three days, wave after wave of intense, personal expression silenced for the last thirty years surged nonstop, "Singing for a New Dawn." They didn't have to say "You have brought me new life" to anyone because each of them powerfully provided it themselves.

Seeing Frank in the crowd, I gently grabbed his arm as he passed me and said, "Frank, this is great. Congratulations." He looked even more troubled than I imagined he would have appeared when we spoke for the first time on the telephone four years before about Ngugi.

Letting him go, I turned around and saw a woman whom I had met earlier—a Malawian linguistics professor who taught in the United States. She shook her head, saying, "The British are driving him crazy. They are complaining to him that they have not been listed properly in the program. They want their names to appear under the 'Poetry Readings' category, even though no one's name is listed. And get this. I was just talking with my friend Judith, who teaches in the English department at the University of Malawi up in Zomba. The roly-poly Brit in the white suit with the bright pink face kept gesturing toward me from his chair where he was sitting with the other two. Finally when I went over to him, he said, 'Can you get us some tea?' I simply walked away, pretending I couldn't hear him."

"Who are they?" I asked.

Her angry tone cooled into a more academic description. "One is the editor of a Penguin anthology of modern African poetry," she answered.

"I know it," I replied. "It's the most popular anthology there is, but it's all in English and—"

She cut me off, saying, "Yes. It should be called the most popular delusion of African poetry. The other is a poet whom I met as we were leaving the president's palace. He invited me to ride with them in their Land Rover and tried to impress me by saying that he wanted to talk with me about some Malawian imagery he was putting in a poem he was writing for the Christmas Festival of Carols at Cambridge. Maybe I should have offered him the poetic detail that six out of seven of my best friends here have AIDS? Christmas in Cambridge and July in Malawi. I mean, what's the difference?! The third one I know nothing about, other than he likes to scowl when no one brings him his tea."

As she spoke I worried to myself: could this happen at the conference in Asmara?

Her final comment gave me an idea for the poetry readings and workshops Frank had assigned me to coordinate. She said, "I am telling everyone

I know only to speak in Chichewa or whatever their mother tongue is when these Brits try to talk with them."

Unfortunately, her plan didn't work because the British Council had already stipulated and required the conference program to state that their workshops—labeled A and B—would be conducted in English only, and membership in the workshops was preassigned and not by choice.

When I began my workshop by asking in English if anyone knew any languages other than English, everyone smiled politely at first, as if I had told a teacherly, unfunny joke. But then I asked, "Would anyone here like to translate 'Singing for a New Dawn' into Chichewa?" The older students laughed, and the younger students shot their hands up. In a few minutes we had three different versions of a Chichewa translation. By the first half hour we also had translations into Tumbuka, Bemba, Kokola, Lomwe, Sena, and Tonga.

Turning the tables, they asked me if I could give them translations in Afrikaans and Portuguese. My asking "Why?" got the biggest laugh of all. The youngest student, dressed in a green and yellow uniform skirt and black polo top blurted out, "Because you are white." When I said I couldn't provide any translation but Italian, she started speaking to me in Italian. Two of the older students offered the Afrikaans and Portuguese translations. Our first session together ended with my asking for a chorus of translations of the words "white," "black," "red," and "green" in all the languages that anyone knew in the class.

At the plenary session poetry readings two days later, the British poets—who barely said a word to Larry and me throughout the conference—had prevailed at listing their names in the program. Workshop C, however, simply listed the titles of a dozen poems, their language, and their one translation into English: "Singing for a New Dawn."

As Larry shot pictures of the poets climbing the stage like "a huge hill, / Cragged and steep" to read in their own languages, the Englishman who wanted his tea served to him scowled and waved his finger, mouthing, "No, no. No, no."

Two weeks later, back in the United States when I called Kassahun to arrange our meeting with Ngugi to discuss the possible conference in Asmara, Kassahun asked, "So what did you learn in Malawi?"

"Too much," I replied. "For starters I can tell you that Malawi's flag is a picture not a symbol. I saw a red sun rising out of two horizontal bars—one green and one red—against a black sky."

"Ah, you got up to the Zomba Plateau, no?" Kassahun responded. "So what did you see in Chingwe's hole? Everyone Banda disappeared? Did you have a rope?"

"No rope, no disappeared, Kassahun," I answered, "but lots of ideas for our conference. When should we meet with Ngugi?"

"As soon as possible," Kassahun said quickly. "I mentioned to him our conversation about the conference. I am leaving for Eritrea tomorrow, but you should call up Ngugi and go and speak with him while I'm gone."

I drove through the streets of Orange, New Jersey, again. Nearly four years had passed since I had first visited Ngugi there with Larry. Last summer Ngugi and his wife, Njeeri, had invited Barbara, our daughters, Alicia and Alexandra, and me to attend the naming ceremony of his newborn son, Thiong'o. As Kamau Brathwaite presided, reciting from memory a long poem that recalled Ngugi's grandmother giving him the Gikuyu name "Kamau," the winds of Limuru blew through Ngugi's "Seven Oaks" backyard with a deep yet gentle chant in Gikuyu rising through the trees and weaving through the smoke of roasting goat. Otherwise, my memories of the place where I was born remained unchanged. Passing the working-class houses of my teenage years musician friends in Orange who were raised to like Frank Sinatra, wanted to be Jimi Hendrix, and sang both, I felt guilty that I had just cut short a visit with my mother to have more time to discuss the prospect of the conference with Ngugi. I made sure to stop first at the Italian bakery down the street from his house to bring him the bread I was raised on, which he enjoyed, and which we had also brought to his son's party. As I sliced him a piece at the party, five-year-old Alicia gnawed on the rib of a goat.

She came with me again today. Ngugi always asked for her and smilingly called her "the little organizer" since the naming party for Thiong'o, when she got all the children together to put on a play with one of Ngugi's daughters playing guitar. We sat at Ngugi's dining room table, where he showed Alicia how to play a game of spinning and flipping quarters for around fifteen minutes until Njeeri came in to invite Alicia to join her in the kitchen. Now came my turn to play "organizer."

As soon as I began to describe the prospect of a conference in Asmara, it felt anticlimactic, since Kassahun had already told me that he and Ngugi had discussed it, and he liked the idea. The conversation picked up when, offering "Against All Odds: African Literatures into the 21st Century" as a possible title for the project, I explained that the phrase most often used to characterize Eritrea's struggle for independence—"against all odds"—struck me as a good way to describe the struggle of African writers in the twentieth century, too. However, as soon as I said it, I felt self-conscious either because the phrase was, after all, a cliché, or it sounded overly dramatic and therefore might offend Ngugi's normally low-key sensibility. His own struggles and major literary achievements notwithstanding, I could never imagine Ngugi—who would just as soon lie on the living room floor or sit on a couch and play quarters with Alicia as discuss postcolonial theory—applying such a phrase to his own efforts. Therefore, hoping to distract him from thinking twice about the title, I quickly added, "It's not hype, Ngugi. When I consider the vastness of the political and social problems of twentieth-century Africa and the likelihood of African writers having achieved so much during the same period, and add on that they were hardly known before, the phrase seems right."

I saw the same skeptical look on Ngugi's face as when I asked him, when I visited him my first time at his home in Orange, why the word "struggle" recurred so much in his writing. "I understand, but the title might be an exaggeration unless it applies to the struggle of African writers in African languages. Look at Heinemann and other publishers. They have served African writers in Europhone languages, including me, rather well."

I couldn't disagree, but I felt that focusing only on African language writers would make the project too narrow and put me in the position of organizing something that, for the most part, I knew nothing about, even if I had heard a lot of Tigrinya in Eritrea, Chichewa in Malawi, and whatever African languages I heard similarly without understanding elsewhere. I recognized, of course, Ngugi's own powerful record on the issue since 1987, when he published *Decolonizing the Mind* and bid farewell to his writing in English. My 1994 conference on him in Reading, Pennsylvania—*Ngugi wa Thiong'o: Texts and Contexts*—theorized and offered a few examples at least of how the Gikuyu language was the ultimate critical context for his work. Beyond this, however, African languages were foreign to me: "Greek," as the saying goes. Even if I did not need any convincing, at least since 1993 when I first spoke with Ngugi in Orange, that the empowerment of African languages in Africa and the world offered unprecedented opportunities and potential for advancement just as vernacular languages instead of Latin and Greek once did in Europe during the Renaissance, I still only knew books by African writers in English or in translation into English. And even though I saw no reason why Malawi's languages shouldn't take the stage in Malawi, African languages as the primary focus of a worldwide, millennial gathering of Africa's greatest writers and scholars, many of whom did not agree with Ngugi's position and the vast majority of whom did not write in African languages, seemed too esoteric. How many African language writers were there, and how many would want to hear them? Did anyone have a list of African language writers the way there were lists of African languages? And who would want to provide funds for such an event to happen?

As I thought I saw my project's hope for success dissolving into air, Ngugi continued, "In my almost forty years as a writer, the conferences on African writing in English that I have been invited to are countless, but I have never been invited to or even heard about a conference called for the sole purpose of discussing literature in African languages."

Knowing that Ngugi's support of the project would be crucial, and despite my feeling that only emphasizing African languages would marginalize it and weaken its chances to be a success, I agreed with him, grasping at least at the notion that the conference would be a first. If Ngugi would lead, I would follow, a little like Don Quixote and Sancho Panza.

"I'm sure I can get Penn State to support us," I replied, wondering if I really could when I only knew of one or two people in the entire university who worked in African languages.

"Ngugi, do you think NYU will support the project?" I asked, a lot more sure about it than Penn State since NYU supported anything Ngugi wanted to do, if only to keep him as one of its most distinguished faculty.

As Ngugi replied, "I will ask," I looked at my proposed first title for the conference in my notebook and, inserting a carat between "African" and "Literatures" added "Languages and" above the line for it to read "African Languages and Literatures into the 21st Century."

Before I could read back the new name to Ngugi, Alicia ran into the room from the kitchen, with Njeeri following her and laughing, "That little girl is smart, Charles. She told me the next time I cook goat, she'll come back and play her violin."

When I went back to Penn State that fall, I visited every possible dean, vice president, and department chair that I could to ask them to support the project with "seed money" based on the success of the Penn State conference on Ngugi in Reading in 1994. By December, I had raised thirty thousand dollars, perhaps because Penn State is one of the largest universities in the United States—with eighty thousand students and twenty campuses—and has a lot of "seed" to spare, but also, I thought, because the project appealed to these administrators for what they considered to be its relevance to their efforts, desperate at times, to promote cultural diversity within the university. Yet again, as I found the argument for the potentially "Renaissance" power for African languages easy to understand, so did I find it easy to explain and, the more and more I explained it, easy to believe in, at least within the confines of the academy.

Meanwhile, Kassahun was flying back and forth to Asmara, where he too was knocking on doors to get local and government support for the project. A key step was to obtain the backing of the president of Eritrea, Isaias Afwerki. I remembered seeing him at the barbershop. Kassahun spoke so warmly and casually about him that I wondered if Kassahun might spot him there one day from the Africa World Press office and walk across the street to ask him. But instead, Kassahun told me that he enlisted the support of someone named Zemhret Yohannes to ask Isaias, and that when they presented the idea to him he liked it so much that he made them promise "to use him" in any way they wanted to ensure its success. Also, Zemhret had agreed to join Kassahun, Ngugi, and me in co-chairing the project.

I wondered if Zemhret was a government economist or treasury official—I had forgotten that Eritrea's Constitutional Commission chair, Bereket Selassie, had mentioned him—but Kassahun told me that his title was director of research and documentation in Eritrea's main political party, the People's Front for Democracy and Justice, the PFDJ. I feared that the distinctly Marxist, revolutionary-sounding name of the party coupled with the amorphousness of Zemhret's title, again much like Ngugi's insistence on stressing African languages, would put off presumably staid, serious, Western foundations like Ford, Rockefeller, and Carnegie that both Penn State's development officers and Kassahun were insisting we should now contact for their support. However, I had to listen, even if I didn't understand, no differently than I had over the last dozen years in Jericho, Cairo, the Sinai, Senegal, Togo, Kenya, Morocco, the barn of straw in Hecla, Casamance, Cameroon, the nursing home room where my father died, Eritrea the first time, and Malawi.

CHAPTER NINE

Red Sea Foam

ARRIVING BACK IN ASMARA IN THE EARLY SPRING OF 1997, FOR THE FIRST time in ten years of traveling to Africa, I didn't feel like a stranger. I wasn't just another name and number to expressionless immigration and customs officials in cast-off clothing: a lonely white man jostled by locals dragging overstuffed suitcases and heavy large boxes bursting their tape; a mere spectator and self-conscious presence amid families and friends embracing, kissing, holding up babies, and soaking each other's shoulders with tears of joy. Instead, as I walked into the unlit parking lot outside of the airport and gazed into the dark and cold Asmara midnight, Kassahun appeared wearing a cowboy hat. He gave me a bear hug and a "Welcome to Asmara."

The next morning, the few blocks between my hotel and the Africa World Press office seemed almost as familiar as Bethlehem, Pennsylvania: this tree, that archway, this crack in the sidewalk, that café, this window, that flower again. Easily finding my way to the Africa World Press office, again I saw Arefine, standing in the heavy iron and plate glass office doorway, across from the busy *Posta Centrale,* and greeting his many friends—including the old man in the heavy double-breasted suit whom I met last visit—poking a head in and out of the office or stopping to exchange a few more words about an illness, a job, a death, or a marriage. When I appeared in the same doorway, again I heard, "*Ah, Charlus. Benvenuto a Asmara. Avete un buon viaggio? Venga all' interno e rendasi comodo.*"

"*Buongiorno, Arefine. Com' esta?* It's great to be back, *un altra volta. Ancora, grazie.*"

Immediately I heard another voice—"Hey, who's this Asmarino wasting our time with Italian talk"—and Kassahun emerged out of a doorway on the side of the office. "Come on back, Charles," he said ushering me into a long room with long, varnished work tables covered with papers on either side and lit up with two banks of overhead room-length fluorescent lights.

"Hang up your jacket," he added, pointing to a deco chrome and ebony coat rack suitable for the design section of any museum of modern art but even more at home in Asmara with its Italian modernist cinemas and ministries and futuristic winged gas station. "Now let's get to work," he continued, as I saw a tall young woman with his mouth and chin and with her hair piled high at a computer set up on the end of one of the tables. "You can check your email, but first I want to introduce you to my daughter, Kidan, who is living here before she starts graduate school." The intensity of her working pushed my eyes toward the end of the room and through an open glass door where I saw shelves and boxes filled with Africa World / Red Sea Press books: *The Invention of Somalia, Silence is Not Golden, Against All Odds, Kebra Nagast, Being and Becoming Oromo, Kush, The Jewel of Nubia, Beyond Survival, The World of Ngugi.* . . . Kassahun was speaking quickly, "Kidan will work with you directly in organizing your schedule. Now I must leave for a meeting. I will see you tonight at the reading." He was out the door before I could go over to Kidan, who was getting up as we shook hands.

With a warm smile, which I tried to return at the same time as I was wondering about the reading Kassahun mentioned, Kidan said, "Hi. My father has told me a lot about you. Did he forget to tell you about the reading?"

"Hello, Kidan. It's a pleasure to meet you," I replied, just catching myself from saying "*Piacere*," which would have sounded ridiculous between us. "What reading did your father mean?" I asked. Kassahun had told me to bring my work for a poetry reading, but he didn't tell me when or where it would take place.

"Yours," Kidan replied. I tried not to seem surprised or anxious as she continued. "I have gotten the Alliance Française to sponsor it. A friend of mine here plays *krar*, and he will join you along with a young woman poet whom a lot of people in Asmara are talking about. Today I have scheduled a series of meetings for you, and we better get started."

Without another word she picked up a file of papers, took her heavy sweater off the coat rack, and went out the door, with me rushing to follow her. As we passed Arefine sitting in the outer office at the long desk covered with Eritrean newspapers in Tigrinya and glossy Italian magazines, he was getting up to greet the same little boy in his school uniform whom I had met during my last visit. Without Arefine's prompting, he ran over to me, kissed the top of my hand and put it to his forehead just like last time. Expecting I would meet him again, I had brought a box of red and blue pens labeled Penn State and reached in my book bag to give them to him.

"*Ciao*, Arefine."

"*Arrivaderci*, Charlus," Arefine replied, raising his hand and quickly twirling it twice.

Over the next two hours Kidan had arranged appointments with Eritrea's ministers of information, education, and finance. Kassahun had managed to open their doors for us, and we entered feeling welcome, receiving warm expressions of support for our project, detailed responses on how it would help Eritrea, and sincere questions on how Eritrea could help us. As when I had first visited Asmara, I was marveling at having such immediate access to the kind of people I would never be able to meet in my own country, when Kidan said, "Okay. Now the British Council."

Even passing the bulging shelves of my favorite writers like Hardy, the Romantics, Marlowe, Milton, and Hobbes in a wide, bright, and clean room with nearly every seat taken by young people reading, I didn't look forward after Malawi to becoming friendly much less asking for the support of someone whose diplomatic disappointment at being relatively powerless in a remote, not very powerful country had made him become more British than most British back home. Outside the director's door, the secretary asked us to wait a moment and if we would like coffee or tea.

I replied antagonistically and a little too loudly, "*Boon,*" meaning Eritrean coffee, meaning Italian, although this would be my fifth so far that morning.

Looking startled, Kidan's eyes opened a little wider than usual. "Nothing for me, thanks," she said.

As I smiled to reassure her I heard, "Dr. *Charlus,* welcome," as the director opened his door, and I was greeted by an Eritrean, Dr. Meles Negusse. "Kassahun has told me all about your project. I have an idea," he added as we entered his office and sat down. "The British Council would like to support the performance of one of Ngugi's plays, *I Will Marry When I Want,* but we also want to do the production translated into Tigrinya." Negusse dispelled the specter of Malawi's British Council in my mind, so that when the coffee arrived, I thought that if he asked for tea, I would have been happy to get it for him.

Walking to the Alliance Française and retracing downhill the walk I first took from the Albergo Italia to find Africa World Press, I remembered my feeling back then like a pilgrim—reinforced again by hearing the clanging bells of the Romanesque-style red cathedral. But now with Kidan I was simply joining everyday Asmarinos streaming past me in a hard day's work.

Nestled beside the Albergo Italia, the Alliance Française in Asmara, like the Alliance Française in Malawi, set a great example of joining the local culture instead of insinuating its own, at least under its present director, who seemed right out of the mold, ideologically and physically, of the students at the barricades in 1968 Paris. "He produced the CD of and is marrying Eritrea's best new pop star, Faytinga," Kidan told me as we ducked under the trellis of the Alliance's lush garden.

When Kidan introduced me, I said "*Bonjour,* Claude." Strikingly handsome with a Charles de Gaulle nose, he ran his long fingers though his floppy dark hair.

"Hi, Kidan. Hi, Charles. Welcome to Asmara. We really look forward to your reading. What can I get you?"

His matter-of-fact friendliness and immediate sense of solidarity that we were all working together and inspired to do so by nothing more or less than the spirit of the new nation of Eritrea itself—a feeling in the streets, in the ministries, at the press, and wherever we went—made me look forward to my reading not as the poet or a professor or someone important but simply to join hands with Eritreans in celebrating a sense of themselves and giving it to one another so that this feeling would never be destroyed here or wherever we called home.

Later at the reading as I heard the electrified high treble twang of the lyre-like Eritrean *krar* and tried to fit into its player's graceful intensity with the refrain I first imagined echoing on the mountainsides of Nefasit two years before—"Without a war, without a war . . ."—the rhythm and the phrase seemed at least momentarily to join in a pattern of eighth note, quarter note, double eighth note, quarter rest, eighth rest, eighth note, and somewhere in the room I heard "A love supreme, a love supreme."

When I finished reading, the *krar* didn't stop but only slowed the pattern, replacing the eighth notes and rests with quarters, and the quarter notes and rests with halves, whereupon the young woman whom Kidan had told me about took the stage. She seemed shy and uncomfortable in a starched Western dress, but hearing her first word, which I didn't catch since I was returning to my seat next to Kassahun, the audience started laughing and applauding.

"What was her poem about?" I asked Kassahun after she finished and I saw Alemseged Tesfai, modern Eritrea's greatest historian and one of its best writers, wiping tears from his eyes as he doubled over in laughter.

Kassahun answered, "The poem is called 'Go Crazy Over Me.'[1] It describes a boy and a girl who don't know one another flirting as one passes the other on the street. They know they're acting crazy, but they don't care and just want to fall in love, no?"

"That's normal enough," I responded.

"And that is why everyone enjoys it so much. This country hasn't seen or heard much normalcy—except war—in a long time," Kassahun replied.

"Speaking of enjoyment," he continued, "Kidan told me you worked hard today. Now that you're the bard of Asmara, why don't we drive down to my family's farm in Nefasit tomorrow. Come to the press after breakfast, and we'll leave from there."

Only a few remaining wisps of foamy clouds scuttled down the steep sides of the escarpment as we began our midmorning descent from Asmara. Kassahun drove a beat-up, white Toyota pickup that, if it had a machine gun mounted in the back, would have exactly resembled the "technicals" driven by Somalia's warlords a thousand miles south. Remembering but not seeing the *beles* or prickly pears I saw brimming out of baskets lining every part of the road with even the shadow of a shoulder, I said, "What will we eat, Kassahun, with no *beles* to buy?"

"We will stop at my sister's," Kassahun said, almost officially. "You remember meeting her husband? We'll eat real *injera*, *zigni*, *schuro*, and even some pasta. Now let me tell you about my meetings this morning and since I've been here. I spoke with Zemhret, and we decided our budget should be at least two million dollars. He said he would ask the NUEYS and NUEW to . . ."

"The what?" I asked.

"One is the National Union of Eritrean Youth and Students, and the other is the National Union of Women. They are civic organizations that carry over a lot of the same values as the EPLF maintained during the war. Zemhret also said that he would ask the minister of transportation to help us transport our guests around the city and the country. I also met the president of the big Eritrean bank who is an old friend of mine and with the head of the Chamber of Commerce, another old friend. Before we go back we need to go to city hall to meet the mayor. I have an appointment tomorrow with my friend Menghis, who is helping to wire the country for the Internet, because he's already called me about our project. He went to Penn. Also, the Rotary Club here called me and wants us to make a presentation at their next meeting. I better slow down around this curve, or the conference will be the least of our worries."

Like the last time I came down the escarpment, a vision of mountain after gorge after mountain after valley stretched endlessly. Only faith would let one think that it led eventually to the Red Sea. I knew the ritual enacted by Kassahun as he rolled down his window and said, "Do you feel it getting warmer? We are almost at Nefasit." He continued, "This trip has shown me that we need to come to Eritrea every few months to make this project work. Next time we need to meet with the foreign embassies and consulates in town. When we get back, you and Kidan should start visiting the hotels in town to let them know about our plans. I have to show you the site where a new five-star hotel is being built, the Asmara Palace. I can also show you the new building for the Sabur Press, which we passed in Asmara on Liberation Avenue as we were leaving. You saw it, no?"

"Where, Kassahun? I'd love to go in someday," I replied.

"We will try before we go back to New Jersey. If not this time, next," he promised. "Now let's turn here and go out to the farm before we go to my sister's house."

From the road winding away from town and following a dry riverbed down a valley, I saw round stone huts, some with and some without conical thatch roofs up on the mountain. "We call them *agudo*," Kassahun said. "Most of them have been destroyed from the war. The government is now allotting a few acres and a one-room house to replace them, no?" The wrecked huts looked grim as I remembered the one-room houses I had seen on the way to Massawa: the towering stalks of corn seeming to grow right out of their roofs and swaying with the warm breeze off the sea in an ancient, newly returned rhythm that also let me hear: "without a war, without a war . . ."

Kassahun stopped the car by a gate, and as we followed a faint path through a thick green tangle filled with yellow thorn birds, he walked me through "the farm." "The war ruined it," he said, "but beneath the weeds you can find a few traces of the buildings. That hole was the swimming pool." I saw a few bands of turquoise concrete the color of the sky in the brush. "I have hired somebody to start cultivating the area again. You should have seen all the terraces back then. Let's look around." Passing through patches of oranges, shin-high coffee plants, black pepper bushes, and banana trees, we came to the riverbed overhung by huge trees along the banks. Its dry, bright pallor made me squint, and in the middle of it I saw a family of nomads. Two old men in dirty white turbans, three younger women in bright pastel robes and head scarves, five children in colorless, tattered T-shirts and shorts, and two camels, with no one holding the ropes on their bridles, stood around a dark muddy spot roughly two feet in diameter. Kassahun continued, "I was always warned to stay out of the riverbed since a violent flood could come rushing down it in a minute and with no warning. I used to sit up in that tree and read, pretending not to hear my name being called to perform various chores around the farm. I only wanted to read and read."

Nine months later as I was planning to return to Eritrea with Kassahun, I recalled that simple scene of a contented reader in a tree overhanging a dry riverbed offering a glimpse of precious water and hoped to go back myself for a breather from the torrent that the idea for the conference had become. Fed by Ngugi's ideas, I had been working with two directors of development at Penn

State who were more responsive, articulate, and helpful than anyone I had met at the university in twenty years. Kassahun had made several trips around Africa, including Eritrea, and to Europe. President Isaias had agreed to serve as Against All Odds' honorary chair and to be joined by Meles Zenawi, prime minister of Ethiopia, and Yoweri Museveni, president of Uganda. The most recent issue of *Time* magazine featured Eritrea as a new and shining example of "Africa Rising."[2] Against All Odds would be a summit of language, politics, and power. As our chief liaison with the government, Zemhret would mobilize the political machinery of Eritrea's PFDJ on Against All Odds' behalf, and he would travel to the United States to join us in making the rounds of present and future supporters. Zemhret would also select the local, Asmara coordinating chair and organizing committee, and he would monitor conference support and participation by university, international, and corporate entities so that they were in keeping with strict Eritrean government policies.

A bigger and bigger cultural coalition was forming around the project nearly every day. Thanks to Ngugi, NYU wanted to partner with Penn State as the project's primary academic sponsors. Kassahun pledged thirty thousand dollars to Penn State to partner with it too. Both universities planned courses around the conference and would send large numbers of their students to attend. The African Literature Association and the African Studies Association endorsed the project and invited us to present it in plenary sessions at their annual conferences. Penn State's development officers produced long lists of foundations and corporations who seemed like likely funders: Ford, Rockefeller, MacArthur, Carnegie, Getty, Soros, and more; Compaq, Siemens, Mobil, Anadarko (who were drilling for oil in Eritrea), Coca-Cola, Lufthansa, Toyota, and other corporations with offices or equipment in Asmara. Kassahun bolstered the list with SIDA, NORAD, Bellagio, the World Bank, the Economic Commission of Africa, the OAU, UNICEF, UNESCO, UNDP, and on and on. We faxed, emailed, Fed-Exed, couriered, and hand delivered dozens of detailed proposals with all kinds of possibilities: satellite transmission of the conference, videotaping and filming for archiving and the making of documentaries, distribution rights, travel and lodging expenses for invited writers, distance-learning hookups, certificate programs, sponsorship and branding opportunities for major events, and linkages with the universities of Asmara, Addis Ababa, and Makerere. We even thought we could get Oprah Winfrey or NBC's *Today* show to broadcast from the conference. When we followed up on our proposals, secretaries recognized our names and put us through to their bosses who asked us to come to their offices to discuss our ideas and how they could help.

A few days before I was about to depart for Asmara in January 1998, Kidan emailed me a preliminary list of countries that had diplomatic representatives in Asmara and with whom I would be meeting. We would also travel to Addis Ababa and Nairobi for additional meetings. When I called Kassahun to discuss our trip, I was wondering why he wasn't saying much when he shocked me. "Charles. Something has come up, and I can't go."

I wanted to ask, "What?" but instead replied, "When should we postpone to, the end of January?" We had already postponed our visit twice, so why not a few more weeks, I thought.

Kassahun shocked me again with his answer. "No. You should go. Kidan will be there. We shouldn't wait any longer."

While I agreed, as soon as I got off the phone I told Barbara about the conversation and asked her, "How can I go alone? Kassahun is the one who everyone knows in Asmara, not me."

The feeling of not knowing a single person on the entire continent that I had had in Morocco a decade before when Barbara went home and I stayed a week to write came roaring back as if my experience in Africa since then had never happened. Was it only in my imagination, merely intellectual, theoretical, "for the sake of poetry," as I wrote back then, and, other than for a few moments in Malawi, perhaps, really about no one but me? What did seeing the ants in the sands of Jericho combined with imagining my grandparents in the steam bellies of steerage on the *Rhein*, the *Scotia*, and the *Rijndam* at the beginning of the twentieth century really mean? Did the relic piles of eyeglasses and shoes at Yad Vashem, the initial strangeness I felt in realizing that all my gods came out of the Red Sea, and saying yes to Barbara and the straw and no to the holy letter of the law change anything? What did Rome teach me? Rome's Rome? Ngugi's ideas? Larry's images? That I would always have my fear of connecting with no one on any shore—the Atlantic Ocean west or east, the Indian Ocean, the Dead Sea or the Red? Were the shadow of Kilimanjaro and the confidence of my father on his deathbed unreal? My word or the African word—did it matter? In practical terms, why did I think I didn't know anyone in Asmara or Eritrea, even after being there twice, and feeling the second time that I wasn't totally a stranger anymore? Twenty-five years before I had thought that I had to know my own culture before I should try to know another. How many more times did I have to be shown that they were not separate but joined? I had to go.

"*Buongiorno,* Arefine. *Kassahun detto ottiene di nuovo a lavoro. Adesso, per favore,* get back to work!" I poked my head into the doorway of the Africa

World Press office and saw Arefine with a worried look as he bent over and read an open *Haddas Eritrea* on the desk counter. The old man in the double-breasted suit also sitting at the counter silently smiled.

Arefine looked up without surprise. "*Ah, Charlus, un altra volta.* Welcome back to Asmara. *Com' esta,* and how is your family? Kassahun just called to tell me you were coming."

"*Buon Natale,*" I said giving Arefine a hug.

"*Buon Natale a lei,* Charlus. You should have brought your family this time," Arefine answered.

"Maybe *la prossima volta,*" I said wishing I could afford it. "*Ma, e troppo caro,* no?"

"Don't worry," Arefine shot back, "Now you can use Eritrea's new nakfa instead of dollars." Eritrea had only recently started to print its own money and had banned any more use of the infinitely crumpled, oily with *injera, zigni,* and berbere Ethiopian birr. I loved handling and folding the crisp, fresh American-designed notes that looked like greenbacks only with Eritrean scenes of its railroad to Massawa, bridges, trees, and smiling Eritrean women and children.

"*Basta* with the birr, right, Arefine? We can forget about them." With a look of mock disdain, Arefine flicked his fingers in the air. "*Grazie per tutto,* Arefine," I said and, as I turned to go into the side office, "Excuse me. I need to check my email."

"*Prego,*" he replied flatly. "Kidan is out, but she said she left your schedule on the table."

Soft gray walls, the high ceiling lined with the room-length fluorescent lights, the futuristic coat hook, the computer, the two long work tables, a comfortable chair, and the stockroom full of books made the office feel like a second home. I found the itinerary and quickly scanned our appointments for the next four days with governments that had representatives in Asmara—Denmark, Germany, Norway, Israel, Sweden, Italy, Egypt, UNICEF, and more. My anxiety about whether I really knew anyone in Asmara disappeared because at least I knew someone who did.

On a separate sheet Kidan had written "Schedule meetings with US ambassador, USAID, President of the University of Asmara." Next to that, I found a USAID pamphlet promoting its accomplishments in Eritrea. Expecting the patronizing articles about how American food aid and mosquito eradication programs would somehow foster democracy in Eritrea, I still found hope in the USAID mission statement, which I copied into my notebook: "The Government of the State of Eritrea (GSE) has called for a change from the historical, paternalistic donor-recipient relationship toward a development partnership of equals; any unilateral initiative and influence by donors and dependency on their largesse are anathema to the current GSE leadership." This certainly described what I understood about the GSE, yet another acronym, but I wondered what my government was doing about it. On a smaller scale, could a "partnership of equals" without any "dependency on their largesse" determine the approach of the Against All Odds project too, whether the players were nations, NGOs, big universities and world languages, or local languages, individual writers—famous or not and wherever they were from—along with students and ordinary Eritreans, whatever the "odds?"

As we went from meeting to meeting and perfected our presentation of the project, Kidan and I were continually amazed at how well we were received. An elderly and dapper Belgian diplomatic at the Office of the European Union, who said that he would be delighted to contribute, commented in thick, British-accented English as he took his fluffy silk handkerchief out of his double-breasted blazer pocket with brass buttons, "A typical American presentation: quick, efficient. You've done it. It will work."

Yet the national stereotypes went both ways. A flush Danish ambassador, who said he wanted to write us a check before we left his office, could have easily fit the part of the drunken King Claudius in *Hamlet*. A buff and righteous blonde Swede, the polite yet superior English, the intellectual and defensive Israeli, the formidably modest but hard-to-read Chinese, the repressed Egyptian, the efficient and all-knowing yet unrevealing German, the bearish yet elusive Russian, the calculating liberal Dutch, the solicitous yet officious UNICEF rep in Asmara, the elegant Italian of all gesture and no substance, and our typical American ambassador—politic, oblivious, sincere, and supremely self-assured. They offered funding for travel, housing, catering, performances, and whatever kinds of media we required; names of directors and assistant directors of more NGOs whose help we could depend on; and more varieties of in-kind support than we could have ever imagined. My once fat folders with copies of our project description and its budget emptied so quickly, and so many diplomatic faces broke into broad smiles without warning as they perused the packets, that I wondered if funding the conference might be easier than getting more copies of our proposal out of the old Xerox machine back in the office.

"*Quando partite per Addis Ababa?*" Arefine asked me as I blew Asmara's highland dust out of the copy machine with a near-empty aerosol can of air in the hope that eventually I would have enough copies to last for the rest of my trip.

"We leave this afternoon, Arefine. But if we don't catch that flight—*questa macchina e disperata!*—we can get the next one at six."

"*Harrai*," Arefine responded, "*tutta va bene, no?*"

"Of course, Arefine. No problem," I answered automatically, but Arefine pushed on: "*Ma faccia attenzione in Addis.* Also, Kassahun called this morning while you and Kidan were at the American Embassy. He wants you and Kidan to see Tadesse at Sabur this afternoon before you leave."

"*Molto bene*, Arefine," I responded. "I've been trying to get over there to see it, and now's my chance."

Tadesse managed Sabur. A blockish, bluish green and windowless building stretching half a block on Liberation Avenue, Sabur printed nearly every book, form, paper, label, ticket, wrapper, and official document that originated in Eritrea.

"Come back to my office," Tadesse said as he opened the glass door into the bland and unassuming reception office where Kidan and I waited impatiently to leave for the airport. As we followed Tadesse, however, in a few seconds I forgot about going anywhere, enveloped in a history of printing in twentieth-century Eritrea. Children's report cards, lunar charts, newspapers, AIDS awareness literature, marriage licenses, pamphlets on the constitution process, restaurant menus, insurance forms, Asmara telephone books, geologic and tidal charts, doctors' scripts, children's readers, pads of restaurant checks, and paper stock of every thickness, hue, and weave spilled out of a labyrinth of rooms, where Tadesse would stop, usually for a pleasantry but sometimes for a quick and deeply grumbled complaint, with two or three Eritrean men or women in inky, dull worn-to-a-sheen brown or green laborer's uniforms. Except on the grimy tin ceilings, I couldn't see a single original surface with more than a square inch not plastered with disconnected, half-ripped flashes of red, green, blue, and yellow graphics—palm trees, Asmara's arched doorways, *agudo,* bathers in the Red Sea, smiling children, grimacing Ethiopian soldiers, mangoes, fishes, impossibly full-flowing rivers, old Fiats, women fighters in big Afros and short shorts, Orthodox crosses, soap advertisements—all creeping with characters of Ge'ez. One room with an unusually low ceiling had two huge, glistening presses like a pair of monstrously yet archaically mechanized basalt slabs, their Italian manufacturer's name in elegant silver cursive under a bright shining wheel. Another room with a much higher ceiling had towering walls with thousands of thin wooden drawers and hundreds of thousands of ink-stained dividers holding millions of cold type Ge'ez, Arabic, and Latin letters.

Tadesse's "So are you looking forward to your trip?" sounded like a voice out of a dream that I awakened from as I sat down on a hard chair in his office as lackluster as his secretary's except for a huge topographical map of Eritrea behind his desk. "I wish we had more time so we could talk," he continued. "Kassahun told me you were coming, Charlus. Hey, Kidan.

Where is the little girl that came up to my knee? Have a great time in Addis. I only wanted to tell you to be careful in Addis airport when you declare how much and what kind of currency you are carrying."

"Careful in Addis"—when I heard the same phrase from Arefine earlier in the day, I didn't acknowledge it. No one had ever warned me about being "careful" about anything in Asmara. I figured that Tadesse was simply offering an obligatory note about using our street smarts in a big city until I noticed his eyes anxiously brighten and his lips grimly purse, but only for a few seconds, which I decided to ignore as he took a few more moments to explain there was a disagreement between Eritrea and Ethiopia about whether the latter would recognize the nakfa as a legitimate form of currency. The problem sounded like a mere technicality or a bargaining ploy to gain an advantage in establishing a rate of exchange but nothing more. "*Che cosa e il problema?*" I would have joked with Tadesse if I knew him better. All currencies put pressure on one another. More importantly, hadn't President Isaias said in an interview the month before that he envisioned an open and virtually seamless border between Eritrea and Ethiopia in the near future, allowing the citizens of both countries to go back and forth without visas?

No one bothered Kidan and me about currency or anything else at Addis airport. The next morning, highland gold and bright blue much like in Asmara, we met with cultural affairs officers in the German, Swedish, and Italian embassies. As in Asmara, they said they wanted to support our project, but when we asked particularly if they would fund Ethiopian writers and scholars—the "Black Lions" and their most promising young pride—we only received in return, in all three instances, hyperbolic praise for Against All Odds' potential for "capacity building."

I had heard the term—thinking it was an oxymoron—for the first time a time a few days before, in the USAID office in Asmara. Responding to our pitch, the director said she would support us because Against All Odds would create, in words that I copied into my notebook since they sounded as if they could easily become a part of our own presentation as we developed it even more, "unique capacity building: a positive condition that would allow lasting and local development of necessary yet still to be realized initiatives including education, health care, agriculture, and democracy itself." I was able to answer her, thanks to my being tutored in such jargon by both Kassahun and my colleagues in development at Penn State, "I really appreciate what you're saying. Against All Odds wants to build capacity for the use of African languages as a source of cultural, social, political, and economic development." I found that the same words combined with hers worked as well in Addis as in Asmara, notwithstanding Eritrea's and Ethiopia's new-found problems in establishing an agreed-upon rate exchange.

Yet our potential Addis supporters' not saying they would engage our primary request for travel support worried me. Unaccustomed to feeling insecure in such situations, I remembered when I had an appointment with the president of the University of Asmara directly after meeting with USAID. When he told me bluntly that as a scientist he was skeptical about the power of African languages "to build capacity" for anything, I responded—panicking a little but hoping that I could still draw off the power that I had felt only an hour before at USAID flanked by a big U.S. and a slightly smaller Eritrean flag—that Against All Odds would stress the power of African languages as a means toward building democracy. Sounding even more skeptical about democracy than about African languages, he responded with a frown, "Capacity building and democracy? I don't see the connection."

For an afternoon meeting in Addis with UNESCO, Kidan and I climbed a steep stone staircase past huge but dry fountains and entered the sumptuous Hall of Africa. Glinting with stained glass, it towered like a cathedral without the need to specify a god. Contemporary African art, blending European modernist techniques of abstraction and collage with African imagery in bright colors, covered the walls. Abstract and animal mosaics flowed across the floors.

Scheduled to meet with the "Chef du Bureau de 'UNESCO" and "Representant aupres de l'OUA, de la CEA, des gouvernements de l'Ethiopie, de l'Erythree et de Djibouti," we opened the door to an imposing office of inner and outer rooms, massive ebony tables, large leather couches, and ceiling-to-floor glass cabinets with African artifacts, books in many languages, and an archive of UN documents and studies. A disembodied voice immediately called us into the innermost office of the chief himself, a huge man in a black suit, heavily starched white shirt, and Dior tie. As he busily rearranged himself behind a desk taking up nearly a third of the large room, two of his assistants joined us.

"Welcome, Professor," one of them cooed softly as the chief looked up for a moment and went back to skimming a letter that he signed five seconds later.

"How can we help you?" droned the other assistant like a monk beginning a psalm.

"Please, Professor," the chief said very slowly, looking up like a distracted academic, "Tell us about your project."

The intimidating environment notwithstanding, I gave him my usual presentation, and Kidan provided what I nervously forgot to say. The chief responded simply: "Yes. This is good. How can we help?"

"Could you fund one hundred writers from around Africa as well as their stay in Asmara?" I quickly replied.

"We cannot fund anyone," he just as quickly answered, "But we can give you assistance." As I wondered what that was, he continued: "Simply write us a formal letter of request. UNESCO will then study the project to see how we can best participate. Do you know about the recent formation of the International Institute for Capacity Building in Ethiopia, the first of its kind in Africa?" I nodded yes, and he continued: "The Institute will emphasize capacity building particularly from the African point of view, with education being of special interest. Against All Odds could benefit from this." As I glanced at Kidan, whose eyes were smiling, I saw the chief smile at our smiling. "UNESCO offices can announce the project and solicit participation worldwide," he said without a pause, "and you can use us to circulate any information you have. We can provide you with linkage and contacts with Francophone and Portuguese Africa. I will personally inform former UN secretary Boutros Boutros Ghali, about what you've told me today. He will love it." With this he got up from his desk, one of his assistants jumped out of the leather chair next to the couch Kidan and I were sitting on, and the chief sat down with us as he clasped his hands and began as if he now felt free enough to think out loud: "Also I will put you in touch with UNESCO's African experts in Paris and Dakar. We have been waiting a long time for such an African-language project as yours. Stress this aspect of your work in your formal letter of request for support, and please send it to me here as soon as possible."

"We have followed the lead of Ngugi wa Thiong'o in this," I replied in awe.

"He's a good man. See? I have all his books on this shelf above my head," the chief warmly responded.

"Great," I continued, becoming too enthusiastic. "I really want to emphasize that our initiative is the kind of broad coalition that values every one of our players, E—"

I stopped in midsentence, about to say "EPLF style," referring to the Eritrean People's Liberation Front to suggest that it was our paradigm for struggle, teamwork, and success. But in the same second and as I looked straight into the eyes of the chief now sitting next to me, I also noticed a penholder with two Ethiopian flags on his desk. Since the EPLF's victory was over Ethiopia, I stopped my analogy and hoped that he didn't see me blink and switch my word to "even," going on to say "even against all odds."

"We are with you, believe me," the chief said, slapping his knees and getting up, with all of us in the room doing the same and immediately shaking each other's hand before the cooing assistant accompanied us out the door.

After the meeting, Kidan and I skipped through the mist of the billowing fountains that had just been turned on and down the steep Hall of Africa stairs that we had labored before to climb and found our car. Riding high on the apparent success of our meeting and buoyed by the wave of our other strong support, we joined the surging life of early evening rush hour Addis around us. "Kidan," I said, "do you know that 1966 interview with Coltrane when he said, 'I want to be a force for real good. . . . I know that there are bad forces . . . that bring suffering to others and misery to the world, but I want to be the opposite . . . the force which is truly for good?'[3] Am I wrong to be feeling that way now?"

I didn't know if she heard me or had to concentrate on her driving as we pulled up to a red light, but she didn't respond. Our car was mobbed with beggars: a ragged mother trying too hard to frown with a small child, a little girl dressed in a flour sack with her hand out, a wizened man with no arm, three kids in filthy jogging suits pounding their fists on the car roof, an ancient woman in greasy billowing robes mouthing a constant stream of prayers and curses.

I had a disturbing moment of clarity. In a war, I would be the first to run away from these people and get in the line of foreigners jumping ahead of each other at the airport to get out of the city. I could make no more real difference here than I could in burying the blossoms of the trees back home to keep them from blooming. Against All Odds would do less for the beggars than I would if I turned the flowered carpets in Haile Selassie's old Imperial Palace backside up. With the walls bursting and collapsing, I was running away from evil in and out of buildings and cars to end up plunging a dull knife without effect into the sole of a foot not mine. If I thought I could upgrade, the better things would only fall apart worse than what was already broken, and my saying so to anyone would only increase the terror he or she expected to experience as a result. The surge of the city offered a better chance for survival simply because it promised another sunrise to man, woman, and child: the teeming and flowing together, back and forth in every direction and at all levels. My delusions condemned me to hell unless I could eat a few of those fresh peas off the branch that someone was pressing to the car window. I couldn't speak because my dry tongue clacked in my dry mouth. I wanted to be back at Mai Wei under the thatch and branches, where I would take a metal cup and drink from the pipe in the cement cistern full of hot, healthy spring water constantly flowing. A thin line of dark sky on top of a dark road blended into a distant clarity wrapped in gold with blue writing I could translate with a little more time. Down on the green terraces with yearlong corn, I entered a coral block building, heard rain spattering the tin roofs, watched peacocks open their tails in the backyard, smelled roasting goat, and saw my daughters, Alexandra, Alicia, and Elizabeth with Barbara looking for me out on the street. I wanted to take the picture I didn't see until it happened: to tell . . .

"Hotel, Charles. Hotel Guyon. Thanks. Charles? Wake up. I'm tired too. I'll meet you in the lobby tomorrow morning to leave for the airport and our flight to Nairobi." I heard Kidan's voice and got out of the car.

The next day as she and I waited in the Addis airport lounge for our plane, I still had twelve birr in my pocket and, knowing I couldn't use them in Asmara, I thought I could buy a few things at the souvenir kiosk to bring home. I could only afford two small sheets of UN / Ethiopian-issue stamps commemorating the fiftieth anniversary of UNICEF. They pictured mothers and children. Some had their sleeves rolled up to be inoculated. Mothers held their cups under a faucet for clean drinking water. Children wrote in Ge'ez on a pad at a desk. Breast-feeding mothers and their babies looked unrealistically plump.

Our project had until now been so well received so widely that, looking at the stamps, I thought that one day Against All Odds could have a stamp, too. It could picture similarly benevolent occasions when African mother tongues would be put to good use, even including words from a variety of African languages themselves. When I got back to Asmara I would email the Eritrean artist Yegizaw Michael, to ask if he would consider making some preliminary designs. He had already sent me a series of sketches for an idea that I was hoping Against All Odds could fund. He pictured parks in Asmara and all over Eritrea with huge sculptures resembling Ge'ez letters and people walking among them and resting on the foot of a "tse," the arm of "qhwa" or the tail of a "kxwa."

In Nairobi I had plans to meet with the chief program officer in the Ford Foundation's office there and with Ngugi's longtime publisher, Henry Chakava, one of Ngugi's oldest and best friends and the director of East African Educational Publishers, whose legendary work I first learned about during the conference on Ngugi in Reading three years before. The Ford Foundation office in New York had insisted that the involvement of at least one of its offices in Africa was vital to a decision about whether we would be funded. I wanted to see Henry to invite him personally to the Asmara conference and to seek his support in helping to bring more Kenyan writers with him.

I had roughly twenty-four hours to stay in Kenya, and as soon as we arrived at our hotel, The Hilton, around noon I began to make calls for my appointments. I would be alone since Kidan let me know she wasn't feeling well and would stay in her room. The Ford Foundation said I could come to its office on Koinange Street at 5:00 P.M. and, after I tried unsuccessfully to reach Henry both at his office and his home, since Ngugi had given me both numbers, his office called me back at 2:00 to meet him at his club in Nairobi at 3:00.

Quiet and elegantly shrouded in trees that were especially lush with Kenya's record rains, the club's verandah was the perfect place for a Tusker. I mentioned to the young waiter that I was there for a meeting with Henry. "I know him well. He said he would read my novel when I have finished it," the waiter responded brightly. Later he wouldn't let me pay for the beer— and two more after it since, although I waited almost two hours, Henry never showed. As I was writing a note for Henry that I had a meeting at Ford at 5:00, the waiter told me that he had called a cab to take me back downtown.

My meeting at the Ford Foundation also flopped. The program officer, I was told by the Ford representative who herself had just arrived in Nairobi from New York a week before, was on an extended conference call with the New York office. Hoping that Against All Odds was a part of the discussion, I sat down with the new representative to explain the project to her, but she only listened for about five minutes before getting up to rearrange a bouquet of flowers on the coffee table and smooth out the tight wrinkles in her Chanel knockoff suit. "I'll be right back," she said without looking at me.

After fifteen minutes, the program officer appeared. A thin and neat Kenyan in a tweed jacket, baggy khakis, and a button-down oxford shirt with a regimental blue tie, he seemed distracted as he apologized for a few seconds and, asking if I could meet him around 7:30 at the bar in the Hilton, ran out of the office to catch the elevator down the hall visible from the door closing loudly behind him.

When I came into the Hilton bar—a pseudo-British pub with heraldic animals on the wall—and saw the Ford program officer, I could barely sit down and say "against all odds" before he replied, "What are you having? This is a great project. It is sure to be successful."

"Great. Thanks. I'll have a Tusker, please."

He responded as he waved to the barmaid, "We don't care if the New York office wants it or not because in Nairobi . . ."

I couldn't hear the rest of what he said because the band—a duo with two keyboards—began playing seventies and eighties rock-and-roll hits that got louder and louder. As he continued to talk without being heard, when his lips would stop I would talk similarly, although in half the time, and nod my head affirmatively. Unsure whether the meeting was a good one or not, I got up to go to the men's room in the hope that by the time I got back the music would be stopped. As I passed a large and stately man with a wide, wild tie on an African shirt, he looked at me and said "Charles!"

"Henry Chakava. It's a pleasure!" I said with a start and not knowing what else to say except, "I have to go to the rest room. Can I meet you back in the pub in two minutes?"

When I returned Henry was sitting with the Ford program officer. I could tell that they were arguing—since they held their heads at sharp angles to each other, and I heard their loud voices—but I couldn't tell about what since the music hadn't stopped. I had rushed back and wanted to talk to them, but now I was torn between which one. Regardless, whatever any of us said couldn't be heard. Instead, all I could focus on was Henry taking and breaking one toothpick after another out of a greasy container on the table and picking his teeth so that he seemed to be wildly snarling any time the conversation turned from him. When I saw him mouth to the barmaid, "Give that man another beer," and gesture toward a drunk in a raincoat and high boots sitting two tables away, Henry pulled me close to him and yelled directly into my ear, "There is the best spy the government has."

Finally the band announced it would go on break. The Ford program officer immediately got up, shook both our hands, and said he had to run to another meeting. "Do you like Chinese food?" Henry offered, turning to me for the first time without a toothpick in his mouth. "We can drive there in my Pajero. There's a great restaurant outside of the downtown."

Rain had continued to pour since the afternoon, and driving through the potholed streets of Nairobi was like being on a safari and navigating the four-wheel through swollen rivers. At dinner, Henry anxiously asked about how Ngugi was doing "in New York" and what role he wanted to play in the project.

"Ngugi is our intellectual leader, and he is our presiding chair," I replied.

"Charles," Henry smiled. "Ideas, yes. But Ngugi an administrator? Who is doing all the work?"

"The co-chairs," I said, "Kassahun, Zemhret Yohannes in Eritrea, and me."

"Kassahun will do a lot," Henry nodded. "Zemhret I don't know, but if the government is behind him, you will be fine. In fact this could be the greatest conference ever held. I will be happy to serve in a consulting role and to provide ideas too, but don't expect too much work from me either. Cheers." With this, Henry raised his glass for a toast.

As I was about to click his glass, he said, "Don't drink it. This is terrible." He picked up a menu. "Waiter," he said, "take back this Pouilly-Fuissé"—I wasn't sure if he might have said "piss-eye" for a joke—"and bring us two bottles of the '95 Rhone." The waiter, dressed like a Ninja, scooped up the open bottle, ran off, and returned in thirty seconds with the two Rhone wines. "Open both," Henry demanded. The waiter sheepishly complied with a frightened smile. "And get me three clean glasses," Henry crossly added. The waiter again quickly did as he was told. Henry poured from one bottle in one glass, from the other bottle in the other glass and tasted both. "Give this one back to your madame," he said, keeping one bottle and thrusting the other into the waiter's hand so hard that he almost dropped it.

As Henry was driving me back to the Hilton and we had to stop at a corner flooded too deeply for us to proceed without making a sharp right, he said in an exasperated tone, "Why doesn't Ngugi come back to Kenya?" I recalled seeing the Ford program officer mouth the same question in our meeting before Henry arrived. Over dinner, when Henry had asked me how Ngugi's youngest children, Thiong'o and Mumbi, were doing, Henry also had brought up Ngugi's decision not to return to Kenya for the death of his first wife. "This was wrong, and it defied tradition," Henry said matter-of-factly.

"I don't know, Henry. Maybe it's the right decision," I countered. "I mean I don't know about tradition here, but maybe Ngugi made the right decision emotionally because he has started a new life, with a new wife and young children after he has suffered so much pain." I didn't want to presume on Henry and Ngugi's long and productive friendship, going back to high school, but Henry's demeanor, even though I barely knew him, demanded more honesty than ceremony. Therefore I continued, "C'mon Henry. Give him a break. Maybe he had to decide, like Blake in the *Proverbs of Hell*, to drive his cart and plow over the bones of the dead."[4]

"But he could still come back now," Henry said quickly, as he took another sharp right to avoid a flooded intersection. "You see those kids over there playing in the water? They are saying worse things about the government than Ngugi ever did or will, and no one's putting them or their parents in prison or forcing them into exile anymore. Time changes some things, at least."

"Maybe you're right," I said to Henry as we pulled into the Hilton's long driveway, "but what about the government's favorite way of dealing with dissidents: arranging for them to be beat up as if by criminals and then expressing mock surprise at what happened?"

"You mean surprise at this," Henry laughed, holding up his hand for me to see the scars where his fingers had almost been cut off for publishing

Ngugi. "Please give Ngugi and Njeeri and the children my regards," he said as I opened the car door, "and see you in Asmara."

When Kidan and I got back to Asmara the next afternoon, we went immediately from the airport to the Africa World Press office. Seeing Arefine rolling his miniature, fold-up Italian bicycle through the doorway, I snuck up behind him and asked, "*E questo Eritrean Airlines?*"

He didn't look surprised, saying, "Kidan, Charlus, *benvenuto di nuovo a Asmara. Avete siete sopravissuto Addis?*"

"*Si*, we survived, Arefine," I answered a little wearily.

"Hey. No bad-mouthing Ethiopian Airlines," said a friend of Arefine's whom I had never met before, the darkest Eritrean I had ever seen. Stout in a safari vest with lots of pockets, he wore polished Italian loafers with tassels and, sitting at the counter and twirling his beaded keychain with a Mercedes key, he added, "All their best pilots are Eritrean."

Arefine continued, "So, Charlus. Did you get lots of money in Addis and Nairobi or only promises?"

"Lots of promises," I replied, beginning to list whom we had met until he interrupted.

"Good, good. I have confirmed your airline ticket at Lufthansa for your return flight to America tomorrow night."

For a second the calm, the companionship, the sense of purpose, and all of the connections I felt in Asmara dissolved into scenes of a frightened stranger lost in a mob at an infernal Air Afrique departure desk in Dakar from nearly a decade ago: "*Non confirme, non confirme. Je suis regrette, monsieur.*"

"How did I get here?" I asked myself before recovering and responding to Arefine. "*Grazie mille*, Arefine."

"*Prego,*" he answered, looking twice at me as if he thought I might not be all right, before he continued. "*Osservi* tired from your *viaggio*, but Zemhret called today. He wants you to meet him at the Embasoira Hotel tonight at eight o'clock. *Va bene?*"

"*Tutta va bene*," I replied.

"*Harrai!*" Arefine concluded, his wide eyes saying that he did not believe me. Finally I would get to meet Zemhret for myself. My doubts about whether I belonged here a few seconds before, or a week before, or even ten years before led to now.

Later that evening as I walked up the hill to the Embasoira, I passed the Asmara Art School where with Arefine two and a half years before I had met Feshaye Zemichael, the director, carrying the prototype sculpture of the trophy that would become the Raimok Award to be given annually to

Eritrea's best artists and writers. Later Kassahun told me that Zemhret had originated and directed the process.

As Kassahun told me more about Zemhret, I began to understand that the work that came with his title, director of research and documentation, involved a wide range of Eritrean arts and culture. Now walking again past the small villa-like, fortified jewelry box in which the Constitutional Commission had been housed, I remembered Bereket Selassie's characterization of Zemhret, the commission's secretary, as a difficult ideologue. However, neither then nor now did I presume to know much of anything about Eritrea's internal politics. I enjoyed and exercised as vigorously as I could the freedoms enshrined in the American Constitution and Bill of Rights. But for the most part I had given up thinking I could bring about political change in my own country other than by casting my vote and trying to teach my students and to remind myself to think critically, imaginatively and humanely long before I first came to Africa.

What little I did know of Eritrea's history made clear that it had suffered more than enough from Eritreans being told by outsiders that they knew what was best for Eritreans better than Eritreans did. Eritreans didn't need any smooth talk from me that objectified their martyr's certificates, disabilities, militarism, and political systems in order to ensure that I could always address them in the safe-for-me third person or, even worse perhaps, with a merely patronizing "you" since I had even less political power here than I had at home. I asked Kassahun once about politics in Eritrea, and he said, "It's like a family. It's a very small country. You know what family politics are like, no?" Yet he seemed to be an important part of the Eritrean family. He worked closely with Zemhret on many Eritrean publishing projects and had a managing role in Sabur. If Zemhret were the ideologue that Bereket bemoaned, Kassahun didn't mention it or told me instead about the graduate from the "University of the Revolution" in the field during Eritrea's armed struggle for independence, which Zemhret joined at a young age, after being brought up a devout Roman Catholic and having served as a faithful altar boy.

Writing, publishing, drama, art, music, and education were all vital elements of the Eritrean revolution. Maintaining and developing culture was a major part of the struggle and life in the field. A whole generation of fighters spent their youth there; a new generation was born and grew up there. Not the gun but the mind of the fighter who pulled the trigger was the most important part of the Eritrean revolution, as Alemseged Tesfai had insisted when I asked him about the relationship between the pen and the sword in Eritrea as we were having drinks after my poetry reading on my last visit. Eritrea's greatest writers, artists, musicians, and educators discovered and developed their artistic skills simultaneous with their becoming fighters, and Zemhret embodied this ethic. With mock exasperation Kassahun would tell me how Zemhret was forever sending him lists of books, magazines, and journals that he had to have, and I always saw a pile of them on Kassahun's desk either ready to be mailed or stuffed in his suitcase on his next trip to Asmara. As I opened the perennially smudged glass door into the hotel, I wished I had brought a copy of one of my books from Africa World Press as a gift but also as some form of credential.

I liked the Embasoira's sprawling and dim lobby: peeling veneer, grimy marble floors, a flickering black-and-white TV, sofas with bedspreads on them, cracked leather chairs, scuffed coffee tables, and groups of three or four mostly Eritrean men in black leather jackets, tweeds, or windbreakers, occasionally with an elegantly dressed and dignified older woman or a scruffy, white aid worker, tourist, or me. I stayed there now and on my last trip to Asmara since the Albergo Italia had been closed to be restored. The Embasoira's long curved reception desk had the feel and the smell of a well-worn wooden pencil. "Ah, Professor Charlus, *buona sera,*" came the usual greeting and warm smile from Mussie, or Negusse, Ghirmai, Ruth, Nanu, or whoever was on duty.

"*Brukh meshet. Kemey alekha,* Mussie. *Per favore,* I have a meeting . . ."

"With Ato Zemhret? He called," said Mussie finishing my sentence: "He is on his way. No wait; he is here."

I turned around. Hearing "Charles, I'm Zemhret," I saw someone my height and build, ten years younger, reddish brown, with a short Afro, round face, small nose and mouth, high cheekbones, high forehead, large and narrow eyes, and wearing jeans, hiking boots, and a leather jacket: in other words, blending in and acting no different than everyone else in the room. "Let's sit and talk. Kassahun tells me you have been traveling and working hard."

Ten minutes later and three-quarters through a summary-like development report on my meetings in Asmara, Addis, and Nairobi, I realized that Zemhret had only occasionally nodded in approval and had hardly spoken. Becoming anxious that he might be thinking that we had not accomplished enough, I began telling him about Penn State's commitment to the project, my meetings with Ngugi, and our plans for meetings at the UN and the Ford and Rockefeller foundations, but Zemhret still said very little, until he broke in with, "I will organize an exhibit on the history of the written word in Eritrea. It goes back four thousand years. Have you seen the inscribed stele south of here? We have sustained culture and moved forward at the same time with a kind of parallel between tradition and change. Our colonial guests have also provided us with many books and papers for our people to learn their languages down through the years: the Arabs, the Italians, the English, the Amharas. In the field we set up mimeograph machines in caves—there are pictures—so that the Ethiopian air force couldn't swoop down and destroy them. There we produced translations into Tigrinya of writers like Dickens, Gorki, Maupassant, and Shakespeare for our fighters to read when they weren't in battle. I will also get together a committee of local writers whom you can meet next time you're in Asmara."

As Zemhret spoke I realized that I had been packaging and pitching my ideas for the conference for so long and so many times, even from when I felt I had to convince Kassahun and Ngugi that I wanted organize it, that I couldn't imagine a meeting like this one until it happened. A stele that old? A tradition of writing that old and continuous? Instead of theorizing, I could now be simply joining local writers to discuss what they wanted to do?

Our different backgrounds—Eritrean, American, African, white, black—didn't matter here: only our inspiration. The phrase from the USAID pamphlet came back to me not as some kind of admonishment but as an unspoken contract: "partnership of equals." Zemhret wasn't interested in anyone's "largesse"—NGOs, universities, other countries, or mine, and he didn't offer any of his own. He wanted "equals": from Eritrea's nine languages enshrined as equals in its constitution to our meeting and talking as equals about a conference to enshrine the African word. On my second visit to Asmara, I felt for the first time that I wasn't a stranger in Africa. Fearing this third time that if I came alone I would be unable to accomplish anything, that I might still be a stranger other than superficially, now for the first time in Africa I felt that I was treated as an equal. Not different, superior, or inferior—but as an equal.

CHAPTER TEN

I Wrestled the Devil

Two months later, I sat in the elegant New York City office of one of UNICEF's highest directors. He had requested a meeting after reading my project description that one of his assistants—whom I had already met with twice, three floors down, since I had returned from Asmara—had strongly recommended he should support. "Eritrea is near and dear to my heart," he said with a long sympathetic breath after "dear" as he looked around the room and made eye contact with everyone. As I sat there and listened intently with two Penn State vice presidents, Penn State's development director, and Kassahun, the comment reinforced an almost magical feeling I had in the gift shop downstairs as I waited for my colleagues to arrive. Since I had been a child, and now for my own children, the word "UNICEF" evoked National Geographic-like pictures of once impoverished and oppressed women and children around the world being helped by donations that paid for new schools, health care, clean water, and adequate housing where there had been none before. Images of tiger, Princess Jasmine, witch, and pumpkin costumes evoked small, orange, fold-up cardboard boxes marked UNICEF to collect pennies, nickels, and dimes at Halloween, which we would turn in at school the next day to be sent to help children like us but who didn't have the advantages of living in a wealthy nation like the United States. Was Against All Odds now a part of such a powerful, hallowed humanitarian effort? Offering an official UNICEF endorsement of our project, the director encouraged us to submit an ambitious proposal asking for UNICEF help with everything from supporting conference participation by grassroots community organizations of African women writers to producing African-language television broadcasts aimed at children to help them realize their human rights. He also wanted us to write into our proposal a request for funding children from Africa and around the world to attend the conference. As we flew back from New York to Penn State on its corporate jet, the UNICEF logo of a woman lifting up a child to the world came into my mind and seemed to make the university logo of a Nittany lion imprinted on the glass of my drink look a little more African than before.

Eritrea might reject any dependency on largesse, but by the spring of 1998 the development of Against All Odds overflowed with such a spirit. Thanks to Ngugi, New York University confirmed that it wanted to co-sponsor the project and hold a launch to announce the initiative to the New York press. The event would take place in September during the meeting of the UN General Assembly to attract the maximum international attention. A former president of the African Literature Association confirmed that the University of Iowa also wanted to become a co-sponsor. Not only did UNESCO and UNICEF now support the project, the United Nations Development Program also wanted to be a part of it. Offering to enlist the support of leaders of the Organization of African Unity (OAU) and of other African governments, the UNDP's director of public affairs offered to fund seventy-five writers in African languages, or at least one from every African country, to attend the conference. He said that he had made similar arrangements for a conference in Africa that involved African women filmmakers.

Ngugi had known the director for several years. A friend of Ngugi, who also knew the director quite well, told me that he always delivered on what he promised. One night we all met for dinner, and the conversation between Ngugi and the director about African languages swirled and soared over Cuban Chinese food on New York's Upper West Side near Harlem. The director and I agreed that with Ngugi as our leader, we would work closely together. His staff would dovetail our project and UNDP priorities. Grasping my forearm, he assured me, "The writers *had to be in Asmara* for such an historic gathering," and so would he.

Meanwhile, the Rockefeller Foundation invited a request for seventy-five thousand dollars to fund Africa-based women writers and scholars to travel to the conference. Governments and NGOs whom we had met in Asmara and Addis were contacting us as a follow-up to our meetings there and proposals. Even the president of the University of Asmara called to let me know that he wanted every one of his faculty and students to participate in the conference and for the university to be a co-sponsor.

Kassahun and I traveled to Washington, DC, to meet with the manager of the External Affairs department for Africa at the World Bank. He warmly encouraged us to submit a proposal for two hundred thousand dollars. He also wanted to help us with obtaining funding from the OAU as well as from the African Development Bank and the Economic Commission for

Africa. He told us to invite the World Bank's vice presidents for the Africa region and that they would definitely attend. Elated with his response, as Kassahun and I took the "down" elevator after our meeting, we felt as if we were going up, up, up!

Our next stop was the Ford Foundation. As we traveled together to New York on the train, Kassahun surprised me with a detailed, million-dollar conference budget. Down to the penny, it covered everything from hundreds of thousands to be spent on broadcasting, video and audio documentation of the event, funding authors' travel to Asmara, venue costs, promotion and advertising, translation equipment, restoration of the Cinema Asmara, insurance, receptions, tours of Eritrea, performances by a variety of African cultural troupes, the publication of conference proceedings, to computers, copiers, paper, pens and pencils for the secretariat and even a Land Cruiser, albeit rented. He projected nearly half a million in conference revenues. The budget's last line listed the amount he thought we should request from Ford: three hundred thousand dollars. "The program officer with whom we are meeting," Kassahun said, "is a Nigerian. I have published one of his books. He is very interested in Eritrea and other African countries as emerging democracies. He believes that African languages play a vitally critical role in the process. He is in the Peace and Social Justice Program at Ford, which is part of Governance and Civil Society."

As I looked out on Newark's beaten, broken, and half-abandoned skyline, the mercury-laced Jersey meadowlands, the backup of planes at Newark Airport and of cars and trucks on the New Jersey Turnpike, the scores of cranes unloading container ships, and the seemingly endless oil depots and refineries opening onto Newark Bay—a landscape I loved as a boy and still loved—I asked Kassahun, hoping that he did not hear any regret or misgivings in my voice, "Will we also be meeting with the Ford people in Education, Media, Arts and Culture? EMAC should love us," but he was dozing and the train went dark as we entered the tunnel under the Hudson.

When Ngugi insisted a year and half before that Against All Odds should focus primarily on writers in African languages, I feared that this would narrow the appeal of the project and discourage those with a more general interest in African literature and culture from supporting us, but I was wrong. Our support was great, even when it might not have been capable of understanding or even concerned with a distinction between African literature and its language. Still, however great the connections between politics and language in African literature, wouldn't a project on African languages and literature be better understood by and, therefore, more likely to receive

Ford support and funding from program officers in art and culture than by a political scientist in peace and social justice?

My qualms faded almost as soon as our meeting began with the program officer's deep, soft vowels opening into praise for our project. From his office we looked through soaring interior glass walls supported by calm brown granite and henna-toned steel girders down to a tropical garden, as if the foundation rooted itself in a fundamental awareness that peace, social justice, art, and culture had to work together to survive.

But on May 6, 1999, in the one-street, hot and dusty, tiny border town of Badme, any questions about peace and social justice, much less art and culture, couldn't be heard through all the gunfire between Eritrean and Ethiopian troops determined to decide who would own the place. A week later the Ethiopian parliament declared war on Eritrea. Three weeks later Ethiopian air force fighter planes bombed Asmara, including the airport. At the same time and almost in the same hour, Eritrean air force fighter planes bombed the Ethiopian city of Mekele and hit an elementary school, causing over forty casualties. More air attacks took place on both sides. The Ethiopian government ordered mass expulsions of Eritreans living in Ethiopia and forced them to walk the last three miles in the one hundred degree Fahrenheit heat of the no man's land where the two country's armies faced each other. Ethiopia's prime minister, Meles Zenawi, Against All Odds' honorary co-chair with Eritrea's president, said even to be his cousin, justified the policy with a statement: "If the Ethiopian government says 'Go, because we don't like the color of your eyes,' they have to leave."[1]

Soon after the outbreak of war, a contingent of U.S. Marines heavily armed and in full combat gear landed unannounced in Asmara and burst out of their airplanes onto the airport tarmac to begin evacuating Americans and Europeans. The soldiers' appearance caused more commotion than the bombing, at least in Asmara. Barely seven years of peace with Ethiopia had elapsed after thirty years of war. Who wanted to face or even imagine it happening again? Not Eritreans—and therefore, so I thought, not us organizing the conference, now less than a year away. I had to repress my anger and frustration, but when I read the Reuters report on the morning of May 6 about the first outbreak of fighting, I went outside and threw a rock at my cat walking in our newly planted garden. As the news reported more and more fighting, I didn't want to see what Yegizaw Michael told me he was now painting: an ominous shut door in the middle of a barren landscape; spikes stirring the brain of a crazed body wrapped in padlocks and knots; blue and black instead of red, gold, and bright brown landscapes; ancient Ge'ez letters cracked apart and rearranged either meaninglessly or like a corrupted spelling of the word "nation."

From then on whenever I would call prospective donors, they were less eager to talk about the conference than the fighting. Instead they would ask, "Had I seen the story in the *Times*?" "Had I heard the report on NPR?" "Was there going to be a full-scale war?" "Did I think the latest mediation effort announced by the United States would change anything?" More difficult than their questions were their answers when I would ask the status of our funding proposals, many of which we were supposed to have already been notified about. Now the replies were "still under review," "circulating to others who would be involved," "opening up a wider dialogue," "moving through the process of gaining support." When I called various deans and department heads at Penn State, NYU, and Iowa who had been planning courses based on the conference and to fund their students to travel to Asmara for the event, instead of a response about how great the experience would be for them, I heard that curriculum committees might not be able to approve the courses soon enough so that they could be offered and that, regardless, university attorneys in "risk management" were beginning to raise questions about the wisdom of sending students to such a potentially dangerous place.

Eritrea and Ethiopia's sudden border conflict and its dizzying escalation never led me to say that the project might not happen, but the similarly sudden standstill in our work to raise money and other kinds of support as a result of the fighting forced us to postpone the event from June 1999 to January 2000. Over the summer I wrote to one particularly shaky yet important supporter that a resolution of the conflict was likely "in the near future and more substantial every day," although I did not really know how—as my stale language confessed—since a UN Security Council resolution condemning the fighting, a peace plan sponsored jointly by the United States and Rwanda, and a high-level OAU meeting in Burkina Faso all proved nothing but the intractability of the disagreement and the inevitability of war. In September the United States announced that, in a new initiative to end the hostilities, it would be sending a former national security advisor to Asmara.

Kassahun and I were already there, despite a U.S. travel advisory that we should not be. Before going, Kassahun assured me we would be fine, but I wondered and felt afraid. Every Western news report highlighted the war of words and the growing number of military skirmishes between the two countries. A report in the *Financial Times* likened the conflict to two bald men killing each other over a comb.[2] Any anxiety I had felt before about going to Eritrea alone seemed trivial in comparison with going there and maybe being killed if the Ethiopian air force bombed my hotel. Kassahun had a family and other business there besides the conference, but did I?

Asmara thrived as usual. What whispers of war? The Red Sea / Africa World Press office buzzed like normal. A stray cloud interrupting the highland sunlight momentarily ripened the avocado facade of the *Posta Centrale* as the bells of the Cathedral of Our Lady pealed brightly as ever.

"Dr. Charlus, *venuto visitarlo ancora?*" Arefine smiled when he saw me from behind the counter and as he closed his new copy of *Oggi*. "*Benvenuto, benvenuto. Si comodo.*"

"*Grazie*, Arefine," I replied warmly. "How can I not be comfortable in Asmara. I'm glad to be back. We have *troppo lavoro.*"

"*Ah, si, troppo lavoro, sempre troppo lavoro,*" he responded, putting his hands together as if in prayer and moving them up and down.

"*Ma*, Arefine. Too much work now, but when the conference is over, and if we survive the war, then we'll take it easy."

"*Che guerra? Dove la guerra?* Where is the war? With the Woyane?" he asked with a smile yet in a soft, serious voice. This was the first time I had heard the derogatory word "Woyane," used to refer to Ethiopians.

"Never again. *Mai ancora*, I hope," I answered.

"*Si, speriamo, speriamo,*" he quickly countered, again moving his mock praying hands up and down as his eyes wandered to the street outside the office.

That evening Zemhret invited us to join him at Eritrea's annual eight-day cultural festival, which he directed. "Now you will see why Zemhret is so important to our project," Kassahun said as we pulled up to the PFDJ party headquarters. "Victory to the Masses" was emblazoned in English and Tigrinya below the cornice of the cubist yet school-like two-story building surrounded by a high and decorative cast iron fence and with two soldiers holding Kalashnikovs at the gate. "Compared with the festival, our project is peanuts," Kassahun added as he ran into the building with a nod to the guards.

Ten minutes later Kassahun slowly wedged his Toyota truck through buses, taxis, cars, vendors at the festival gate, and a throng of tens of thousands of people of all ages and from all walks of life.

"Let's park and get out," Zemhret said, pointing to a place behind the gate where an aging, turbaned war veteran in a long heavy coat with a walking stick was already gesturing that we should enter. "The festival theme this year is 'Inheritance,'" Zemhret continued as we joined the crowd rolling and surging like a powerful if temporary Eritrean river during the rainy season. "People should be able to see their cultural heritage. We may not be wealthy in the eyes of the West, but we are very rich."

As a cordon of festival workers gathered spontaneously around us, each wanting to ask Zemhret a question yet none but one or two daring to do so,

I asked Kassahun, "Where are we going? Where is everyone going? We're all moving in the same direction?"

"To a poetry reading," Kassahun answered, slowing down our pace as Zemhret did.

"This many people going to a poetry reading?" I responded, although Kassahun didn't hear me as we stopped at the edge of a huge crowd and an Arabic poet's voice boomed from the podium loudspeakers. The area seemed to be shaped like a huge basin, with children—whom I didn't expect to see at such an event—packed into the middle, and the poet and the audience at opposite edges. After a minute or so I could see that the arrangement was really just a platform with a podium, and the audience gathered in a flat place in front of it. Still, my initial misimpression was telling. Eritrean poetry was at the center of the festival, and I had never experienced poetry in this way before—so public, performative, respected, engaging, high quality, and popular: all at the same time. The audience and the reading space seemed physically raised up to be even with the poet who was reciting. Furthermore, following the example of the children in the middle, a lot of the crowd was joining the poets in their lines, at times either anticipating or echoing them with obvious pleasure and understanding.

"Wait until you hear this one," Kassahun said as he pointed to the next poet ascending the podium: tall and thin, with a much-grayed Afro, hollow eyes, a long sharply angular face, and wearing a dark tweed sport jacket with a classic white Eritrean blanket or *gabi* draped over his shoulder and wrapped around him.

"What is his name?" I asked.

"Reesom Hi . . . ," Kassahun replied, but I didn't hear the whole last name as the crowd cheered the poet's announcement of the first poem he would read. The Tigrinya rattled from the loudspeakers through the crowd like a rivet machine securing smiles, laughs, and a few tears on all the faces. One word kept recurring, *gewaal*, with a kind of faint guttural pause or half-breathed caesura between the "g" and the "a," which the crowd picked up on and started repeating every time they heard it.

Turning away for a second from the reading, I noticed that Zemhret and Kassahun seemed to be talking seriously with one another about something other than the poetry we were hearing, but I interrupted: "What is the poem about?"

"The title of the poem could be translated as 'Your Sister,'" Zemhret responded. "The poem keeps repeating the word 'daughter' and calls for respecting women's rights."[3] I wondered how the poem's rather serious message still sparked so much hilarity.

"The woman of Eritrea love him for this, and a lot more too," Kassahun half-joked with a leer.

As the applause and the cheers for the first poem began to recede, the poet reached his long arm out to them and, as he formed a wide swirl with the icon-like dark gold fingers of his hand, slowly intoned, "*Alewuna,*" to which the crowd responded in near ecstatic unison but in the exact same tone, "*Alewuna.*" The poet countered with "*Alewana*" the same way, again as did the crowd, which triggered another *staccato prestissimo* performance interrupted roughly every ten or twelve syllables with the more slowly pronounced refrain, "*Alewuna, Alewana,*" echoing back and forth between the poet and the crowd.[4] As soon as he finished and as another poet took the podium, Zemhret insisted, "You must meet this guy."

"That was the best poetry performance I've ever seen," I said as I shook the poet's hand and introduced myself.

He responded in a polished, light British accent, "It's the people who make the performance in Eritrea," and started joking with Zemhret and Kassahun in Tigrinya.

Again I interrupted, "Reesom, I would like to talk with you about your work and a project we're working on. I'm in town for the next week."

"Where are you staying?" he replied.

"The Embasoira," I answered.

"So am I," he responded, continuing, "Let's have breakfast. Tomorrow? The next day?"

"How about not tomorrow or the next day but the next?" I said, remembering that for the two upcoming days I would have time for nothing but making my rounds of meetings with the conference's supporters in Asmara, starting with the president of the University of Asmara at 8:00 A.M.

As Kassahun was driving me back to the Embasoira later that evening, we talked about the reading. "Could you tell me the poet's last name again?" I asked.

"Haile," Kassahun responded and continued. "Reesom Haile. He came back to Eritrea like we all did in the diaspora after the war. He grew up here and went to Addis to go to school and work in radio. He ended up in New York, got a Ph.D. in Communications and now works as a development consultant with the UN and various other NGOs. Still, he seems to be spending most of his time in Asmara these days and, as you saw, his poetry is really catching on."

"Maybe I could translate him," I responded, "and you could publish a book of his poems. What do you think?"

Kassahun seemed to hesitate. "I would love to, but Tigrinya poetry is tough if not impossible to translate. All the levels of meanings and wide range of linguistic references might not carry over, but you could try. Ask him."

"I will at breakfast the day after tomorrow," I answered, "but what were you and Zemhret talking about so seriously about at the reading?"

"It wasn't that serious." Kassahun stretched his fingers on the steering wheel dismissively as he pulled into the Embasoira's carport. "Only that Zemhret said he was encouraging and supporting Reesom because he performed his work so well, even though it differed from most contemporary Eritrean poetry. Zemhret also wanted him to start and develop a series of writing workshops. I told Zemhret that I thought this was a great idea. I had never heard a poet in Tigrinya like Reesom. Hey, see you bright and early tomorrow at the office. Kidan has showed me your schedule."

My meetings over the next two days ranged from the sublime to the ridiculous. The president of the university welcomed me literally with open arms into his spacious and comfortable, book-lined and high-ceiling office. He invited me to deliver a lecture to the entire faculty and student body of arts and sciences later that week and to discuss both intellectual and practical issues related to the conference and to invite everyone in the audience to both help with and participate in the event. The Eritrean director of the British Council had convinced Alemseged Tesfai to do the translation of Ngugi's *I Will Marry When I Want* into Tigrinya, and the British theater director Jane Plastow, who had worked with many Eritrean actors and theater students before—most of whom had also formerly been fighters—at the University of Leads, to come to Asmara to direct the play along with one of Eritrea's leading actors and best director, Msgun Zerai. Originally written in Gikuyu, the play in English—translated by Ngugi himself—would serve as a median or vehicle from one language into another—since Alemseged didn't know Gikuyu—so that via a global language two African languages would speak to one another as never before. The head of the Alliance Francaise was planning three concerts by top West African bands.

Less positive, the World Bank representative in Asmara told me he couldn't understand why the External Affairs for Africa manager in Washington had not answered his two queries about the meeting Kassahun and I had had there since that office had always been prompt and efficient in the past. The UNICEF representative reported roughly the same, only he doubled the lack of response by mentioning New York and Addis, accenting the last syllable and raising the pitch and volume of his Nigerian voice so that I thought of "Dis," the legendary city of Hell. Still less positive than that, the vice president of Anadarko Petroleum in Asmara, a quiet and thoughtful Texan who had promised such a substantial financial contribution that the

Penn State director of development thought it would require that both of us should fly to Texas, told me he was spending his last day in the office since every sample drilling site he had tried was dry.

After a few more appointments, I recognized three early signs following in rapid succession that would indicate a meeting was to go badly: first, an opening comment about "how things had changed in Asmara since . . . [my] last visit"; second, an instantly summoned look of deep yet quizzical concern; third, a rhetorical question that I was somehow expected to answer: why would the Eritrean government go to war again? I couldn't determine if the purpose of such performances—their only variations being whether the accent of the speaker was Dutch, German, Egyptian, Israeli, Swedish, Chinese, or American—was to discourage me from ever returning or to encourage me to share some insight that my questioner thought a powerful political figure like Zemhret had shared with me.

Nevertheless, the most comic performance went to the Italians, with the Danish as runner up. I entered the latter's clean white office with modern teak furniture and remembered the words of the chief consul at the conclusion of my first meeting there: "If I had my checkbook I would write you a big check right now," which his statuesque and attractive assistant with long, flowing hair confirmed, bowing three times in her seat. But now I met only her. Performing the first three meeting-to-go-badly signs, she rose to a new height and asked in an abruptly tearful and almost hysterical tone, hoping to wring me as hard as she was wringing her hands, "What will you do if the Ethiopian air force bombs the conference, and the children attending it are killed?"

To increase the drama, I wanted to respond, "I will call Zemhret, who will call the Eritrean air force," but I said instead, "I am confident we will be safe in the hands of the Eritrean government."

After the dapper, jaunty, and young first secretary at the Italian Embassy performed the "change / concern / why war?" routine punctuated with chaotic flare by three phone calls and his secretary in a huge Benetton sweater and spike heels barging into his cubicle to insist that he had to sign three letters "*subito, subito*," he surprised me with "The ambassador wants to meet you now. *Andiamo.*"

As I entered his bright, airy office, the dark, elegantly suited, and gold-tied Italian ambassador got up from behind his desk, the size of a big Italian family's dinner table, to greet me at the center of the room hung with Italian flags of various sizes and large framed posters of tourist sites in Rome on the gleaming white walls. We moved to a black leather couch, where I sat, and a huge stuffed, slightly elevated chair—unlike the Embasoira lobby furniture, without a trace of wear—clearly for him. Although he began our meeting with a "change / concern / why war?" recital, instead of worrying about children being bombed, he let his eyes fill with tears as he protested his and Italy's love for Eritrea as its *primo genitore*, or first parent. Unfortunately, he continued, while he appreciated my proposal that Italy fund an architectural restoration of the Cinema Asmara or, less expensive, an exhibition of Eritrean artists or a concert by Eritrean musicians, his government's *politica ufficiale* was only to support Italian culture. However, he asked, might people attending the conference be interested in buying a CD on the architecture of Asmara that the embassy had just produced? If so, perhaps he could arrange for them also to get tickets for an Italian "festival *gastronomico*" sponsored by the embassy. Without waiting for me to respond, he continued: "I have noticed your last name is Italian. From where did your parents originate?" When I told him my Italian grandparents came from the mountains outside Avellino and my father from Newark, New Jersey, he beamed: "Newark! My wife and I got married in Newark when I was serving there as a consular officer."

I wanted to respond with, "You mean until black people in Newark forced you out with a lot more violence than they did in Asmara?" Instead I said, "*Daverro. Grazie,*" as he ended the meeting with an invitation to join him and his wife for dinner next time I was in Asmara, and as I censored my response once more, only thinking in my head, "I will join you only if you promise to put a lot of berbere in the tomato sauce." The good Italian bread in Asmara, the pasta, the locally made provolone and prosciutto, the Fiats, so many Italian words dappling Tigrinya, the Franciscan-like monasteries, and ochre villas surrounded by vineyards with groves of cypress and citrus perched on the hilltops in the Eritrean countryside, Arefine acting the supreme Italo-phile and his telling me that he had heard of one "Cantalupo" who had been a plumber in Asmara and another who had run a *salumeria* in the city of Keren—they all fed my Italian nostalgia richly. However, the ambassador's performance killed it, at least until the end of the day when I saw Zemhret and told him about the meeting. It made him laugh so hard—he also hissed when he laughed—that I had to laugh too, although a bit less, because I knew I would follow every suggestion for possible funding that the ambassador recommended, even when I was 99 percent sure that it would be a cul-de-sac. He would outfox me because Italians like him invented the role and knew how to play it better than anyone else: *il volpo*. My Italian grandparents ran away from him to America, and he almost found them again in Newark.

The next morning, as I shuffled down the wide and circular marble staircase of the Embasoira and greeted the usual chamber maids looking up from their scrubbing, their foreheads each tattooed with an orthodox cross,

I hoped that breakfast with Reesom Haile would be more relaxing, less dramatic, and less disappointing than most of my meetings the day before.

"Good morning," I nodded to Negusse as I passed the reception desk.

"Ah, good morning, Professor Charlus," he replied, as if we were following a script that he but I didn't know.

"You are meeting Dottore? He has told me. I just brought him some aspirin in the dining room. He is waiting for you."

As I saw him and sat down, realizing that my weariness would only be matched by his hangover, I feared the worst.

"What brings you to Asmara?" he asked as he lit a cigarette, breaking the silence after we ordered. Blinking from the bright sunlight in the restaurant and occasionally twitching while he protracted his neck as if from a chronic pain in his back, he listened patiently as I hurried through a description of the conference to end with a question.

"Would you like to be a part of it?"

Lighting another cigarette and looking at me coldly, he responded, "Yes, of course," and smiled, adding as he rubbed his gray stubble, "After twenty years of exile, I returned to Eritrea in 1994. Our languages and our poetry had been targeted for extinction, and they had been battered, but they survived. After all, we carried them in our memories and our voices, and we used them as our best weapons to defend ourselves throughout the struggle."

From the moment I saw him ascend the podium at the festival three nights before, I knew he was a natural for our project, surely as Zemhret knew when he invited Kassahun and me on that particular night to the festival, but now I felt like taking notes on what Reesom said since he so clearly understood and expressed what Against All Odds was trying to accomplish: "I like the way you are simply and directly addressing the demand side of the question, reaching out to a natural constituency of writers, teachers, and readers in local languages—the vast majority of Africans—to encourage and enable all kinds of information dissemination in African languages."

As he paused to wave and smile at someone across the room and getting up to leave, I asked him, "Have you always written poetry in Tigrinya?"

"Not really," he responded, "I only started a few years ago."

Before I could ask "Why then?" he continued.

"Reading a poem in Tigrinya on the Internet, I suddenly fell in love with the image of someone reading it in Asmara and thought, 'What if I wrote like this too?' It was like going back to what God has given you and saying, 'I'm not going to give it up.' It's your freedom, your speech, your self-definition, and your self-expression. You cannot give it up. If you lose your language, it isn't just the language you lose. It's the cultural codes embedded in that language. It's the values, the sense of community, and the sense that I am responsible for my brother, my sister, my mother, and they are equally responsible to me. This is what I do not want my people to lose. Shall we go?"

I still had one more question, maybe the most important in my mind. "Sure, in a minute," I answered. "But I wanted to ask you. Has anyone ever translated one of your poems in Tigrinya?"

"No," he said matter-of-factly, adding, "It would be too difficult. Tigrinya has too much to get across."

Remembering that Kassahun had been similarly discouraging about Tigrinya, I didn't care or didn't believe that it was so different from other languages that it couldn't be translated. "Still, I'd like to try," I answered as Reesom lit another cigarette and started to get up.

"All right," he said over his shoulder, "I'll email you a poem."

Four months later, in the middle of February 1999, it appeared in an email from Reesom—the original Tigrinya in Latin letters with a half literal / half doggerel version in English. I opened the email in the business center of my hotel in London just before I was to meet Kassahun for breakfast. I saw "Alewuna, Alewana"—the title of Reesom's most famous poem—below a brief message saying "sorry for the delay" and "as promised in Asmara." In the Tigrinya version, nearly every line seemed to rhyme. Also, the singsong version in English settled on abstractions and generalities without a single image.

"Maybe you are right about Tigrinya being too difficult to translate," I said to Kassahun when I told him about the email as we emerged from the Piccadilly Tube station to walk to the British Council headquarters, International House, for our meeting.

"Still, you can try. You poets only speak your own language to yourselves anyway," he replied as I thought about the rhythm of the poem I had heard in Asmara—"eZM! Z-eEZM! eZM! Z-eEZM! eBUM! Z-eEZM! eBUM! Z-eEZM!" It made the jostling Piccadilly crowds seem unreal, and I felt like a ghost passing among them. Even as we sat with the director of the British Council, well known for his work in African literature and whose rumpled demeanor enhanced his OBE status and supreme position in Britain's cultural bureaucracy, his words and promises of support seemed no more substantial than the steam rising at first from the surface of our tea in comparison with the original Tigrinya rhythm I kept hearing behind my eyes. I worried about getting it into English instead of getting more than verbal support for our project from the patronizing director. Yet since he began our meeting with an impeccable "change since we had first spoken about our project . . . my profound concern . . . and why war?" performance, I expected nothing, even while realizing that he as well as our project's other supporters had more reason than ever to worry. Over the two weeks leading up to our meeting and as we spoke, total war had broken out between Eritrea and Ethiopia, with thousands of soldiers already dead and more dying every day. On the underground on our way to the meeting, I quizzed Kassahun about whether he had heard anything about the war other than what we could hear on television in our rooms. I also wanted to escape into the rhythm of Reesom's poem, making London and our meeting seem so unreal in comparison, because the news every day from the Horn of the aerial bombardment of cities on both sides, trench warfare, massive attacks, counterattacks, charges of ethnic cleansing, Eritrea redeploying its forces in a "strategic retreat," and Ethiopia trumpeting "total victory" threatened to make the idea of the conference I had been working on for three and half years seem most unreal of all. Any initial joy about the project quickly transformed into dread unless I was talking with Ngugi, Kassahun, Larry Sykes, our colleagues in Asmara, or the somewhat drunk members of the audience whom I would meet after the poetry readings I also gave on this trip to London.

We had already postponed Against All Odds six months. Did we now have to cancel it? Prospective corporate supporters no longer answered our calls. The Ford Foundation still supported us but had cut our initial grant in half, as did Rockefeller. The World Bank would contribute less than a tenth of its first offer. Even Alemseged Tesfai was reporting absolute carnage on the battlefields of southern Eritrea. I thought, although I never said it to anyone, "How could we go on?"

Still I clung to our project's clichéd title: Against All Odds. Hadn't most African writers of the twentieth century struggled and written their great works against high odds like those the project now faced, and worse? If "against all odds" characterized these writers' efforts, who were we to cancel our project simply because now it had to begin living up to its name? We had not planned on such an effort, but who were we to turn around and stop, if the writers themselves didn't? The Eritrean landscape itself seemed inscribed with their spirit. Our project would have to live up to it or die. Didn't the war now create the conditions that could ironically demonstrate our project's greatest success and why it had to happen? Maybe the title Against All Odds wouldn't be a cliché after all?

The sinking fortunes of Against All Odds fared worst of all, perhaps, at the UN. UNICEF acted as if all of its offers to fund conference programs as well as writers, children, and many of its own staff members to go to Asmara existed only in my imagination. Regardless of whether Eritrea was really "near and dear" to UNICEF's heart, a newfound regulation appeared on the formerly friendly director's lips—or rather on his representative's now in a cursorily worded email—to rule out even a mere endorsement of our project. A few days later as I was reading the *New York Times* on a bus from Manhattan to Bethlehem, I saw a full-page ad for Special Olympics. A healthy bunch of supporting organizations' endorsements appeared at the bottom of the page, the UNICEF logo included. Seeing the familiar silhouette of a mother holding up her child, I felt like Against All Odds was a child out of the picture whom the mother had rejected.

Hoping to salvage UNESCO's support of the project and happening to glance at the postage stamps I had bought in the airport at Addis like they were a kind of holy card a believer might use to provide an extra leap of faith, I realized at once why my meeting there in the cathedral-like Hall of Africa with UNESCO's *chef d'bureau* would also retain no more reality than a dream. In Ge'ez and English inscribed on the bottom of the stamp, the word "Ethiopia" balanced the United Nations name and logo at the top. The joint issue signified a connection between Ethiopia and the UN—with its African headquarters in Addis—that even Eritrea, much less our project, could never come between or threaten.

Our greatest hope at the UN, the United Nations Development Program and one its most important directors, also blew away in the winds of war. The day before we were supposed to meet him in his office, I received a call from Kassahun in Asmara, where he had brought Ngugi for his first visit, that their departure would be delayed.

"How is Asmara with the war?" I asked Kassahun through the crackling phone connection.

As he replied, "There's nothing. We're fine. Ngugi has been having a great time meeting people," and I was thinking of Arefine's response when I had asked him a similar question six months earlier—"*Che guerra?*"—I realized that I would have to go to the UN meeting alone, especially when Kassahun said, "Please give the director our sincere apologies, best wishes, and assurances that we will meet with him as soon as we get back."

Arriving in the director's office high in UN Plaza and overlooking the East River, I hoped that the gray cashmere sweater and business-like strand of pearls on the director's elderly secretary assured respect for whomever entered the door. Warmly welcoming both my being there and my offering Ngugi's and Kassahun's apologies for their absence, she said, "I will tell the director that you're here and that your colleagues cannot make it." Since she knew better than me that the director would not be pleased, I wondered why she acted as if I hadn't called the day before and told her, as soon as I had heard from Kassahun, that he and Ngugi couldn't be there. Perhaps she feared to tell him or hoped for the best? She returned saying that our meeting time had to be cut short due to an unexpected emergency meeting elsewhere in the UN.

Ushered into the director's office, again I relayed Ngugi's and Kassahun's apologies. They were received with smiles, at least for a few seconds, as wide as Vice President Gore's and Secretary of State Madeline Albright's posing with the director in several pictures on the wall, until the director abruptly turned from shaking my hand and quickly moved back behind his desk as if for protection from a germ. "I have asked two UN economists from Africa to listen to your proposal and to provide feedback," he said matter-of-factly, following with a command, "Now tell them," which I did as I had at least a hundred times before and at least twice to him. Upon completion, I looked around the room: two polished, African economists darker than their expensive suits; the director dressed as usual in lavish African robe and cap. Who was I to tell them about the power of African languages, as if they didn't know—even if they didn't? Persisting, I turned to the director, but he turned to the economists and spoke French.

One of them said to me, "I've read your proposal and now I've heard it. But what's the punch line?"

I barely uttered, "The punch . . ." when the director broke in to apologize: "I have to go, I'm sorry. Let's meet again soon. We'll be in touch." As he swept out of the room, the economists quickly falling in behind him and leaving me alone, I looked down on the whitecaps in the East River and identified with them. Ten seconds later, the director's secretary entered the room with my coat and a "Thank you so much for coming under such difficult circumstances."

I saw the director for a last time, and then only to speak in meet-and-greet formalities, when he came to the Against All Odds project launch a month later, provided by NYU in an elegant downtown New York City setting with generous food and drink. Grandly entering the room in his elegant robes like springtime in New York, he was surrounded by women in African dress who seemed to greet his warmth like happy songbirds. As he came to the podium and praised the project by detailing his long relationship with Ngugi and promising more support than ever, how could I believe him, even against all odds?

At the same time, in translating the poetry of Reesom Haile, I was finding the opposite of empty words, broken promises, and sinking expectations: an independent voice steeped in Eritrean oral poetic traditions and, as the poet Rimbaud—who may have lived in or at least passed through Eritrea in the 1880s—demanded, "absolutely modern,"[5] yet in a way I had never experienced and had to learn. For example, "*Alewuna, Alewana*" in Reesom's eponymous poem meant "we have, we have," the "u" and the "a" signifying gender, respectively men and women. Since the words recurred so frequently in the poem, in my first translation I set up a kind of grid, with "We have" positioned at the corners and key points, as in concrete poetry. Next I had them feed into the poem's second recurring words—"men" and "women"—via the poem's third most recurring word, "Who," which led to a verb describing what men and women could do to rebuild Eritrea: sacrifice, gather, provide, lead, grow, study, persist . . . and so on. Along the lines of the innovative twentieth-century poet Charles Olson, I imagined the poem as a kind of field of energy filled with the poet's spontaneously projected language.

When I emailed my translation back to Reesom, he rejected it in an email the same day. As I read past the rejection and Reesom explained what he was looking for instead, I thought of Kassahun's contention about the twentieth-century Ethiopian writers collected in the book *Black Lions*: that they were modern but in ways that still weren't recognized. I also recalled what Zemhret said in our first meeting: that he looked for a parallel between tradition and change. I had to find an English approximation for the poetic process of writing in Tigrinya that Reesom in his email described as

> not something that has left our tongue and lived in the books for a very long time. Our poetry is participatory. When I recite my poetry at home, the people listening to me will say, "add this to that, add this to that." It is participatory. It's not something that we put on the wall and say "Oh, this is pretty." Our traditional poetry form is *ad hoc*. Someone will just get up and say something to try to capture the spirit of that particular time. And people will add, "why don't you say so, why don't you add this, why don't you extend it." It is very much part of the tradition. I am putting it on paper because I think it is about time we start storing it for the next generation.

The poetry Reesom wanted had few critical equivalents in English, especially not modern: spontaneous, fresh, oral, unforgiving, accessible, and public without becoming empty words, broken promises, and sinking expectations: a kind of daily bread or common currency for all kinds of people—writers, children, artists, young professionals, working people, the elderly, government people—to create a universal rapport of give-and-take.

Seeing and hearing Eritrea and its diaspora caught up in the indomitable rhythm of self-affirmation in "Alewuna, Alewana" instead of a sense of inevitable doom brought on by yet another round of war with Ethiopia, I found the closest English equivalent for the poem's spirit in a phrase, which I slightly altered to sound more modern, from Paul's epistle to the Philippians, traditionally thought to have been written when he was a prisoner in Rome: "Rejoice in the Lord alway; and again I say, Rejoice" (4:4). It epitomized Eritrea's irrepressible self-determination more lyrically than any phrase I knew or could invent in English. Yet I rejoiced, too. Working on Against All Odds continued as my day job: a kind of nine-to-five, only usually beginning earlier and ending later, conducted for the most part from my attic office at home via telephone, Internet, and fax. But now I had an antidote against the project's daily grind and mounting odds. Nearly every morning I would receive an email from Reesom with a new poem transcribed from Ge'ez and typed in Latin letters, accompanied by a translation into literal doggerel. I would translate it—transform? transmit? transcreate?—into an English poem and return it to him by the end of the day. Exemplifying Eritrea's liberated spirit, Reesom's poems flying back and forth between us also happened to liberate my own poetic spirit, even if it had to embrace a style as foreign to my own—more abstruse, compressed, and private—at least at first, as Tigrinya itself. Reesom's poetic devotion to all things Eritrean made him intolerant of anything more obviously experimental or discursive than the demotic English of a New York beat inflecting the epigrammatic sense of the *Greek Anthology.*

Poem after poem detailed a kind of Eritrean genome of cultural resiliency: resisting the Italians by making them dependent on Eritrean eggs for their omelets; rejecting foreign aid because one had to beg for it; tasting lemon, orange, and bitterness in knowledge; realizing too late that change came yesterday although it was expected tomorrow; recognizing that "the sauce / With spicy melted butter / Berbere . . . / . . . sea salt"[6] and big bones of Tigrinya itself could also be like "communion" without genuflecting—"straight / From the heart" and "simply understood / To resurrect / The nation."[7] Such a "voice" or *dehai*, even online, unlike any other could set its speaker free like an eighth beatitude, "To think in poetry."[8] Furthermore, Reesom wrote as if believing that history, God, Satan, priests, political leaders, NGOs, the next generation, soccer players, exiles, families, friends, enemies, thinkers, drinkers, Africans, Rome, and more would respond, "Why don't you say so, why don't you add this, why don't you extend it." They would also listen. Tigrinya finally would be heard and recognized not only locally but worldwide, like Eritrean nationalism after decades and centuries of being denied.

By June the Eritrean and Ethiopian armies had fought each other to a standstill, a tense cease-fire prevailed, the UN and the OAU made sporadic attempts to help maintain it, and I had to get back to Asmara with the conference only six months away. What about Kassahun's emergency angioplasty keeping him home, personal doubts whether I could be effective on my own in Asmara, fear of getting caught in a war zone? I had no excuses for not being there, as long as I had Arefine, Kidan, Zemhret, and Reesom on my side.

After traveling for twenty-eight hours, I still couldn't sleep the first night I arrived at the usual 11:00 P.M., looking forward to the next day, until "*La Illah Allah, wa Mohammed rashul Allah*" through the loudspeakers of the Great Mosque calling the faithful to prayer sounded to me like the greatest sigh of relief. Ten hours later, I woke and followed the tweets and the cheeps of the swallows circling from my balcony all the way down to the red brick dome of the cathedral and through a half-open, tall steel-and-glass shop door to hear the voice that first grafted me here four years before.

"*Dr. Charlus, ancora benvenuto. Il piu nuovo Asmarino ritorna,*" Arefine proclaimed, looking up from his *Oggi*.

"*Sono stato,*" I began, and he finished, "*andato troppo longo.*"

"Too long, too long," I continued, "but now that the fighting is over . . ."

He interrupted, "*Pensa di si?*"

"I hope so," I replied, knowing how he would respond, already beginning to laugh.

"Ah, *speriamo, speriamo.*" He moved his mock praying hands up and down.

"If you need me to fight, I can try that too," I added.

"*Harrai,*" Arefine responded, making a fist, trying to look tough and, as usual, visibly enjoying rolling the "rr's."

"Arefine," I asked, "You always use that word. What does it mean?"

"It means something like '*va bene,*' only *fortissimo molto. Capito?*"

"*Si, capo,*" I answered as Kidan emerged from the side office.

"Hey Charles. We've been waiting for you. Here's your schedule. You're getting popular. Zemhret and Reesom have already called here and want you to call them back."

For the first few days, as I resumed my now familiar role of Lazarus begging at the door of the various embassies in Asmara, I sensed hostility, resentment perhaps, unlike before. It made me feel insecure. Maybe they were thinking, "Why was this naive, brash professor from a rich American university back again?" Or "Didn't this idiot know there was a war on?"

I also witnessed another round of international, diplomatic performances that made me feel, as in Baudelaire's famous phrase from his *Journal Intime,* "the wind of the wing of madness."[9] After the Italian ambassador invited me to sit down in his stuffed chair while he took the couch and began, "As an Italian you must be very bitter to come all this way and still receive nothing from us," he started weaving circles in the air above his head and said, gently closing his eyes and as if to offer me some consolation, "Perhaps it was all a dream." The first secretary to the Egyptian ambassador asked me more seriously than ever, almost to the point of demanding, what I could tell him about how to seduce American girls. The Egyptian ambassador had a new obsession: wrinkles on his coattails. He had a ramrod and scowling servant who would lift them whenever he sat down and follow him around the room just in case he might require any more rearranging. The Danish consul who warned me last time she would hold me responsible if any children were bombed during the conference looked more distracted than ever: her long hair in tangles and her Laura Ashley look disheveled with a few too many scarves and sweaters, Asmara's warm June weather notwithstanding. As she paced around the room and never sat down once during the entire meeting, I expected her to start singing like Ophelia toward the end of *Hamlet*, "They bore him barefac'd on the bier, / Hey non nonny, nonny, ney nonny, / And in his grave rain'd many a tear."[10] But pointing to the door as she tried to look me straight in the eyes, she declared coldly and slowly, "I would advise you to consult with your American military attaché at the United States embassy before you go any further."

Since I had protested the Vietnam War all through high school and college, this would have been the last person whose assessment of the situation I would have trusted, but I replied, "Thank you. I have a meeting at the American Embassy later today."

That afternoon the American ambassador was passive-aggressive. As I sat down on a pilling couch and he settled behind his perfectly clean desk, he "harrumphed" and seemed to announce in a radio-style deep voice—although I was the only one in the room with him—that he "was happy to give me the good news that the United States would support Against All Odds by funding an American professor to attend the conference."

"Thank you," I responded, at hearing his name. "He is legendary and a great Africanist."

The ambassador remained silent, as if he wanted me to get up and pledge allegiance to the oversize flag in the corner behind him at such generosity. When I asked instead, "Would there be any possibility of funding for additional professors?" he waved off my question and offered his own.

"Did you ever collect pigeons? I do. I must run and take care of mine now. Please keep me posted on your progress." With this he got up from his desk, and his secretary simultaneously entered the office to escort me out.

No mention of the American military attaché's assessment of the war was necessary for either of us.

Zemhret wanted me to meet him at his office at PFDJ headquarters at the end of the day. The sentries with machine guns at the gate knew me by now. One of them was pouring tea from a thermos as I entered. I couldn't understand all the words of his invitation, but I could make out "Professor Charlus. *Shahi?*"

"No, *Grazie. Yegniyeley,*" I replied, unsure if I had offended him.

"*Genzebka,*" he smiled, as I saw that he had no left eye.

As I settled into the black vinyl chair to wait for Zemhret outside his inner office, I watched ruling party officers and officials rushing in and out. Some of them shot "Who the hell is he?" glances my way as I chatted with Zemhret's longtime secretary, Rhigat, about her family and mine until the phone rang. "Zemhret says come in please," she said softly.

Wearing his usual jeans, outdoor jacket, and hiking boots, he leaned back in his chair and said, "Who is this strange American who comes to Asmara during a war? He must be a poet. Would you like some tea?"

"Yes, please. But I am not a poet," I said. "'I am a beggar at the doors of the ambassadors of Asmara.'"

"Then prepare to beg some more. It is the way of rich Western countries," he said laughing. He laughed even harder when I told him of my meetings. "At least they are entertaining," he concluded, "but you will not need to bother yourself with them anymore. I have established an office for you here, a secretariat to be run by two excellently qualified women. One has a master's from UCLA and studied at the Sorbonne. The other is a tremendous organizer, very intelligent and responsible. Her mother is one of our most famous authors. Kassahun has published her. We will take care of things here. Don't worry. I have arranged for you to meet with them tomorrow. You know that tomorrow is also Martyrs Day. Here is an invitation. I will see you there."

The Penn graduate, Kassahun's friend, who owned an IT company gave us one of his offices in a starkly black and white modern building that also housed the German Embassy and Lufthansa Airlines. "I get a little worried that the conference is so close, and we still have so much to do," said Tsigye Hailemichael as she greeted me at the door the next morning, "but welcome to the Against All Odds office." It had a computer, fax machine, telephone, two large desks and a shelf of office supplies. She wore an expensive Parisian suit and had her hair in a traditional Eritrean style of tightly bound braids angled in straight lines at the top with the bottom wildly flared *au naturel*. She continued with only a faint tone of concern, "But when I tell this to Zemhret, he only replies, '*Dehan, dehan.*'"

"Meaning?" I said.

"Don't worry," she said with a laugh.

I remembered that I had also heard Arefine use the phrase and that when I asked him what it meant, he answered in Italian, "*Non si preoccupi.*"

"Perhaps we should call Zemhret Mr. Dehan Dehan?"

With this she gave me an unsure look, as if I couldn't be serious, or at least I better not be. But then she laughed, saying, "I'll be happy when Ruth Mesun gets back to Asmara and joins us. She will help us a lot."

As dusk fell and I sat on the balcony outside my room at the Embasoira, I sensed in the long arcs of twittering swallows extending across Asmara a kind of circular rhythm that I could use for a translation of a poem on Martyr's Day that Reesom had sent me just before I left for Asmara. Called "My Freedom," it began with a version of the oath I had first heard about at the Constitutional Commission, which I passed again as I walked down from the Embasoira to Liberation Avenue for the day's official, solemn observance, Zemhret's invitation in my pocket: "By the flesh of my martyrs . . ."[11] On the way I saw several teenagers wearing the T-shirts Reesom had told me he was planning to have made. They had the poem emblazoned in Tigrinya and in the red, blue, gold, and green colors of Eritrea's flag on the front. Pensive-looking policeman closed off the main street, and it filled with more and more Eritreans of all ages from adjoining side streets with everyone walking in the same direction and holding a candle.

"Where does this procession end?" I asked a college student wearing one of Reesom's T-shirts.

"At Bahti Meskerem," he responded, as if I was an unwanted distraction. I remembered the charmless and utilitarian small stadium and parade ground—known as Red Square during the Ethiopian occupation—at the end of the street and assumed that this was where Zemhret wanted me to meet him. Not wanting to bother the student again, I still wanted to ask him where I could get a candle, but then the streetlights went out. At the same time, the crowd seemed to close in more tightly than before but, still flowing as one in the same direction, the candles' glow in people's faces transformed them into masks. Intensely sad and intensely glad almost impossibly at the same time, they reminded me of the expressions of St. John and the Virgin Mary in an Italian medieval painting for which I had a holy card from a trip to Florence in 1972 that I still carried in my wallet, although I had looked at the image differently ever since I found myself in the shadow of Kilimanjaro a dozen years before.

Candles and more candles glowed brighter and brighter, one candle lighting another, coming out of the darkness, the edges of their flames brimming with more and more people's faces marching into an ever increasing light now coming from all directions—one glorious beam and millions of eyes commemorating martyrdom and death. It so overwhelmed me when I saw the piled-up graves and little paths winding through the cypresses and fountains of Martyrs Cemetery outside of town, that I had to turn away. But not here. As I joined the vast procession of a candlelit crowd in the early evening of the summer solstice, I realized that they wanted more than anything else to refuse death and to restore, adore, and rejoice in life. As the crowd reached the square and fanned out into the bleachers, the streetlights went on. Finding a seat in the bleachers next to the president of the University of Asmara, I saw Zemhret down on the parade ground. Wishing that I could understand the speech he was giving in Tigrinya, I remembered the conclusion of Reesom's poem, which I translated as "I am freedom / Forever / By the flesh of my martyrs."[12] Forever? Who could know that? I pictured Arefine saying, "*Speriamo, speriamo.*" At least there was freedom now.

After the ceremony, the surrounding crowd was just as large as I retraced my steps in the opposite direction out of the stadium, but now the streetlights glowed and Liberation Avenue jumped like one big party. "Joiner, Joiner, Joiner. Over here." I recognized the voice. Standing in a group of six or seven young men and women dressed up for the party swirling around them, Reesom with his gray Afro like an ashen halo and his white *gabi* as usual draped over his gray tweed sport jacket waved to me. "Joiner, join us. They want to hear my poems," he said, adding, "But I have told them I must restore my powers after sitting through the Martyrs Day pageants in the square."

He held the door open for me to follow him beneath a sign that read "Bar Gurgusum." "My heroes! Good evening," Reesom announced as we went in. Men with glum expressions suggesting that they had been drinking for too long looked up and smiled. Catching their eyes and now smiling broadly, Reesom scanned the room and asked so everyone could hear, "But where are the women who fought?" For a second the men's smiles froze and then grew broad as they returned to their drinks. We passed a table by the window with a man slumped over it and passed out. "One of our best generals," Reesom turned to me and said as we sat down against a corner wall so that he could see the entire room and vice versa. "*Ciao*, Rita," he exclaimed as a swarthy women with long, full dark hair and tight clothes accentuating her big, beautiful body came toward us and, as she erupted with an "*Amore!*" hugged him. Reesom abruptly became serious, saying, "Please help me out. A White Horse or a cold one with the old-style Melotti cap? And Joiner, what can I get you, a scotch or our local Asmara beer?"

Before I could answer, Rita stood up straight, threw back her hair, thrust out her chest, and, flashing her eyes, admonished him. "*Amore!* Do what you like. Don't ask me. Peace. It's a free country." A few minutes later, she brought us two glasses and a bottle of Johnnie Walker Black. For the next few hours, we seemed to share it and at least three more with several other tables in the room, but we never paid.

"Joiner," Reesom said as we left the bar, "I am going to Seghenyetti and Quhaito with some friends tomorrow. I'll bet you have never been to either place since you're always traipsing around in a suit and a tie with a briefcase of papers from office to office and begging for Against All Odds." We walked down a now empty Liberation Avenue at 1:30 A.M. He was right. The next day was Sunday, and I was anxious to get out of the city for a change.

"*Grazie*, Reesom," I responded immediately, a little louder than I should have due to too much scotch. "I miss being a tourist and my old life of visiting places and writing poetry about them. I used to love communing like a vulture with no one but the dead and for nothing but my own spiritual and poetic salvation."

"You will have plenty of," he began but then stopped as a scary, hulking man weaved toward us and getting closer started slowly intoning in slurred syllables, "*Alewuna, Alewana, Alewuna.*" He stopped only to bow deeply as he passed us and to greet Reesom by looking straight into his eyes and saying once more, "*Alewuna, Alewana,*" as if it were his name.

As we turned up the hill to the Embasoira, Reesom laughed, "Another one of my happy readers. He is a great photographer too."

The next day, Reesom's best friend, Solomon Abraha, who owned a travel agency in Asmara, which we planned to use for Against All Odds, picked us up in his Pajero just before dawn. Beside him sat Yosef Libsekal, an archaeologist and the director of Eritrea's national museum. "Let's go to Seghenyetti for breakfast, and then we'll have the strength to continue on," Solomon said, looking straight down the road as we left Asmara behind for wide dry fields that eventually began to roll higher and higher until they became mountains. Changing his position every few minutes as if to relieve the pressure on his back from a combination of the SUV's bad shocks and the bumpy road, Reesom spoke in Tigrinya with Solomon almost without stopping the first half hour as Yosef stared quietly out the window, and I dozed off and on.

Finally Reesom stopped, nudged me out of my drowsiness, pointed to Yosef, and whispered so he could hear, "Do not disturb. He is reading."

"What?" I asked, not wanting to be rude but seeing Yosef smile.

"You will see," Solomon interjected. "We will soon be passing through fields that he will read like books."

"Joiner," Reesom added. "Yosef is like a medium, echoing voices in the gravel, flint, and potsherds."

"They say this," Yosef said turning to me, "because I have told them that by looking at the grass, I can tell what's under it. Short grass means short roots, which means that they can't grow because something is under it. That something may be a rock, but it may be an archaeological ruin too, like a building or a wall. We have one of the oldest cultures on earth to settle in one place. Dig anywhere out here and you're likely to find an ancient site."

Solomon continued. "And Reesom makes their language live again, in the flesh and singing in all the people who still live in these places, who take care of them and love them, because they reveal the spirit of their ancestors and their children as one unbroken line named Eritrea that we live in now, after how many decades of struggle and blood?"

I looked up and saw a boy in tattered clothes standing in an empty field and holding the tether of a donkey. Reesom rolled down his window and waved. The boy called back, "*Alewuna, Alewana.*"

"Ah, Seghenyetti. Let's get coffee," Solomon said, pulling into a bleached and dusty lot and yanking up the emergency brake as if he wanted to stay forever.

"You see the sign on the café?" Reesom said pointing to it. I read "*Va bene* Bahta" scrawled in Italian and Tigrinya over the doorway. He continued, "During colonial times, an Italian captain named Sanguinetti entered the area to assert his jurisdiction as its overseer. He also wanted men and women recruits for the upcoming Italian invasion of Ethiopia. The local people and their leader gathered to meet him. In full regalia and with great stateliness, the captain walked through the crowd to personally confront and to intimidate his Eritrean counterpart into submission. His name was Bahta, and he had previously won renown by fighting the Tigreans and the Turks. Although he had accepted an Italian appointment as a local administrator to please his family and friends, this was against his better judgment. The demands and demeanor of Sanguinetti were the last straw. As soon as Sanguinetti reached Bahta to face him down, Bahta leveled him with a single, powerful blow to the head and ordered that his guards be jailed. Dazed, the captain got up and said, '*Va bene* Bahta.' It is an expression of triumph in Seghenyetti and throughout Eritrea even today. Yet the macchiato in this café is better than any you can get in Italy."

"Joiner," Reesom continued as we got back in the car and stared out the window as if he weren't talking to me, "Eritrea will show us who we are today. Black, red, white, Eritrean, American—you will hear many voices and one voice. Welcome to the land of Punt." We drove on quietly—as if the coffee opened our eyes to close our mouths—and I began noticing huge trees on the side of the road. Some of them seemed to be growing out of granite, and some of the granite seemed also to be growing up into the trunks of the trees.

"*Sicomoro.* I love this place," Solomon said, turning left onto a dirt road.

"The Valley of the Sycamores," Reesom added. "Over there is the one pictured on our five-nakfa bill." As Solomon turned around to hand me one, he got out of the Pajero and we walked toward the tree. Yosef wandered to an almost circular spot of land where nothing grew. He started scratching the hard dirt. Reesom stood in a patch of dry weeds, breaking and tasting them one by one.

The sycamore had a presence like the Wailing Wall in Jerusalem—and stretched as wide—with a trunk as big as a room. I felt I had to circle it cautiously yet reverently. As I looked up into the massive tangle of monumental limbs, I saw all four seasons at once and as they took place simultaneously all over the world: buds and blossoms, green leaves, fruit, the dry and the dead. As I stepped behind the tree, its immensity, the space it filled, and the bits of sky like stars of daylight shining through the branches engulfed and drove me to my knees to pray, placing my hand on the trunk to touch its power yet also to keep myself from falling prostrate on the roots. My children's names, Barbara's, my parents' and grandparents', more family, friends, ghosts from whom I came, loves, fears—they all touched my lips, as if their names came from here, and as if I did too. But what could this really be? Could I read it like some great document from the top and reread it from the deep as did Yosef poking through the garbage that filled an ancient well he showed us a few hours later at the site of Quhaito? Could I follow this message back through the sand where water used to run, leading back to an equally ancient dam called Safra and still in use: a girl, a boy, a jug, a dip, a word, and stone containing the "I am" without the fire? Could I pocket this feeling like a couple of potsherds—one with a little glaze and the other with the broken stem of a handle—lost amid the countless broken stones, columns, statues, and houses, so cold and high on the plateau they seemed only to answer to the Red Sea on the horizon and the sky, since no one knew who carved them, made them home, or broke them into pieces and tried to plow them under? A little later could I look up at the four-thousand-year-old stele in Belew Kelew that Zemhret had once told me about and with Yosef's fingers in the air trace its letters and translate them as *strug 1agains al od s wi* inscribed beneath a sun and quarter moon?

"Adulite. Joiner, here we begin to write," Reesom declared as we gazed at the dry hills and tunnels stretching out behind the stele.

As I turned to Yosef to ask him, "What is Adulite?" I wondered if the tears in his eyes were only caused by looking into the sun to read the stele.

"We are excavating an ancient seaport south of Massawa named Adulis. It's mostly a mystery so far," Yosef replied softly, "but we are looking at a time stretching long before the Axumite period in the second century A.D. Did the Egyptians learn mummification from the Eritreans of that time? The evidence is mounting. We are naming it the Adulite period and—"

Reesom interrupted, "Scratch the surface anywhere in this country, and you get a different answer every time."

Two months later when I heard Ngugi say to Kassahun, "It's a mystery so far," I thought of Yosef's face and teary eyes as he confessed that even he, as Eritrea's greatest archaeologist, didn't really know what he was excavating. Meeting in Kassahun's office, we now had two hundred thousand dollars from the Ford and Rockefeller foundations to fund African-language writers to come to Asmara. Who would they be? I turned to a clean sheet of paper to write down the names. Recalling my serious doubts three years before about whether an entire conference could be devoted to African-language writers, I thought to myself, "Maybe this is a good time to confess them to Ngugi and Kassahun? Did they sense them at the time or since?" I certainly didn't have any now. Against All Odds was going to happen. We had our funding. A lot less than what we had planned for but only because of the war and not because we were focusing on African-language writers. On the contrary. Our primary emphasis on African languages was our strongest point with Ford. Rockefeller liked it too, although for that we had to add African-language *women* writers to get the funding.

I turned to another blank page in my notebook and said, "Ngugi, did I ever tell you . . . ," but Kassahun interrupted.

"You know, now we may have a problem. Whom should we invite? I can think of three or four in Tigrinya and many more in Amharic but . . ."

Now Ngugi interrupted, "Yes, I have several names of Gikuyu writers, both in Kenya and here. Of course there are many Swahili and South Africans."

I wrote down the names Kassahun and Ngugi suggested and said, "Who else?" Neither Ngugi nor Kassahun spoke. Hoping they weren't expecting me to add any names, I said, if only to break the silence, "I'm trying to remember the name of the writer in Chichewa whom I heard in Malawi."

"We will need help," Kassahun sighed, smiling and shaking his head.

"Yes," Ngugi answered, rubbing his hand on his forehead. "Who do we have in Mande, Akan, and Hausa?"

"And Yoruba, Sotho, Wolof, and Xhosa," Kassahun added.

"We have so many, too many, but who are they? Where are they?" Ngugi responded, his voice trailing off, "It's a mystery so far. . . ."

Kassahun picked up. "We shall have to contact our colleagues from different African countries to ask them, and hopefully they will give us some names. We will find them."

As I listened I turned to another blank page and started writing: "Look up names. Make list. The *Norton Anthology of African Language Writers*, the African Language Writers' Association, books by African Language Writers, the Academy of African Language Writers, contemporary African-language authors, the *African Languages Review*." I crossed off each one as Ngugi got up to put on the brown sport jacket he wore with the "Haggar" label still on the cuff.

Kassahun's cell phone rang. "*Iwe*. Yes, I'll be there in November. It would be great. I want you to see my country. In ten years it could all be over. Yes, Charles leaves soon."

A week later, as I settled into the now familiar bed in the Embasoira's Room 211 around 1:00 A.M. after the long flight back to Asmara, I worried that I wouldn't be able to fall asleep, listening to Asmara's dogs barking for many an hour, at least until I heard *La Illah ila Allah, wa Mohammed rasul Allah* reaching up over the city below from the Great Mosque. I sat up, turned on the twenty-watt lamp, reached for my notebook, and turned to the page I had written from my last meeting with Ngugi and Kassahun. Wondering why I had written "*Iwe, Iwe, Iwe*" at the bottom, I turned to a fresh sheet and started thinking about what I wanted to accomplish on this trip, starting tomorrow. I needed to make a list and started writing.

CHAPTER ELEVEN

A Draw

"Ah," I heard myself saying as I opened my eyes in the dim room: Asmara, my notebook, a blank page, the call to morning prayer: *La Illah ila Allah, wa Mohammed rasul Allah.*

"Charles, you look tired," Zemhret said four hours later as he got up from behind his desk. "Will you have some coffee? I think that mankind was not meant to fly. How are things going?"

"Ah," I heard myself saying again and yawning before I began to tell Zemhret about meeting with Kassahun and Ngugi the week before and how we had to work to get more names and contacts for African-language writers to come to the conference. "We don't have that difficulty here," he smiled. "All of our writers use African languages, except our fathers, the Italians."

"They are not the problem," I responded with a laugh. "Far worse are my fathers at Penn State. They say they have not received enough registration fees, as I promised them. Therefore, when they come to Asmara for the conference, the man and two women who have been collecting the registrations in Pennsylvania want to be at the registration desk here and keep whatever fees are collected. So far I have been unable to convince them that they may have trouble getting through the Asmara airport if they are carrying bags full of nakfa."

As Zemhret poured some tea from a thermos into a well-worn Duralex glass, he smiled again, "Let them try."

A dark, slight, straight-haired girl in a lime-colored, nylon waitress jacket opened the door into Zemhret's office. Her eyes seemed locked, looking right. Under her jacket she wore a T-shirt with an Eritrean soldier's arm holding a torch. She brought my coffee in a small, handleless cup beside a tin sugar bowl on a enamel-coated metal tray decorated with bright flowers. Years past, it might have been made in Italy or Addis, but now the faint print I saw on the bottom as she set down the coffee and sugar read, "Made in China." Later I would buy two in the market to take home: one to use and the other to hang on the kitchen wall. As I asked, "What is new here, Zemhret?" and savored a first sip of bitter and then sweet, I relaxed in a way I hadn't been able to for months, in fact for years. Against All Odds would happen because Zemhret was here. *Dehan dehan—non si preoccupi—* enough worrying—*harrai.*

Pushing aside a summer issue of the *New York Review of Books* and a pile of books and journals with Ngugi's latest book, *Penpoints, Gunpoints, and Dreams* on top, Zemhret put his hands on the desk and looked up. "On this trip you don't have a whole lot to do here, Charles. This afternoon you should go see a wonderful woman who has contacted me from the Norwegian Embassy. She is married to an Eritrean and wants us to apply for a grant from NORAD to document the entire conference, both audio and video. The Audio Visual Institute of Eritrea will handle the filming and recording."

Recalling that I had written many letters, made many phone calls, and visited many UNESCO and UNDP offices to ask for help in creating a video and audio archive for the project and to make a documentary on it—and that many times I was told, "Yes. We would love to help you with this"—I started to say, "How many times the U . . ." Since Zemhret kept talking, I let it go.

"Alemseged has made a wonderful translation into Tigrinya of Ngugi's play. They are rehearsing it at the Cinema Asmara if you want to stop in. There you will also see work being done on a lot of the plumbing and some other repairs. You have impressed your friend at the German Embassy with your CIA credentials, and she has authorized a grant, but we are not yet sure how much." As I thought back to my first visit to the theater with Arefine and to how I watched its painted muses dancing in the cupola to the music of pipes dripping onto the stage, Zemhret continued. "This play is now surely to become one of the most influential works in Tigrinya drama. We will also have a new theater in Seghenyetti. They are building it now out of local stone under one of the sycamores. Emmanuel at the World Bank has helped us. You should go out and see it. Sbrit, our national cultural group, which will give a concert the same night as the Alliance Francaise group from Cote d'Ivoire at the Cinema Odeon in Asmara, will also perform in Seghenyetti for the conference. Solomon Tsehaye, who is the director of our Cultural Affairs Bureau—you might have met him in his office in the Cinema Asmara—is coordinating all the concerts and Seghenyetti too. The conference will conclude with a banquet in the ballroom at city hall. In our secretariat, Ruth is arranging all the receptions. Tsigye has told me that her father will be able to convince

UNICEF that it should do something for us, since he is a former director. Probably it will fund local women to attend the conference. Have you met him?"

"Not yet," I responded, "but I should have twenty-five thousand miles ago. . . .'"

Zemhret finished my sentence and continued, ". . . instead of hoping to taste globalization's forbidden fruit. It lets us forget that we can eat what we grow. I am still collecting materials for 'The Book in Eritrea' exhibition to show the development of writing here."

I broke in, "Did I tell you that I saw the stele in Belew Kelew last June when I was here?"

Zemhret smiled. "Ah, Charles. I am glad to hear you are already a tourist in our young country. Friday is the feast of Meskerem, our new year. You should enjoy it. One more thing before I forget. Kassahun called. He wants you to pick up the proofs of your book with Reesom at Sabur. It has moved, you know, from downtown to right behind the Asmara Palace, the new Intercontinental. I don't like to go there. It's not for me, but it's almost finished and will be ready for all of our guests when you come back in January for the conference. You should also stop in there to see it."

"Their room rates are still too high," I replied, starting to worry again. "We'll have the conference meetings there, and the auditorium will be great for the plenary sessions since it has translation facilities for at least four languages and earphones at every seat. Tsigye is finding our translators. We can also use people attending the conference for Yoruba, Gikuyu, Akan, Swahili, Zulu, and whatever else we can find. But the hotel rates are killing us. Maybe you would have time to come with me to the Intercon to meet with Tewolde, the owner, and see if he can give us a better deal."

"Maybe," Zemhret said, the enthusiasm draining from his voice before concluding. "Let me know when you go."

"Joiner, I have been looking for you." Reesom's voice hummed at the other end of the phone. His call woke me up. After meeting with Zemhret and then with Tsigye at the secretariat office, I went back to the Embasoira for a nap. The balcony curtains and glass doors were closed, although I remembered that I had left them open to hear the afternoon sounds of traffic, Tigrinya, sporadic Italian and English, children, and, somehow just as soothing, the noisy departures and arrivals of various NGO representatives in the carport below. "Have you eaten?" Reesom asked. The time on my laptop read 1:30 P.M., meaning 8:30 P.M. Asmara time. Before I could respond,

Reesom continued, "Come to the Shamrock. It is my office now, and I am always working late. Solomon is here and will order for us."

"I have the best fusilli for them to make," Solomon said to me when I met him in the doorway of the back room in the Shamrock, which, if not my office like Reesom's, had become my dining room. Solomon got me a chair to join the Shamrock owner's wife, her friend who managed the restaurant, the minister of telecommunications, Reesom, and a revolving slate of three or four regulars—businessmen, their wives, colonels in the army, fans of Reesom, various assistant ministers, bank presidents—who always claimed they knew me and whose friendly faces seemed familiar but whose names in Tigrinya I never could remember, to my embarrassment.

Reesom wanted Solomon's attention and raised his voice from his corner seat at the table. "I want meat, meat. Forget your vegetables." I knew he meant it, but the words also came from one of his poems.[1]

"Meat, yes meat," Solomon replied, smiling and turning to the manager so that she could hear him.

"Meat. *Zigni*. Hot *injera*," Reesom continued and then started singing,

Lete Michael, Lete Michael,
Cornrows on your head,
And thighs to comfort
My heart like a morsel of bread.[2]

"Joiner," Reesom said, greeting me with his eyes sparkling, "you see what these Italians thought about our women? Thighs like bread? Bread? Forget it. Why not spicy meat? *Injera*, at least."

"Meat. We want meat," Solomon laughed, shaking his head. "Like lions. Or call us tigers."

"Or just plain cats," Reesom answered. He started singing again but to a different tune that sounded as if he made it up on the spot. "Innards and bones. Cut fresh and dried. We tear it apart. Meat. Forget your vegetables. eZM! Z-eEZM! eBUM! B-eBUM!"

Solomon continued to smile and turned to me. "Meat. Meat. I'm going into the kitchen to make sure about our fusilli so we can eat before it gets so late that we can't have our scotch before we leave. Tomorrow Reesom wants to go to Seghenyetti again, not too early, but we won't be returning to Asmara too late because we have to be back for Meskerem and to ring in the new year. Come along. I'll pick you up."

The next morning I read "*Va bene,* Bahta" over the familiar café door as we drove at about the same speed as the brass of Manu Dibango's

"Wakafrica" playing on the cassette. "I have never seen Eritrea so green," I said out loud to no one.

"Joiner, I've heard you say this six times since we left Asmara. But you're here at the right time. Our rainy season could have been a lot better this year, but we have still been blessed."

Just before we turned off the main road into the valley I saw two little boys and a girl climbing and playing in one of the sycamores. She sat on a limb above them. Clinging to the half granite and half wood trunk, they tried to reach up and pull her down.

"Look. Work has started," Solomon said as we bounced down the rain-rutted dirt road, and he pointed to two huge piles of stones in front of a sycamore around half the size of the tree on the five-nakfa note. "*Il Teatro Seghenyetti,*" Solomon proclaimed.

How about "*Teatro Sicomoro?*" I responded.

"*Mbwa,*" Reesom harrumphed. "Let it be *Teatro Cantalupo.*"

"An Italian name? *No, grazie,*" I demurred as Solomon pulled up to the great tree, "*Aveti avuti abbastanza Italiani.*"

"Welcome to springtime in Eritrea," Reesom said getting out of the car. "Here I begin. I don't know who she is or where she takes me: whether she is dark or light, tall or short. But when I say 'Meskerem,' I feel her power."

As I walked toward the tree, I turned around and saw him stop in the same patch of weeds he stood in last time. Like last time, too, I circled to behind the tree and prayed, letting my voice trail off with "more spirit in us," again as if this had now become my Wailing Wall. Solomon had disappeared, but then I saw a man walking up a nearby hill and knew it was he from the limp, the result of an untreated wound when he was imprisoned in Expo for three years during the Ethiopian occupation.

Coming out from under the tree, I saw Reesom still standing in the weeds and tasting them again as he did last time, only now they glowed green and flowery. "*Meskerem'ya ezi Kulu tgebr, / Kab men tnewH, / Kab men tHaSr. kab men tQeyiH kab men tTqr,*" he intoned between bites.[3]

"This sounds familiar. What are you singing?" I asked.

"You know it but maybe don't remember the Tigrinya," he said, looking up as if surprised.

"This is the poem 'Meskerem,'" I said, feeling embarrassed.

"That's it, Joiner. 'Sky no more tears. Earth meet the sun / And prepare to feast.'"

"We are the guests," I said, finishing the stanza.

Reesom handed me a red flower. "Taste it. We call it Tahbeb. Look at all the bees here. Someone nearby will soon have plenty of white honey."

"Yes, I can taste the honey," I said, chewing a few petals. "But it's very strong."

"Now try this," he said, breaking off a piece of stick-like orange flower growing out of an aloe.

"Bitter," I said, "but they go together."

By now he had gathered an armful of greens. "Our Meskerem salad, Joiner."

"To go with 'the meat and butter,'" I answered, remembering the next line in the poem.

We started trading excerpts, his in Tigrinya, mine in English.

"*Netom qolU nefaTat afnCa, / Enku eske blU blU qanCa.*"

"Come, children. / Chew some cane / With your runny noses."

"*NA nhbi nI Cru nU nferu, / AytHferu dlaykum gberu.*"

"Weaver birds . . . / Come fly. / No one can be shy."

Walking back to the car where Solomon was now standing, Reesom started singing, "eZM! Z-eEZM! eZM! Z-eEZM!"

As we were getting back to Asmara in the late afternoon, Solomon turned to me in the back seat and said, "We might have time to stop to take a look at the Intercontinental."

"The proofs!" I exclaimed in a non sequitur, remembering that Zemhret had told me they were ready to pick up at the new Sabur building behind the hotel. "Can we see it tomorrow instead, Solomon? I have to go to Sabur. Can you drop me off?"

"Why Sabur?" Reesom asked.

"The proofs of our book are ready, and I want to pick them up. Do you want to come in?" I responded.

"I will let you do the proofs, Joiner. I have already corrected the Tigrinya originals on the camera-ready copy I gave to you at first. Meskerem calls me now. "*Meskerem boKri Ameta / . . . aye entezreKba bhyweta / mes meskerem mesker Alem—anes nata!*"

"I only know her shadow," I said, remembering one of the lines as I got out of the car with Reesom singing, "eBUM. Z-eEZM. eBUM. Z-eEZM."

The ink, cold type, and paper warren of Sabur in downtown Asmara had been reincarnated as a kind of industrial park with two cavernous, sand-colored warehouses. Shuffling to open the gate, an old man with a short gray beard and wearing a bulky sweater and baggy pants greeted me: "*Buon-giorno, posso aiuto?*"

Now was the time for Italian. "*Si, grazie. Desidero venire a contatto di Tadesse circa il mio libro.* Is he here? He told me to come."

"*Si, si, si,* " the gatekeeper nodded as his eyes glittered. "*E en su la sul secondo pavimento.*"

"Second floor, *grazie*," I replied over my shoulder as I ran through the door. I couldn't wait to see the proofs. I found the steps upstairs to my left, but to my right and behind a huge plate glass window, I saw newly installed presses from Sweden that dwarfed what I had seen in Sabur before. They hummed and groaned as if they knew they might never be allowed to stop. Pausing to watch, I noticed behind me a museum-like room also behind glass and lined with the floor-to-ceiling thin wooden boxes I had seen at the old Sabur of cold type Ge'ez, Arabic, and Latin letters, their inky dividers still keeping them separate but of no further use since the new presses could typeset without them. A few of the drawers hung open, slanting toward the floor as if their finely oiled grooves and hinges would rather imagine their worse nightmare before—spilling their contents to be scattered in confusion—than to be shoved back forever closed in their final resting place.

Hearing the mechanized continuo of the new presses yet the awful stillness of the antiquated cold type even more loudly, I ran up the stairs until, distracted by my own footsteps' tap and slide on the marble like a drum and cymbal, I stopped on the landing. What was I thinking? Did I think my reason for flying up and down the stairs was any more substantial or necessary in Eritrea than so many other ideas or schemes that eventually faded or disappeared? Even the stairs themselves seemed more important. If armies and empires that came here could last little longer than a cloud over the highlands, some foam on the Red Sea shore, or water in the torrid Sahel, did I really think a book of poetry, a meeting of writers, or any kind of theory could do more? Was there any kind of explanation, expression, or behavior that could sort out, evaluate, make use of, or forget whomever or whatever came and went better than what simply remained?

Outside the landing's window, I saw the other warehouse stacked and crammed with colossal rolls of paper. Beginning with the ants in the sands of Jericho and leading to here, at least I knew I had come far enough to be on one of the rolls. I came from the other direction, made a connection between both sides that only the journey could provide, and I arrived in Rome's Rome, where camels roamed, with an interpretation. I carved a dream and wrestled the devil.

"Here are the proofs, Charlus. Tadesse is out on the floor, and he told me to give them to you." Tadesse's secretary recognized me. Her smile, as she gently handed me the envelope off her desk, made me feel grateful. If only for a moment, I found a little shade from the glaring highland sun. At least I scuttled in the Red Sea foam. An olive tree in the sweltering lowlands needed a little but not much water.

I left the office, sat down on the stairway's landing, and wanted to take a look, unsealing the waxy brown envelope. The lines of my translations looked spindly and light compared with the deep black and thick font of Reesom's Tigrinya, almost double in size. Yegizaw Michael's drawings full of black spots and shadows on many of the pages reinforced the feeling of too much ink contained in each Ge'ez letter, even though I had tapped some of it for mine on the facing page. Was there too much white space between them? I forgot about it later on, walking through downtown Asmara back to the Embasoira. I saw Eritrean brides celebrating Meskerem out in the streets. Wearing gauzy gowns with gold, red, blue, and green ribbons trimming their necklines and hems, the young women met their men, who held torches of twigs to be thrown on the ground and jumped over as they sang, "*Hoye-hoye. Hoye-hoye.*"

CHAPTER TWELVE

A Medallion

"THE CONCEPTION AND DEVELOPMENT OF AGAINST ALL ODDS WERE inspired by the visionary language and educational policies of Eritrea. We the organizers felt that if Eritrea can do it, so can other African countries. We felt, and many argued with us, that the terrible shackles of colonialism have to be broken first and foremost in the minds of African people."

Seated onstage behind Kassahun as he delivered the opening speech for the conference, I looked out on a packed Intercontinental auditorium. Beside me Ngugi was going over his notes, and Zemhret looked disinterested as he scanned the crowd of over a thousand: at least half of them women and two-thirds of the audience being everyday citizens of Asmara; elders in their traditional white *gabis,* students from the University of Asmara and high schools all over the country, Eritrean artists and journalists, local bank presidents and prominent business and civic leaders, out-of-work curiosity seekers, and a phalanx of disabled Eritrean war veterans or *tegedelti,* images of whom—in their Italian-built, red wheelchairs that looked like bicycles modified to accommodate whatever particular limbs they hadn't lost— uncontrollably flooded my mind at the beginning of every meeting I ever had with a possible donor or supporter of the project.

As I picked out the roughly 250 writers and scholars from twenty African countries and around the world—the most uniform and easily recognizable audience members in their Western academic tweeds or blouses, except for similarly recognizable Nigerians and Ghanaians in more colorful dashikis and bubus with headdresses—I wondered how many felt incongruous, self-conscious, and even intimidated squeezed shoulder to shoulder into such a diverse gathering. At least I felt that way. I never expected such a spectacle, regardless of all of the planning for the last four years. However, Zemhret's look of calm and detachment let me know that he had, as he scanned the auditorium's first row filled by Eritrean government ministers and party officials as President Isaias got up to approach the podium while Kassahun sat down beside us.

From Isaias's first word, unlike with Kassahun, all the non-Eritrean members of the audience rustled in their seats to find and put on their earphones. I followed a line that had been taped to the podium and dais of orange and brown Against All Odds' posters: the thick characters of Tigrinya—*Antsar Kulu Mesenakhlat: Afriqawi Qwanqwatatn Sine:tsuhufatn Nab Mebel 21 Zemen* written in Ge'ez—emblazoned at the top with the English below; below that the Hausa Fulani translation of *Shawo Kan Matsalodi: Harsunan Afrika da Adabin Afrika har Karni na Ashirin da Daya;* next the Kiswahili version of *Dhidi ya Vikwazo Vyote: Lugha na Fasihi za Kiafrika katika Karne ya Ishirini na Moja;* and below that the conference title written in Zulu, French, and Arabic.

I watched brown, black, tan, red, yellow, and white fingers nervously dialing their own languages on the earphone switches embedded in the elbows of their seats. As Isaias took his place, also as in the background of the poster, I heard the traffic hum and honk outside as it passed the stately royal date palms lining Liberation Avenue, echoing all the way to the hotel on Warsay. I also imagined, as the poster showed, the sun like a timeless orthodox icon illuminating Asmara and all of Africa with light in the form of the word for "language" in still more African languages: *mutauro, ede, okasa, asusu, lolemu, lakk, lugha* . . . I dialed English and heard Isaias's guttural "qwanqwa" become a precise female voice stating with no emotion, "African intellectuals and in particular linguistic researchers have great responsibilities in this millennium to better understand the uses of languages, thereby to expand and deepen African languages by adding beauty to cultural diversity in order to enhance the development of our continent. When I say this, it is to underline the importance of this conference."

As Isaias took his seat in the first row of Eritrean officials, I saw all of the ambassadors to Eritrea from foreign nations smiling in the row behind him, and I smiled too. The representatives of Denmark, Italy, the Netherlands, Sweden, China, Egypt, Israel, and the European Union, all of whom gave nothing despite their plentiful promises, thought they were attending a little, African Vanity Fair. Pretending to be serious and hoping to conceal their incredulity that such a project could and would take place in Asmara, the ministers' official reasons for freeloading included lack of funds, shortness of time, and reluctance to commit at a time when the border war had yet to be resolved. The American ambassador trumpeted the last excuse loudest of all, especially when Kassahun and I traveled to meet him at the State Department in Washington, where an air force F-16 suspended from the lobby ceiling looked as inviting as the smile he flashed now. Outshining even the

Italian whom he sat next to on the aisle, he gave me a wink and a nod—his only answer to the grant proposals he had encouraged us to submit to the embassy's red, white, and blue Special Self-Help Program and Democracy and Human Rights Fund.

Catching the American ambassador's performance, the French ambassador two seats away from him eyed me for a response. I winked at him and smiled, remembering our conversation in his office the day before. He had recently replaced Claude, who, although he married the Eritrean singer Faytinga, had been transferred to Washington without her. The new ambassador, a cinephile whose last posting was Benin, where he heavily subsidized the Ouagadougou film festival, took back all that Claude had promised except one concert by an Afro-pop group from Cote d'Ivoire, for whom obtaining the visas and fighting the French bureaucratic red tape became so intense and all-consuming that, when I asked Ruth in our secretariat about them, she glared at me and changed the subject.

In our meeting, as the ambassador scanned the program and chain-smoked Gitanes, he gently complained, "Why are there so few Francophones?" When I reminded him even more gently that Tsigye and I had given him the names of a dozen Francophone African writers and scholars and that he had supported only one—who wasn't even on our list—to come to Asmara, he looked up ruefully and exhaled a cumulus of smoke. "Ah *oui,* my old friend at the Sorbonne. He is brilliant. But here. Look at these figures. They don't lie. I have no more francs." His nicotine-yellow fingers pounded a blue calculator labeled "Made in France." Since neither of us had any more to say about the conference, I wanted to take a closer look at the calculator. I hadn't seen one *not* from Asia in years. As I picked it up, his gnarly cheeks imploded with another heavy drag and emitted with a long sigh, oblivious to the Against All Odds mission, "*C'est la vie.* You know in West Africa we really don't have a problem with African languages. Everyone speaks French. Their own kind of French, but French nevertheless."

As the French ambassador turned away his eyes to chat with the Norwegian ambassador in the next seat over, she gestured toward the two AVIE cameramen on stage. His eyebrows rose. She must have been telling him about the huge NORAD grant for us to film all seven days of the conference to create a video archive of the project and a documentary about it. I made a mental note to have one more meeting with him before he or I left Asmara so that I could ask his help in getting the documentary to be shown in the future at the Ouagadougou festival. I would also tell him that we would like to show a second documentary we had made with the NORAD funding: a film of the production of Ngugi's *I Will Marry When I Want* in Tigrinya.

Sitting on the left side of the Norwegian ambassador, the Eritrean head of the British Council, who funded the play's translation and the production, and the World Bank representative in Asmara leaned toward each other. They looked like they were exchanging comments on what the president had just said, but maybe Negusse's telling Emmanuel about the production at Cinema Asmara prompted him to respond that he was happy to help pay for the theater's renovations after the Germans backed out of their commitment when Zemhret told them it was too small (although we did use it for conference T-shirts and name tags).

I remembered my last meeting with Emmanuel. I had complimented the beautiful restoration of the pink stucco, cubist World Bank villa, including its huge satellite dishes just below the American Embassy. Implying that the work appeared too lavish, he said he felt guilty that the World Bank gave us so little. When I responded that we were happy and grateful that he had been able to finance our building the amphitheater under the sycamores in Seghenyetti, he perked up and said, "When the conference is over, let both of us visit UNESCO to support an initiative to make that area along with Belew Kelew and Quhaito a World Heritage site." Recalling that Asmara was also being considered as a World Heritage site due to its architecture, I wondered why Emmanuel thought UNESCO could move mountains—or at least preserve huge sycamores. Trying for four years on three continents to win UNESCO support, I was told from Addis to Paris to New York that we would. But in the end it was only, in the words of UNESCO's deputy director general for education, a "symbolic sum," barely enough to pay for the printing of our Against All Odds programs—even at Sabur rates.

To the left of Emmanuel, Tsigye sat with her father. Thanks to him, UNICEF had paid the conference registration fees of the nearly seven hundred everyday Eritreans—men, women, and children—who filled the auditorium.

The applause for Isaias leaving the podium blended seamlessly into Ngugi approaching it, which I knew made him uncomfortable since he disliked being perceived as backing or endorsing African political leaders. However, Ngugi's tone was immediately personal and not official; and in contrast with Isaias's charcoal suit, blue button-down oxford shirt, and sober Italian silk tie, Ngugi wore a gold, black, and lace African tunic, which was his wife's since his luggage had been lost at the airport. Ngugi gripped the podium when he began, as if to hold on to the earth. He spoke in English, but I saw several of the younger Gikuyu-language writers whom we had funded to come to Asmara dialing their earphone controls to hear if we were translating him into Gikuyu, which we were.

Ngugi spoke slowly.

For me this is a great day, both as an African and as a writer. It certainly is one of the happiest days of my life. I began writing novels, short stories, plays, and essays in 1960 when I was a student of English at Makerere University, Uganda, then an affiliate of London University. I have been writing for the last forty years or so. From 1960 to 1977, I wrote in English, even though all the books were mostly about Kenya and Kenyan people. But from 1977 until the present, I have written my novels, short stories, plays, and books for children in Gikuyu language. So half of my writing life was taken up by English and the other half by Gikuyu language.

As I followed Ngugi's timeline of his literary development, I looked at the first row of Eritrean dignitaries and noticed some of them shifting in their seats while they listened intently. Were they replaying their own last forty years in their minds? While Ngugi had been writing, they had been fighting. The year 1977 was critical for them too, since the Marxist takeover by the Derg in Ethiopia led to a powerful, armed intervention by the Soviet Union in a war that Eritrea was on the verge of winning. Instead, Eritrea had to make a sudden retreat—back then called a "strategic withdrawal"—by the men and women I was looking at twenty-three years later in the front row. I remembered once asking Zemhret about it. "Do you know the battle of Dunkirk," he answered shaking his head but unblinking? "We faced the possibility of total defeat. How were we going to combat black Africa's biggest army now backed by the Soviet Union? Were we out of our minds to continue fighting? Except for Eritreans, everyone thought so, including the Ethiopian government. It had ten times as many troops and twenty times as many armaments when we retreated to the mountains of Sahel. But we knew the terrain and, contrary to what the experts thought, from there we knew we could change the situation. It took almost ten years. Between 1978 and 1983, we withstood seven Ethiopian offensives and, in October 1985, an eighth. After that, we regained the initiative, but we were always sure that we would win."

The silence as Ngugi paused to take a drink of water made me start listening to him again. "Since the sixties of the last century, when African countries started getting their independence, European languages have become the ones setting the terms of the debate on the literature of the continent."

Ngugi's working up to his point that African languages had to determine the course of African literature and African development in general if there were to be true African independence reminded me a little of a new poem by Reesom about the variously and ultimately unsuccessful attempts to colonize Eritrea that I had translated before coming to Asmara for the conference. Scanning the audience to find him, I saw his sharp angular face and gray Afro bobbing ever so slightly on the aisle three rows back from the ambassadors. I could almost hear him: "The Italians said, 'Eat but don't speak.' The English said, 'Speak but don't eat.' The Amharas said, 'Don't speak but don't eat.' eZM. Z-eEZM. eBUM. B-eBUM." Europeans, Ethiopians, Turks, and Egyptians had all tried to tell Eritreans what to do. But the attentive and unchanging faces I looked into in the front row responded, as did their ancestors. They all wanted independence, and now they had it.

I had never heard Ngugi raise his voice quite as loud as now. "I've said it before and I say it again that we must do for our languages what all intellectuals in history have done for theirs by producing the best that can be written and thought in the world. And may this conference be the beginning of better things to come for our languages, for Africa, for the world." The auditorium burst into applause with nearly everyone glowing and smiling, from the front row to the back, up and down the aisles and from the balcony to the podium. They joined Ngugi and each other in a struggle against all odds facing everyone. They wanted what intellectuals throughout history had done for their languages, what Africans still had to do for their languages, and what Eritreans did for Eritrea.

The next speaker, Nawal el Saadawi, reached the podium before Ngugi sat down, and they embraced. When Kassahun and I were thinking about whom to ask to serve as Against All Odds' presiding chairs with Ngugi, we knew that she would accept our invitation only if it came personally from him. Physician, novelist, essayist, political activist, and former health minister of Egypt, she had been imprisoned by Anwar Sadat in the eighties and driven from Egypt in the nineties by fundamentalists who put her name on their hit list. Kassahun had met her at the Asmara airport two nights ago and told me yesterday morning that Lufthansa informed her that the first-class seat on her return flight to Cairo had to be cancelled due to overbooking, and Nawal was very unhappy about it. Could I do something? I called the Egyptian Embassy for help, but the first secretary, as usual, was more interested in hearing about American girls than about the bad back of Egypt's and Arabic's leading woman writer. Would I introduce him to some American female college professors in Asmara for the conference? I said I would if he would give me the ambassador's home phone number.

When I called him, we spoke for an hour. He cheerily let me know that he had just said good-bye to Nawal and her husband, Sherif Hetata—himself a novelist, her translator, and a labor organizer who had been imprisoned in Egypt for ten years. They had come to his house for dinner. "But getting her first class?" he said, oozing false modesty. "I cannot do it. I have already called Lufthansa, and the seats are taken by several very important Arab businessmen."

"But isn't Nawal important?" I countered, adding, "And what if she has to be carried off the plane in Cairo on a stretcher due to her bad back and taken away in an ambulance?" As Nawal began speaking, I could see the Egyptian ambassador looking at me and barely nodding yes.

Wearing a tartan scarf flung across her blue blazer over a check shirt on her small frame with a full mane of white hair, Nawal seemed to burn even more brightly than the unclouded sun outside in Asmara's two-kilometer high air. I had the just-published first volume of her autobiography, *A Daughter of Isis*, back in my room. She held her head high, a woman full of pride based on five-thousand-year-old words spoken to Isis by her mother Noot, goddess of the heavens: "I say to you, my daughter who will inherit the throne after I am no longer here, be a merciful and just ruler of your people rather than a goddess who depends for her authority on sacred power."[1] Yet Nawal began by invoking the ground and in Egypt the life-giving mud of the Nile. "We say in Egypt the neocolonizing powers are globalizing from above, and we are globalizing from below." The deep lines in her face followed her arm going up and down as she smiled and pursed her lips. I turned to Zemhret, and for the first time all morning, I saw him smiling and his Eritrean colleagues in the front row smiling too. If anyone knew globalization from the bottom up, they did.

From the outset, we conceived of Against All Odds as a global or international gathering. As the laughter and applause at Nawal's great one-liner died down, I scanned what I had written and rewritten, repeated and repeated and nearly memorized, which appeared on the back of the Against All Odds poster I had folded in the notebook I was holding:

Countries, universities, corporations, publishers, writers, scholars, artists, students, and children will converge for a weeklong conference and festival at a crossroads of centuries and a crossroads of cultures to make a historic intervention in Africa and the world. . . .

Premised on the belief that the African verbal arts are a vital source of traditional and future social change and individual self-realization, Against All Odds will be a call for action by national, international, academic, and corporate institutions and foundations to promote the continued growth and development of African languages and literatures into the 21st century.

Nawal had moved on from her funny comment about globalization, but reading the Against All Odds description made me want to keep laughing. Sounding good at the time, the description seemed totally out of place and embarrassing here—even false. Against All Odds was finally happening not because a kind of global coalition had converged, although it helped. Our real power was local. Most of the national, international, academic, and corporate institutions and foundations who said they wanted to support us didn't, and if they did, it was with a lot less than we were originally promised. War or no war, we needed help if we were to continue. Most of it came from one source: Eritrea.

I thought again of the speech by Theseus near the end of Shakespeare's *A Midsummer Night's Dream*. Four years of hectic planning, Ngugi's consummate vision of African languages, Kassahun's wheeling and dealing, and the eighty conference sessions I slapped together between Christmas and New Year's had the unreality of "The poet's eye, in fine frenzy rolling / . . . from heaven to earth, from earth to heaven / . . . as imagination bodies forth / The form of things unknown." Eritreans had the real power to turn—or join—"[t]he forms of things unknown . . . / . . . to shapes and give . . . to aery nothing / A local habitation and a name."[2] Zemhret's credentials as an African freedom fighter and Marxist revolutionary notwithstanding, to make Against All Odds actually happen in Asmara, he had to act a lot like the nineteenth-century Scottish American Andrew Carnegie, paying less attention to what people said than to what they did. Not merely in the audience listening, Eritreans mobilized, performing all the work such a gathering required: students and faculty from the university, the unions of Eritrean youth and women, local writers, musicians, dancers, businesses, clubs, state and city workers, *tegedelti*. As a result, once any writer or scholar with any idea about African languages or literature from whatever state and country got on a plane and landed in Asmara, they could not leave without knowing that Eritrea would never be destroyed. Five years before, when I first visited Asmara, I had a similar experience on my own. Inside Eritrea, the conference's happening was never "against all odds"—only outside. Eritrea's confidence that it would win its struggle for independence, despite its forced "strategic withdrawal" and the eight massive Ethiopian offensives that followed, all of which were expected to end the war once and for all—as Zemhret had explained to me back in September, the day before Meskerem—sustained our project, too. Virtually no one in the world—friend, enemy, or indifferent—thought that Eritrea could triumph in its struggle for independence—except the people of Eritrea. Whatever the odds against our project, they had dealt with infinitely worse. How could they let us fail, mere child's play in comparison? For Zemhret and his "compatriots," a word he used affectionately, the project's taking place was never in doubt. Against *what* odds? Three and half years earlier I had hesitated to tell Ngugi that the venture would be named "Against All Odds"—too much hype. He said it wouldn't be, as long as we were talking about the efforts of African-language writers. But calling the project "Against All Odds" here and now in Eritrea, after all the odds it beat and the tremendous human cost to win the war, shouldn't I feel even more foolish?

For a moment I wanted to bolt from the stage, but my way would have been blocked by the Ghanaian poet Kofi Anyidoho approaching the podium. Transporting people into Eritrea from other countries had become our biggest problem. Kofi got a big laugh from the crowd as he described his journey and all its stopovers "from Accra to Copenhagen to Rome to Amman to Sanaa and finally to Asmara." For him, simply getting to Asmara felt "against all odds" the most. The dean of my university followed the same route, only she picked it up in Rome from New York and Pennsylvania before that. As I greeted her and her group as they arrived in Asmara airport after a forced overnight in a state hotel in Yemen, I wondered if her chillier than usual greeting meant I might not have a job once I got back to Pennsylvania.

That same afternoon Kassahun and I had been thrown out of the Yemeni Airlines manager's office on Liberation Avenue when, as we argued that the forced overnight should not be necessary if the planes were running even close to schedule, he and Kassahun began trading insults—with both of them equally vehement in Tigrinya and Arabic—until I tried to step between them, which the manager took as a sign I was about to beat him for insulting Kassahun. Worse still, most of the South African delegation of writers—including Zulu's greatest writer, Mazizi Kunene, and the poet and ANC leader Mongone Wally Serote—had never received their airline tickets to fly to the conference from Johannesburg, again via Sanaa. Yet the other half of the delegation—including another one of conference's presiding chairs, Mbulelo Mzamane—was now stranded for two more days in Sanaa, until the next Yemeni flight to Asmara. Previously, most flights to Asmara came through Addis, a commuter hop away, but the war had shut down the airspace between the two countries completely.

The roundabout routes that most travelers from Africa now had to take to reach Asmara affected the West Africans the most. In addition to their mileage being nearly tripled, they needed special visas to stop in Europe. Furthermore, even with their visas, European embassies in Cameroon and Nigeria prevented writers—whose tickets we had paid for and sent them, and whose visas we had arranged—from boarding their flights. The embassies thought that once the writers landed in Europe they would not continue with their flights to Asmara but leave the airport and become illegal immigrants.

I couldn't remember the name of the cultural affairs officer I knew in Cameroon, I doubted if she would still be stationed there, and I doubted even more if she could help. Nevertheless, I called her from the Africa World Press office, and at Kassahun's urging, even though the phone call would be very expensive. I hoped that my somewhat unusual last name and previous visit to Yaounde might be recalled. Hearing "Embassy of the United States" crackle through the receiver, I answered, *"Buon' giorno. Mi chiamo Dottore Charlus Cantalupo. Ho visitato parrechi ani fa, e sono un amico dell' ufficiale culturale di affair. E la, per favore?"*

"Oui," the operator responded flatly, *"mais elle n'est pas,"* she continued, only I couldn't understand her French.

"Why the hell is she speaking French?" I said in exasperation to Kidan who, writing an angry email to one of our wayward travel agents, looked up and replied, "Maybe because you're speaking Italian?"

At this, Arefine popped his head in the door and said smiling, *"Ma tutto il mundo parla Italiano, Charlus, no?"* At this point, I wondered why I had automatically thought that I had a better chance of getting a response from the American Embassy in Cameroon by sounding like an Eritrean colonial Italian than an American academic.

I interrupted the embassy operator still speaking in French. "No, please wait. I am Dr. Charles . . ." As I translated what I had said before in Italian, I tried to give it an extra American twang.

"Yes, Professor," she said in a light voice, "I remember. She is here, and I will put you through."

"Professor Cantalupo," I heard two seconds later, "How are you?" Hearing the patrician New England intonation of my name by the cultural affairs officer, I realized immediately that our case was hopeless if I felt lucky to be speaking with her.

After exchanging pleasantries and as I explained the conference to her, she responded, "Yes, I have heard about it. A wonderful idea. I wish I could be there." Feeling flattered for a moment, I said, "I wish you could be here, too, but maybe you can help me?" "Please," she responded, "I will be happy to help in any way I can."

As I explained the dilemma of the three Cameroonian scholars not being allowed to board their flight in Douala, the silence on the other end grew louder and louder until I asked, "Are you there," but there was no answer.

The line went dead, and when I tried to call back three times, the line was busy every time.

As Kofi concluded his remarks, his large and heavy body elegantly draped in a tangerine and white lace Ghanaian tunic, I awakened from my travel nightmare to a more promising dawn. He recalled,

> Several years ago when I attended the famous Rotterdam international poetry festival, the organizers decided to focus on Africa, and twenty, maybe thirty of the poets invited were from Africa. When the Swedish poet was called upon, naturally she presented her poetry in Swedish. Our Chinese colleague was called upon. Naturally he presented his poetry in Chinese. The reading went around the world until it came to Africa. When our colleague from South Africa was called upon, he presented his poetry in English. Our colleague from Senegal was called upon, and he presented his poetry in French.

With this Kofi stopped. Turning from the podium to address the Kiswahili poet Abdulatif Abdalla, who was sitting next to Ngugi, Kofi held out an arm almost twice as big as any Eritrean's. "With the exception of our brother here, who made a powerful presentation in Kiswahili," he continued, and the audience broke in with applause.

Jumping like a fish out of a deep pool in the morning light, Abdulatif answered, "Foreign languages are languages of expression to us, and African languages are languages of being. Once we cease to use these languages, we cease to be. And once we cease to be, who are we?"

His question, "Who are we?" over the conference's next seven days echoed from session to session and from stage to stage, translating as naturally as night to day into different answers in every language yet with little if any separation among them, even between "I" and "we," at least for these few days. "Who are we?" I thought and felt chills as the audience from all over Africa and the world in the Cinema Asmara, with its red walls glowing and its stage lights blazing, stood and rushed the stage to dance with the actors at the conclusion of Ngugi's *I Will Marry When I Want* as they waved Kenyan flags and sang Mau Mau songs translated into Tigrinya that only the Eritreans in the audience could understand.

"Who are we?" I thought, as Alemseged Tesfai spoke the next day about "The Pen and the Eritrean Armed Struggle."

"A gun or a pen," Senait Lijam, who served on the central committee of the Union of Eritrean Women, said to me when I asked her about Alemseged's talk: "Posing such a question is like asking me to choose between my mother and my father, who have equally contributed to my life and who are equally dear to me." In her elegant black-and-white check, Dior-knockoff dress, big hair, and Eritrean heart earrings, she looked more like a graduate from a fashion institute than from the University of the Revolution in the field where she had fought so fiercely.

Similarly Alemseged couldn't think of the pen and the sword separately. Could any Eritrean? Could anyone in the world if they thought realistically about it? But instead of finding the relationship as close to home as his mother and father, Alemseged invoked the parents of every writer—word and thing—as he found his inspiration between their yearning for each other in the most violent moment of his wartime experience. "In 1988," he recounted, "I was assigned to report for an EPLF magazine on the course and outcome of one of the great battles of the revolution, the battle to capture Afabet. It was tremendous, very fast, and all-encompassing, and the EPLF accomplished its goal in the set time of forty-eight hours."

Scenes from ERI-TV's late night broadcasts of black-and-white war footage, which usually put me to sleep, now ran through my mind as Alemseged spoke. Wearing ripped fatigues or tight short-shorts, rubber sandals, and huge Afros, Eritrean soldiers filed across barren landscapes, fired machine guns, fell in the dust besides leafless bushes, got up, and fired again.

Alemseged continued. "I was there. I couldn't follow what was happening. I didn't understand how they did it. They were my comrades. I was there with them. Everything happened so fast. I tried to jot down notes, and then something happened."

Standing at the podium in an open shirt and sport jacket, wearing glasses and a graying beard, he looked like the college professor he surely would have become if he remained at the University of Wisconsin in the sixties instead of feeling compelled to go back to Eritrea and fight for his country's independence. But if he didn't go back, he would only have his utter bafflement at war—like most of the college professors, especially the Western, in the room—instead of a little more of an answer. "Who are we?" I asked myself and answered, "We should be like him," as he continued.

My companion and I walked with Ali Ibrihim, the commander of the central flank, an engaging EPLF general who regrettably died two weeks after this, his day of victory. We were reveling side by side when we came across a miracle. Any writer, especially one as perplexed as I was about what to write that morning, will agree that what we saw was nothing short of a miracle. For at the gates of Afabet, under an indistinguishable shrub, lay a piece of flesh amid a pool of dried and curdled blood. The three of us paused to bend down to examine it. It was a human heart, complete with aorta and arteries: one that had poured out what blood it had been pumping into the veins of a fighter who had been blown to pieces by falling enemy artillery fire. The morning sun had not yet worked on its freshness, and the crows and vultures were not yet up and around, so it lay there red and oily as if clinically extracted by an able surgeon. Disturbing to look at or talk about even today, nearly a dozen years on, that ugly product and specimen of unwanted and unnecessary violence expressed something deep, but for me as a writer its profundity lay in what it did not express. Separated from the body it had given life to, it was not attributable to any particular name or face. It had no gender, no linguistic original identity, no religion. It was just a simple heart: the heart of an African freedom fighter that had exposed itself as if to remind us of what the Eritrean struggle was all about or should be all about. We did not bury it. There was not time for that. Ethiopian jet fighters and helicopters were screeching and hovering over our heads threatening to lift us up by the collar. We left the heart lying there, triumphant and heroic, but strangely in that hour of total victory and glory, also lonely, lonely and defiant.

Walt Whitman and Stephen Crane describing the wounds not of national pride but of ordinary soldiers in the American Civil War; Wilfred Owen and Isaac Rosenberg first looking and wheezing at modern trench warfare in World War I; Homer on Achilles dragging the body of Hector in the dust and stones of the plains of Troy; Alemseged at Afabet. "Who are we?" I thought, feeling hopeless, suddenly knowing that Eritrea and Ethiopia would now fight again and afraid that the Danish Embassy and the U.S. military attaché could be right to warn me against holding such a conference in a country about to fall back into a war from which it might never again emerge, until I realized that Alemseged was still speaking.

In most of our Eritrean languages, the heart is not just a life-giving organ. In Tigrinya, a wise man or wise woman is called *lebam,* and wisdom is *lebona.* They both come from the word *lebi,* which means heart. In Tigre, *laleb* is the word for a wise person. It comes from *leb,* which means the heart. In Billen, a wise person is called *labekukh,* which comes from *labahkah,* which means the heart. Like all humanity we think with our heads, but we say we think with our hearts. The heart is the creator. The pen is the creation of the heart. When I speak of the pen, I speak of the heart. I speak of how the Eritrean heart acted throughout the struggle. Performance also is the performance of the heart. Eritrean history is a struggle between forces that have been trying to write off Eritrea as a nation, to simply ignore it as something that did not exist, and the heart of Eritreans that refused to bend to these forces of destruction. As a writer I will speak from the heart.

For Alemseged, Eritrea would never be destroyed because he saw quite literally that the Eritrean heart would never be destroyed—even if it had no bone, muscle, or any more body parts attached—and, just as important, the Eritrean words for heart would never be destroyed. Or at least, from the stele at Belew Kelew to now, such wisdom had not yet been destroyed. I remembered trying to translate the fragment: *strug 1agains al od s wi.*

"Who are we?" I thought again the next afternoon, on the conference's third day, titled, "African Women's Writing," as I heard Nawal el Saadawi speak from the heart, unable to separate it from the words she remembered hearing her grandmother say sixty years before, "*Rabina hawal adel aerifuhu bi-elaqel.* God is justice and we know God by our heart."

She reached this conclusion through a disclaimer: "We all have brains," she began.

> Writers are ordinary people, not geniuses. Political systems try to make them geniuses and heroes. I don't believe in heroism. Or, all of us are heroes, and we are all fighting. Even the very poor and illiterate woman in her home, in her hut is fighting. I was brought up in a poor family, and I was born female, poor, in the village of Kafr Tahla by the Nile. Since I was born female, poor and in the village, I decided that I should change my life.

Had I heard her right? Wouldn't the more common assumption around the room be that most women born in oppressed and remote circumstances did not have the power to change their lives? What did she think superseded the center versus the marginalized polarity that had been dominating most of our discussions until now?

Nawal continued.

> I was inspired by my grandmother. My peasant, illiterate grandmother gave me the first lesson in religion and philosophy when she was fighting the mayor. She stood in front of him, and he was carrying the Koran. He told her, "You ignorant, illiterate woman. Go home and be veiled. That is what the Koran says; that is what God says." My grandmother, a poor woman with no shoes—I was five years of age and she was holding my hand—told him, "I know God more than you. God is not a book. God is justice. He is here. She is here. I hear God inside me."

As she spoke, imitating the actions of her grandmother, Nawal raised her index finger as powerfully as Plato in Raphael's famous Vatican fresco, *School of Athens.* She creased her face with all the hardship that her grandmother, Sittil Hajja, had ever faced and triumphed over, and with all the hardship her great-grandmother, beaten to death for humiliating the village headman, had faced too.

"*Rabina hawal adel aerifuhu bi-elaqel*," Nawal said, pressing her fingers to her heart.

> We are killing in the name of God. My name was put on the death list because they said I was against Islam. I am not against Islam. My father graduated from Al-Azhar, the highest institute of Islam in Egypt. He taught me Islam. Islam, like Christianity, like Judaism, like Buddhism, like all religions—like all human religions—is based on three human principles: justice, freedom, and love. If any religion contradicts justice, freedom, and love, I'm not ready to believe in it.

Globalizing from the bottom up, Nawal not only fought the crush of globalization from the top. She also struggled against radical strains of religion that she saw all around her and that choked more and more life every day.

As I left the room, I ran into Reesom in the hallway. Having barely seen and not having spoken to him since the conference had begun, I missed him and wanted to get him more involved. "Reesom, where have you been? How is the conference?"

"I've been here," he answered, sounding a little distracted, "but I have had nothing to do. Give me something to do."

I felt guilty. Had I become too involved in the conference organizing and forgotten poetry? How could I have neglected him? Therefore, I asked, "Would you like to read a poem tonight at the Union of Eritrean Women's banquet and *guyla*?"

Reesom lit up. "I would, Joiner. I will read first, and it will be about love to bring poetry back to where it belongs—up front and from the heart. eBUM. Z-eEZM. eBUM. Z-eEZM." Along with the rhythm, he started moving his shoulders up and down, right and left. I was looking forward to the *guyla* too, when the entire crowd would be dancing the same way—Eritrean style, in a rotating circle.

As Kassahun and I approached the Expo hall that evening for the huge dinner and dance, we were a little late since we had stopped at the Africa World Press office to call Mbulelo in Sanaa. He told us that he would finally be arriving the next day and that Yemeni Airlines had lost his luggage.

"At least he will be here," Kassahun quipped. "And we will give him a makeover to look like an Asmarino."

"Then he had better learn fast how to speak Tigrinya," I was about to answer when I saw Reesom and Zemhret arguing with one another at the door to the banquet hall. "What the . . ." I said softly instead.

"Just keep walking," Kassahun whispered to me without moving his lips. "Pretend you don't notice."

I looked straight ahead and emotionless until we were inside. "What do you think happened?" I asked, taking Kassahun by the arm. "And please don't tell me not to be too concerned because politics here is like a family argument."

"Don't worry," Kassahun responded, mirroring the panic in my eyes with his, but otherwise seeming calm. "You probably should have checked with Zemhret before you invited Reesom to be the first reader tonight."

"But he told me he had a great love poem, and that it would fit the occasion. I thought people would enjoy it. You know what a performer he is," I replied.

Kassahun answered as if he didn't want to. "The poem itself is not the problem. Zemhret is telling him that by coming to you he was interfering in the program because he wasn't scheduled to be a part of it. Zemhret is asking him to please stop being disruptive, and Reesom is saying he's not."

"*Va bene,*" I nodded wearily, preferring to eat, drink, and dance instead of facing what I had sensed more and more in the past six months: Reesom's star was starting to sink in Eritrea. He had alienated Zemhret, his biggest supporter, as I witnessed myself when he first brought Kassahun and me to hear Reesom perform at Expo a year and a half before. Reesom's poetry performances were no longer on state-sponsored occasions or in municipal forums, except for his two conference appearances scheduled for the next day and the next. The plan for his creative writing workshops had stalled.

I worried. Would the enmity between Reesom and Zemhret prevent me from working closely with them, or if not with one, then the other? Zemhret clearly had the political power; Reesom had the power of poetry. One of my greatest joys in translating his poetry derived from its seeming inseparability from the politics of Eritrea. He would update and reinscribe the stele Belew Kelew with his poetry's own raison d'être: "The Eritrean struggle of independence is the primary motivating force for my art. It's a continuation and expansion of the Eritrean struggle for self determination."[3] Political poetry in the United States and Europe was like an oxymoron—polarizing the many, persuading only the few, and nearly always preaching to the converted. Reesom's poetry in Eritrea seemed different. His "Alewuna, Alewana" rallied the nation, from its ordinary citizens to the office of the president, whom he addressed with "You wear our crown of leaves / As long as we're free / To say *yes* without force."[4] He was the *getamay,* the "Mighty Joiner"—as I often addressed him in our emails—who joined the language of real political power with a genuine language of poetic power to humanize the former and popularize the latter for the betterment of all. Sometimes I felt that I could have been back twenty years ago in my studying the English Renaissance, only it was now and in Tigrinya, and I was actually working with Eritrea's Wyatt, Sidney, Raleigh, Marlowe, and Spenser—at the center of a vibrant culture amid a swirl of young, tried-and-true nationalism and a vigorous vernacular beginning to flex its muscles and feel its strength. Other times as I worked side by side with such poets, political leaders, and ministers, with every door open and easily entered, even the president's, the smallness of the place yet the powerful blooms of art, state, and vernacular language all around—based on a sense of a renewed ancient past invigorated by political and military victory—I felt like a kind of Lorenzo Alberti, returning to Florence during the Renaissance, only this was Asmara in Africa. Simply by walking down a street, I was hearing new kinds of music, ideas, and poetry coming from the doors and windows of buildings that were architecturally new and filling up with ways of making images that had never been tried before. But as I now walked into the banquet I worried: what if I were wrong?

The next evening when I saw Reesom at a poetry reading at the university, I asked him, "Mighty Joiner, are you all right? I saw you arguing with Zemhret last night outside the banquet hall, but I didn't know what to do. I hope I have not gotten you into trouble."

Smiling and unperturbed, he said, "Don't worry. I have promised myself not to be distracted by politics over poetry. Let's go in and listen."

"*Harrai*," I responded, mimicking Arefine, and seeing Bob Holman, the only white American poet other than me at the conference. He wore his trademark porkpie hat, black baggy suit, black frame glasses, and skinny tie. Taking his hand, I wanted to introduce him to Reesom, but when I turned around to find him, he was gone.

"Bob, are you ready for the reading?" I said as we hugged each other.

"Why didn't you tell me that I've been getting ready for poetry in Eritrea all my life? This place makes us know who we are," he whispered.

"Where are you sitting?" I asked, looking around amazed at the huge crowd.

"I'm not," he replied walking toward the front of the audience and holding up his video camera—the smallest I had ever seen. "I'm recording."

Voices thronged within the university's inner courtyard, but at this point none became intelligible since the overamplified singing and kora of Al-Haji Papa Susso, a griot from Gambia, drowned them out. The well of his sound opened deeper and deeper, until thirteenth- and fourteenth-century Mandinka history and fables plucked louder and louder from the kora's twenty-one strings seemed to be on the lips of everyone speaking at once and echoing through the surrounding two stories of *portici* packed with students, many of whom dangled their legs over the marble railings.

Born and raised on the Gambia River—as far away from Asmara as New York from Dakar—Papa fit Asmara and Asmara fit him as if it were his home—as if the only difference between them were a few letters in the spelling of his kora and its Eritrean equivalent, the *krar,* and the number of their strings. Descended from a long line of griots in the Susso family, who invented his instrument—as if the inventor of the Western keyboard also fathered a line of composers for the instrument from medieval times until now—Papa had been telling me for ten years, since I first met him soon after my second trip to Senegal, that he was my personal griot. He would laugh, his voice looping to an unearthly high, and I would laugh in response. Traditionally griots had been attached to West Africa's most royal courts and served as the praise singers and historians for kings. Yet Papa reversed the traditional ratio of power. Since the days of such kings had long passed, he did not have to recognize royalty. He conferred it, as he did now. Everyone who heard him felt like royalty. He said, "I am your griot" to whomever recognized his power. The time and place no longer mattered. The way his words overpoweringly echoed here, they echoed all over Africa, America, and anywhere else he was invited to perform: "*Manjugulong! / Manyinijugalong!*" (I don't know who is my enemy / I don't know who is my friend).[5] He didn't need to know when he sang, only when he did not. Therefore, we wanted him with us in Asmara and performing every day: his one-man riffs of Mandinka and kora setting a triumphant and timeless example of work in an African language to be enjoyed as if any odds either for or against could not equal or even affect what we were hearing.

Stopping abruptly, he boomed "Peace and love" into the microphone, adding, "Now please listen to my new friend." Following his lead, the crowd quieted as abruptly. Opening the program and looking at the list of readers I had scheduled seven days ago and seven thousand miles away—or was it seven thousand years ago on another planet?—I wondered whom he meant?

"*Lwam!*" Tigrinya reverberated around the chamber, and a young woman in traditional Eritrean dress held the microphone. Who was she? Two bold, wide bands of rusty red brocade ran up and down her gauzy, V-necked, floor-length dress instead of horizontally around its neckline or hem. Her thin Eritrean gold necklaces and bracelets trembled and glittered as she stretched high, bent low, swung, and held out her arms as she performed. Yet the large silver pendant tied tightly to her neck—the same shape as her earrings—hung as steadily as her words, like Papa Susso's, echoing as if they would not, could not die: "*Lwam. Ata lwam. Lwamah gedteefah . . .* "[6]

I knew she wasn't on my list, yet I knew her, although not from the way she looked but the way she sounded. The shy girl in a kind of crinoline dress who had stolen the show with her poem "Go Crazy Over Me" when I read in Asmara three years before, now stole the show again. I saw Bob Holman in the front row turn around and wide-eyed mouth the words "diva" and "Who is she?" to me. I noticed that the eyes of the student sitting next to me—who wore an Against All Odds T-shirt—shined as brightly as Bob's yet reflected not only the excitement of the performance itself but also the crowd that she scanned as if knowing that they could not react any other way. "What is she saying?" I asked, leaning over to her before realizing that I shouldn't interrupt what she was experiencing. Without turning her eyes toward me but continuing to look at the stage, she responded in a steady voice as if she wanted to make me sure that I was aware that I was hearing history.

"Our Saba Kidane is telling us who we are. She says a country needs a woman to find peace. That only a woman is willing to sacrifice enough. She'll fight as hard as anybody, but she never loses sight of peace. She'll give birth, and she'll fight like a lion for her kids. She may forget if she's alive or dead and catch fire on the battlefield, but even there she never forgets peace."

As the student's voice trailed off, Saba swayed and her free arm gestured from the sky to the ground and back to the sky again, with her large eyes opening and closing as if following her arm. Her poem's last word, the same as her first, "*Lwam,*" set off a burst of applause and cheers. As I joined in, the student turned to me and said slowly and authoritatively, "We would never have won the war without our women fighters. My mother was one. She is not here tonight, but she will join us in Seghenyetti tomorrow. Will Saba be performing there too?"

"For sure," I responded, knowing that, as here, I hadn't scheduled her.

"She must," the student responded. "She must be a big part of . . . what did you call it? 'The Big Conversation?'"

"Yes," I answered, "Orature in the Valley of the Sycamores: The Big Conversation. We thought there could be no better place to celebrate Against All Odds' sixth day."

The student put her arm around three friends who had gathered around her, all of them wearing Against All Odds T-shirts, but each a little differently: one with the sleeves rolled up, the second tied at the waist, and the third pulled up to her breasts and over a red sweater. "We will all be there to see Saba," she said.

Early the next morning as I drove to Seghenyetti with Zemhret and his young son, Emmanuel—the radio on and tuned to the government station as always—Zemhret asked me as if he had been thinking about the question for the last few miles, "Charles, can you get Bob to perform his poetry again today? He's great. We need to hear him."

"Of course, I will," I replied, knowing that Bob would be happy to. "But Zemhret," I continued, "I overheard some people last night in the audience at the university say after Bob performed that they didn't need to hear any white poets and crazy ones at that."

"These people know nothing," Zemhret replied turning up the news on the radio: "If they complain, you must tell them, 'Light the lights,' like you do in that poem of yours."

"I will try," I answered. "But Zemhret," I added, noticing that we were passing the famously named café, "My name is not Bahta. *Va bene?*"

"*Va bene,* Bahta," he laughed, "Now look. They are expecting us."

Children in turquoise and green school uniform shirts lined the road. They laughed, clapped, and chanted at each passing car. Standing beside them, their mothers ululated and waved from beneath their gauzy and ribbon-trimmed gowns. Many of the students waved palm branches and some held signs that read "We love African languages" in Tigrinya and English. At the turnoff for the valley of the sycamores, one of the older students waved a large Eritrean flag. Their presence, singing, and chanting made the normally dry and brown January landscape bloom as bright as Meskerem. "*Va bene,* Bahta. Zemhret, this is amazing," I said as the Land Cruiser bumped down the dirt road.

"They have worked hard to get it ready," he nodded as we parked.

Solomon Tsehaye approached us. "Sbrit is almost ready. Many of our oral poets are here," he said, "Come see." The two large piles of stones I observed on my last trip had become four curving, deep set rows—actually ridges sloping up from beneath a huge sycamore that provided a roof and a backdrop for the stage. Ge'ez graffiti covered a few of the limbs, and as I looked up and around, once more I followed the progress of the seasons— budding, flowering, greening, drying, dying. Sbrit instrumentalists with drums, electrified *krars*, flutes, long horns, zithers, bells, rattles, and a huge hanging gong were warming up like the members of a symphony orchestra taking their seats and tuning as the crowd streamed into a concert hall— only Eritrean style. "Look, they are coming now," Solomon said, gesturing back toward the road.

"The buses could not handle the dirt road and have emptied," Zemhret added, "Let's meet them."

As I watched a cloud of dust approaching, another cloud enveloped me from behind. "All the local villages are here with us," Solomon said, putting his hand on my arm. A wave of Sbrit instrumentation almost obsessively repeating the same three measures combined with a seemingly chaotic flock of ululation pushed me forward, and the two clouds became one. More musicians with long wooden flutes and sword-waving elders with spindly legs and their traditional Eritrean dress girded up to their loins led processions within processions, circling under a rain of popcorn thrown out of large baskets by women in brightly colored dresses and veils starkly contrasting their very dark skin. The entire conference and what seemed like half of Asmara with them flooded the area to be greeted by nearly everyone who lived there. I picked out Kassahun wearing his cowboy hat, surrounded by dancing drummers and striding with a group of Nigerians—Akinwumi Isola, Tanure Ojaide, Abdul Rasheel Na'Allah. They all waved and gave the thumbs up sign to the crowd. Papa Susso in a glittery green Gambian robe and playing his kora had joined the Eritrean musicians and dancing elders. A din of clapping broke in and out of unison. Ngugi, his wife Njeeri, their daughter Wanjiku, and half a dozen Gikuyu writers formed a kind of eddy in a vast stream of faces of all ages and colors speaking dozens of languages and inevitably pushing toward the stage. I turned around and saw the rows of the amphitheater already filled, with huge straw mats and blankets unrolled and covering the ground up behind them. Extending far beyond the tree limbs and into the sun, the slope teemed with children. They quickly became wild. Men in custodial uniforms chased them and wielded long, thin sticks. The crowd continued to flood in until no one could move. Finding a place behind the musicians and leaning against the tree, I saw Larry taking pictures in the field behind it also overflowing with the crowd. Beside him stood two of the students with whom I had talked about Saba at the university.

Solomon passed me as he climbed onto the stage to begin. "Solomon, do you have the list of the performers?" I asked.

Holding up a paper written in Tigrinya, he replied in a serious tone, "I have the names of the traditional performers here. Zemhret has also just given me a new list."

Wondering if I should ask him about it, I said, trying to gauge my tone to his, "Is Saba on it? Is Bob? And the African American women who want to sing a spiritual?"

"Yes," he answered with a nod and a tightening of his lips to suggest that the list was too long. "They are all there, along with the Gikuyu, Ngugi, Mbulelo, Abdulatif, the two Kofis, and you be ready too."

Jumping onstage, Solomon ran to the center. He casually greeted and took the arm of a small, old woman with a large gold ring in her right nostril and draped in a huge red scarf folded over her head to her feet. Guiding her to the microphone, he began speaking, but I couldn't hear until a stage monitor placed up in the tree got connected, and I caught him in midsentence: ". . . a very known oral poet."

I knew she had to be Mother Zeineb. Who better to begin? A veteran fighter from the war and mother of nine now in her early eighties, she was among the first to challenge the tradition of a male-only EPLF army and made women's rights in Eritrea her lifelong mission as a fighter and as an oral poet. I remembered her famous line, which became the title of one of the first books Kassahun had given me in 1995 about Eritrea: "Even the stones are burning," her response to a journalist to describe a battle for her village.

Solomon continued, "She fought against the enemy, which finally enabled us to achieve independence. Mother Zeineb." As he spoke she almost scowled, with eight thick lines of flesh descending horizontally from her thick lower lip. As if beginning to feel comfortable at the microphone once she was alone, she brightened, lifting her right arm and pointing her fingers up and down as if she was spelling every word and punctuating every phrase.

"She is Tigre," I heard a voice say next to me: "Meet my mother." I saw the student with whom I sat at the reading the night before standing next to me and gently pushing the arm of a middle-aged woman next to her toward me.

"Hello," I said taking her outstretched hand. She wore a black sweater and jeans, smiled, lowered her eyes, and looked up. I did the same. In the background, Mother Zeineb sounded as if she were telling us that even though the stones had cooled, we should still be careful. "Do you know Tigre?" I asked, looking back and forth between the student and her mother.

Looking at each other, they laughed and began trading the phrases of Mother Zeineb filling the air. "I'm burning. You should boil like delicate, raw meat in freedom," the mother said.

"I'm too old for the army. Too weak to be the minister of education," her daughter responded.

"But this damn world makes me too bold," the mother concluded, forgetting her initial shyness.

After a pause, the daughter picked up again: "Now she is cursing the Woyane and their new war."

"And now she is singing of victory and peace," the mother added.

When Mother Zeineb stopped, the audience responded with surges of applause, cheers of "*Amandla!*" and hundreds of clicking cameras. Palm branches waved in the sky and women's ululating weaved like wild ribbons through the crowd. Every performer after her received the same, yet more and more, with Sbrit knitting an ever denser thicket of rhythm and song before and after each one. They all took the stage as if it was the entire African continent. Arabic to Akan, Gikuyu to Zulu, bebop to "Swing Low Sweet Chariot"—however various the African languages, the people, all the people, understood.

Around midway through the performances when Solomon at center stage turned around, grabbed the microphone, and raised his heavy eyebrows so that they extended well above his thick-framed aviator sunglasses, I knew it was my turn. "Light the lights,"[7] I began as he handed me the microphone, and I leaned over to speak into it while he still held it, prompting him and the audience to respond "Light the lights." "Light the lights," I said again and again, each time with the audience replying louder and louder until we reached a level that, when we stopped, made the silence stark. Yet at this point, when I would normally continue with the lines of the poem, they seemed stale, and I thought of standing under the sycamores my first time, when I silently spoke the names of everyone dear to me as if they came from here. "Light the lights because the names come from here," I continued. "Light the lights," the response came back in a somewhat muted tone. "Light the lights for your names. Light the lights." "Light the lights," came back a surer response. I replied, "I say your name. Please say your name here. Your name. I am Charles. Light the lights. Say your name." I looked out and saw people saying their names, first into the air and looking at me but then to each other, louder and louder.

The four hours of performances passed like four minutes, at the end of which Solomon emerged and, without showing even a hint of weariness, announced, "Now we must share Eritrean bread." Eritrean women in their white, billowing, and ribbon-trimmed robes and scarves appeared with huge baskets of flat huge circular loaves baked from corn especially for the occasion. The oldest woman took out a loaf and, offering it first to Ngugi, signaled to him to break off a piece, which he did, also breaking it to give half to Njeeri. The woman also signaled to him, as she did to Mbulelo who joined Ngugi, to break off more pieces and to continue handing it out, as if they were priests offering communion, yet a bread only aspiring to be the word, the African word, and not flesh. Meanwhile, additional baskets and loaves fanned out similarly through the crowd. Solomon took the microphone for a last time. "There is more to eat under the next tree. Please, everyone follow us there." He held a chunk of bread as he came backstage to where I stood, jumped down, and gave some to the student, her mother and me. "It makes us hungrier than we were," he smiled.

"Then let's go," I answered as we were already being pushed and pulled with the crowd in a kind of spontaneous procession—only now with no music but each other's voices—to the biggest sycamore, the one pictured on the five-nakfa bill and which had felt so sacred to me when I had stood under it before. Now it seemed ready as if with the biblical loaves and fishes to feed everyone who came to it. Blankets and benches appeared for people to rest and lounge in the shade. The Ethiopian and Eritrean armies' faceoff a mere thirty kilometers away couldn't disturb this African Renaissance of the word and sharing in the fruits of peace.

Still, as if to remind us not to be too blissfully unaware, five skinny young men with manic and menacing looks in their eyes stripped down to their shorts and started a group wrestling match, compelling us to form a circle around them. One of them standing with all of the others thrown in the dust signaled the end of the match. But as I turned away, an old man and woman entered the circle: he in a long, soiled white robe and cracking a whip; she in a leather skirt, white tunic, blue beads around her long neck, and with roughly pulled back hair. They seemed to stalk each other, exchanging songs as she raised her hand and threw it down in disgust, and he threatened her with his whip. At one point he came after her, and she ran behind a row of three similarly dressed women who emerged from the crowd to protect her. They made me wonder if the performances by the young men and the old man and woman had been planned or took place spontaneously—or even if they were performances. I saw Zemhret but felt too foolish to ask him, saying instead, "Are we ready to leave?"

"Yes," he replied. "And we must get some rest for tomorrow if we are to write our declaration." He, Kassahun, Mbulelo, Ngugi, and I had met for lunch the day before. Reesom had suggested to me a few days before the conference began that we should issue a kind of joint statement at the end of it on what we had accomplished. When I mentioned it to Kassahun, he said that Ngugi was already planning to write something, and we should all meet to work on it. Nawal had flown back to Egypt already, but Kassahun also said that before she left she told him that she would be happy to read it, offer her own suggestions, and sign her name. Over *berbere tagliatelle* and *zigni*, we decided that we would hold a previously unscheduled plenary session beginning at noon on the conference's last day to ask for suggestions on what we should include in the document. As we talked, Ngugi took out an envelope and started writing "a preamble," as he called it. When I asked to see, he responded by pulling back the paper, "Not yet. I'll show you tomorrow."

"Hey, you guys, slow down," Mbulelo laughed as if to admonish us. "We will have more than enough to add tomorrow when we hear from our colleagues."

Kassahun smiled, "I am afraid of that. We will get plenty of advice, no?"

At this, Zemhret nodded, "More than enough, for sure."

Around three the next afternoon as I sat at a long table onstage in the Intercontinental auditorium, I turned to Kassahun, seated at the end of the row after Ngugi and Zemhret and ducked behind the high pile of papers in front of me. "Too much. Too much. *Basta cosi,*" I silently mouthed to him behind my hand. Kassahun nodded and rolled his eyes. Standing at the podium for the last three hours—and looking regal throughout while exhibiting his ANC-perfected skills of decisive empathy to the hilt—Mbulelo asked the packed house for suggestions about what we should write in the declaration, and a hundred hands were still raised. As he called on nearly everyone, he also asked each person who stood to write his or her suggestions and leave them on the podium, which I gathered as a kind of impromptu secretary.

Doubt over who was actually directing the conference vanished as speaker after speaker—women, students, veterans, Asmarinos, everyday Eritreans, and unknown writers as well as established professors and writers whom we invited—all stood up like generals, matter-of-factly acknowledging the bravery of their troops but upbraiding them with the new and more difficult challenges ahead, including the real possibility of death, before issuing their ultimate order: attack!

Colonial languages should not be speaking for Africa. African languages should. It was their duty and responsibility. The future of Africa's people depended on them, as did Africa's economic life. Only African languages could unify Africa, and dialogue among them, including translation, was essential. Equally essential was the use of African languages in educating Africa's children and developing the use of African languages at all levels of education, especially in research. Science and technology also had to be applied to African languages, and vice versa. Furthermore, African democracy could only be achieved through African languages, while social equality and justice—including an end to all forms of discrimination, particularly against women—must also flow from the same source. The decolonization of African minds and any notion of an African Renaissance depended on the empowerment of African languages more than on anything else. Last but not least, Against All Odds could not end but had to continue and should meet again in different parts of Africa too. Yet no longer merely a conference,

Against All Odds had to become a movement. Whatever we wrote we had to translate into as many African languages as possible and submit it to the OAU, the UN, and all international organizations that served Africa so that they could develop their policies accordingly and join us in our efforts to bring about "the beginning of better things to come for our languages, for Africa, for the world"—as Saba Kidane said, when she stood up and quoted what Ngugi had said the first day, who now delighted everyone when he greeted her from the podium as "my new Eritrean daughter."

By 4:30 P.M. the pile of suggestions I had been trying to keep intact had multiplied over the entire table. I didn't even hear Mbulelo end the plenary session but only realized it had finally stopped when he started to walk away from the podium and I saw Ngugi and Zemhret standing up. Kassahun gathered the suggestions at his end of the table, as we all did at our places, looking at each other with our hands full. Wondering how we could write the declaration in the hour and half that remained before the final banquet began at City Hall at 6:00, I heard Zemhret say to Mbulelo, "That was a good idea to announce the postponement of our banquet until 8:00. People will need some time to rest, and now they will have it."

"Only we will not rest," Mbulelo replied in his deep voice and with a wide yet weary smile. It reflected our own weary looks: happy to be reaching the end but unsure about what to do next.

"Where should we go to write? Do we need a break?" I asked.

"We should start writing right now," Ngugi shot back, adding, "Can we meet right here?"

"There are too many people," Kassahun replied, gesturing out into the auditorium, where half of the crowd still lingered.

"Is there a place in this hotel where we can be alone?" Zemhret wondered aloud.

"What about the utility room in the back, where the journalists have been typing their stories this week? Now it's our turn. Can we go there?" I asked.

We followed Kassahun past the Intercontinental banquet rooms and down a dark hall where he opened the door. We had to kick away the trash of crumpled papers, empty cups, and boxes around our feet as we each found a chair. Small with blank white walls, a table and a computer screen at which I sat down and typed the first words we all agreed on—"The Asmara Declaration on African Languages and Literatures"—the room set the stage for a history painting illuminated by the long fluorescent bulbs overhead. We needed a relatively simple, clear concise statement that could be read three hours later at the closing reception and offered for ratification.

Unfortunately, the room had no printer—as I remembered several of the journalists complaining to me during the week—and I had to start writing by hand. Luckily I had a long legal pad. Where to begin? We looked at the piles of suggestions and Ngugi took out an envelope, on the back of which he had written a complete draft of his preamble. As he read, we all made excited suggestions, no different than our colleagues in the auditorium a few hours before. I listened and wrote what Ngugi said, crossed out, doubled back, inserting carets, arrows, boxes, and circles to reflect the consensus as it spontaneously appeared. Finishing and revising each other's sentences in the air, no one seemed to have an ego. Either we had come too far together or there was simply no room or time for it. We could see and feel the pressure of Ngugi mentally compressing thirty years of his writing about African languages into a few basic principles. We deferred to Mbulelo's all-inclusive vision while he patiently read through the piles of suggestions as if they formed a hypertext with myriad links to African voices that had been but would no longer be silenced. At times when their clamor seemed to suck all of the air out of the room, Kassahun would break in and lift our spirits like a fresh breeze, recounting in barely a few sentences the grandest narratives of emancipation and enlightenment cleansed of their neocolonial debasement by what we had been hearing for the last seven days. When we doubted whether what we were proposing was realistic, Zemhret revitalized our convictions by telling us specifically how they could be achieved, step by step, starting with his own actions when he returned to his office tomorrow. As I worked in bits and pieces of the tenets of Against All Odds that I had been repeating for years like mantras, our prose spontaneously emerged: the preamble, ten articles culled from hundreds, and in conclusion a three-paragraph call to action.

As I looked around the room, I was reminded of paintings in American museums of members of the Continental Congress who met in Philadelphia and joined together in a room to sign the Declaration of Independence. The "Asmara Declaration," however, was a statement of African-language independence for the entire continent.

For a "Cantalupo" to appear in a painting of the signing of the American Declaration of Independence or the composing of the Asmara Declaration seemed equally incongruous, but there I was at the latter. I listened and wrote, struggling as if I were a child trying to keep the paper neat, the tip of my tongue clenched between my teeth. Two and a half hours and three drafts later, I handed Mbulelo what remained of the legal pad: four long sheets half attached to a piece of damp cardboard. "I can read this," he replied, adding with a smile, "The nuns have taught you well, my pink brother."

Thousands packed the big-as-a-football field banquet hall of Asmara City Hall. Its glistening chandeliers reflected off the rich coffered ceiling, the mirrors on the walls and in the plenty of wine and beer, and most of all scotch, freely flowing. Arriving a little late, I heard Sbrit playing as I entered the main doors. Immediately I spotted Larry, his head taller than anyone, weaving through the crowds and taking pictures. Wearing billowing white robes and turbans, Sbrit entwined half a dozen different, electrified string instruments into a trebly pattern laced with a single flute and rooted to the ground between a pair of conga and bongo drums. On the floor directly in front of them, four lithe young women danced, lifting tightly pleated pale blue capes above their heads. Slinking in circles, their movements seemed patterned after strange birds poured into shimmering lavender gowns cinched at the waist with wide black belts to accentuate their breasts and hips. With a crescendo, the music ceased and they froze, their wings outstretched.

Loud applause and cheers, with a few already drunk hoots, filled the room and quickly fell apart into too many loud conversations as Mbulelo came on stage. He wore a black and white, oversized checkerboard vest. His eyes flashed as he looked up from the legal pad and spoke into the Sbrit microphone. "I shall begin by reading our preamble and proceeding to the ten points that we put together in summary of your recommendations this afternoon. The declaration reads as follows: 'At this historical conference. . . .'" He sounded as certain as Moses, only more friendly. The crowd quieted and parted like the Red Sea—a hundred miles away down the escarpment—to receive his message.

> We writers and scholars from all regions of Africa gathered in Asmara, Eritrea from January 11 to 17, 2000 at the conference titled *Against All Odds: African Languages and Literatures into the 21st Century*. This is the first conference on African languages and literatures ever to be held on African soil, with participants from East, West, North, Southern Africa and from the diaspora and by writers and scholars from around the world. We examined the state of African languages in literature, scholarship, publishing, education and administration in Africa and throughout the world. We celebrated the vitality of African languages and literatures and affirmed their potential. We noted with pride that despite all the odds against them, African languages as vehicles of communication and knowledge survive and have a written continuity of thousands of years.[8]

More loud applause and shouts of approval punctuated every sentence. At the end, Mbulelo requested ratification. The crowd cheered for five minutes in response, until Sbrit started playing again. At this point an old woman hooded and wrapped in her billowing white and beribboned traditional Eritrean dress offered another huge flat loaf of hard corn bread—as she did at Seghenyetti—to Mbulelo on the stage. He called up Ngugi, and again they began breaking it into pieces to travel all over the room. Sbrit sped up the tempo and lifted the volume. Everyone started dancing. As more and more people flooded onto the stage, I decided to join them. We danced, swayed, held hands, and sang, trying not to fall off the overly crowded stage. An Eritrean businessman in suit and tie jumped up from the audience and pasted a one-hundred-nakfa bill on Ngugi's forehead. The student's mother whom I met in Seghenyetti jumped next out of the audience and pasted another one-hundred-nakfa bill on the forehead of Papa Susso, whom I was dancing next to. He reached into his kora, brimming with nakfa bills, and pasted another hundred on mine.

Back in my room at 3:00 A.M. and listening to the usual chorus of dogs barking all over Asmara all night long, I couldn't sleep, too hyper from the day. Not wanting to stay awake until I heard "*La Illah ilah Allah, wa Mohammed rasul Allah*" through the loudspeakers of the Great Mosque, which I knew if I were patient for a few more hours would finally put me to sleep, I tried to read.

I had brought the *Iliad* with me to Asmara. The renewed war between Ethiopia and Eritrea and the history of Eritrea's armed struggle made me think that I should try to understand better than I did the relationship between poetry and war. I thought reading the *Iliad* would be a good place to start, since Simone Weil famously called it "*le poème de la force,*" "the poem of force."[9] Reesom didn't write much about war, at least about directly experiencing it, but nearly all the other Eritrean poets I had met and had been hearing read their work at the conference did. They seemed to know firsthand and write about, in Weil's words—which I had copied into the book when I was back in Pennsylvania—the "washed out halo of patriotism" descending on their dead heroes.[10] Solomon Tsehaye had showed me a few, rough English translations from his first book, *Sahel,*[11] and Weil's description of the *Iliad* seemed to apply to his lines perfectly: their true subject, their center was force. Force used by people; force that they thought they could handle but which blinded them; force that all flesh shrunk away from; force that enslaved their users as it destroyed their victims.[12] My best friends in Eritrea knew such force. They used it and survived it, as I saw when I first came here. Now I wanted to understand it better. Certainly Zemhret knew it, although he didn't say so to me. Since Homer talked about it, I thought I should start with him to learn to talk about it, too.

I had not opened the book since I read it on the airplane over ten days ago, when I left off with the struggles to retrieve Patroclus's body. They seemed too hard to follow or remember now. I flipped ahead to book 18 and, quickly turning the pages, found the part where Thetis, the mother of Achilles, begs Hephaestus to make him a new shield, to inspire him to fight again. Ever since I had first seen the Eritrean metal market, Medeber, five years before, I pictured Hephaestus, the blacksmith of the gods, as if he could be there, or all its metalworkers in the *Iliad*. Arefine's telling me the Eritrean word for poet, *getamay,* and Reesom telling me repeatedly how it really meant something more like a "joiner" reinforced this association in my mind even more. Yet now as I read Homer's famous description of the shield, it reminded me of Against All Odds. Africa and certainly Eritrea had seen its share of what W. H. Auden had depicted in a poem revisiting Homer's description but also seeing

> A plain without a feature, bare and brown,
> No blade of grass, no sign of neighborhood,
> Nothing to eat and nowhere to sit down,
> Yet, congregated on its blankness, stood
> An unintelligible multitude,
> A million eyes, a million boots in line,
> Without expression, waiting for a sign.[13]

Before I left for Asmara, I also had made a copy of Auden's poem and had inserted it in the book. He could have been describing a scene at the Expo prison during the Ethiopian occupation:

> Barbed wire enclosed an arbitrary spot
> Where bored officials lounged (one cracked a joke)
> And sentries sweated for the day was hot:
> A crowd of ordinary decent folk
> Watched from without and neither moved nor spoke
> As three pale figures were led forth and bound
> To three posts driven upright in the ground.[14]

But didn't Against All Odds promise Africa something better? Couldn't African languages provide Africa with a better world, more like the idyllic descriptions Homer also offered in the original, which Auden in his updated description said that Thetis missed, and which many thought Africa would also never see again?

I looked up from my reading and saw my father, framed by a gold sun rising out of the Red Sea behind him. His forehead draped in shells, he carried a book, *The Autobiography of Benvenuto Cellini,* the only book he had ever told me that he loved. I asked him, "Do you have the shield of Against All Odds?" Shaking his head no, he put his hand to his chest and held up a medallion. Engraved upon it, a huge sycamore spread over its upper half and a crowd just as large gathered beneath it with a poet standing in between.

CHAPTER THIRTEEN

The Poem

"THEY'LL USE YOU AS A SYMBOL," REESOM GROWLED OVER THE PHONE from Belgium, where he now lived in exile again from Eritrea, a mere two years after Against All Odds. "They'll parade you around as evidence that the country is still open and encouraging freedom of expression. They'll use you for propaganda."

I had called from Bethlehem to ask his advice about accepting an invitation from Zemhret to come to Eritrea to translate and edit an anthology of contemporary Eritrean poets. "But Reesom," I replied, "if I read a poem that sounds like propaganda, it can't be a good poem. And I'm not going to translate bad poems. Still, I haven't made up my mind about going yet."

Our conversation ended abruptly, and it was our last. The days of our "Mighty Joiner / Joiner" sweet talk had ended. Our near daily emails—his sending me a poem in the morning, with my returning a translation by the end of the day, including many emails of rough drafts in between—dried up worse than an Eritrean river, and a rainy season to make it flood would never come again.

A year later, a week before he died of lung cancer, I heard he was fatally ill in Brussels and didn't want to see anyone. I knew that since I had decided to go back to Eritrea to work on the anthology, he considered it a betrayal of our work together and of Eritrea itself, since he thought that the Eritrean government had betrayed the nation and the ideals of its armed struggle for independence, and if I worked with Zemhret, it meant that I worked with the government too.

Even though Reesom and I worked closely together for four years—translating over two hundred poems, exchanging countless emails, performing poetry readings, sharing many a joyful meal, and traveling a lot together with many nights of carousing along the way—I couldn't imagine that he would want to see or hear from me now. The foreboding that I felt the night of Against All Odds when I saw Reesom arguing with Zemhret outside of the banquet hall—that I had been wrong in thinking that Reesom embodied an ideal in Eritrea that poetry and politics could thrive together rather than end up like Cain and Abel—came true. Even though he told me not to worry when I saw him the next night at the poetry reading at the university because he had promised himself "not to be distracted by politics over poetry," it was a promise he could not keep.

Yet it was a promise that in working on the anthology of other contemporary Eritrean poets I was simultaneously discovering that many of them did keep, and that this allowed them to keep writing and keep being heard in Eritrea. Reesom's being distracted by politics in Eritrea was fatal, if not to his poetry—which was still widely if not officially appreciated in Eritrea—then to his life as a poet there, since by the end of 2000 he became a persona non grata, neither welcome to perform publicly nor, soon thereafter, to enter the country. He responded with a poem called "Intifada," likening himself to David—"With a challenging song / And a stone / Flying from his sling"—which was never published.

If only from hearing how Reesom sounded over the phone as I spoke with him, I knew he felt his rejection acutely. Did it contribute to his unexpected, early death? In five years, he went from exile to return to renown to rejection and again into exile.

After hearing he was fatally ill and then that he died, I found a poem I had translated but again that we had never published, called "Shakespeare, Enough," in which he talked about "what makes a poet," meaning an Eritrean poet: "The love of Eritreans / For green Eritrea . . . / the story of my poems." At the end of the poem, Reesom claimed that even if he lived as long as the biblical Methuselah, "God would call me home / Before I could end this song." Regardless of whether politics was a distraction or inseparable from it, Reesom hadn't ended his song when he died at 57. Nor would he have ended it if he lived to 557.

After Against All Odds, his poetry became a kind of one-man Asmara Declaration, but whereas the official document we had composed in the Asmara Intercontinental's storeroom had to struggle to be noticed after the conference, Reesom's poetry attracted attention in much the same way that it did the first time I heard him perform at the Expo festival in Asmara in 1998, only now internationally. He became Eritrea's best-known—in fact, first known—poet in the West. Kassahun published a second edition of *We Have Our Voice*, we made a spoken-word CD of it, and Kassahun published another collection twice as long: *We Invented the Wheel*. Proportionally, in Eritrea as suddenly as Reesom's poetic star sunk, it rose dramatically in the

United States and Europe, and not only in literary journals, poetry circles, small presses, universities, and literature conferences and festivals. Reesom's poetry might have lost its place at the center of Eritrean politics and power, but now CNN, BBC, NPR, VOA, Deutsche Welle, RAI, Radio Vatican, South Africa's SABC, and Australia's SBS all featured interviews with him.

Accustomed to seeing poetry as a marginalized art—not in itself marginal but marginalized in popular contemporary culture—I had never seen a living poet get such mainstream media attention. Furthermore, I had never expected that I would hear it featuring my translations since, although Reesom would always insist that his inspiration was in Tigrinya, which he would also read, the interviews inevitably would include him reading my English. After the CNN interview, he took the bus from New York back to Bethlehem, walked the five miles to our local brewery, and appeared at my front door. He held two gallon jugs of beer to celebrate. With his poetry in prime time, they made sure we would not be distracted by politics, but not for long.

Far from being a distraction from poetry, Zemhret's invitation in 2002 for me to come to Eritrea to begin working on the anthology seemed like the perfect, much needed distraction from politics—in Eritrea and in the world. Five months after Against All Odds, in May 2000 Ethiopia launched the massive military offensive that we all had worried might take place before or during the conference. Before the fighting ended, the Ethiopian army came so close to Asmara that many feared it might be captured before Eritrean resistance stiffened once again, although not without Ethiopia occupying most of the disputed sections of the border and other, previously undisputed parts of Eritrea, including the towns of Tserona and Senafe and, just outside it, Belew Kelew, the site of the ancient stele, which Ethiopian tanks pulled down.

As a result of the war and Eritrea's difficult struggle to survive it, thirteen leading Eritrean professionals, academics, and intellectuals—including Kassahun and Reesom—met in Berlin and drafted a letter to Eritrea's president to question the future course of the country. Responding equivocally at best, at least at first, the government and its most vocal supporters soon began to vilify the letter's signees as traitors. Six months later, a group of fifteen political leaders in Eritrea, including former and current government ministers, wrote their own, open letter to the president. They accused him of violating the Eritrean constitution and acting illegally. Four months later, Eritrean security forces arrested them in predawn raids, and at the same time the government shut down all eight privately owned newspapers and detained their editors and reporters.

Zemhret's invitation also seemed like the perfect distraction from the failing fortunes of Against All Odds, although the anthology also seemed like a perfect application of many of its most important principles. The outbreak of war in May 2000 meant the end of our international support, which had already dwindled before the conference due to the war in 1998, and which only Zemhret's mobilization of Eritrean resources had compensated for. Clearly he was in no position now to bail out the project again.

When I had returned to Asmara two years before the invitation, in September 2000, nine months after the conference, and three months into an uneasy peace agreement, or at least a "cessation of hostilities," in the words of the OAU, I asked people there what it was like during the invasion. Arefine's eyes no longer sparkled. "*Molto diffetoso, sfaverole, peccato*—but we have survived worse," he said slowly and in a low voice as he shook his head. His nephew, the father of the little boy who always kissed my hand and put it to his forehead, had not yet come home from the war front and no one had heard from him for weeks.

My friend who managed the Shamrock whispered as we sat in the Intercontinental lounge, her eyes full of fear and tearful, "I never imagined it would come back, so close. I will probably stay, but my sister has already gone back to Holland, and she says she is never coming back."

Tsigye said, "I wasn't sure what to think," and laughed nervously. She wore a kind of khaki suit. It looked like but was not officially military. I would see her wearing it again as the broadcast anchor reading the news on ERI-TV that night.

Alemseged Tesfai, who had visited Tserona after the battle for it, said that he never imagined he would see so many dead bodies.

Solomon Abraha, instead of being his usual philosophical self, looked angry and seemed to begin and end every observation he made with a "*Mbwa*" of disgust. "*Mbwa*. This war makes me sick. Why do we need it? Where is my friend, Reesom? Have you heard from him? We will need to eat a lot of meat before we feel better, if we can afford it. *Mbwa*."

Solomon also complained about the rampant inflation in Asmara since the war. It ruined the economy. Displaced persons, bombed-out cities, starvation, and deserted fields gone fallow at the time for planting would make things worse. The governments of Eritrea and Ethiopia had agreed to a demilitarized zone between the two countries, but it would be on Eritrean soil. UN peacekeeping troops would be in charge. Some Danish soldiers were on my plane coming into Asmara. Italian troops stayed in my hotel, with racks of dry-cleaned uniforms lined up outside of their rooms every afternoon. I had never seen so many white Toyota Land Cruisers in one place except on the docks of Port Newark, New Jersey, from where the vehicles made their ways to American suburbs and shopping malls.

Zemhret called the troops "the crusaders." Did they and did the countries they came from think they would save Eritrea? If so, from whom? In the past, Eritrea had already saved itself from Ethiopia, repeatedly. In the past, Eritrea had also saved itself—repeatedly—from the colonial aspirations many of the same countries whose troops came once more, only now labeled as peacekeepers.

Yet the presence of the troops also suggested that Eritrea needed to be saved from itself. Their clean boots, pressed uniforms without a spot of dirt, and ascots represented a political order for the most part without political detentions, students allegedly murdered for demonstrating, the banning of a free press, the imprisonment of journalists, the postponement of elections, and a constitution put on hold. If all the major news outlets that once featured Reesom reported now on Eritrea at all, they either focused on the political stalemate over its disputed border with Ethiopia or Eritrea's internal political repression. When I asked Ngugi and Kassahun—my two friends who had taught me nearly all I knew of African literature—what they thought about my going back to Asmara to work on the poetry anthology under such circumstances, they also questioned it, although much less vehemently than Reesom.

"I remember when I was in exile in London," Ngugi said when I called him in California, since he had left NYU to direct a translation and writing center at the University of Irvine. "I received a generous offer from South Africa to produce *I Will Marry When I Want*. I felt I had to refuse it because the financing came from an institution of apartheid at a time when there was a worldwide movement to boycott anyone and anything with such a connection. Yet I knew that the play's producer and director was a South African who himself was struggling against the same system and would be hurt by my refusal."

Calling Kassahun, I knew that he had suffered personally and professionally from the political changes in Eritrea. He could no longer return and feel safe. The Red Sea / Africa World Press office near the *Posta Centrale* would be closed. Most of all, his family there depended on him. "Kassahun, what should I do?" I asked, feeling guilty.

"No one can tell you," he answered gently. "Maybe we were fools with Against All Odds. We were certainly little, unimportant people. But we put ourselves forward with ideas about freedom of expression, and we can't turn back. No?"

Taking this as discouragement, I answered, "But Kassahun. I will make sure that the poems I translate *are* freedom of expression. I will also make sure that the book will include Reesom because—"

Kassahun interrupted, "Hey, Charles. I wish I could go. You should feel confident with Zemhret."

Reesom, Ngugi, and Kassahun suggested in different ways that I now had a kind of public identity—be it symbolic or "little"—that could be viewed as supportive of the questionable internal politics of Eritrea if I accepted Zemhret's invitation to visit and begin work on the anthology. If I were no longer the lone poet of ten or fifteen years ago visiting an African country to write what I saw in order to be published in an English-speaking journal with a few readers and in a book with a few more, did I too have to be distracted—maybe even consumed—by politics over poetry?

I had one more friend to call for advice: Larry Sykes. "You like it too much," he said slowly over the phone from his basement studio in Boston. I could picture his serious smile, and I knew immediately what he meant. Larry always told the story of a profitable, old Ghanaian merchant in Kumasi. Larry had returned there in 1982, not knowing that Ghana at the time was suffering a depression and out-of-control inflation. The merchant had quoted Larry a price on some item, and Larry humorously scolded him that he wanted too much money. The merchant responded sheepishly but also brashly, "You are right. I like it too much. I like the money too much." Larry was right. I liked Eritrea too much—too much not to go. "If it's a political minefield," he added, "and you think you can get through it, why not try, especially if you can get past the sentinel, when maybe no one else can. You have to go back. It's a part of the story you'll be missing all your life if you don't."

When Zemhret and I met in his office a few months later, we didn't discuss the war or Eritrea's internal politics but, in addition to the idea for an anthology, the next steps for the Against All Odds secretariat in Asmara, once we got more funding. We would commission the translation of a classic of African fiction into four, geographically representative African languages. We would similarly commission the translations of a notable African woman writer, a famous African play, and a celebrated African poet. We would establish a literary prize for African-language writing: Pan-African and nationally, both at the student and professional level. We would plan for a second and third conference, to be held in South Africa in 2003, and in Ghana in 2006. Also, we would establish a permanent Against All Odds archive in Asmara, including the conference papers, audiotapes, videotapes, and even the other papers and correspondence so that we could fully document Against All Odds' means of cultural production.

"*Dehan, dehan,*" I was thinking an hour later, when I found whatever had been left in the now closed secretariat office in seventeen large boxes piled up in a hot and stuffy room in back of PFDJ party headquarters. Already the material looked and smelled dry and dusty. Papers crumbled in my fingertips as I pulled them out. Despite our big plans, as I inventoried the contents, I wondered if anyone or I would ever want to look at them again. My day job from 1997 to 2000 had been planning and making Against All Odds happen, but it was an act of love with a budget and time off from teaching. Now I had neither.

Zemhret's invitation to work on an anthology also seemed like a perfect distraction from the politics of 9/11 and their aftermath: the attack on the World Trade Center and the subsequent "war on terrorism," Afghanistan and Iraq; or, if not a distraction, an antidote to the poison—or at least some understanding—of the fear, hatred, and overwhelming evil that most Americans, including me, were feeling faced with war. Recognizing the success Reesom and I had with his poetry, if no longer his biggest supporter, Zemhret said that he hoped that an anthology of contemporary Eritrean poets would allow more Eritrean poets, in addition to Reesom, to receive the attention that they deserved. At the same time, Zemhret told me that many of them had become annoyed at hearing Reesom called Eritrea's poet laureate, although his designation was not official but proclaimed first by some of his most ardent fans and then by himself.

"Maybe these poets are jealous," I said to Zemhret.

"Accuracy, not jealousy, is the issue," he replied. "Reesom is a unique and powerful performer, but to consider his work alone as representative of Eritrean poetry is incorrect. This is not jealousy we are dealing with—but a misconception. He is not considered our best poet in Tigrinya. We have many poets in Tigrinya. What they write needs to be heard, too."

"Like what?" I asked incredulously. "Reesom writes about more different subjects than anyone I know. What else can there be?"

Zemhret looked as if he weren't going to respond so that I could find out for myself, but then he said, "These poets write a lot about the field and about war. And yet war isn't only about fighting. And it's not all about death. That's too restrictive. They write about friendship and the perennial issues of love and life. War has that, too."

Reesom didn't write about war, if only because he was in exile during Eritrea's armed struggle for independence. Could the poetry Zemhret was recommending really be any good? Not only did his insisting that war poetry need not only be about fighting and death not persuade me—I immediately forgot what he said. Instead, I recalled that I had tried to read Homer's *Iliad* in the hope that it would help me understand the relationship between war and poetry, which I had begun to see was so important to

Eritrean poets other than Reesom. However, like most readers of poetry in Western countries, I wasn't sure if my appetite for a poetics of force could be contemporary or extend beyond the form of ancient or medieval epic. Horace's famous tag line in Latin, *Dulce et decorum est pro patria mori*[1]—To die for one's country is sweet and honorable (or satisfying)—had been deconstructed long ago, so that it could be heard only as ironic, as in Wilfred Owen's poem based on this line in 1917. No quality poem of World War I, World War II, or subsequent wars in the West had been able to proceed after Owen and recover the heroic tone of Horace's phrase, and even that was suspect since he had himself been accused of running away from battle. I thought of my own country, the United States at war—in Afghanistan and Iraq. How could great contemporary literature about war, its waste and its trauma, be anything but ironic? Did Eritrean poets know? Did I want to know? Did anyone need to know?

Five and a half years after Against All Odds and ten years since I first came to Eritrea, I sat in my usual room, 311, in the Intercontinental and looked over the anthology's proofs one last time before I would return them to the printer the next day. Overheating the small office attached to the room and gilding its semicircular windows, the late Sunday afternoon sunlight of Asmara washed out the text on my computer, to which I was comparing the pages from Sabur. But the conflicting images of what I was remembering—which had led to me to this moment—seemed clearer than ever.

I had just returned from a Saturday overnight in Massawa and had a few hours before I would be attending a huge poetry performance and reading in the banquet hall at the Expo fairgrounds, where the annual Eritrean arts and culture festival had just begun. I would also be meeting a director and several cameramen from AVIE to shoot a documentary on the event, featuring the poets reading their poems from the anthology.

In Tigrinya, the journalist Meles Negusse would read his lament for the Eritrean muse, Mammet, during the war. Was she still "Among the hills and cliffs / . . . [she] ruled with . . . [her] poetry" or "in her grave / Along with her rhymes?" Would Eritrea's poets "waste away / To nothing, silenced / And forever abandoned?" Or would she, "for the sake of art / . . . fall from the sky / . . . and open . . . [their] hearts / With . . . [her] secret poetry's sacred key?"[2]

Also in Tigrinya, the short-story writer and employee in the Cultural Affairs Bureau, Angessom Isaak, would read what finally winning the war felt like:

I saw a color
Unbelievably bright
And like a powerful wind
Encompassing the sky
Mirrored across the sea
And pouring freedom
All around me.[3]

Isaak would go on to describe his vision now—"black, / Blacker than a crow's eye"—and wonder if his "vision has changed / Or if . . . [he] has become smarter" to see and experience "Freedom. . . . / As more than one color" and "More than . . . he . . . [has] ever seen / . . . ever heard" or "can explain."

In Tigre, the *Haddas Eritrea* editor, Paulos Netabay, would memorialize all the places in Sahel where Eritrean fighters took refuge and many died when there was no place else to hide from the Soviet air force and tanks: Baquos, Ela-babu, Itaro, Amerberbe, Halibet, Hishkib, Himbol, Hager, Arerb, Hal-hal, Arag, Nakfa, Rora-habab, Asry, Marsa-gulbub, Marsa-teklay, Ayget, Quatat, Denden, Ashorm, Tikse, Koken: "Rough song in a rough land / Where lions also lived."[4]

In Arabic, the novelist and poet Ahmed Omer Sheikh would rewrite the story from Genesis of Abraham brought out into the wilderness by Yahweh, who promised him a nation as numerous as the stars in the clear desert sky, only now the promise would be a future for Eritrea. Or was it only "wind in a palm tree— / Restless, stirring, wandering // And lost in a wilderness," or even "Just another hallucination"? Still the poet would resolve to "find the voice to bring it back."[5]

The film would also have the festival as a backdrop, to reinforce the idea of the centrality of poetry in Eritrean culture, as I had first experienced seven years before when Zemhret took Kassahun and me to the festival to hear Reesom perform. Writing the first scene in the documentary, I wanted to reproduce a similar experience of someone arriving at the festival, entering, and being caught up in the excitement—the mob scene at the gate, the buses, the cars, the many different kinds of Eritreans and culture already on display—and his or her being swept into the flow of people, eventually arriving at the poetry performances. Against the same backdrop, the documentary would also feature interviews with the poets from the anthology after their reading in the banquet hall. I would ask them when they wrote their poems and why.

I also planned to join a few poets onstage to read translations of their work after each had read the original. Solomon Tsehaye, who would be there too, told me that I should be prepared to be introduced to the crowd and to offer a few words of my own, like "Light the Lights" perhaps, since many of the people there would remember me from Against All Odds and the performances at Seghenyetti.

I looked forward to reading a few of my translations of the originals by the Eritrean poets who would be reading, since we had become friends in the process of working together on their translations. Some of them had even been published already in American and British literary magazines that offered an honorarium. When I converted it from dollars to nakfa and gave it to the poets, they responded half jokingly that they never thought the poems they wrote as fighters in the harshness and waste of war in the Sahel would make them literary celebrities in the West. Saying they especially enjoyed telling their friends back in their old neighborhoods, the poets added, "That's the real Asmara we want to show you, Charlus." I wasn't sure if I wanted an Asmara any more real than what I had.

Yet I felt anxious that I would be reading even a few lines of my own poetry—which would only be in English—in front of many of Eritrea's greatest and oldest oral poets: the *getamo* and *getemti,* who would be wearing their traditional robes, suits, and *gabis,* and who would also be in the banquet hall to perform their work in various Eritrean languages. The contemporary poets who wrote their work now knew me, and I knew them. But the oral poets still intimidated me, since I barely knew them beyond their hallowed names. What could I do to please them?

Maybe I was too tired from the trip to Massawa to go over the proofs. I turned the pile of paper back to the title page: *Who Needs a Story? Contemporary Eritrean Poetry in Tigrinya, Tigre and Arabic.* It would be a first in a world where literary anthologies of contemporary American poetry, Irish poetry, French poetry, Italian poetry, British poetry, in short the poetry of most developed nations were abundant. Like many poets who wrote in African languages, Eritrean poets writing in their own languages or in translation could not be found on the shelves of the world's bookstores and libraries. But now contemporary Eritrean poets would be on their way to being known and enjoyed throughout Africa and the world, much as poets of other countries—South American poets in the 1960s, Eastern European poets in the 1970s—had achieved, however belatedly, worldwide recognition.

Zemhret was right. More Eritrean poets in addition to Reesom did deserve to be known outside of Eritrea. I had sensed it from hearing some of them read at Against All Odds, but coming back at Zemhret's behest to meet them and more convinced me immediately that the project should go forward. The poets represented a wide cross-section of Eritrean society, including men and women from their twenties to their eighties as well as scholars, professional writers, journalists, social scientists, cultural activists, teachers, actors, theater directors, and performers. Furthermore, Ghirmai Negash, the author of the amazing and the first history of Tigrinya litera-ture, had moved to Eritrea from Holland with his wife and twin daughters to establish and chair a department of Eritrean languages and literature at the University of Asmara, and Zemhret had convinced Ghirmai to be the book's co-editor.

With Ghirmai we decided that trying to include all of Eritrea's nine languages would be impossible, making the book too long and requiring good translators for all of them. We limited ourselves to Tigrinya, Tigre, and Arabic: producing a book in two local and two international languages. Ghirmai and his university colleagues handled the first round of translations in Tigrinya. He also had colleagues who knew Tigre, and we relied on Mussa Aron, who was writing the first dictionary of Tigre.

Toward the end of my first trip, Zemhret had directed me to make an appointment with the director of the press department in Arabic at the Ministry of Information, Said Abdulhay. I knew rationally that the suspi-cion and phobia in the United States of all things Arabic due to the attacks of 9/11 were wrong, but I also felt insecure and a little insincere when Said began by defending Arabic and the Koran against popular American misconceptions about them that both he and I knew came into his office with me. Arabic newspapers and books outnumbered the Tigrinya piled up around us. Beginning to feel defensive myself, I half remembered a passage from the Koran about how Allah made people different so that we could love one another for our differences. It seemed pale in comparison with the bloodshed we both knew.

Bolstering myself with a sip of coffee and tasting cardamom, I said instead, "How did you like Nawal el Saadawi at Against All Odds? *"Rabina hawal adel aerifuhu bi-elaqel?"*

Said's dark eyes brightened as he nodded and ran his finger over his moustache, saying the phrase slowly and adding, "She is right. Her grand-mother was right. The rest is all distraction. God is justice, and we know God by our heart. Let's talk poetry. The look on your face tells me that you never tasted our traditional lowlands coffee until now."

Three years later and for the moment unable or unwilling to give more than a desultory look at the anthology's proofs, I turned to one of the Arabic poems we had translated: "Singing Our Way to Victory" by Mohammed Osman Kajerai. A leading Eritrean intellectual and poet, he had died in 2003 in his early eighties—although the exact year of his birth was unknown—in Kassala, just over the Eritrean border with Sudan. Returning to Eritrea after its independence, Kajerai worked briefly in Asmara as a teacher and journalist but became sick and impoverished.

A few days ago I had wanted to visit for one last time the office in Eritrea's Research and Documentation Center. Ghirmai and I had finished the anthology there, moving between the originals and their translations laid out on three long tables in a cavernous room with ceiling-to-floor gleaming veneer cabinets lining the walls and naturally lit by large windows looking out on the surrounding rooftops. As I stood there again and saw the empty tables, Said walked in with a huge folder of papers under his left arm. Surprised and happy to see each other again, we grabbed each other's right hand and bumped our right shoulders, a traditional form of Eritrean greeting among former fighters, which now I felt comfortable exchanging too. We agreed that we were happy with the final outcome of the anthology. But as he put the overstuffed file on one of the tables, he reached into it and pulled out two sheets of paper. "I am still wondering about these lines," he said calmly, holding the original Kajerai and the translation, and then began to read the English softly:

> I plant the landmines for our struggle
> To continue, raising our flag
> As the gunpowder explodes
> Into fire and smoke—The valley of death's shadow
> Making white mercury purple,
> Suffusing the horizon
> And lingering in the air like chrysanthemums.[6]

When I first began working on the poem a few years before, its violence made me uneasy. Also, when I first read the literal translation, the mention of mercury confused me until I looked up landmines on the Internet and found out that they often contained mercury. I hoped that my searching for information on landmines and Arabic poetry at the same time would not trigger any over zealous adherent of the antiterrorist Patriot Act or an FBI officer who might be spying on my use of the Internet. "Have I made the poem too violent? I asked Said nervously.

"Not at all," he said shaking his head, "If anything you have not made it violent enough, but that's okay. The flower is what bothers me. Don't you call it a gardenia instead of a chrysanthemum?" I had no idea. We let it go for a better scholar, a reviewer or a future translator to solve.

Translating Reesom from Tigrinya, I always worked—totally trusting and helplessly grateful—from his first literal translation. Translating now from three languages in which again I had no proficiency but some experience where they were spoken, I similarly had no choice but to depend on Ghirmai, Mussa, Said, Rahel, Nazreth, Adem Saleh, a translating institute in Beirut, and whoever else might read an original and my version in English and offer a correction or a suggestion.

I listened to all of them like the three Orthodox priests I met at Arefine's house on one of the four trips I made to Asmara to work on the anthology. The priests had been expected without being invited to join Arefine and his male friends for a large, midday meal on the feast of the birth of Mary, the mother of Jesus. Gathering in a small, unadorned, one-room building on the side of his yard, we sat on low benches at a low table and each of us drank *sewa* in the traditional half-liter, enameled tin cup—called *wancha*—imprinted with the coat of arms of Haile Selassie.

The cup's quaint design signified the claim of successive Ethiopian governments that they descended from Solomon, Sheba, and their son, Bayna-Lehkem, which none of us took seriously. Ancient, medieval, or modern, they failed to recognize that Sheba and her son ultimately cared more about their home than about Solomon, which is why they left him in Israel and returned to the Red Sea. The same sense of home extended to this simple room in Asmara. Claims to divine or political and military might had no place here.

Weathered and barefoot, white robes girded up to their loins, carrying walking sticks and wearing threadbare suit jackets, the three gangly priests entered and gave us and the food—*injera*, *zigni*, and *schuro*—their blessing. As we ate together, one priest tried to explain to me how Mary and the Ark of the Covenant were the same thing since it was feminine and called "Our Lady." He didn't realize or care that I didn't speak Tigrinya. The two other priests gently argued about the precise spot and time that Sheba gave birth to Bayna-Lehkem on the banks of a nearby river. "*Mai Bela*," the third priest joined in.

Arefine's friend with the safari vest and tasseled Italian loafers translated their Tigrinya into English. "They all have different versions of the story," he said, smiling skeptically.

"I love the differences," I replied, "and I couldn't believe the priests without them." He looked at me as if I were crazy.

When everyone had eaten and drunk their fill, the priests again offered their blessing and got up to leave. We exchanged thanks, hugs, and laughter, with less than a handful of Tigrinya and English words in common. One priest and I exchanged pens. American stars and stripes emblazoned what he gave me.

Below the glass table that also reflected the late afternoon sunlight outside, I now reached for my briefcase. As I dug to the bottom to find the pen that I had carried like a talisman ever since I got it, I heard Barbara's voice echo, "For or against?" around the room, which made me miss her as much as I did on the shores of Morocco almost two decades before. Putting my hands on the proofs to steady myself, I said out loud what I remembered I had said to her when she first took off my religious medals as we made love one of our first times, and she asked me the same question: "*For* protection and *against* harm." As before I couldn't answer the question, "Protection and harm from what?" Maybe the proofs contained a few Eritrean answers and mine as well?

At least that was how I had been presenting the poems during the last week as I traveled around Asmara and to Keren and Massawa to give lectures about the work. The American Embassy had sponsored my trip to Eritrea and invited me to speak about the poetry anthology as an example of American and Eritrean interaction and cooperation. In comparison with Against All Odds, the anthology required a lot less of it or might only be viewed as a microcosm of what happened at the conference: a mere putting into practice of some of the principles of the Asmara Declaration. Nevertheless, the embassy now said in its invitation, which seemed to echo what I had written seven years earlier when I sought U.S. support for the conference, that the objective of my lectures should be to demonstrate American interest in, and respect for, Eritrean indigenous literary traditions and to promote mutual understanding between the two countries by strengthening their literary and academic links. In short, I was to be a goodwill ambassador at a time when mutual understanding between Eritrea and the United States was at its lowest point since Eritrean independence in 1993. "Now even literary understanding is better than nothing," I laughed when I told Kassahun about the invitation the previous fall.

The United States had been equivocal during the renewed fighting with Ethiopia, ineffective in trying to prevent it, and now failed to support, much less help to enforce, a demarcation of the disputed border based on a decision—which both Eritrea and Ethiopia had agreed would be "final and binding"—by an international commission set up in the Hague. When it awarded the ostensible flashpoint of the war—the tiny border town of Badme—to Eritrea, Ethiopia balked, denounced the decision, and asked the Security Council to review it, which meant to change it in Ethiopia's favor.

When I met with the current American ambassador the day after my arrival, I sat on the same couch, drank the same brown dishwater American coffee, and surveyed the same room of bookshelves with useless diplomatic reports, bland paintings of American landscapes on the wall, and the gold-tasseled, too big, and therefore garish American flag serving as a backdrop behind his desk. Following our mutual and formal exchange of admiration and enthusiasm for each other's efforts, he brought up the border dispute. "Policy talk instead of pigeons," I thought to myself, remembering the last ambassador as his current replacement got up from behind his desk and sat down on the couch opposite from me.

"You will be asked many times," he said, leaning over and clasping his hands, his lips like a wide jar lid atop his neatly trimmed, full beard, "why the United States is not doing more to resolve it, but I want to tell you that we are working night and day for a solution. The Eritrean government is making our lives difficult. It arrests members of our staff, limits our travel throughout the country and refuses any overture to discuss the border decision until it is enforced. We respect the commission's decision and the Eritrean government's frustration at this point, but even after a divorce, the two parties need to meet to work out the details."

I neither expected to be asked such a question—and I never was—nor planned to defend American foreign policy in Eritrea, since I didn't agree with it. More importantly, at least for me, the ambassador's politics—anyone's politics—could only be a distraction from the trust and communication I had with Zemhret; the Eritrean poets and scholars with whom I was working; friends like Arefine and Solomon; audiences of all kinds of Eritreans; and even with the Kalashnikov-bearing guards whose tea I shared outside of PFDJ headquarters.

"Who needs a story, especially the American ambassador's story?" I thought to myself as I now started shuffling through the proofs again. Looking up and seeing the last bolts of late afternoon Asmara sunlight bury themselves in the vast red clay field outside my window, I marveled at the golden beam that spread across the page of Arabic and its English translation that my fingers rested on.

I sing for the children of Ar,
Of a love in the forest and caves
Of Goluj—a painting finished
With the barrel of a gun—the soldier,
Abraham, shot, carrying out the body
Of his hero, Mahmuday.[7]

Mohammed Mahmoud El-Sheikh (Madani), a few years younger than me, was a well-known poet in Sudan and the Middle East and now lived in Saudi Arabia. He created a kind of history painting of the death of one of Eritrea's most famous war heroes.

Yet the book was full of poems about dead Eritrean war heroes: Fessehaye Yohannes, one of the journalists now in jail, wrote about his "like a pearl. . . . [a] stately shade tree. . . . [a] pillar of light. Gold . . . / [a] compass. . . . [a] diamond. . . . [the] riches of / Grass or flesh. . . . The mighty lion."[8]

Solomon Drar, one of the PFDJ's fiercest ideologues, wrote about his, whose name was Merhawi, "Buried in the ground / Heaped with stones / Silent and at peace," yet still alive "In the whirlwind / Of the revolution / . . . Harvesting the fields of gold."[9]

Mussa Mohammed Adem, a radio broadcaster in Tigre, wrote about his, "The Invincible," with "that true killer look" and "dirges play[ing] like soundtracks in his head . . . / constantly / Making him think, 'Encircle, attack, attack.'" He

> . . . sees enemies like sorghum bending
> And breaking, their heads spilling out all red.
> . . .   . his bullets
> Fall like rain . . . and it floods
> As in the days of Noah, only with blood.
> . . . He's blinding . . .
> Like July lightning, thunder, downpours and
> Fifty days straight of sandstorms uprooting
> Boulders like arrows . . .
> . . . mercilessly slashing
> The tendons, crushing and splashing the marrow.[10]

The violence was excessive, endless, and timeless. Adem reveled in his fallen hero's

> . . . entire flesh
> Bloody and broken with wounds and lead as the field
> Where he stands unafraid, letting no one
> Flee as he fulfills the ancient lines,
> Playing and singing them too: history
> Repeating itself, prophecy come true . . .
> Welcome to free Nakfa, Setit and Belissa.

The conclusion reminded me of the banner I saw in the Asmara airport the first time I came to Eritrea ten years ago: "Welcome to Free Eritrea."

Unable to resist drifting back into proofreading and putting my pencil under every word and letter to make sure it was right, I paused at Madani's word, "shot." Despite the Stars and Stripes pen and whatever other charms I carried in my briefcase, I had almost been shot the day after I met with the ambassador when I needed to go to Sabur to get copies of the final proofs so that I could read from the poems during my lectures. I could see the Sabur building now outside my office window in the waning light at the end of the red clay field traversed by families come back from downtown, children leading donkeys, and the few people who worked on Sunday making their way home.

The afternoon when I went for the proofs had been rainy. The field had been a patchwork of small lakes and big puddles through which I had to walk a zigzag pattern to keep my feet relatively dry. Sabur also stood contiguous to a UNICEF outpost wrapped in barbed wire, enclosing six huge satellite dishes and three communication towers. The path leading to Sabur's gate also led to the UNICEF encampment. As I approached, I saw two UN guards—they looked Indian—get up and start walking toward the heavily barricaded gate. One turned around and spoke, although I couldn't hear him, and two more guards followed. They looked Irish. All four wore blue helmets. At the time I didn't make the connection that the guards might be walking toward me. I thought they were only checking the gate, which the puddles all around compelled me to walk straight toward. Around ten yards away, I saw the two Irish guards raise their guns and heard the safety catches—click, click—removed from their triggers. Turning around to see if anyone was behind me, seeing that there wasn't and continuing to walk, I realized the guards were pointing their guns at me. At the same time, a deep puddle cutting off the path forced me to make a sharp turn to the left around five yards from the UNICEF entrance to the Sabur gate. Two old men attended it. They immediately swung it open and welcomed me in Italian: "*Entra qui.*"

I wanted more than the proofs, which the printer happily gave me. I also asked if he would let me copy the book's electronic files—including all four languages and the cover, which Larry had done—on my flash drive. "*Iwe, Charlus. Riddu.* I will be delighted to do it for you."

His cheerful willingness made me ashamed of my reason for asking. But I thought: what if Eritrea's political situation suddenly worsened, due to another Ethiopian invasion or even a coup? Would the book ever be published? Could it be lost? It had been delayed over a year. The obstacles I had to overcome finally to hold the proofs in my hand and see the electronic files on the printer's screen made me paranoid. I didn't have a book. It was a one-of-a-kind, perishable artifact. Ghirmai also worried that the book might never appear. He had been in Asmara since the project began. Working firsthand with the printer, the poets, and the translators, he experienced everyday the politics that almost led me to decide not to work on the book in the first place.

Waving uneasily to the UN guards as I left Sabur, I stepped lightly and felt like a thief after a grand heist with the flash drive in my breast pocket and the folder of proofs in my bag. Publishing most books anywhere encounters problems in delays, editing, printing schedules, and more. But getting to this penultimate point so that *Who Needs a Story?* could finally become a book felt like another "against all odds." We had to invent "the wheel," as the title of my last book with Reesom seemed to predict, to publish a high-quality book of poetry in four languages and three fonts requiring different programs and new technology. On the first proofs, different fonts and lost characters of the Arabic, English, and Ge'ez alphabets strayed like lonely derelicts on pages where they didn't belong, as if the poems they had once happily lived in had been lost.

We had to push to obtain the recognition that as a writer from the West I thought was automatic at least since the eighteenth century: copyright. It was something new in Eritrean publishing. An author's claiming his or her copyright reeked of ego and individualism, which Eritrea's thirty-year armed struggle for independence deemed counterproductive, and which the government still frowned upon. It had denied Alemseged the copyright on one of the books of Eritrean history he had written.

We had to push even harder to obtain the recognition that books all over the world now required if they were to compete in the global marketplace and appear in electronic databases and any other records of books in print: an ISBN number. Kassahun was the only Eritrean publisher who had ever used one. The stele at Belew Kelew four thousand years ago might have been the beginning of Eritrean literature, but it still needed to learn basic lessons in twenty-first century publishing and technology to be read outside the nation's borders.

When I got back to my room in the Intercontinental, I locked the door and began slowly turning page after page of the proofs. Their orderly and proper appearance as they documented in poetry the near unspeakable thirty-year Eritrean experience of war dispelled my paranoia at the prospect of their loss and my guilt over not trusting Sabur with the work.

As with Against All Odds, without Zemhret's support and timely intervention in the problems we had with publishing the book, it would never have happened. His "*dehan dehan*" had come true over and over. Stealthily obtaining the electronic files of the book, I should have known better. Maybe I needed to know the original Sabean on the stele at Belew Kelew to really understand it: that poetry in Eritrea had always thrived and always would, whatever politics, problems, and new ways of presenting it might come and go—*dehan, dehan.* I should have remembered the evening a night before Meskerem that Zemhret had organized at Asmara's most famous traditional restaurant, Giday's, during my last trip to work on the book.

He gathered all of the poets he could from the book; we sat at long tables and drank *sewa* out of *wanachu* like traditional Eritrean *getamo* and *getemti,* but no one wore traditional dress. We all had held the same kinds of jobs to be found in any major city around the world, and we all wore similar Western clothes with little obvious connection to the traditional Eritrean carvings, pictures, animal heads, and tapestries running riot on the wall. Each poet performed his or her work in the original. Ghirmai and I alternated following them and reading our translations. Working our way through the book, when we came to a poem whose author wasn't in the room—for whatever reason, simply logistical or due to illness, death, disaffection, imprisonment, or exile—another poet from the audience would volunteer to read the original. No one could read "Alewuna, Alewana" as well as Reesom, but it was heard, since we included two of his poems in the anthology, too.

We also heard the poem "Naqra," by Fessahazion Michael, who died in action in 1980 at age twenty-six. In the 1970s he wrote about the infamous island prison, a barren rock in the Red Sea, "Lonely in the distance, / Graceless / Smelling of death / And hell" and where "our people / Fighting for our country . . . / Succumbed in despair."[11] Ghirmai's reading the original in a flat and uneventful tone gave way to a moment of silence, as if the tragedy of the place had to be remembered again for the sake of those who perished there; as if everyone in the room also felt a part of themselves had perished there. Following Ghirmai, I read the English translation impassively, depending on its harshness and skeletal form to be true to the disappointment, despair, and defeat that the place and the poem in the Eritrean struggle invoked and protested as vital, even when it could not prevail.

After reading the English, as I sat down I remembered one of the last things I ever heard Reesom say, as he argued with me about whether I should go to Asmara and work on the anthology. "When the powers that be are preaching exclusion even of their own flesh," he said loudly over the phone, "Joiners, *getamo* like me and you have to tell them they are wrong. There is another meaning of *getamay* you must remember: challenger." I did remember it, I wanted to say. Now I saw that every poet—alive or dead—who was heard that evening at Giday's remembered it, too. No dynamic of poetry—triumph or defeat, praise or dissidence, love or hate—was new to Eritrea or had not been already wielded by the *getemti,* and contemporary poets shared in their legacy.

Yet I had seen the *getamay* assuming the role of challenger as naturally as he breathed even more clearly a few days before the reading at Giday's, when Ghirmai took me to a wedding in Senafe, again near Belew Kelew, from where the Ethiopian army had only recently withdrawn, even though over four years had passed since the end of the renewed fighting in 2000. The bride's father was one of the most famous traditional oral poets in Eritrea.

Entering the gate of a multitiered backyard and house that seemed to have no center, we joined hundreds of guests divided into groups of seven or eight gathered to eat communally from a tiny metal table with a base of iron latticework to hold our cups of *sewa* and *mies,* a strong local wine made from honey. Straw covered the floor, and smoke from the cooking fires filled the air. Halfway through the feast, the bride's father, dressed in his billowy white, traditional suit, wearing a straw, short-brimmed hat and with a *gabi* draped gracefully around him, rose from his seat and delivered a stately yet spontaneous-sounding epithalamion in praise of his daughter and her groom. When he stopped and I expected applause, a grizzled old man at the next table, dressed similarly, except that his clothes were dirty, stood up and began reciting his own poem that clearly berated the father. The father cut him off halfway through with an equally blistering response. Three more *getamo* joined the fray, reciting their own poems, all to the silent eaters' delight.

Night had fallen now in Asmara, and I had to get ready to go to Expo for the performances and readings. Remembering the wedding in Senafe lessened my anxiety about performing in front of the oral poets. If they tolerated so much from each other, surely they would tolerate me. I looked forward to seeing and hearing them carry on, much more wildly than any of the poets who would read from *Who Needs a Story?* Far from finding that great poetry might be threatened, not truly possible, not enough, or even objectionable amid the disturbing political realities gripping Eritrea since Against All Odds in 2000, I found that poetry, perhaps more than anything, thrived.

Earlier in the week, before I went with Solomon Tsehaye to Massawa, the American Embassy gave us a car and a driver to go to the city of Keren, where an "American Corner" had been set up in the municipal library, which we were to draw attention to by talking about the anthology and reading poems from it. Before we left the next day, Solomon wanted to go to the outdoor market, famous for its camels and for its delicious mangoes. He wanted to buy a bushel of them to take back to Asmara. I bought some green chilies and tomatoes for lunch. As I held the bag on my lap in the car, Solomon suddenly remarked, "That's my poem!" When I asked "Where," he said, "On the bag," which the poem's three stanzas in Ge'ez script decorated, although not without an error in one line, which Solomon corrected with a pen I had given him with a request that he autograph the bag. When I first came to Eritrea, occasions to write poetry seemed to be everywhere. Now I was finding that performing and writing poetry were everywhere, too.

Once more I looked at the book's title—a question—on the first page of the proofs: "Who Needs a Story?"

"Who needs a story? No Eritrean I have ever met here," I said aloud, as I neatened the pages for the next day. I couldn't wait to hear the film director and songwriter Isayas Tsegai also answer the question, a little later when he would read "I Am Also a Person" in the banquet hall, where we would film him too:

> When I saw the world didn't care
> If I was stripped of everything,
> Even my dignity,
> And beaten like a slave
> Less than human,
> I lost all sense of peace except in saying
> *I'm a person. I'm an Eritrean.*[12]

I also looked forward to seeing Ghirmai Yohannes again, who wrote the poem "Who Needs a Story?"—which gave us the title of the book. Whenever I met Ghirmai, one of Eritrea's most famous comedians and TV stars—nicknamed "San Diego" for the T-shirt with the American city's name on it that he never seemed to take off during the fourteen years he fought in the war—our conversations never lasted very long because inevitably he would attract a crowd of fans who would break in.

San Diego's poem told a story that any poet could identify with, but in the process it applied to Eritrea too and, perhaps, to anyone concerned with the age-old aphorism: *Know thyself.* His poem began, "I needed a story," and asked the most basic questions: "What can I write? / . . . What do I have to say?" All too familiar excuses put off an answer. It required a lot more thought: "so many words / And ideas"; a lot more style: "I need . . . art"; and more time: "Tomorrow I . . . [will] start."[13] San Diego sounded like Sir Philip Sidney in the first sonnet of his Astrophil and Stella sequence from the

1580s: another poem about writing a poem, containing the same excuses, only draped in Elizabethan diction. Sidney depicted a similar struggle with too much to think about: "I sought fit words . . . / Studying inventions . . . / Oft turning others' leaves"; style: "words came halting forth, wanting invention's stay"; and time: "great with child to speak . . . helpless in my throes."[14] Furthermore, both poets condemned such a struggle, implying self-condemnation. Sidney's "Biting . . . [his] truant pen" and "beating . . . [himself] for spite" translated into San Diego's thinking, "All this time and hard work— / For what?" The original question, "What do I have to say," allowed for only one answer, and it required self-redemption. For Sidney, it meant that he had to "look in . . . [his] heart and write." San Diego had to realize, "I already have a story / That nobody knows and it's great— / I am the story."

Sidney gave the credit for his discovery to "my muse." San Diego depicted his discovery as a self-discovery, yet it seemed a quintessentially Eritrean discovery, or as if the Eritrean armed struggle had been his muse. For decades, centuries, and millennia other nations had been trying to tell Eritrea what its story should be instead of what was inscribed on the stele in Belew Kelew and continually recounted by the *getemti,* the joiners, all the way up to the poets we included in the anthology and more whom we could not fit. They knew their own unique story—the story of a free and independent Eritrea—before anyone else did. They also knew at least four thousand years of their own story before that. If Eritreans didn't know their own story and didn't know how to tell it, first to each other and then to the world, how could they form a nation? In the twentieth century, the world took thirty years until it finally heard them telling their story through the barrel of a gun. Could the story now be heard instead in a book of poems?

After the party at Giday's, Zemhret came up to me and said, "Your translation of San Diego's 'Who Needs a Story?' is missing something at the end. He doesn't like how he acts in the poem. He needs a story, but he has one. It's great, but no one knows it. He is the story. But he tries other stories. At the end of the poem he says he hates himself because he hasn't told his own story. Can he tell it? He should. He challenges himself."

I recalled the last part of the literal translation of the poem that I worked from had hinted that the poet was frustrated with himself and depressed that he had to struggle so much just to get to the point of realizing that he had his own story to tell, a great story. But I thought that the translation might have strayed from or unnecessarily diluted the poet's triumph in the end of simply realizing, "I am the story." However, when I looked at the translation again, and inserted "I hate myself for thinking this," the poem struck me as not merely being San Diego or Eritrea or echoing Sidney's sonnet from another time and place. I identified with the poem myself.

"I needed a story" thirty years ago when I decided that I had to dedicate myself to learning about my own, Western culture before going to any other. I too asked "myself all day" and "all night . . . / What do I have to say," and I "emptied so many words / And ideas out of my brain" that "It would have floated away / If not tied to my heart." Also, I thought that if I were going to know what to write or what I had to say, "I needed art." Anyone following such a course was bound to lose his or her story, as Sidney, San Diego, and many other poets portrayed, but as I only began to realize when I looked down at my feet and saw the ants tunneling in the sands of Jericho where twenty cities had come and gone. I also could have said to myself then, "Wait. / What is this all about?" And at this point, I hated myself, too. I looked back on the "time and hard work" I had put into my learning, my writing, my religion, and my marriage. What did they amount to? Any more than the dust at my feet? Seeing the ants, I asked, "For what?" I needed a story—my own story. As I walked away, I began to find it. It was about Africa but also about me. I couldn't separate them.

But now, twenty years later, I was going to be late for the poets performing at Expo if I didn't get going. Through my hotel terrace windows I heard the traffic and saw the crowds rushing down Warsai Avenue outside under the palm trees and streetlights. Instead of halfheartedly going over the proofs and daydreaming, I should have started working on the poem I wanted to write about being in Massawa yesterday and this morning. Again I traveled with Solomon Tsehaye, sponsored by the American Embassy, to give a lecture on the anthology at the local library and to read a few of the poems.

"At least I should write down his response," I thought: an aphorism that he repeated in Tigrinya and English when I told him about my walk this morning.

"*Senbet'se bahri ikwa te'ref,*" Solomon said in a voice of weary satisfaction. I asked him to write it in Latin and Ge'ez script in my pocket notebook.

As he added, "In English you could say, 'On Sunday even the sea rests,'" I heard the phrase transform itself into first two lines of a poem: "Sundays in July, nothing moves / In Massawa—not even the sea."

I got up early since the heat after breakfast would make it almost impossible to stay outside for long. Total stillness engulfed me as I stood on a quay near the hotel. Black-headed storks, ravens, and, I imagined, enemy planes glued themselves solid to the sky, which had the texture of brittle paper and the same color as the sea, if bleached-out had a color. Bamboo shades sealed whatever coolness the night had introduced into the coral villas without a single window or door open. Any news, information. or political issues we heard the day before when we traveled with people from the American Embassy didn't matter now: food aid supposedly rotting on the docks; a naval frigate's port of call; dehydrated mothers at the health clinic, according to the medics; the Eritrean government's being run by an incurable bunch of rebels while suicide bombers recruited at the bus stops, according to a U.S. intelligence officer I drank with at the hotel bar; the amputee *tegedelti* or veterans being denied their benefits, according to the BBC reporter who traveled with us for awhile. Solomon was right. "Sundays in July, nothing moves in Massawa—even the sea." Massawa, Eritrea's busiest port? The word "port" no longer applied. All the security precautions around the American ambassador? Who needed security now? The two women shuffling down the street? The two men taking a swim? Selassie's useless palace on the other side of the quay? The tiny grain by grain of salt already beginning to add to the heaps of it on the edges of the ponds fed by the Red Sea? The unidentifiable car plowed into a palm tree that seemed neither dead nor alive? Still life ruled the day. Memories of the liberation and the bodies blown apart in battle equally faded away like ideas, not things. Nothing moved. Differences didn't register: the air and sea temperature the same; long phrases droning from the mosques and the four St. Mary's churches ringing their bells; stray cats and wandering camels; the rich tourists who would later relax on the beaches and the girl dressed in rags chasing a chicken past a row of huts made out of crooked sticks, ripped blue plastic, and a sheet or two of sharp, rusty metal; the ruling party, the only one allowed, a skinny donkey and two wizened men drinking from the same well, with no change to come. Busyness, bulletins, machines, schedules, marching, and longing for something more had no place here: no one to show what they meant; no one who wanted to know; no one who felt anything except being unreal. Sundays in July in Massawa, nothing moved—even the sea. I had to weep with so much peace.

I Came to Carthage

Veni Karthaginem.

—ST. AUGUSTINE, *CONFESSIONS* 3.1

I came to Carthage from the other direction,
From Rome back to Rome's Rome.
I wrestled the devil to a draw and won.

I had more than the need of a god and moved on.
Newark, Cairo, Dakar, Nairobi, Asmara, home:
I came to Carthage from the other direction.

The journey provided interpretation.
Connection made both sides of the poem.
I wrestled the devil to a draw and won.

A beam in an old house had a medallion
I carved in a dream out of Red Sea foam.
I came to Carthage from the other direction.

Local marble, corn, spring-like voice, sun,
Safe city and a hilltop where a camel roams—
I wrestled the devil to a draw and won.

All these Bethlehems so full of passion—
Why had I lived so long in a catacomb?
I came to Carthage from the other direction.
I wrestled the devil to a draw and won.

Notes

PREFACE

1. Charles Cantalupo, *Light the Lights* (Lawrenceville, NJ: Red Sea Press, 2003), 21.
2. Ribka Sibhatu, "Abeba," in *Who Needs a Story? Contemporary Eritrean Poetry in Tigrinya, Tigre and Arabic,* translated and edited by Charles Cantalupo and Ghirmai Negash (Asmara, Eritrea: Hdri Publishers, 2005), 29.
3. *The Iliad,* translated by Robert Fitzgerald (Garden City, NY: Anchor Press, 1974), 450–54.
4. Ghirmai Yohannes, "Who Needs a Story?" in Cantalupo and Negash, *Who Needs a Story?* 79.

CHAPTER ONE. FROM THE OTHER DIRECTION

1. All biblical quotations are from the King James Version, unless noted otherwise.
2. Samuel Taylor Coleridge, *Biographia Literaria* (1817; New York: William Gowans, 1852), 2:378.
3. Tsegaye Gabre-Medhim, *Collision of Altars,* in *Modern African Drama,* edited by Biodun Jeyifo (1977; New York: W. W. Norton and Company, 2002).
4. W. B. Yeats, "Sailing to Byzantium," in *The Poems of W. B. Yeats,* edited by Richard J. Finneran (1928; New York: Macmillan, 1983), 193.
5. Ted Hughes, *Tales from Ovid* (New York: Farrar, Straus and Giroux, 1997), ix.
6. Ngugi wa Thiong'o, *Homecoming* (New York: Lawrence Hill and Company, 1972), 150.
7. Chinua Achebe, "An Image of Africa: Racism in Conrad's *Heart of Darkness,*" *Massachusetts Review* 18.4 (1977): 788.
8. Edward Said, *Orientalism* (New York: Vintage, 1978), 7.
9. Ibid., 11.
10. Ibid.

CHAPTER TWO. CONNECTION

1. *Symposium*, translated by Michael Joyce, in *The Collected Dialogues*, edited by Edith Hamilton and Huntington Cairns (Princeton, NJ: Princeton University Press, 1961), 543.

CHAPTER THREE. BOTH SIDES

1. Ezra Pound, *ABC of Reading* (1934; New York: New Directions Books, 1960), 29.
2. Edmund Spenser, *The Faerie Queene*, edited by J. C. Smith (1596; Oxford: Clarendon Press, 1909), II.xii.83, p. 340.
3. Edward Said, *Culture and Imperialism* (New York: Knopf, 1993), 312.
4. G. W. F. Hegel, *The Philosophy of History*, translated by J. Jibree (1837; New York: Dover, 1956), 93.
5. Edward Said, *Representations of the Intellectual: The 1993 Reith Lectures* (Vintage: London, 1994), xii.
6. Francis Bacon, *Meditationes Sacrae*, "De Heresibus," in *The Works of Francis Bacon* (1597; London: 1826), 10:308.
7. George Herbert Walker Bush, in *The Greek Miracle*, by Diana Buitron-Oliver (Washington, DC: National Gallery of Art, 1992), 7.

CHAPTER FOUR. THE JOURNEY PROVIDED

1. George Orwell, "Politics and the English Language," in *The Orwell Reader* (1946; New York: Harcourt, Brace and Jovanovich, 1956), 363.
2. Francisco López de Gómara, quoted in *Christopher Columbus and the Conquest of Paradise,* by Kirkpatrick Sale (New York: Knopf, 1990), 225.
3. Adam Smith, *An Inquiry into the Nature and Causes of the Wealth of Nations* (1776; New York: E. P. Dutton, 1921), 2:121.
4. Wole Soyinka, "Twice Bitten: The Fate of Africa's Culture Producers," *PMLA* 105.1 (1990): 114.
5. John Donne, "Elegy XIX, To His Mistris Going To Bed," in *The Elegies and The Songs and Sonnets,* edited by Helen Gardner (1669; Oxford: Clarendon Press, 1965), 1.25–27, p. 15.

6. William Shakespeare, *Hamlet*, in *The Riverside Shakespeare*, edited by G. Blakemore Evans (1602; Boston: Houghton Mifflin Company, 1974), III.i.78, p. 1160.

CHAPTER FIVE. INTERPRETATION

1. Ngugi wa Thiong'o, *Ngugi wa Thiong'o Speaks*, edited by Reinhard Sander and Bernth Lindfors (Trenton, NJ: Africa World Press, 2006), 360.
2. Quoted in Ngugi wa Thiong'o, *Decolonising the Mind* (Oxford: James Currey, 1986), 86.
3. Frank Chipasula, "Singing like Parrots," in *The World of Ngugi wa Thiong'o*, edited by Charles Cantalupo (Trenton, NJ: Africa World Press, 1995), 233–34.
4. Ngugi wa Thiong'o, "Moving the Centre: An Interview by Charles Cantalupo," in Cantalupo, *World of Ngugi wa Thiong'o*, 213.
5. Ngugi wa Thiong'o, "*Matigari* and the Dreams of One Africa," in *Moving the Centre* (London: James Currey, 1993), 166.
6. Ibid., xiv.
7. Ngugi, "Moving the Centre: An Interview by Charles Cantalupo," 221–22.
8. Charles Baudelaire, *Journaux Intime* (1887; Paris: G. Crès, 1920), 45; Charles Baudelaire, *Intimate Journals*, translated by Christopher Isherwood (1887; New York: Howard Fertig, 1977), 53.
9. Thomas Hobbes, *Leviathan*, edited by C. B. Macpherson (1651; Harmondsworth: Penguin, 1968), 75.
10. Ibid., 717.
11. Ngugi, *Moving the Centre*, xvii.
12. Ngugi wa Thiong'o, *Penpoints, Gunpoints and Dreams* (Oxford: Clarendon Press, 1998), 100.
13. Ngugi, "Moving the Centre: An Interview by Charles Cantalupo," 221.
14. Hobbes, *Leviathan*, 712.
15. Ngugi, "Moving the Centre: An Interview by Charles Cantalupo," 221.
16. Ibid.
17. Ngugi, *Moving the Centre*, 156.
18. Ngugi, "Moving the Centre: An Interview by Charles Cantalupo," 221.
19. Ngugi, *Moving the Centre*, 8.
20. Ibid., 10.
21. Ibid., 11.
22. Ibid., xvii.

23. *World of Ngugi wa Thiong'o,* 133.
24. Ibid., 132.
25. Ibid., 58.
26. Ibid., 44.
27. Ibid., 226.
28. Ibid., 44.
29. Ibid., 92.
30. Ngugi, *Moving the Centre,* 10.
31. Ibid., 27.
32. Ngugi wa Thiong'o, *Matigari,* translated by Wangui wa Goro (London: Heinemann, 1987), ix.
33. John Keats, letter to John Hamilton Reynolds, May 3, 1818, in *The Selected Letters of John Keats,* selected by Lionel Trilling (New York: Doubleday and Company), 141.
34. Ngugi, *Moving the Centre,* 10.
35. Ibid., 11.
36. Henry Chakava, "Publishing Ngugi: The Challenge, the Risk, and the Reward," in *Ngugi wa Thiong'o: Texts and Contexts,* edited by Charles Cantalupo (Trenton, NJ: Africa World Press, 1995), 23.
37. Kamau Brathwaite, "Limuru and Kinta Kunte," in Cantalupo, *Ngugi wa Thiong'o: Texts and Contexts,* 2.
38. Amiri Baraka, "Brother Okot 1931?1983," *Ngugi wa Thiong'o: Texts and Contexts,* 90.
39. Sonia Sanchez, "Coming Full Circle," in Cantalupo, *Ngugi wa Thiong'o: Texts and Contexts,* 367.
40. Ibid., 372.
41. Ngugi, *Moving the Centre,* xvii.
42. Quoted by Edward Wiltse, "The 'Mau Mau' in Hollywood: *Something of Value* and Counterinsurgency from Algiers to Alabama," in Cantalupo, *Ngugi wa Thiong'o: Texts and Contexts,"* 73.
43. Ngugi, *Decolonising the Mind,* 3.
44. Quoted by Annie Gagiano, "Blixen, Ngugi: Recounting Kenya," in Cantalupo, *Ngugi wa Thiong'o: Texts and Contexts,* 100.

CHAPTER SIX. ROME'S ROME

1. Reynolds Price, "Numbers 12," in *A Palpable God: Thirty Stories Translated from the Bible* (San Francisco: North Point Press, 1985), 94.

2. *Holman Christian Standard Bible* (Nashville, TN: Holman Bible Publishers, 2003), 928.

3. *A Modern Translation of the Kebra Negast,* compiled, edited, and translated by Miguel F. Brooks (Lawrenceville, NJ: Red Sea Press, 1996), 3.

4. Ibid., 2.

5. Ibid., 3.

6. Ibid., xiii.

7. Ibid., 33.

8. Ibid., 38.

CHAPTER SEVEN. WHERE A CAMEL ROAMS

1. Edgar Allan Poe, "The Raven," in *The Selected Writings of Edgar Allan Poe,* edited by G. R. Thompson (1845; New York: W. W. Norton and Company, 2004), ll. 43, 41, 48, p. 59.

CHAPTER EIGHT. I CARVED A DREAM

1. William Shakespeare, *A Midsummer Night's Dream,* in *The Riverside Shakespeare,* edited by G. Blakemore Evans (1595?96; Boston: Houghton Mifflin Company, 1974), V.i.14–17, p. 242.

2. Amiri Baraka, *Eulogies* (New York: Marsilio Publishers, 1996), vii.

3. Ibid., 50.

4. Ngugi wa Thiong'o, *Moving the Centre* (London: James Currey, 1993), xvii.

5. Tim Jeal, *Livingstone* (New York: J. P. Putnam's Sons, 1973), 336.

6. Ibid., 344.

7. William Garden Blaikie, *The Personal Life of David Livingstone* (1881; Santa Barbara, CA: Greenwood Press Reprint, 1969), 162–63.

8. David and Charles Livingstore, *Narrative of the Expedition to the Zambesi and its Tributaries; and of the Discovery of the Lakes Shirwa and Nyasa 1858–1864* (London: John Murray, 1865), 9.

9. John Donne, "Satyre III," in *The Satires, Epigrams and Verse Letters*, edited by W. Milgate (1633; Oxford: Clarendon Press, 1967), ll. 79–82, p. 13.

CHAPTER NINE. RED SEA FOAM

1. Saba Kidane, "Go Crazy Over Me," in *Who Needs a Story? Contemporary Eritrean Poetry in Tigrinya, Tigre and Arabic,* translated and edited by Charles Cantalupo and Ghirmai Negash (Asmara, Eritrea: Hdri Publishers, 2005), 33.
2. Johanna McGeary and Marguerite Michaels, "Africa Rising," *Time,* March 30, 1998, 34–46.
3. Quoted by Amiri Baraka, "John Coltrane (1926–1967)," in *Eulogies* (New York: Marsilio Publishers, 1996), 2.
4. William Blake, "Proverbs of Hell," in *The Complete Poetry and Prose of William Blake,* edited by David V. Erdman (1790; Berkeley: University of California Press, 1982), 35.

CHAPTER TEN. I WRESTLED THE DEVIL

1. "The Horn of Africa War: Mass Expulsions and the Nationality Issue," in *Human Rights Watch,* 15.3 (2003): 20.
2. Michela Wrong, "Prickly Horn of Africa States Threaten to Fight Over Border," *Financial Times,* May 21, 1998.
3. Reesom Haile, "Your Sister," in *We Have Our Voice: Selected Poems of Reesom Haile,* English translation with Charles Cantalupo (Lawrenceville, NJ: Red Sea Press, 2000), 2–3.
4. Reesom Haile, "We Have," in *We Have Our Voice,* 44–45.
5. Arthur Rimbaud, *A Season in Hell and Other Works / Une saison en enfer et oeuvres diverses,* edited and translated by Stanley Appelbaum (New York: Dover Publications, 2003), 43.
6. Reesom Haile, "Our Language," in *We Have Our Voice,* 72.
7. Reesom Haile, "Tigrinya," in *We Have Our Voice,* 74.
8. Reesom Haile, "Voice," in *We Have Our Voice,* 12–13.
9. Charles Baudelaire, *Intimate Journals,* translated by Christopher Isherwood (1930; New York: Howard Fertig, 1977), 56.
10. William Shakespeare, *Hamlet,* in *The Riverside Shakespeare,* edited by G. Blakemore Evans (1602; Boston: Houghton Mifflin Company, 1974), IV.v.165–67, p. 1174.
11. Reesom Haile, "My Freedom," in *We Have Our Voice,* 78.
12. Ibid., 78.

CHAPTER ELEVEN. A DRAW

1. Reesom Haile, "Meat," *We Have Our Voice: Selected Poems of Reesom Haile*, English translation with Charles Cantalupo (Lawrenceville, NJ: Red Sea Press, 2000), 108.
2. Reesom Haile, "Lete Michael," in *We Have Our Voice*, 92.
3. Reesom Haile, "Meskerem," in *We Have Our Voice*, 112–15.

CHAPTER TWELVE. A MEDALLION

1. Nawal El Saadawi, *A Daughter of Isis: The Autobiography of Nawal El Sadawi*, translated by Sherif Hetata (New York: Zed Books, 1999), 4.
2. William Shakespeare, *A Midsummer Night's Dream* (1595), in *The Riverside Shakespeare*, edited by G. Blakemore Evans (1595?96; Boston: Houghton Mifflin Company, 1974), V.i.14–17, p. 242.
3. Reesom Haile, *We Invented the Wheel*, translated by Charles Cantalupo (Lawrenceville, NJ: Red Sea Press, 2002), 226.
4. Reesom Haile, "The Leader," in *We Have Our Voice: Selected Poems of Reesom Haile*, English translation with Charles Cantalupo (Lawrenceville, NJ: Red Sea Press, 2000), 38.
5. Papa Susso, translated by Bob Holman: http://bobholman.com/poems/01frame.htm.
6. Saba Kidane, "War and a Woman," translated by Charles Cantalupo and Ghirmai Negash, *UniVerse:* http://www.universeofpoetry.org/eritrea_p2.shtml.
7. Charles Cantalupo, *Light the Lights* (Lawrenceville, NJ: Red Sea Press, 2003), 21.
8. "Asmara Declaration on African Languages and Literatures," http://www.outreach.psu.edu/programs/allodds/declaration.html.
9. Simone Weil, *L'Iliade ou la poème de la force* (1940); Simone Weil, *The Iliad, or, the Poem of Force*, translated by Mary McCarthy (Wallingford, PA: Pendle Hill, 1983).
10. Ibid., 4.
11. Solomon Tsehaye, *Sahel* (1994; Asmara: Hdri Publishers, 2006).
12. Ibid., 3.
13. W. H. Auden, "The Shield of Achilles," in *Collected Poems*, edited by Edward Mendelson (New York: Random House, 1976), 454.
14. Ibid.

CHAPTER THIRTEEN. THE POEM

1. Horace, *Odes and Epodes,* edited and translated by Niall Rudd (Cambridge: Harvard University Press, 1994), 144.
2. Meles Negusse, "We Miss You, Mammet," in *Who Needs a Story? Contemporary Eritrean Poetry in Tigrinya, Tigre and Arabic,* translated and edited by Charles Cantalupo and Ghirmai Negash (Asmara, Eritrea: Hdri Publishers), 1–3.
3. Angessom Isaak, "Freedom's Colors," in Cantalupo and Negash, *Who Needs a Story?* 23–26.
4. Paulos Netabay, "Remembering Sahel," in Cantalupo and Negash, *Who Needs a Story?* 83.
5. Ahmed Omer Sheikh, "A Song from the Coast," in Cantalupo and Negash, *Who Needs a Story?* 131–33.
6. Mohammed Osman Kajerai, "Singing Our Way to Victory," in Cantalupo and Negash, *Who Needs a Story?* 99.
7. Mohammed Mahmoud El-Sheik (Madani), "Singing for the Children of Ar," in Cantalupo and Negash, *Who Needs a Story?* 119.
8. Fessehaye Yohannes, "If He Came Back," in Cantalupo and Negash, *Who Needs a Story?* 51.
9. Solomon Drar, "Who Said Merhawi is Dead?" in Cantalupo and Negash, *Who Needs a Story?* 71.
10. Mussa Mohammed Adem, "The Invincible," in Cantalupo and Negash, *Who Needs a Story?* 87–92.
11. Fessahazion Michael, "Naqra," in Cantalupo and Negash, *Who Needs a Story?* 27.
12. Isayas Tsegai, "I Am Also a Person," in Cantalupo and Negash, *Who Needs a Story?* 9.
13. Ghirmai Yohannes, "Who Needs a Story?" in Cantalupo and Negash, *Who Needs a Story?* 79.
14. Philip Sidney, from "Astrophil and Stella," in *The New Oxford Book of Sixteenth Century Verse,* edited by Emrys Jones (Oxford: Oxford University Press, 1992), 303.